W9-AQN-997

macromedia®

FLASH® 8

ActionScript

Training from the Source

Jobe Makar

Danny Patterson

ADOBE
PRESS

Adobe

ST. PHILIP'S COLLEGE LIBRARY

TR
891.7
· M3495
2006

Macromedia® Flash® 8 ActionScript
Training from the Source

Jobe Makar

Danny Patterson

ADOBE
PRESS

A Adobe Press books are published by:

Peachpit

1249 Eighth Street
Berkeley, CA 94710
510/524-2178
800/283-9444
510/524-2221 (fax)
Find us on the World Wide Web at:
www.peachpit.com
www.adobe.com

To report errors, please send a note to errata@peachpit.com

Copyright © 2006 by Adobe Systems, Inc.

Notice of Rights

All rights reserved. No part of this book may be reproduced or transmitted in any form by any means, electronic, mechanical, photocopying, recording, or otherwise, without the prior written permission of the publisher. For information on getting permission for reprints and excerpts, contact permissions@peachpit.com.

Trademarks

Flash, Dreamweaver and Macromedia are registered trademarks of Adobe Systems, Inc.

Throughout this book, trademarked names are used. Rather than put a trademark symbol in every occurrence of a trademarked name, we state that we are using the names in an editorial fashion only and to the benefit of the trademark owner with no intention of infringement of the trademark.

Notice of Liability

The information in this book is distributed on an "As Is" basis, without warranty. While every precaution has been taken in the preparation of the book, neither the author, Macromedia, Inc., Adobe Systems, Inc. nor the publisher, shall have any liability to any person or entity with respect to any loss or damage caused or alleged to be caused directly or indirectly by the instructions contained in this book or by the computer software and hardware products described in it.

Printed and bound in the United States of America

ISBN 0-321-33619-4

9 8 7 6 5 4 3 2 1

Credits

Authors
Jobe Makar
Danny Patterson

Macromedia Press Editor
Angela C. Kozlowski

Editors
Robin Drake
Robyn G. Thomas

Technical Editor
Alfio Raymond

Production Coordinator
Becky Winter

Copy Editor
Nancy Sixsmith

Compositors
Rick Gordon, Emerald Valley Graphics

Debbie Roberti, Espresso Graphics

Indexer
Joy Dean Lee

Cover Design
George Mattingly, GMD

Proofreader
Mark Kozlowski

Dedications

This one is for Emmet.

—Jobe Makar

This book is dedicated to my wife Melissa, for putting up with the long hours I spend in front of the computer.

—Danny Patterson

This book and all my work are dedicated to the joyous totality that is present in each moment.

—Joy Singh

Bios

Jobe Makar is the lead programmer and co-owner of Electrotank, Inc., and winner of several international game awards. The creator of more than 100 Macromedia Flash games, Jobe has been working with Flash since version 3. He has authored or co-authored several books on Flash, including *Macromedia Flash MX 2004 Game Design Demystified.* He has been the lead programmer at Learnimation for four Small Business Innovation Research Awards from the National Science Foundation and the U.S. Department of Education. Jobe currently lives with his wife and entirely too many animals in Elm City, North Carolina.

Danny Patterson is a consultant specializing in Flash and Web technologies. He also works as a Senior Architect with Schematic, the industry leader in the development of multimedia content and applications using the latest Macromedia tools and technologies. He is a Partner/Author at Community MX and a Member of Team Macromedia Flash. He has also been published in the *MX Developer's Journal.* He is a Certified Advanced ColdFusion MX, Flash MX and Flash MX 2004 Developer. He has worked on Flash projects for many large companies, including Microsoft, IBM, Dell, Adobe, Starz, and Virgin. You can check out his blog at *DannyPatterson.com.* Danny currently lives with his wife in Minneapolis, Minnesota.

Joy Singh has a passion for art in all forms. She considers ActionScript an art, and she is as passionate about ActionScript (and teaching ActionScript) as she is about her painting. She's also a songwriter and composer, and she loves to work in her home recording studio. Joy lives in Southern California where she takes full advantage of the year-round sunshine and temperate weather by getting outdoors as much as possible. Joy's website is *www.joysingh.com.*

Acknowledgments

It's a wonderful feeling to have completed this book. Macromedia gave us many great new features to write about in Flash 8! Thanks to Joey and Danny for creating some useful lessons. As always, we could not have accomplished this monumental task alone. There are some really talented people whose efforts and support have contributed as much during the creation of this book as the authors'. Thank you, Angela, for coordinating and keeping us all on track. Robyn, you really have done an excellent job with the editing and your attention to detail. Thanks also to the editors Robin Drake, Alfio Raymond, Nancy Sixsmith, and Becky Winter. My Electrotank.com colleagues Mike Grundvig and Robert Firebaugh often provide me with conceptual help when creating new exercises; thanks guys!

It has been a crazy year and I couldn't have stayed focused without the support of my wife, Kelly, and my mistresses, Anna and Hayes. And of course, thanks to my fuzzy dog Free for forcing me to throw a ball for him every two hours to clear my thoughts.

–Jobe Makar

I'd like to thank all the programming influences in my life, but there are far too many to count. Thanks to Angela and Robyn for being flexible and giving me freedom in my writing. Thanks to the technical editors for the time and effort they spent in proofing my work. And finally, I'd like to thank Macromedia for continuing to push the Flash platform and developing great tools for us to use.

–Danny Patterson

Joy thanks her parents and her sister for their continual love and support. She thanks all her many friends that surround her with beauty. She would also like to thank Robyn Thomas for all the edits, insightful comments, and patience. Thanks go to Angela Kozlowski for the opportunity to work on this project. She'd also like to acknowledge Margot Hutchinson at Waterside for her help with the project. Of course, Joy thanks Danny and Jobe for their work on the book. Thanks go to all the readers that make this possible. And she sends endless thanks to the infinite source.

–Joy Singh

Table of Contents

Introduction

ActionScript is the programming language that enables you to use Macromedia's popular Flash to create highly interactive multimedia-based websites, product demos, teaching materials, and more. If you're familiar with the logic of other programming languages, especially JavaScript or Java, ActionScript will seem quite familiar. After you learn the logic behind how scripting works, as well as the many things it allows you to create and do, chances are you'll wish you had started sooner. Creativity isn't reserved for artists and designers, after all; scripting is another form of creativity and is equally as rewarding. With a thorough knowledge of ActionScript, you can express yourself in many ways you may never have imagined.

This *Training from the Source* course introduces you to the major elements of ActionScript by guiding you through a wealth of step-by-step projects that thoroughly explain not only what's happening but also why and how. The focus of each project is the teaching of ActionScript; therefore, in nearly all the projects, most graphical elements and other objects not directly related to the lesson are already set up for you. Their purpose in the project, as well as brief descriptions of what they do (if necessary), are always included.

There are two versions of Flash: Flash Basic 8 and Flash Professional 8. Flash Basic 8 has a very limited feature set and is not intended for the development of rich applications. As such, this book uses Flash Professional 8 and all the exciting features that come with it!

Outline

The curriculum of the course is approximately 20–25 hours in length and includes the following lessons:

Lesson 1: Introduction to ActionScript 2.0

Lesson 2: Functions

Lesson 3: Conditional Logic

Lesson 4: Arrays and Loops

Lesson 5: Built-in Classes

Lesson 6: Custom Classes

Lesson 7: Events, Listeners, and Callbacks

Lesson 8: Dynamically Creating Assets

Lesson 9: Bitmap Features

Lesson 10: UI Components

Lesson 11: Advanced Object-Oriented Design

Lesson 12: Data Validation

Lesson 13: External Data Connections

Lesson 14: XML and Flash

Lesson 15: External Interface

Lesson 16: Sound and Video

Lesson 17: Printing and Context Menus

Lesson 18: Maximum-Strength SWF Files

Standard Elements in the Book

Macromedia Flash 8 ActionScript: Training from the Source contains more than 60 separate projects, each designed to teach you a specific aspect of ActionScript. These projects are fun, useful, and practical examples of how ActionScript can be used in real-world situations. Each lesson begins with an overview of the lesson's content and learning objectives. Lessons are divided into individual tasks that help you learn and utilize various aspects of the lesson's topic.

This book is part of the *Training from the Source* series. It contains conceptual information, in-depth material, and step-by-step explanations. In addition, each lesson includes the following special features:

Italicized text: Text that should be *entered* by the reader as well as *new* vocabulary that is introduced and emphasized in each lesson appears in italicized text.

Code text: To help you easily identify ActionScript, XML, and HTML code within the book, the code has been styled in a special font that's unique from the rest of the text. Single lines of code that are longer than the margins of the page allow wrap to the next line. They are designated by the turnover character (¬) at the end of the broken line and are indented on the next line. For example:

```
this.attachMovie("Example", "exampleClip",¬
   this.getNextHighestDepth());
```

Menu commands and keyboard shortcuts: There are often multiple ways to perform the same task. The different options will be pointed out in each lesson. Menu commands are shown with angle brackets between the menu names and commands: Menu > Command > Subcommand. Keyboard shortcuts are shown with a plus sign between the names of keys to indicate that you should press the keys simultaneously; for example, Shift+Tab means that you should press the Shift and Tab keys at the same time.

Notes: Notes provide additional information pertaining to the task at hand.

Tips: Tips contain shortcuts for carrying out common tasks and discuss ways you can use the skills you're learning to solve common problems.

This course is developed to help you build your skills progressively as you work through each lesson. After you complete the entire course, you'll have a thorough knowledge of ActionScript, including its syntax, capabilities, and the logic behind the way to make it do what you want it to do. As a result, you'll have the skills necessary to create dynamic, highly interactive Flash content.

The accompanying CD-ROM contains all the files necessary to complete each lesson. Files for each lesson appear in a folder titled with the lesson number. It is strongly suggested that you create a folder on your hard drive and transfer all lesson files to that folder prior to beginning the course because you'll occasionally be asked to test your work using Flash's Test Movie command. This command creates a test file in the same directory as the Flash file that is being authored. If the authored file were opened from the CD, Flash would attempt to create the test movie on the CD. In almost all cases, this is impossible and will result in an error.

Each lesson folder contains two subfolders: Start and Completed. If the Lesson uses media files, a third subfolder named Assets is included in the lesson folder. The Assets folder contains any media required for projects in the lesson. The Start folder contains any initial Flash files needed for the lesson. The files you need are identified at the beginning of each lesson. The Completed folder contains completed files for each step in the project as well as intermediate files built in each exercise so that you can compare them to your own work or see where you're headed.

The directory structure of the lessons you will be working with is as follows:

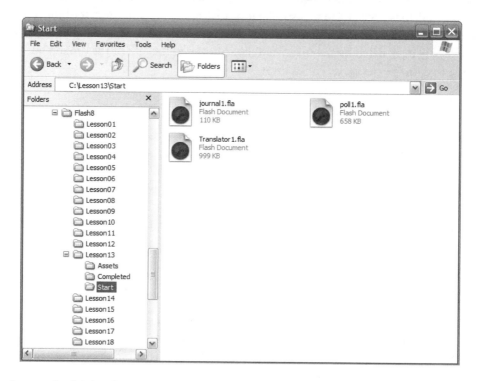

The lessons in this book assume that the following statements are true:

- You're familiar with using menus, opening and saving files, and so on for either the Windows or Macintosh operating system.

- Flash Professional 8 is already installed on your machine.

- Your computer meets the system requirements listed in the "Minimum System Requirements" section.

- You're generally familiar with Flash's interface, movie and authoring concepts, creating and using movie elements, using the Timeline, using basic actions, and working with the Actions panel. If you're not comfortable with any of these tasks, be sure to check out other books from Adobe Press and Peachpit Press.

Macromedia Training from the Source

The Macromedia *Training from the Source* and *Advanced Training from the Source* series are developed in association with Macromedia and reviewed by the product support teams. Ideal for active learners, the books in the *Training from the Source* series offer hands-on instruction designed to provide you with a solid grounding in the program's fundamentals. If you learn best by doing, this is the series for you. Each *Training from the Source* title contains hours of instruction on Macromedia software products. They are designed to teach the techniques that you need to create sophisticated professional-level projects. Each book includes a CD-ROM that contains all the files used in the lessons, completed projects for comparison, and more.

Macromedia Authorized Training and Certification

This book is designed to enable you to study at your own pace with content from the source. Other training options exist through the Macromedia Authorized Training Partner program. Get up to speed in a matter of days with task-oriented courses taught by Macromedia Certified Instructors. Or learn on your own with interactive, online training from Macromedia University. All these sources of training will prepare you to become a Macromedia Certified Developer.

For more information about authorized training and certification, check out *www.macromedia.com/support/training*.

What You Will Learn in This Book

As you work through these lessons, you will develop the skills you need to create and maintain your own websites.

By the end of this course, you will be able to do all of the following:

- Plan an interactive project
- Understand ActionScript syntax and how it works
- Use event handlers to create a variety of activities
- Use and understand built-in classes, properties, and methods
- Manipulate text and numbers dynamically to perform specific tasks
- Use functions to centralize your code
- Create custom classes
- Employ conditional logic in your movie to react to varying circumstances

- Use loops to automate scripting tasks
- Use and customize user interface (UI) components
- Use object-oriented techniques
- Increase the performance of your applications using the BitmapData class
- Move data in and out of Flash using text files and XML
- Script your applications to communicate with a third-party Web service
- Use the ExternalInterface class to communicate with JavaScript
- Validate all types of data
- Dynamically control movies using scripting rather than the Timeline
- Script sounds to make your project more engaging
- Load and unload various types of media from your projects
- Create an application that uses a third-party tool to enhance its functionality beyond Flash's built-in capabilities
- Print Flash content using ActionScript

Minimum System Requirements

Windows

- 800 MHz Intel Pentium III processor (or equivalent) and later
- Windows 2000, Windows XP
- 256 MB RAM (1 GB recommended to run more than one Studio 8 product simultaneously)
- 1024 × 768, 16-bit display (32-bit recommended)
- 710 MB available disk space

Macintosh

- 600 MHz PowerPC G3 and later
- Mac OS X 10.3, 10.4
- 256 MB RAM (1 GB recommended to run more than one Studio 8 product simultaneously)
- 360 MB available disk space

1 Introduction to ActionScript 2.0

Introductions form the start of any great relationship. Get ready, then, to be introduced to your new best friend: ActionScript! We believe you'll find ActionScript a satisfying companion—especially as you delve deeper into the relationship. Although you might not necessarily think of scripting as a creative endeavor, a working knowledge of ActionScript can spark all kinds of ideas—ones that will enable you to create dynamic content that can interact with your users on myriad levels. Best of all, you'll get the satisfaction of watching your ideas grow into working models that fulfill your projects' objectives.

In this lesson, we'll show you some compelling reasons for learning ActionScript, as well as what makes it tick. And if you're feeling a little shy, sometimes the best thing to do is jump right in—which is exactly what you'll do here as you create and test a complete interactive project before lesson's end.

Use your arrow keys to move the balloon!

We'll create several projects in this lesson, including this interactive scene that moves the balloon with key presses.

What You Will Learn

In this lesson, you will:

- Use the Actions panel
- Create variables
- Learn the various elements that make up ActionScript

Approximate Time

This lesson takes approximately two hours to complete.

Lesson Files

Media Files:

None

Starting Files:

Lesson01/Start/Balloon1.fla
Lesson01/Start/AnsweringMachine1.fla
Lesson01/Start/Navigation1.fla

Completed Projects:

Lesson01/Completed/Balloon2.fla
Lesson01/Completed/AnsweringMachine2.fla
Lesson01/Completed/Navigation2.fla

What Is ActionScript?

If you've been using Flash for a while then you've probably heard of ActionScript. You might not know exactly what ActionScript is or why it's important—just that it seems to be a hot topic. In this section, you'll learn what ActionScript is used for and will be introduced to some terminology and syntax.

ActionScript is a programming language. It allows you to break your application out of the static mold by enabling your Flash application to react uniquely, based on user input, external data, and even the time of day! It bridges the gap between what you understand and what Flash understands. As such, it allows you to provide both action-oriented instructions (do this) and logic-oriented instructions (analyze this before doing that) in your Flash project.

Like all languages, ActionScript contains many different elements, such as words, punctuation, and structure—all of which you must employ properly to get your Flash project to behave the way you want it to. If you don't employ ActionScript correctly, you'll find that interactivity either won't occur or won't work the way you intended. This structure is called *syntax*.

To begin to understand how ActionScript works, look at this sample script, which contains many of the essential elements that make up a typical script. After the script is a discussion of these elements and their role in the script's execution.

As an example, let us assume that there is a button that a user will click to submit an order, and the button has an instance name of checkout_btn. Now consider the following script:

```
checkout_btn.onRelease = function() {
  //set the cost of the mug
  var mugCost:Number = 5;
  //set the local sales tax percentage
  var taxPercent:Number = .06;
  //determine the dollar amount of tax
  var totalTax:Number = mugCost * taxPercent;
  //determine the total amount of the transaction
  var totalCost:Number = mugCost + totalTax;
  //display a custom message
  myTextBox_txt.text = "The total cost of your transaction is " + totalCost;
  //send the cashRegister_mc movie clip instance to frame 50
  cashRegister_mc.gotoAndPlay (50);
}
```

ST. PHILIP'S COLLEGE LIBRARY

Although at first glance this may look like Latin, after you become acquainted with some of its elements, you'll understand. Now you'll be introduced to some terms. The preceding script will be explained as you go.

Events

An *event* is when something happens. There are predefined events that the Flash player gives you access to, such as the act of moving or clicking the mouse. And there are custom events made for special uses, as you'll see later in this book.

Events occur during the playback of a movie and trigger the execution of a particular function. In the preceding sample script, the event that triggers the script is onRelease. This event signifies that when the checkout_btn button instance is released, the script will execute. Every script is triggered by an event, and your movie can react to numerous events—everything from a button being pressed to text changing in a text field to a sound completing its playback, and more. We will discuss events in depth in Lesson 7, "Events, Listeners, and Callbacks."

Actions

Actions form the heart of your script. An *action* is usually considered to be any line that instructs Flash to do, set, create, change, or delete something.

Here are some examples of actions from the sample script:

```
var mugCost:Number = 5;
cashRegister_mc.gotoAndPlay (50);
```

The first line creates a variable named mugCost, sets its data type as Number (data typing is discussed later), and sets the value of the variable to 5. The second line tells the cashRegister_mc movie clip instance to begin playing at Frame 50 of its Timeline.

Generally speaking, most of the lines in a script that are within curly braces ({}) are actions. These lines are usually separated by semicolons (we'll discuss punctuation shortly).

Operators

Operators include a number of symbols (=, <, >, +, -, *, &&, etc.) and are used to connect two elements in a script in various ways. Take a look at these examples:

- var taxPercent:Number = .06; assigns a numeric value of .06 to the variable named taxPercent using the assignment operator, =. This operator assigns the value of what is found to the right of it, to the variable on the left.

- amountA < amountB asks if amountA is less than amountB.
- value1 * 500 multiplies value1 times 500.

The operators >, <, >=, <=, ==, !=, ===, are known as *comparison operators*. They'll be discussed in Lesson 4, "Arrays and Loops."

Keywords

Keywords are words reserved for specific purposes within ActionScript syntax. As such, they cannot be used as variable, function, or label names. For example, the word on is a keyword and can only be used in a script to denote an event that triggers a script, such as on (press), on (rollOver), on (rollOut), and so forth. Attempting to use keywords in your scripts for anything other than their intended purpose will result in errors. Here are some other keywords: break, case, class, continue, default, delete, do, dynamic, else, extends, finally, for, function, get, if, implements, import, interface, in, instanceof, new, null, private, public, return, set, static, switch, this, throw, try, typeof, undefined, var, void, while, and with.

Data

A dynamic script almost always creates, uses, or updates various data during its execution. Variables are the most common data found in scripts and represent information that has been given a unique name. After a variable has been created and assigned a value, that value can be accessed anywhere in the script simply by inserting the variable's name. The value of a variable is data.

Note *Variable names are case-sensitive: firstname and firstName are not the same.*

In our sample script, we created a variable named mugCost and assigned it a value of 5. Later in the script, the name of that variable is used to refer to the value it contains.

Curly Braces

Generally, anything between opening and closing curly braces signifies an action or set of actions the script needs to perform when triggered. Think of curly braces as saying, "As a result of this—{do this}." For example:

```
on (release) {
    //set the cost of the mug
    var mugCost:Number = 5;
    //set the local sales tax percentage
    var taxPercent:Number = .06;
}
```

The preceding could be viewed as a sentence that says this: As a result of releasing the button, create two variables called mugCost and taxPercent.

Semicolons

Appearing at the end of most lines of scripts, semicolons are used to separate multiple actions that might need to be executed as the result of a single event (similar to the way semicolons are used to separate thoughts in a single sentence). This example denotes six actions, separated by semicolons:

```
var mugCost:Number = 5;
var taxPercent:Number = .06;
var totalTax:Number = mugCost * taxPercent;
var totalCost:Number = mugCost + totalTax;
myTextBox_txt.text = "The total cost of your transaction is " + totalCost;
cashRegister_mc.gotoAndPlay (50);
```

Dot Syntax

Dots (.) are used within scripts in a couple of ways. One is to denote the target path to a specific Timeline. For example, _root.usa.NorthCarolina.ElmCity points to a movie clip on the main (_root) Timeline named usa, which contains a movie clip named NorthCarolina, which contains a movie clip named ElmCity.

Because ActionScript is an object-oriented language, most interactive tasks are accomplished by changing a characteristic (*property*) of an object or by telling an object to do something (*invoking a method*). When changing a property or when invoking a method, dots are used to separate the object's name from the property or method being worked with. For example, movie clips are objects; to set the rotation property of a movie clip instance named wheel_mc, you would use the following syntax:

```
wheel_mc._rotation = 45;
```

Notice that a dot separates the name of the object from the property being set.

To tell the same movie clip instance to play, invoking the `play()` method, you would use this syntax:

```
wheel_mc.play()
```

Once again, a dot separates the name of the object from the method invoked.

Parentheses

Parentheses are used in various ways in ActionScript. For the most part, scripts employ parentheses to set a specific value that an action will use during its execution. Look at the last line of our sample script that tells the `cashRegister_mc` movie clip instance to go to and play Frame 50:

```
cashRegister_mc.gotoAndPlay (50);
```

If the value within parentheses is changed from 50 to 20, the action still performs the same basic task (moving the `cashRegister_mc` movie clip instance to a specified frame number); it just does so according to the new value. Parentheses are a way of telling an action to work based on what is specified between the parentheses.

Quotation Marks

Quotation marks are used to denote textual data in the script, called a *string*. Because text is used in the actual creation of the script, quotation marks provide the only means for a script to distinguish between instructions (pieces of data) and actual words. For example, `Kelly` (without quotes) signifies the name of a piece of data. On the other hand, `"Kelly"` signifies the actual word "Kelly."

Comments

Comments are lines in the script preceded by two forward slashes (//). When executing a script, Flash ignores lines containing comments. They indicate descriptive notes about what the script is doing at this point in its execution. Comments enable you to review a script months after it is written and still get a clear idea of its underlying logic. They do not affect the outcome of a script.

You can also create multiline comments using the following syntax:

```
/* everything between
here is considered
a comment */
```

Indenting/Spacing

Although not absolutely necessary, it's a good idea to indent and space the syntax in your code. For example, the following:

```
on (release) {
var mugCost:Number = 5;
}
```

executes the same way as this:

```
on (release) {
   var mugCost:Number = 5;
}
```

However, by indenting the second line of code, you make it easier to read. A good rule is to indent anything within curly braces to indicate that the code within those braces represents a *code block*—or chunk of code—that is to be executed at the same time. (The AutoFormat feature of the Actions panel takes care of most of this formatting for you.) You can *nest* code blocks within other code blocks—a concept that will become clearer as you work through the exercises.

For the most part, white space is ignored within a script. For example, the following:

```
var totalCost:Number = mugCost + totalTax ;
```

executes in the same way as this:

```
var totalCost:Number =mugCost+totalTax;
```

Although some programmers feel that extra white space makes their code easier to read, others believe it slows them down to insert spaces. For the most part, the choice is yours. There are a couple of exceptions: variable names cannot contain spaces; nor can you put a space between an object name and an associated property or method. Although this syntax is acceptable:

```
myObject.propertyName
```

this syntax is not:

```
myObject. propertyName
```

In addition, there must be a space between the var keyword used when creating a variable and the actual name of the variable. This is correct:

```
var variableName
```

but this is not:

```
varvariableName
```

You have just gotten your first taste of ActionScript. You have learned a little about what ActionScript is needed and you have been introduced to the various elements that make up ActionScript. Don't worry if the code snippets that you have seen don't make much sense—they aren't supposed to yet! We just talked about what makes up the code, not the logic that goes into creating it. In the coming sections you will learn more about ActionScript and will get a chance to write some yourself.

In this exercise, you will take a look at the ActionScript in an existing Flash file. You'll inspect the elements that make up the code and add a few lines yourself. The goal of this exercise is just to let you poke around in some ActionScript first-hand so that you can relate what you've seen here to an actual simple application.

1. Open the *Balloon1.fla* file, found in the Lesson01/Start folder.

The first things that you'll notice when you open this file are the colorful landscape background and the hot air balloon on top of it. When complete, this application will allow you to use the four arrow keys on your keyboard to navigate the balloon through the air. The file already has the necessary ActionScript to allow the left and right arrow keys to control the horizontal movement of the balloon. In the steps to come you will inspect the existing ActionScript and will add a few more lines that let the balloon move vertically as well.

There are four locked layers in this file. The first one is called actions. It is used to store the ActionScript. The second layer, called text, holds a text field that will display text generated by ActionScript. The text field has an instance name of instructions_txt. The next layer, called balloon, contains the balloon image in a movie clip with an instance name of balloon_mc. The bottom layer, called background, simply contains the background image.

2. Click Frame 1 in the actions layer. Select Window › Actions to open the Actions panel.

The Actions panel will be discussed in great detail in the next section. For now, it's enough to know that it is used to edit ActionScript in a Flash document.

You should see 13 lines of ActionScript in the Actions panel. Some of the lines have text that is completely gray, and some of the lines are multicolored. The grayed-out lines start with //, which means that they are comments. Comments are not considered code; they are usually used to provide a description of the next line (or lines) of ActionScript.

The multicolored lines are lines of ActionScript. You'll notice that ActionScript lines end with a semicolon, and comment lines do not.

3. Look at the operators in lines 2, 4, 6, 9, and 11.

These lines contain the assignment operator, =, the addition operator, +, and the subtraction operator, -. Operators are used to connect to elements in a script. In line 2, the = operator is used to add text to a text field. In line 9, the + operator is used to increase the x position of the balloon by an amount.

4. Look at the curly braces, { and }, on lines 6, 8, 10, 12, and 13.

Curly braces are used to group lines of ActionScript. Whenever you have an open curly brace, {, it must eventually be closed by }. The curly brace opened in line 6 is closed on line 13. All lines of ActionScript contained within those curly braces, 7–12, are grouped together. That group of ActionScript will be executed together when the time comes.

In line 6, we capture an event called the onEnterFrame event. This event occurs once per frame, at the frame rate. This file is set to 24 frames per second (fps) and so the `onEnterFrame` event will occur 24 times per second. All the code that is grouped within its curly braces will be executed 24 times per second.

The ActionScript on lines 8–12 checks for one of two conditions. It first checks to see whether the right arrow key is currently pressed. If it is not, then it checks to see if the left arrow key is pressed. If the first condition is met, line 9 is executed. If the second condition is met, line 11 is executed. If neither condition is met, neither line 9 nor line 11 is executed.

There is one other thing to take note of here. Code that is grouped by curly braces is tabbed in one time for every open and closed curly brace in which it sits. Line 9 sits within two sets of curly braces, so it is tabbed in by two tabs.

5. Notice the dot syntax on nearly every line.

In ActionScript, *objects* are containers that hold data. They can hold other objects, variables, and functions. Some objects have visual representations, such as movie clips, but most do not. You will learn more about these in the coming sections and lessons.

This is line 2:

```
instructions_txt.text = "Use your arrow keys to move the balloon!";
```

Let's look at this line of code, reading from left to right. The first element is the instance name of the text field found in the text layer, followed by a dot. The dot means that what comes next is *inside* the text field object. Then there is an = operator followed by a string. The whole line of code sets the text inside of the text field instance equal to the string found to the right of the = operator.

6. On line 12, click just to the right of } to move the cursor there. Press Enter to add a new blank line to the ActionScript. Type this onto that blank line:

```
//move vertically if the UP or DOWN arrow keys are pressed
```

You just added a comment, which always starts with //. In the next step, you will add ActionScript to enable the balloon to move vertically when the up and down arrow keys are pressed.

7. At the end of line 13, press Enter to add a new blank line to the ActionScript. Type the following four lines of ActionScript:

```
if (Key.isDown(Key.UP)) {
    this._y = this._y - speed;
} else if (Key.isDown(Key.DOWN)) {
    this._y = this._y + speed;
}
```

These four lines of ActionScript look very similar to lines 8–12. The only differences are that they refer to the *y* position of the balloon instead of the *x* position, and they check for the up and down arrow keys instead of the left and right arrow keys.

It is not expected that you will fully understand ActionScript at this point in the book. The purpose of this exercise is let you gain a little experience in working with ActionScript.

8. Generate a test SWF file by selecting Control > Test Movie. Use the four arrow keys to see how the balloon reacts.

The balloon should move left, right, up, and down when those arrow keys are pressed. It's amazing how interactive Flash can be with such few lines of ActionScript!

9. Close the test movie and save your work as *Balloon2.fla*.

You should now be familiar with the various ActionScript elements. It will definitely take a little time, practice, and experience to really feel comfortable writing and editing ActionScript. Fortunately, you have this book and the step-by-step exercises to help you through it!

Next, you'll be formally introduced to the Actions panel. And then you'll start writing variables.

Using the Actions Panel

You know that you can add ActionScript to your Flash application, but you might wonder how you add it. There is a panel, called the Actions panel, for just that purpose.

The Actions panel allows you to view or edit the code on anything that you have selected. If you have a frame selected, the Actions panel shows you the code that is on that frame and lets you edit code on that frame. If you have a symbol on the stage selected, such as a button or a movie clip, the Actions panel allows you to view/edit the code that is on this symbol. A later section in this lesson, called "Code Placement," discusses in greater detail where you can add code in your application.

Launching the Actions Panel

The Actions panel can be opened in three ways.

- Use the toolbar in Flash; choose Window > Actions.
- Use the hotkey F9.
- If the Actions panel is already open, but minimized, you can click the word *Actions* to expand the panel.

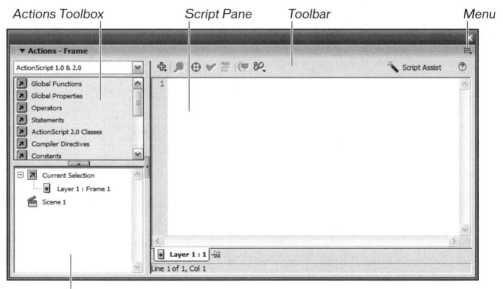

Many people prefer to undock the Actions panel so that it can be easily dragged around as needed. You can do this by clicking and dragging the panel by its *gripper*, which is the small area just to the left of the panel title *Actions*. Just drag the gripper onto the Stage area until you see a ghosted image of the panel appear to be undocked, and then release.

Actions Toolbox   *Script Pane*   *Toolbar*   *Menu*

Script Navigator

The Actions panel is made up of several pieces shown in the screen shot. They are explained in the following sections.

Script Pane

The *Script pane* is where you manage ActionScript. If a frame is selected and there is code on that frame, it can be viewed and edited through the Script pane. You can select another frame that does not yet contain ActionScript and then add ActionScript to it.

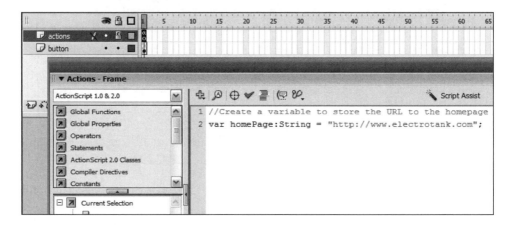

In this image, Frame 1 in the actions layer is selected. That frame contains some ActionScript, so it is visible in the Script pane of the Actions panel.

Toolbar

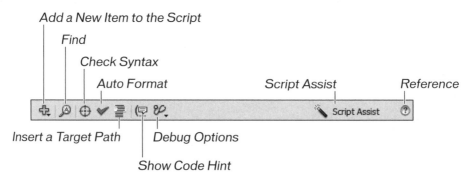

The Actions panel toolbar is found at the top of the Actions panel. It contains several buttons that can be useful while writing and debugging ActionScript. We'll briefly cover them here.

Add a New Item to the Script

This button provides a way for you to add pieces of ActionScript into the Script pane without having to remember exactly how to type it. You'll see this in action, along with the Script Assist option, in the exercise at the end of this section.

Find

This button launches a search window. You can search your ActionScript to find certain words or variables. You can also use this window to find and replace one grouping of characters for another! As a developer of ActionScript, you'll find that this tool comes in quite handy.

Check Syntax

If you have programmed using improper syntax, when you test or publish, you will be informed of a syntax error. If you want to check for syntax errors before publishing, just click the Check Syntax button. It checks the syntax of the currently selected script. If it finds errors, you'll be informed. The Output panel appears and displays an error message.

Auto Format

Formatting your code with tabs, carriage returns, and spaces is considered by many to be a good practice. It makes your code more easily readable. If you would like to have Flash search through your currently selected script and auto format it by placing tabs, carriage returns, and spaces where it thinks is best, then click this button.

Insert a Target Path

When you want to use code to control a symbol, you must refer to its instance name. You can type in the path to this symbol instance or you can use this button to launch a window to help you do this visually. This window allows you to navigate to the symbol of interest and to select that symbol. Once you have selected the symbol, the target path is automatically inserted for you.

Show Code Hint

Code hints help you easily select from a list of methods and properties of a class instance stored in a variable. They are discussed briefly in the section on creating variables.

Debug Options

The Actions panel allows you to set a breakpoint in code. A *breakpoint* helps you when you are trying to debug your application. With this toolbar option, you can set a breakpoint, remove a breakpoint, and remove all breakpoints.

Script Assist

By default, you add code to the Actions panel by typing it in. If you click the Script Assist button, the Actions panel no longer lets you manually enter code into the Script pane. You edit code another way. This is discussed in greater detail as follows and in the exercise at the end of this section.

Reference

This button is used to launch the Help panel. If something is highlighted in the Actions toolbox area of the Actions panel when this button is clicked, help for that item is displayed. The Help panel is a very useful tool.

Menu

There is a menu button found on the far right of the toolbar. If you click it, you see a long list of options, many of which are also represented in the toolbar.

Reload Code Hints	
Pin Script	Ctrl+=
Close Script	Ctrl+-
Close All Scripts	Ctrl+Shift+--
Go to Line...	Ctrl+G
Find and Replace...	Ctrl+F
Find Again	F3
Auto Format	Ctrl+Shift+F
Check Syntax	Ctrl+T
Show Code Hint	Ctrl+Spacebar
Import Script...	Ctrl+Shift+I
Export Script...	Ctrl+Shift+X
Print...	
Script Assist	Ctrl+Shift+E
Esc Shortcut Keys	
Hidden Characters	Ctrl+Shift+8
✓ Line Numbers	Ctrl+Shift+L
Word Wrap	Ctrl+Shift+W
Preferences...	Ctrl+U
Help	
Group Actions with	▶
Close Actions	
Rename panel group...	
Maximize panel group	
Close panel group	

Here are a few of the other options and what they do:

Import Script

This option allows you to browse to a text file that contains ActionScript. This script is then loaded and added to the Script pane.

Export Script

This option allows you to easily save the script currently showing in the Script pane to a text file.

Line Numbers

If selected, line numbers show in the Script pane to the left of each line of code. This can come in handy when you are communicating with another programmer about the ActionScript or if you just like to know how many lines of code you write.

Word Wrap

Sometimes lines of ActionScript can be quite long, extending wider than the visible area of the Script pane. If you don't want to have to scroll horizontally to be able to read that line of code, you can select Word Wrap. The entire script is then word-wrapped into the visible area in the Script pane.

Preferences

Selecting this option launches a new window that allows you to configure ActionScript preferences. Keywords, comments, and other special cases are colored in the Script pane. You can customize these colors as well as the preferred font and font size. In addition, you can also customize how the ActionScript is autoformatted.

Actions Toolbox

The Actions toolbox is found in the upper-left corner of the Actions panel. It contains a highly organized list of all built-in functions; classes; and the methods, properties, and events of those classes. We'll look into this a bit more in Lesson 5, "Built-in Classes."

A drop-down list at the top of the Actions toolbox lets you select which version(s) of ActionScript you want to appear in the list. By default, it is set to display ActionScript 1.0 and ActionScript 2.0.

The Actions toolbox is used as an easy way for you to drill down to find what ActionScript is available for specific classes. It can be used to add code to the Script pane by double-clicking an action. I personally use it the most to highlight a specific action and then get help on that action by clicking the Reference button in the toolbar.

Script Navigator

In some Flash files, ActionScript is placed in a number of areas. If it is your job to open such a file and edit the ActionScript, you might find it difficult to locate exactly where the ActionScript exists. The Script navigator, found in the bottom-left area of the Actions panel, helps you see at a glance where code exists.

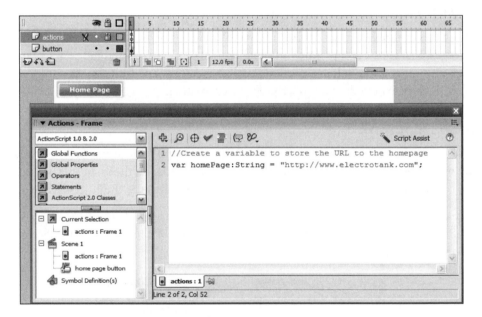

The Script navigator shows you a tree view of the elements that contain ActionScript in your current file. You can click anything in that tree to view/edit the code that is attached to it. The previous image shows a frame that contains some ActionScript and a button that contains some ActionScript. In the Script navigator, you can see that both Frame 1 and home page button appear. If you click home page button, you would see the ActionScript on that button.

Script Assist

The default setting for the Actions panel allows you to type all of the ActionScript that you need right into the Script pane. If you are new to programming, remembering all the syntax rules can be daunting. There is an alternative to writing code manually: Script Assist.

The Actions panel is switched to Script Assist mode by clicking the Script Assist button. This mode helps you to add ActionScript in an easy way so that you don't have to worry about the syntax or formatting rules. Using the Add a New Item to the Script button in the Actions panel toolbar, you can add lines of code. Script Assist then gives you fields to fill out to customize the script.

To create a new variable using the Add a New Item to the Script button, select Statements > Variables > var. A blank variable template appears in the Script pane with fields to fill out above the Script pane.

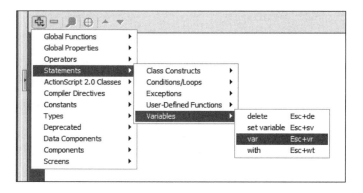

The first field is called Variables. Type the name of the variable, an equal sign, and the value of that variable. On the next line, you'll find a field called Type. You can type the name of the data type or you can find it in the drop-down list. To add a second variable, follow the same process. The Script Assist tool helps you by enforcing proper syntax and formatting.

You've now been formally introduced to the Actions panel. The various areas on the panel as well as its buttons have been explained. So now, it's time to use it! In this exercise, you use Script Assist to add ActionScript to a frame.

1. Open *AnsweringMachine1.fla* from the Lesson01/Start directory.

This Flash application is a simple answering machine. When the application is complete, you'll click a button to have your phone messages played back to you. You'll be able to click another button to stop the message playback and another one to rewind the messages.

The file has five layers. The topmost layer, called actions, is where you'll add the ActionScript. The second layer is sound clip, which contains a movie clip with an instance name of messages_mc. That movie clip holds the sounds of the answering machine messages. There are four answering machine messages.

The third layer down holds a movie clip that plays an animation of a blinking number 4. The next layer, called buttons, contains three buttons with instance names of play_btn, stop_btn, and rewind_btn. These buttons will be used to control the answering machine playback. The final layer simply holds the rest of the images.

2. Click Frame 1 in the actions layer. Open the Actions panel by selecting Window > Actions, or by using the hotkey F9. Click the Script Assist button.

The Actions panel should now be open and showing no ActionScript because none has yet been added.

Over the next few steps, you'll be making this application interactive by adding ActionScript to handle the user interacting with the play, stop, and rewind buttons. So far, you only typed ActionScript into the Script pane. In this exercise, you'll be using Script Assist to add ActionScript. This is the only exercise in the book in which Script Assist is used.

You'll use the Add a New Item to the Script button to add chunks of ActionScript to the Script pane.

3. Click the Add a New Item to the Script button.

Move the cursor over ActionScript 2.0 Classes > Movie > Button > Event Handlers > onRelease and click it.

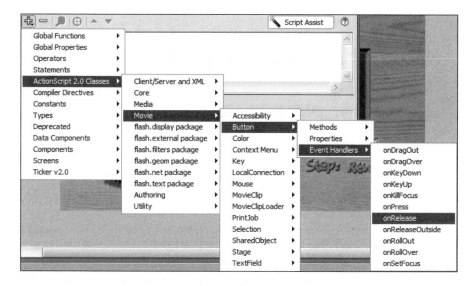

Two lines of ActionScript have been added to the Script pane. They are templates that need to be filled out. In Script Assist mode, you can select any line of code and see the custom fields for that code above the Script pane.

4. Click the first line of ActionScript and then click the Object field. On the Actions toolbar, click the Insert a Target Path button.

Select play_btn and click OK.

The ActionScript that you added in the previous step is a template for capturing an onRelease event; that is, when a button is clicked and released. This template needs to know which button instance to work with. You just told it to use the play_btn button. Any ActionScript that you add between the curly braces will be executed when the play button is clicked.

5. Click the Add a New Item to the Script button. Move the cursor over ActionScript 2.0 Classes > Movie > MovieClip > Methods > play and click it.

A new line of ActionScript has just been added between the curly braces. When the play button is clicked, this line of ActionScript will be executed. It is a template to play a movie clip. It will be filled out in the next step.

6. Click line 2 and then click in the Object field. Click the Insert a Target Path button and choose the Absolute radio button. Find messages_mc and click OK.

This line of ActionScript is executed when the play button is clicked. It tells the messages_mc movie clip to play. That movie clip contains the sounds for the answering machine. As the movie clip plays, you can hear the messages.

You chose the Absolute radio button when locating messages_mc. When you learn more about ActionScript and scope, this choice will make sense. But here is a brief explanation.

The event handler that you added to the play_btn instance is scoped to that instance. By default, that button only sees itself. For the event handler on that button to talk to another movie clip, it must look outside of itself. By choosing Absolute, the target path put _root in front of the instance name, which tells the event handler that the messages_mc instance is on the main Timeline.

Tip *In this exercise, you will see that we use _root three times. For this exercise, that is ok. But it is considered a best practice to avoid using absolute paths unless absolutely necessary.*

The Script pane should now show this ActionScript:

```
this.play_btn.onRelease = function() {
  _root.messages_mc.play();
};
```

7. Click line 3 of ActionScript and then click the Add a New Item to the Script button. Move the cursor over ActionScript 2.0 Classes › Movie › Button › Event Handlers › onRelease and click it. Fill out the Object field to point to **stop_btn**.

In this step, you're doing the same thing that you did several steps ago. You first add an event handler template and then you associate it with a button instance. So you are capturing the onRelease event of the stop_btn instance. Now let's give it something to do.

8. Click line 4 and then click the Add a New Item to the Script button. Move the cursor over ActionScript 2.0 Classes › Movie › MovieClip › Methods › stop and click it. Click the Object field and add an absolute path to **messages_mc**.

You just added a new line of ActionScript between the curly braces of the stop_btn onRelease event handler. When the stop button is clicked, the messages will stop playing. If you click the play button again, the messages will continue where they left off.

9. Click line 6 and then click the Add a New Item to the Script button. Move the cursor over ActionScript 2.0 Classes › Movie › Button › Event Handlers › onRelease and click it. Fill out the Object field to point to **rewind_btn**.

Just as with the play and stop buttons, you have added an onRelease event handler for the rewind button. In the next step, you'll make it do something useful.

10. Click line 7 and then click the Add a New Item to the Script button. Move the cursor over ActionScript 2.0 Classes › Movie › MovieClip › Methods › gotoAndStop and click it. Click the Object field and add an absolute path to **messages_mc**. Click the Frame field and type the number 1.

This line of ActionScript that you just added sends the messages_mc movie clip back to the first frame. That essentially rewinds the messages. To play the messages again, you'll have to click the play button.

11. Choose Control > Test Movie to test the application. Use the buttons to test your work.

When you click the play button, you should hear a beep and then the first message. After the first message, there will be a slight pause, and then another beep and the second message. There are four messages in total.

If you click the stop button, the messages will stop playing. If you then click the play button, the messages should continue playing from where they left off. Finally, if you click the rewind button, the messages should rewind to the beginning, but not automatically play.

12. Close and save your work as *AnsweringMachine2.fla*.

In this exercise, you added button event handlers and gained some experience using Script Assist in the Actions panel. We will not be using it for the remainder of the book. But at least you know it's there if you need a little extra help when programming!

Creating Variables

In this lesson, you were introduced to the concept of ActionScript, saw its basic syntax, and were teased with a few lines of code. Now it's time to start learning how to write some ActionScript yourself! It all starts with understanding variables and how to create them.

When creating an application there are many pieces of data that need to be managed. For instance, a Visit Website button would take a user to a specific website after the click. The URL of this destination website needs to be stored somewhere in the application so the ActionScript for that button knows where to take the user after clicking. A variable is needed in that situation. Here is an example script:

```
var destinationWebSite:String = "http://www.electrotank.com";
visitWebsite_btn.onRelease = function() {
getURL(destinationWebSite);
}
```

The function getURL is built into the Flash player. It launches a new web page when a user clicks and then releases the button. As you can see in the preceding example, variables are used to store data. The first line of code creates a new variable called destinationWebSite. The next few lines capture the onRelease event of a button and execute the getURL function as a result. As you can see in the third line of the code, the destinationWebSite variable is fed into the getURL function. The getURL function looks at the value of this variable, sees that it is http://www.electrotank.com, and then opens a new web page to that URL.

Variables can be used to store any type of data available in Flash. There is no reasonable limit to the number of variables that you can use in your application. Some types of variables are useful to be created and destroyed as the application progresses, and some you'll want to stick around the whole time. Through the course of this book, you'll encounter these situations and gain experience working with variables in a number of ways.

You'll see how to create variables and the types of data that they can store in the next section.

The Syntax

If a line of ActionScript is a sentence telling the application what to do, then operators (=, +, -, etc.) are verbs, and variables are nouns. A variable is a named reference to a piece of data. For instance:

```
var firstname:String = "Jobe";
```

The name of the variable is firstname. The data, also known as the *value* of the variable, is "Jobe". Notice that :String appears after firstname. This is called *data typing* and will be discussed in the next subsection.

To create a new variable, first type the characters var and then add a space. This tells the Flash player that you are declaring a new variable. Then type a name for that variable— this is your choice. After the name, you can strictly type the variable by typing a colon and then the data type (discussed as follows). Next, you need to assign the variable a value, which is done using the assignment operator (=). Following the =, you type the data that you want to store. And as with all other actions, it ends with a semicolon.

When declaring a variable properly, you are telling the Flash player three things:

- **Its existence.** You inform the Flash player that from this point forward, within the current scope, a variable with this specific name will exist. Scope is something that will be discussed more in Lesson 2, "Functions."

- **Its scope.** As mentioned previously, we will discuss scope more in Lesson 2. For now, it's enough to understand that a variable can be created but seen only in certain areas. For instance, the variable firstname can appear with different values in many areas of the application.

- **Its data type.** Data types will be discussed in the next subsection. A variable can store a name, such as "Jobe," but can also store numbers, dates, and many other types of data. As you'll see, it is to your advantage to define a variable's data type.

The value of a variable doesn't have to be typed in. You can have the value of the variable driven dynamically by the values of other variables. That is the power of ActionScript! Here is an example:

```
var firstname:String = "Jobe";
var welcomeMessage:String = "Good morning "+firstname+"!";
```

In this example, two variables were created. The first one, firstname, stores a name. The value of the second variable, welcomeMessage, is dynamically generated based on the value of firstname. In this case, the final value of welcomeMessage is Good morning Jobe!

Data Types and Strict Data Typing

Variables store data, which can be text (such as the name of a city), a number (such as the age of a person), and so on. These different types of data are called *data types*. When declaring a variable, it is recommended to also assign it a data type, which is *strict data typing*. Strict data typing is a simple concept.

```
var variableName:DataType = someValue;
```

You have seen the preceding syntax several times in this lesson. Strict data typing comes into play in the syntax after the variable name. It is the :DataType part. Let's start with a few lines of code and then explain them:

```
var catName:String = "Anna";
var ageInYears:Number = 3;
var ageInMonths:Number = ageInYears*12;
var isSpayed:Boolean = true;
```

In this example, four variables were created using three different data types. The first one is a String, which is data that should be treated as text. The second variable is typed as a Number, which is a type of data that stores an actual numeric value. The value "3" is a String, which is different from 3. One is treated as text, and the other is treated as a number. The third line of ActionScript is typed as a Number as well. Notice that this variable's value is set by the product of two other numbers.

The final line of ActionScript types the variable isSpayed as a Boolean. If you are completely new to programming, the concept of a Boolean value is probably new to you as well. A Boolean value is either true or false, and that is it. It cannot contain any other values. They are used to store information that can have only two states. As an example, you might store a value in your application that indicates whether the user has logged in or not. You might call this variable isLoggedIn. If its value is true, the user has logged in; otherwise, it's false.

In addition to String, Number, and Boolean, dozens of other data types are used in ActionScript. In fact, as you learn how to build your own custom classes (see Lesson 6, "Custom Classes"), you'll see that you create your own custom data types!

Note that data typing is not required. You can leave off the :DataType part of your variable declaration. Before you abandon strict data typing, however, please read the rest of this section to see why it's so important. We'll use strict data typing throughout this book.

Now you should understand the *how* of data typing. But because data typing is not required, you might wonder *why should I data type?* There are a few very compelling reasons why you should data type. These reasons are very important even if they might not seem so to the novice programmer.

- **Workflow.** When you work on an application, you'll very quickly reach dozens, hundreds, or even thousands of lines of code. When adding to your code or revisiting it months later, you'll thank yourself for properly declaring variables with a data type. This gives you more information about a script that you are looking at than you would normally have. The combination of commenting your code and data typing variables will help your workflow or a coworker's stress level as code enhancements are needed.

- **Compile-time errors.** This is huge. Strict data typing can happen in areas of your script that we haven't yet discussed. You'll see more about this in a later lesson. If you data type in every area of your code that allows data typing, then when you publish or test your SWF file, the compiler will perform a certain level of error checking for you. For instance, consider this:

```
var catName:String = "Anna";
var age:Number = 3;
var ageInMonths:Number = catName;
```

  In the third line of the preceding script, the variable was declared as a number. But we tried setting its value from a variable that was declared as a String. If this script was in your Flash application and you tried to publish or test the SWF file, you would receive an error. The previous example is extremely simplified. As you create more-complex scripts, you'll find the fact that you receive an error a good thing. It's better to be told that there is an error while you are creating the application, than to let the SWF be published as "error-free," only to find the bug at some later date.

- **Code hints.** If you strictly type a variable, you can gain access to code hints as you use that variable. We haven't yet discussed classes, methods, or properties. But for now, it's enough to know that by strictly typing a variable, you can make your life a little easier. With code hints, the Actions panel can predict certain things for you as you type. Code hints are automatically shown for a variable in a drop-down list if you type a period (.) after the variable in a line of code.

In this section, you learned the syntax used to properly create a variable. In this exercise, you will create some variables and will use strict data typing.

1. Open *Navigation1.fla* in the Lesson01/Start folder.

This application is a very basic Flash website navigation example. There are three buttons that are used to navigate between three frames. Variables will be used to dynamically size the logo and to display a welcome message on the home page screen. The three buttons will be made interactive to handle navigation.

There are seven layers in this file. The first layer is called labels. Frames are numbered, but they can also be labeled. Using ActionScript, you can tell the movie to go to a specific frame number or to a frame label. This movie has three frame labels in this layer: Home Page, News, and Contact Us.

As with the previous exercises, an actions layer holds the ActionScript. The three buttons, homePage_btn, news_btn, and contactUs_btn, are on the nav buttons layer. The logo for the website, which is large and seen in the upper-left corner of the Stage, is contained on the logo layer. It has an instance name of logo_mc.

The nav bar layer contains the graphic for the navigation bar, and the background layer contains the graphic for the background image. The content layer contains the content that is frame-specific. There are three key frames, one for each frame label. On the Home Page label, there is a text field with an instance name of welcome_txt. On the other content frames, there is only static text.

2. Click Frame 1 in the actions layer. Open the Actions panel by selecting Windows > Actions or by using the hotkey F9.

You just opened the Actions panel. There is not yet any ActionScript on this frame. If you have Script Assist enabled from the previous exercises, make sure that you deselect that option. In this exercise, you'll be typing directly into the Script pane.

3. Add a stop action to the Script pane. Type this: *stop();*

A SWF file that has more than one frame will automatically play. If you were to test this application before adding a stop action, you would see the movie jump from content screen to content screen as the movie plays continuously through all of the frames.

A stop action tells the Flash player to stop playing through the current Timeline. You will use stop actions very frequently to ensure that your application flow is controlled by ActionScript, not just by animation.

4. On the next line, declare a new variable called **logoScale**, type it as a number, and give it a value of 55.

So, enter this ActionScript:

```
var logoScale:Number = 55;
```

You probably noticed that the logo doesn't fit nicely within the navigation bar; it is just too large. Using ActionScript, we'll make the logo movie clip smaller to fit within the navigation bar.

You just created a variable called logoScale. We will use the value of this variable to assign a new size to the logo_mc movie clip instance.

5. To size the **logo_mc** instance, add these two lines to the script:

```
logo_mc._xscale = logoScale;
logo_mc._yscale = logoScale;
```

Movie clips have a property called _xscale. This property contains the percentage of the movie clip's current width, as compared with its natural width. Movie clips are not resized, so the _xscale value would be 100, because its width is 100 percent of the natural width.

You can set this property, as is done in the first line that you added previously. By adding that line of ActionScript, you are telling the logo_mc movie clip instance to change its width to 55 percent of its natural width. It is 55 percent because the value of logoScale is 55.

The second line of code you added does the same thing as the first, but for the _yscale property. The end result is a movie clip that has scaled to 55 percent of its original size.

6. Next, create a new variable called **welcomeMessage**, type it as a string, and give it a string value of **"Welcome to Science Now!"**. Then populate the **welcomeMessage_txt** field with this value.

To do this, type these lines of ActionScript,

```
var welcomeMessage:String = "Welcome to Science Now!";
welcomeMessage_txt.text = welcomeMessage;
```

Here you have created a new variable called welcomeMessage. It contains a string that will be displayed in the welcomeMessage_txt text field.

In the previous step, you changed the value of the _xscale property of a movie clip to alter the way it looks. In this step, you are changing the value of the text property of a text field to alter the way it looks. The act of assigning a new value to this text property displays it on the screen within that text field.

You have now created and used all the variables that are needed for this exercise. The rest of the steps deal with something you have done before: capturing the onRelease event of buttons.

7. Add button event handlers to capture the **onRelease** event of the three button instances. In each event handler, add a **gotoAndStop** action to send the movie to the appropriate frame label.

To do so, add this code

```
homePage_btn.onRelease = function() {
    gotoAndStop("Home Page");
};
news_btn.onRelease = function() {
    gotoAndStop("News");
};
contactUs_btn.onRelease = function() {
    gotoAndStop("Contact Us");
};
```

In the previous exercise, you added onRelease event handlers to buttons using Script Assist. Here you get a chance to type them using the correct syntax. Events and event handlers will be discussed in greater detail in Lesson 7, but you will also learn more about them along the way.

The gotoAndStop global function sends the current Timeline to a specific frame. You can feed it a number or a frame label string value. In this case, you are using frame labels.

8. Test the movie by selecting Control > Test Movie, or by pressing Control + Enter. Notice the welcome message and the size of the logo. Click the navigation buttons to check your work.

The welcome message should be displayed on the home page. The logo movie clip shows on all content frames. When you jump from the home page to another screen and then back to the home page, the ActionScript on that frame is again executed. If it were not executed again, the welcome message wouldn't show up when you leave the home page and then come back.

9. Close and save your work as *Navigation2.fla*.

In this exercise, you created variables to store values. You then used those values to manipulate the way the application displays.

Code Placement

In this lesson, you have learned about the Actions panel. You've seen that you can select a frame and add code to that frame by using the Actions panel. This section discusses other places where you can add ActionScript. We'll also discuss best practices for programming. Just because you can put code somewhere doesn't necessarily mean that you should!

Frames

You have already gained experience adding ActionScript to a frame. ActionScript can be added only to a key frame. If you select a frame in theTimeline that is not a key frame and enter ActionScript into the Actions panel, it will attach itself to the nearest key frame at a lower frame number.

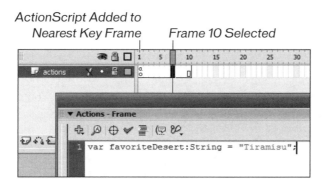

Buttons

If a button is selected and the Actions panel is open, you can add code directly to the button. Because the purpose of a button is to capture specific events, such as release, rollOver, and rollOut, all actions added to a button must sit within code that captures a button event.

The syntax for capturing a button event is this:

```
on(someEvent) {
   //actions go here
}
```

Instead of the word someEvent, you enter the event you want to capture. For example:

```
on(release) {
   getURL("http://www.electrotank.com");
}
```

You can add ActionScript to a button to capture several events:

```
on(rollOver) {
   this._xscale = 200;
}
on(rollOut) {
   this._xscale = 100;
}
on(release) {
   getURL("http://www.electrotank.com");
}
```

If the preceding ActionScript is added to a button, it gets twice as wide when the mouse is over it, it returns to normal size when the mouse leaves it, and it launches a new web page if clicked.

Movie Clips

You can add code to frames. Movie clips contain frames. Adding ActionScript to frames within a movie clip is the same as adding it to the main Timeline. You select the frame and the type in the code.

With movie clips, however, there is another place where you can add ActionScript. From outside of the movie clip, you can select the movie clip, open the Actions panel, and then enter ActionScript to attach the code to the movie clip itself.

With buttons, you have to put the code within a button event handler code. For movie clips, you must put the code within a *clip event* handler. Some example clip events are load, enterFrame, mouseDown, and mouseUp. The syntax to attach ActionScript to a movie clip is this:

```
onClipEvent(someEvent) {
   //add actions here
}
```

Instead of the word someEvent, you type the name of the event you want to capture.

```
onClipEvent(enterFrame) {
   //add actions here
}
```

You can capture several clip events on a movie clip like this:

```
onClipEvent(load) {
  //add actions here
}
onClipEvent(mouseMove) {
  //add actions here
}
```

Best Practices

A *best practice* is an idea or procedure that is generally accepted as a good way to approach a certain task. With ActionScript there are several best practices, two of which are discussed here.

Best Practice 1

You can add code to frames, directly to buttons, and directly onto a movie clip. One best practice in ActionScript, which is used in this book, is to ensure that *no code should ever be placed directly onto a button or movie clip*. If you want to capture button events or clip events, you can do that by adding code to a frame. For instance, if you want to launch a new web page when a user clicks a button, you can add this code to a frame:

```
visitWebPage_btn.onRelease = function() {
  getURL("http://www.electrotank.com");
}
```

The only extra thing that you have to do is to make sure that your button or movie clip has an instance name. Without an instance name, you can't talk to it using code.

This practice emerged as a best practice because many Flash applications were developed with code in dozens of locations all throughout the document. When you needed to edit the code, it proved to be a nightmare to even find the code, let alone edit it. With this best practice, you still might have code in a few locations throughout your application, but knowing where to look for it just got a lot simpler.

Best Practice 2

ActionScript should always be placed on its own layer with a name of actions or something similar. This layer should not contain any assets; it should be completely blank except for the code. The layer should be locked so that you do not accidentally add an asset to that layer. It is also common to make this layer your top layer or one of the top two layers.

This emerged as a best practice for two reasons:

- It takes the first best practice a step further. Not only does someone looking in your file know that your code is on a frame somewhere, but this person knows it will be on a blank layer called actions (probably at the top of the layer stack).

- Keeping the layer empty of assets helps keep you from accidentally adding ActionScript to a movie clip or button. Also, if you mix assets onto the actions layer and then want to delete all the assets on the layer, you might be tempted to delete the layer itself, which would remove the code!

Understanding Objects, Classes, and Scope

This section introduces you to some new concepts. It will be useful for you to be exposed to the ideas here before moving on to the following lessons. We will not go into much detail with objects and classes here because there are later lessons devoted to these topics.

Objects and Classes

An object is a container. When created, the object is empty. Variables can be added to this object. A variable that "lives" in an object is called a *property*, but you'll still frequently see it referred to as a variable.

A *function* is a grouping of code that is given a name. By using special syntax, that grouping of code can be executed any number of times and at any time. A function can be added to an object. A function that lives in an object is called a *method*.

Now imagine an object that has certain properties and methods that are useful for a special purpose. For instance, imagine an object that had these properties: firstname, lastname, and age. This object also has the methods speak(), eat(), and sleep(). This fake object represents a person. The person can have a first name, a last name, and an age. This person can be told to speak, to eat, and to sleep.

What if we want to have an object like this, with these specific properties and methods, but for an unlimited number of unrelated people? It would be a pain to start off with some basic object and create properties and methods every time we need them. That's where a *class* comes in, which is a blueprint for a custom object. The previous example might be called the Person class. If we defined a new class called Person with the properties and methods described here, we can easily create new instances of this class when we need them.

In Flash, there are many classes built in. Here are a few that you've already seen: MovieClip, String, Number, Boolean, and Button. Some of the classes have an asset on the screen

(MovieClip and Button), but most do not. Some properties of the MovieClip class are as follows:

- _x—The *x* position of the movie clip
- _y—The *y* position of the movie clip
- _rotation—The rotation in degrees of the movie clip
- _name—The instance name of the movie clip

As a quick recap, we have seen that

- An object is an empty container to which you can add properties and methods.
- A class is a blueprint for a new copy of an object that has a custom set of properties and methods.

In Lesson 5, "Built-in Classes," and Lesson 6, "Custom Classes," you will learn a lot more about the built-in classes and will create your own custom classes!

Scope

Let's say you have two movie clips on the stage with the instance names cat_mc and dog_mc. As mentioned, all instances of the MovieClip class have a property called _x. Because a property is just a variable on an object, here we have two movie clips, and so we have two _x properties.

The _x property represents the *x* position (horizontal) of the movie clip. It makes sense that the value of the _x property of dog_mc should not be the same as that of cat_mc, unless of course they are on top of each other. In this case, we have two variables of the same name that exist separately.

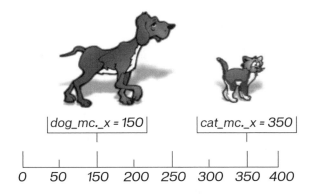

The scope of a variable is where that variable exists. No other variable of the same name can exist within the same scope. A variable is scoped to the object in which it is created. An _x property was created separately for the cat_mc object and the dog_mc object. Those properties are scoped to the object in which they reside.

Even if something is scoped to a specific object, it can still be seen by other scopes if it is referenced using *dot syntax*. Consider that this ActionScript on Frame 1 of the timeline contains cat_mc and dog_mc:

```
var cat_x:Number = cat_mc._x;
var dog_x:Number = dog_mc._x;
```

These lines of code create two variables whose values are the _x properties of cat_mc and dog_mc. It illustrates how you can reference the properties in one scope from another.

What You Have Learned

In this lesson, you have:

- Been introduced to the various elements that make up ActionScript (pages 3–12)
- Used the Actions panel to enter ActionScript manually, or with Script Assist (pages 12–24)
- Created variables that change how an application looks (pages 24–30)
- Learned where it is legal to place code, and what best practices for this are recommended (pages 31–36)

2 Functions

When programming, you might find yourself using the same chunks of code repeatedly—either by copying and pasting them or by rewriting the same lines of ActionScript. There is a way to write ActionScript just once and reuse it any time with a single action. You do this with *functions*, and the action by which you execute a function is a *call* or a *function call*. Functions are real time-savers—during both development and code maintenance—because they reduce the amount of code you need to write or modify. Think of a function as a mini-program that serves a specific purpose within another application. You can use it to perform a set of specific actions, you can feed it information and output a result—or you can do both. Functions provide a powerful and versatile way to script your project.

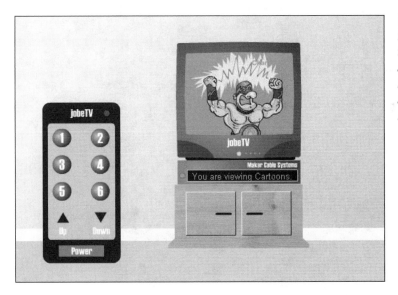

You will create several functions that allow you to turn a Flash-TV on and off and change its channels. A Flash-TV is a simple Flash app that acts like a TV and remote control.

In this lesson, you'll learn how to create and use functions while developing a remote control for a Flash-made television set.

What You Will Learn

In this lesson, you will:

- Create a function
- Call a function
- Add parameters to a function
- Create a function that returns a result
- Use local variables

Approximate Time

This lesson takes approximately one and one half hours to complete.

Lesson Files

Media Files:

None

Starting Files:

Lesson02/Start/television1.fla

Completed Projects:

Lesson02/Completed/television4.fla

Creating Functions

Before you use a function, you must create or define it. You can do this by using one of two possible syntaxes.

Syntax 1

This code describes the first syntax:

```
function myFunction (parameter1:DataType,parameter2:DataType,etc.) {
  //actions go here;
}
```

The code represents the most common way of creating a function, as well as the syntax we'll use most frequently in this lesson. You'll see that the function declaration begins with the word `function`, followed by the name of the function (which can be anything you choose, as long as it follows typical naming conventions). Following the function name is an area enclosed by parentheses. You can leave this area blank or you can fill it with information (parameter data) that the function can use. By leaving the area within the parentheses blank, you create a "generic" function—that is, one that performs the same way whenever it's called (used). If your function contains parameters, it will perform in a unique way each time it's called based on the parameter information it receives. Giving the function information in this way is called *passing in arguments* or *passing in parameters*. You can use as many parameters as you want. We'll tell you how to use parameter data a bit later in this lesson.

Following the optional parameter area is an open curly brace, followed by a carriage return and then some actions before the curly brace that concludes the function. In the space between the curly braces, you write the actions that you want your function to perform. These actions can also make use of any parameter information passed to the function (as you will see soon).

Syntax 2

This code represents the second syntax for creating functions:

```
myFunction = function (parameter1:DataType,parameter2:DataType,etc.)
  {/* actions go here */
};
```

You would use this syntax to create a function dynamically or to define your own custom *method* of an object (which we'll discuss in Lesson 6, "Custom Classes"). The only difference between this syntax and Syntax 1 is in the way the function name is assigned: The function name appears first, and the syntax for defining how the function will work follows the = assignment operator.

Now that you understand the basic syntax for creating/defining a function, let's look at how a function is used, or called.

If a function contains no parameters, it can be called using the following syntax:

```
myFunction();
```

When you call a function, you're telling Flash to execute all the actions within that function. If myFunction() contained 20 actions, they all could be executed by using this single line of script.

If a function has been defined to accept parameter data, you can use the following syntax to call it:

```
myFunction(parameter1, parameter2);
```

If parameter1 had a value of cat and parameter2 had a value of 36, those two values would be sent to the function for use by the actions within the function definition. At a later time, the same function could be called, but different parameter values sent. This would result in the same function working in a slightly different way from the first example because the actions within the function would be making use of different parameter values.

The foregoing examples assume that the function and function call reside on the same Timeline. Just as each Timeline contains its own variables and objects, each Timeline also contains any functions you've defined there. To call a function on a specific Timeline, you need to place the target path to that Timeline in front of the function call like this:

```
_root.clip1.clip2.myFunction();
```

In this exercise, you'll create a Power button on a television remote control. With this button, the Flash TV can be toggled on and off using a function.

> **Note** A function can be called dynamically based on a value—for instance,
> _root[aVariableName]();. Thus, if aVariableName had a value of "sayHello",
> the function call would actually look like _root.sayHello();.

1. Open *television1.fla* in the Lesson02/Start folder.

The movie's structure has already been created. The Actions layer is where you will include all of the ActionScript for this exercise. On the TV layer, a movie clip instance named tv_mc has three layers on its Timeline: the bottom layer (Television) is a graphic, and the layer above that (Screen) contains a movie clip instance called screen_mc (which is then masked by the layer above that). The screen_mc movie clip instance, which includes two layers and two frames, contains graphical content that represents the various "programs" seen when changing channels on the TV.

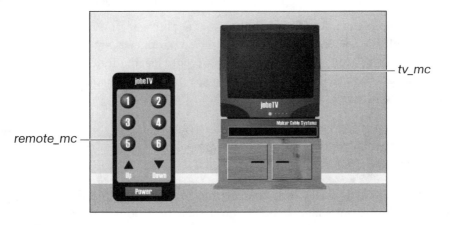

On the main Timeline, a layer named Remote contains a movie clip instance named remote_mc. Inside remote_mc, you'll find a layer that contains most of the remote control graphics, including a movie clip with an instance name of light_mc, as well as another layer that contains the buttons for the remote. The numbered buttons have instance names of channel1_btn through channel6_btn. Under the numbered buttons are the Up and Down channel buttons whose instance names are up_btn and down_btn, respectively. The bottom button, Power, has an instance name of power_btn.

2. Select Frame 1 of the Actions layer on the main Timeline. With the Actions panel open, add the following script:

```
var tvPower:Boolean = false;
function togglePower() {
  var newChannel:Number;
  if (tvPower) {
    newChannel = 0;
    tvPower = false;
  } else {
    newChannel = 1;
    tvPower = true;
  }
  tv_mc.screen_mc.gotoAndStop(newChannel+1);
  remote_mc.light_mc.play();
}
```

The first line of this script creates a variable named tvPower, which is used to track the current state of the TV. A value of true means the television is on; false means the television is off. The television will appear off initially, so tvPower is set to false.

The next 11 lines represent a function definition for togglePower(). When called, this function will toggle the television power on and off. No parameters are passed into this function. Because this script exists on Frame 1, our togglePower() function is defined, and a variable called tvPower is set to false as soon as the frame is loaded (that is, when the movie begins to play).

Note *Because functions must be defined before they can be called, it is common practice to define all functions on an early frame in your movie so that they can be called at any time after that.*

The first part of the function uses an if statement to analyze the current value of tvPower. If tvPower is true (TV is on) when the function is called, the actions in the function change it to false (off) and set the value of the newChannel variable to 0; otherwise (else), tvPower is set to true and newChannel to 1. Using the if statement in this manner causes the value of tvPower to be set to its opposite each time the function is called, thus toggling the value of newChannel. By the time this statement is finished, newChannel has a value of 0 or 1.

Note *We use if statements—conditional logic—in a few places throughout this lesson. They are not formally covered until Lesson 4, "Arrays and Loops." For now, it is enough to know that they are used to determine whether a certain condition is met. If that condition is met, extra code will be executed.*

The function then sends the screen_mc movie clip instance (which is inside the tv_mc movie clip instance) to a frame based on the current value of newChannel + 1. You must add 1 to the value of newChannel to prevent the Timeline from being sent to Frame 0 (newChannel sometimes contains a value of 0, and there's no such thing as Frame 0 in a Flash movie Timeline). In the end, this part of the function will send the screen_mc movie clip instance to Frame 1 (showing a blank TV screen) or Frame 2 (showing Channel 1).

The function finishes by telling the light on the remote control to play, which causes it to blink, providing a visual indication that a button has been pressed.

There is now a function on Frame 1 of the main, or root, Timeline. Although this function contains several actions, none of them is executed until the function is called.

3. **With the Actions panel still open, add this script to the end of the current actions (after the function definition):**

```
remote_mc.power_btn.onRelease = togglePower;
```

```
▼ Actions - Frame
                                                    Script Assist   ?
 1  var tvPower:Boolean = false;
 2  function togglePower() {
 3      var newChannel:Number;
 4      if (tvPower) {
 5          newChannel = 0;
 6          tvPower = false;
 7      } else {
 8          newChannel = 1;
 9          tvPower = true;
10      }
11      tv_mc.screen_mc.gotoAndStop(newChannel+1);
12      remote_mc.light_mc.play();
13  }
14  remote_mc.power_btn.onRelease = togglePower;
15
 Actions : 1
Line 14 of 15, Col 1
```

The Power button for the remote control has an instance name of power_btn (and it exists inside the remote_mc movie clip instance). This line of ActionScript assigns an onRelease event handler to the Power button: our togglePower function. Every time the Power button is clicked, the togglePower() function is called, causing the actions within the function to be executed.

4. Choose Control > Test Movie. Then click the Power button several times to view the TV on/off functionality you created.

Every time you press the Power button, the togglePower() function is called so that all the actions within that function are performed. As mentioned, the actions within the function toggle the state of the TV.

5. Close the test movie and save your work as *television2.fla*.

You have now created and used a function! In the next section, we'll build on this idea to create a more powerful and versatile function.

Adding Parameters to Functions

In the preceding exercise, you learned how to create a function and call it. In this exercise, you'll add parameters to a function and learn how to use them. Here's the syntax for creating a function that accepts parameters:

```
function convertToMoonWeight (myWeight:Number){
   var weightOnMoon:Number = myWeight/6.04;
}
```

The sole parameter for this function is named myWeight. The value of that parameter is also used *within* the function definition (near the end of the second line), just as if it were a preexisting variable. Notice that you should associate a data type with the parameter in the function definition. In this case, the parameter myWeight represents a numeric value.

Here's an example of the syntax used to call this function:

```
convertToMoonWeight(165);
```

Here you can see that we added a numeric value of 165 to the function call. This value is sent to the function being called so that it can perform its specified functionality, based on that value. In this example, the value of 165 in the *function call* is assigned to the myWeight parameter in the *function definition*. The result looks something like this:

```
function convertToMoonWeight (165){
    var weightOnMoon:Number = 165/6.04;
}
```

Thus, in our example, sending a value of 165 to our convertToMoonWeight() function would set the value of weightOnMoon to 165/6.04, or 27.32.

The myWeight parameter is replaced with the value sent to the function when it is called. The great thing about this is that whenever we call our function again, we can send it a different value, which will result in the weightOnMoon variable being set to a different value as well. Take a look at these function calls to the convertToMoonWeight() function:

```
convertToMoonWeight(190);
convertToMoonWeight(32);
convertToMoonWeight(230);
```

Each of these function calls is to our single function, but because different values are sent to the function in each call, the function performs the same action (converting that value to moon weight) using the different values.

Note *Parameters you define for a function have meaning only within that function. In our example, myWeight has no meaning or use outside of the function itself.*

When sending values to a function, you can also use variables in your function call, as in the following:

```
convertToMoonWeight(myVariable);
```

When you do this, the current value of the variable is passed to the function.

Functions can also be made up of multiple parameters, like this:

```
function openWindow(url:String, window:String){
getURL(url, window);
}
```

This function definition contains two parameters, url and window, separated by a comma. The function contains a single action, getURL(), which makes use of these two parameters. Making a call to this function looks like this:

```
openWindow("http://www.yahoo.com", "_blank");
```

The function call also *sends* two values, separated by a comma, to the function: a URL and the HTML target for opening the specified URL. These parameter values are used by the function to perform its specified functionality. In this case, the function call would result in *yahoo.com* opening in a new browser window.

When defining multiple parameters in a function definition, remember their order within the parentheses. Respective values that are defined in the function definition should be listed in that same order in the function call.

Here's a function call to the openWindow() function that won't work because the parameters of the function definition dictate that the URL should be listed first in the function call:

```
openWindow("_blank", "http://www.yahoo.com");
```

Note *When a function is called, a temporary array called* arguments *is created. This array contains all parameters passed to the function—even if you specified none when defining your function. Here is an example of how to access the* arguments *array:*

```
function traceNames() {
   trace("This function was passed " + arguments.length + "arguments");
   trace("The value of the first argument is: " + arguments[0]);
   trace("The value of the second argument is: " + arguments[1]);
}
traceNames("Kelly","Chance");
```

In this example, these strings appear in the output window:

```
This function was passed two arguments
The value of the first argument is: Kelly
The value of the second argument is: Chance
```

Accessing the arguments array enables you to create functions that can adapt their functionality based on how many parameters are passed to them. For more information about arrays, see Lesson 4, "Arrays and Loops."

In this exercise, you'll add functionality to the numeric keypad on the remote control and to the TV channel Up and Down buttons, allowing them to change the channel displayed on the TV screen. The numeric buttons work by calling a function and passing in the number of the channel to jump to. You will also modify the `togglePower()` function slightly.

1. Open television2.fla.

We continue to work with the file you completed in the preceding exercise. Before we do, however, it's important to note the structure of the `screen_mc` movie clip instance, which is inside the `tv_mc` movie clip instance. The `screen_mc` movie clip instance's Timeline has graphical content on Frames 1 through 7. This content represents the "off" state of the TV (on Frame 1), as well as six channels of programming that our TV will be set up to receive.

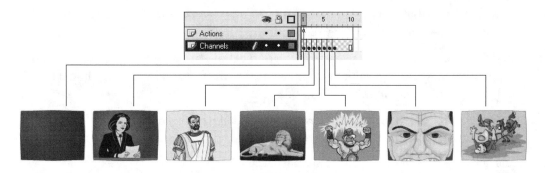

2. Select Frame 1 of the Actions layer on the main Timeline and open the Actions panel. Add this ActionScript just below the line that reads `var tvPower:Boolean = false;`:

```
var currentChannel:Number;
```

In this exercise we create functions that change the channel of the TV, including incrementing and decrementing the TV channel. To increment or decrement a channel, you need to have the current channel stored. The script declares a new variable called `currentChannel`, which will be used to store the numeric value of the current TV channel.

3. With Frame 1 still selected, add this script just below the end of the last function definition:

```
function changeTheChannel(newChannel:Number) {
  if (tvPower) {
    currentChannel = newChannel;
    tv_mc.screen_mc.gotoAndStop(newChannel+1);
    remote_mc.light_mc.play();
  }
}
```

```
1   var tvPower:Boolean = false;
2   var currentChannel:Number;
3   function togglePower() {
4       var newChannel:Number;
5       if (tvPower) {
6           newChannel = 0;
7           tvPower = false;
8       } else {
9           newChannel = 1;
10          tvPower = true;
11      }
12      tv_mc.screen_mc.gotoAndStop(newChannel+1);
13      remote_mc.light_mc.play();
14  }
15  function changeTheChannel(newChannel:Number) {
16      if (tvPower) {
17          currentChannel = newChannel;
18          tv_mc.screen_mc.gotoAndStop(newChannel+1);
19          remote_mc.light_mc.play();
20      }
21  }
22  remote_mc.power_btn.onRelease = togglePower;
23
```

You have just created a function that accepts a parameter. This function changes the TV channel based on the parameter value received (newChannel). All the actions the function performs are enclosed in an if statement, which is used to allow channels to be changed *only* if tvPower is true. The function then sets a variable used to store the current channel of the television to the value of the parameter value sent to the function.

The next two lines should be familiar from the togglePower() function we discussed in the preceding exercise: They set the frame in the screen_mc movie clip instance (causing the television to change channels) and instruct the light on the remote control to blink. To understand how this function works, consider a simple example. Assume that this function call is made:

```
changeTheChannel(4);
```

The function would ask whether tvPower is true (TV is on) before doing anything else. If it is, currentChannel is given a value of 4 (the same as the parameter passed to the function). Next, the screen_mc movie clip instance is moved to a frame based on the parameter value passed to the function, plus 1 (or 4 + 1). The screen_mc instance is moved to Frame 5.

Your newly created function is ready for use. Next, we'll add onRelease event handlers to each of the numeric buttons to call changeTheChannel().

4. Add this script to the end of the current script on Frame 1:

```
remote_mc.channel1_btn.onRelease = function() {
  changeTheChannel(1);
};
remote_mc.channel2_btn.onRelease = function() {
  changeTheChannel(2);
};
remote_mc.channel3_btn.onRelease = function() {
  changeTheChannel(3);
};
remote_mc.channel4_btn.onRelease = function() {
  changeTheChannel(4);
};
remote_mc.channel5_btn.onRelease = function() {
  changeTheChannel(5);
};
remote_mc.channel6_btn.onRelease = function() {
  changeTheChannel(6);
};
```

You just added an event handler function to each of the numeric buttons on the remote control (remember that remote_mc contains six buttons named channel1_btn through channel6_btn—thus the basis for the syntax used). When one of those buttons is clicked, it calls the changeTheChannel() function and passes it a channel number. In this way, we can use the same function with several different buttons and have the result depend on a parameter that was passed in.

> **Note** *Functions that are created as the result of the assign operator (=) are considered to be actions. All actions should be terminated with a semicolon. Therefore, each function definition above ends with a semicolon, whereas the normal function syntax does not.*

5. Choose Control > Test Movie. Press the Power button on the remote control to turn on the TV and then use the numeric keypad on the remote control to change the channels.

If you press the channel buttons before turning on the television, the changeTheChannel() function will not perform the change request. If the television is on, and you press one of the channel buttons, that button number is passed into the changeTheChannel() function and the screen_mc movie clip instance moves to the correct frame (channel).

6. **Close the testing movie to return to the authoring environment. With the Actions panel open, select Frame 1 of the Actions layer.**

This frame now contains two function definitions: one for turning the TV on and off, and another for changing channels using the numeric buttons on the remote control keypad. However, you'll notice some redundancy between these functions: Both are set up so that when either is called, it tells the remote control light to blink and sends the screen_mc movie clip instance to the correct frame. It's best to fix this type of redundancy whenever possible, so we'll correct this problem now.

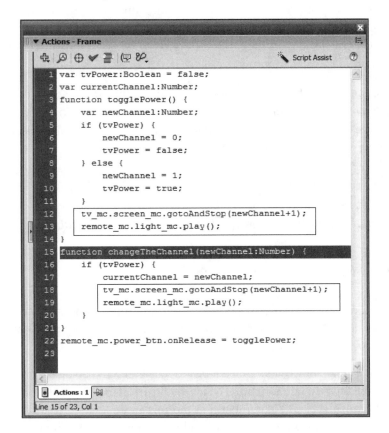

7. With the Actions panel still open, modify the `togglePower()` function to read as follows:

```
function togglePower() {
    if (tvPower) {
        changeTheChannel(0);
        tvPower = false;
    } else {
        tvPower = true;
        changeTheChannel(1);
    }
}
```

This function now makes use of the `changeTheChannel()` function to change the channel when the power is turned on or off. When the TV is turned on, the `togglePower()` function makes a call to the `changeTheChannel()` function and passes in the number 1. This means that every time the TV is turned on, it starts on Channel 1. When it is turned off, it goes to Channel 0 (the off state of the TV screen). This demonstrates how one function can contain a call to another.

Note Notice that in the first part of the `if` statement in Step 7, the call to the *changeTheChannel ()* function happens before *tvPower* is set to *false*. This is because we defined the *changeTheChannel ()* function so that it works only if *tvPower* is *true* (which it is if this part of the statement is executed). If *tvPower* were set to *false* first, the function call of *changeTheChannel (0)* would do nothing. The *else* part of the statement works just the opposite: The value of *tvPower* is set to *true* first, before the function call. Once again, this is because *tvPower* must have a value of *true* before the function call will have an effect.

Let's create some functions that will allow us to increment and decrement channels using the Up and Down arrows on the remote.

8. Select the first frame of the Actions layer on the main Timeline and open the Actions panel. Insert this script in the frame, just below `tvPower:Boolean = false;`:

```
var numberOfChannels:Number = 6;
```

This line of code creates a variable called `numberOfChannels` and assigns it a value of 6. This variable will be used in a function (which we'll create in a moment) that increments channels each time it's called. Remember that the `screen_mc` movie clip instance contains graphics representing only six channels; this value of 6 represents the total number of channels our TV can display and will be used to prevent the incrementing of channels beyond Channel 6. Let's see how this works.

9. Add this script at the end of the currently selected frame:

```
function channelUp () {
    if (currentChannel + 1 <= numberOfChannels) {
        changeTheChannel (currentChannel + 1);
    }
}
```

This function—which does not accept parameters—bumps up the channel by 1 each time the function is called. However, it uses a "safety mechanism" to prevent going beyond Channel 6. Recall that a variable named currentChannel is set every time the changeTheChannel () function is called (refer to Step 3). The value of this variable represents the channel currently displayed minus 1. Thus, if Channel 4 is currently displayed, this variable's value is 3. Before the channelUp() function executes, it uses an if statement to determine whether the current channel incremented (the value of currentChannel + 1) is still less than or equal to the upper channel limit (the value of numberOfChannels, or 6). If the condition is satisfied, the changeTheChannel () function is called with a parameter that has a value of the current channel plus 1, which causes the next channel to be displayed. This if statement contains no accompanying else statement: If the condition is not satisfied, Channel 6 is currently displayed and no further actions are performed.

10. Add this script at the end of the currently selected frame:

```
function channelDown () {
    if (currentChannel – 1 >= 1) {
        changeTheChannel (currentChannel – 1);
    }
}
```

Like the channelUp() function, this function does not accept parameters. When called, it determines whether the value of the currentChannel variable *decremented* by 1 is greater than or equal to the lower bound of 1, thus preventing the user from "channeling down" beyond Channel 1. If this condition is satisfied, the changeTheChannel () function is called and passed the value of the currentChannel minus 1. This procedure causes the previous channel to be displayed. As with the if statement in the channelUp() function definition, this if statement contains no accompanying else statement. If the condition is not satisfied, it means that Channel 1 is currently displayed, and no further actions will be performed.

It's time to add function calls to the Up and Down buttons on our remote control that will use the channelUp() and channelDown() functions we created.

11. Add this script at the end of the current script on Frame 1:

```
remote_mc.up_btn.onRelease = channelUp;
```

This line of ActionScript assigns an event handler to the onRelease event of the up_btn instance inside the remote_mc movie clip instance. Every time the button is clicked, the channelUp() function is called. When the current channel reaches its upper limit (as defined by the numberOfChannels variable), the channels no longer increment.

12. Add this script:

```
remote_mc.down_btn.onRelease = channelDown;
```

As with the Up button in Step 11, this script assigns an event handler to the down_btn button instance in the remote_mc movie clip instance. Every time this button is pressed, channelDown() is called, and the currentChannel variable is decremented (as long as it's greater than the lower limit). The television is then set to the correct channel.

13. Choose Control > Test Movie. Turn on the television using the Power button, and use the Up and Down buttons to change channels.

Notice that you can select any channel, and from there use the Up and Down buttons to change the channels. Using a variable that stores the current channel and functions, as you have done here, makes this type of functionality simple.

14. Close the test movie and save your work as *television3.fla*.

You have created a functional remote control for a television. In the next exercise, you'll use functions in a new way while adding functionality for the cable box in our project to display a text description of the current channel's content.

Using Local Variables and Creating Functions that Return Results

The variables you've created and used so far can be accessed at any time by any script in the Flash movie. In contrast, *local* variables are special variables you can create and use only within the scope of a function definition. In other words, a local variable is created within the function definition, used by the function when it's called, and then deleted automatically when that function has finished executing. Local variables exist only within the function where they are created.

Although local variables are not absolutely required in ActionScript, it's good programming practice to use them. Applications that require many and frequent calculations create a lot of variables and slow applications over time. By using local variables, however, you minimize memory usage and help prevent *naming collisions*, which occur when your project gets so big you unknowingly create and use variable names that are already in use. However, local variables in one function definition can have the same names as local variables within another function definition—even if both definitions exist on the same Timeline—because Flash understands that a local variable has meaning only within the function definition where the variable was created.

There is only one way to create a local variable manually. Here's the syntax:

```
var myName:String = "Jobe";
```

This variable becomes a local variable by simply being declared *within* a function definition using the keyword var.

To better grasp this concept, consider this example. In the previous exercise, we declared (created) the variable currentChannel on Frame 1 of the main Timeline using the following syntax:

```
var currentChannel:Number;
```

Because the line of script that created the variable was on Frame 1 of the main Timeline, and it *didn't* exist within a function definition, currentChannel became a variable of the main Timeline. If we place this exact syntax within a function definition, `currentChannel` is considered a local variable (belonging to the function only); it exists only when the function is called and is deleted immediately upon the completion of the function's execution. Think of local variables as temporary variables for use within functions.

If you need to create a Timeline variable from within a function, do not use the `var` syntax when declaring it. Declare the variable like this:

```
name = "Jobe";
```

> **Note** It's best to create Timeline variables outside of function definitions. Declaring a Timeline variable outside of a function is considered good practice because you group all your Timeline variables together. When coming back to your code months later or having another programmer look at your code, this variable organization will be appreciated.

Multiple local variables can be declared within a function definition on a single line using this syntax:

```
var firstName:String = "Jobe", lastName:String = "Makar", email:String = ¬
   "jobe@electrotank.com";
```

Returning Results from a Function Call

Not only do functions simply execute sets of actions but they can also be used like mini-programs within your movie, processing information sent to them and returning values. Take a look at this function definition:

```
function buyCD(availableFunds:Number, currentDay:String):Boolean{
   var myVariable:Boolean;
   if(currentDay != "Sunday" && availableFunds >= 20){
     myVariable = true;
   }else{
     myVariable = false;
   }
   return myVariable;
}
```

The values of two parameters—`availableFunds` and `currentDay`—are sent to the function when it is called. The function processes those values using an `if/else` statement. At the end of this function, `myVariable` contains a value of `true` or `false`. Using the `return` statement (as shown at the bottom of the function definition), the value of `myVariable` is returned to where the function was called. To understand this, take a look at how this function is called in the following script:

```
var idealCircumstances:Boolean = buyCD(19, "Friday");
if(idealCircumstances == true){
  gotoAndPlay("Happiness");
}else{
  gotoAndPlay("StayHome");
}
```

Pay particular attention to the line that reads as follows:

```
var idealCircumstances:Boolean = buyCD(19, "Friday");
```

To the right of the = sign is our actual function call, which sends the values of 19 and "Friday" to the buyCD() function for processing. If you recall how our function was defined, these values are used to determine a true or false value for myVariable. Sending these particular values (19, "Friday") to the function causes myVariable to evaluate to a value of false. Because the last line of code in our function says return myVariable;, the value of myVariable is returned to the script where the function was called. The following is the result:

```
idealCircumstances = false;
```

In essence, we used a function call to assign a value to the variable idealCircumstances, which happens in a split second. After a value has been assigned, the value of idealCircumstances can be used in the rest of the script, as our example demonstrates.

idealCircumstances:Boolean = **buyCD(19.00, "Friday")**

↓

buyCD(availableFunds:Number, currentDay:String)

```
var myVariable:Boolean;
if (currentDay != "Sunday" && availableFunds >= 20.00) {
        myVariable = true;
} else {
        myVariable = false;
}
return myVariable;
```

idealCircumstances = **false**

Tip   *You can use the* return *action to return any data types, including variable values, arrays, or any other objects.*

Now that you understand that functions can return values, it's a good time to point out a minor addition to our function definition syntax. The first line of our buyCD() function definition looks like this:

```
function buyCD(availableFunds:Number, currentDay:String):Boolean{
```

Between the closing parenthesis and the curly brace on the end, we placed the syntax :Boolean. This addition is to indicate that the function returns a value whenever it is called. In this case, the function returns a true or false value, hence the reason for using :Boolean. A function set up to return a numeric value is written this way:

```
function myNumberFunction(param1:Number, param2:Boolean):Number{
  //actions
}
```

A function set up to return a string value is written this way:

```
function myNumberFunction(param1:Number, param2:Boolean):String{
  //actions
}
```

A function set up to return an Array object is written this way:

```
function myNumberFunction(param1:Number, param2:Boolean):Array{
//actions
}
```

And so forth.

If a function doesn't return a value at all (like the functions used in this lesson's projects so far), the function should be written this way:

```
function myNumberFunction(param1:Number, param2:Boolean):Void{
  //actions
}
```

Notice the use of :Void to indicate that this function does not return a value.

Although the functions we used in this lesson do not make use of this syntax (they still work properly), using this syntax is considered good practice and should improve the speed of ActionScript execution. The speed increase may be noticeable only if your project contains many functions.

In this exercise, using both local variables and a function that returns a value, you'll script the cable box display in our project, which displays the name of the current channel. You'll create a function that builds the text to be displayed on the cable box.

1. Open television3.fla.

This file continues where the last exercise left off. We'll focus on the movie clip that has an instance name of `cableBox_mc` (and that looks like a cable box). This movie clip instance contains a simple graphic and a text field with an instance name of `cableDisplay_txt`. This text field will be filled with different channel names, depending on the channel selected.

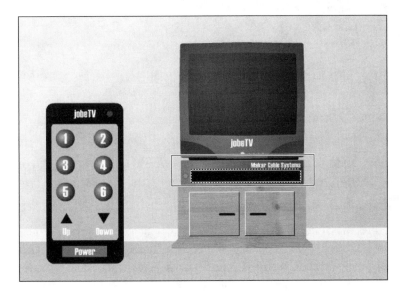

2. With the Actions panel open, select Frame 1 on the main Timeline and enter this script just below where it says `numberOfChannels = 6;`:

```
var channelNames:Array = ["","News","Classics","Family","Cartoons", ¬
    "Horror","Westerns"];
```

You just created an array named `channelNames`. This array contains names that will be dynamically inserted into a string of text that will be displayed inside the cable box. The seven string elements in this array are separated by commas (the first may not be easily discernible because it's an empty string of `""`). Each one of these elements has an associated *index* value, beginning with 0. For example, `channelNames[0]` = `""` (empty), `channelNames[1]` = `"News"`, `channelNames[2]` = `"Classics"`, and so on. This is important to understand as we progress.

> **Note** *For more information on arrays, see Lesson 4, "Arrays and Loops."*

Let's create a function that uses the text elements in this array to display a message in the cable box.

3. **With the frame still selected, enter this script at the end of all scripts on Frame 1:**

```
function displayCableText():String {
  var displayText:String;
  if (currentChannel != 0) {
    displayText = "You are viewing "+channelNames[currentChannel]+".";
  } else {
    displayText = "";
  }
  return displayText;
}
```

| Note | *Although the displayCableText() function is defined after the other functions but before the event handler assignments, it really doesn't matter where it's defined. It's just a matter of preference to have it one place over another.* |

This script defines the displayCableText() function, which accepts no parameters. It is used to dynamically build a string of text that will eventually appear in the cableDisplay_txt text field within the cableBox_mc movie clip instance. The function then takes this string and returns it using the return action. The function contains a conditional statement that checks to make sure that the television channel is not the channel associated with the TV being in the off state (0). If the condition is satisfied, a local variable named displayText is created, and a line of text is dynamically built from the channelNames array as well as the current value of currentChannel. For example, if the value of currentChannel is 4 at the time this function is called and executed, this would essentially be the same as the following:

```
displayText = "You are viewing " + channelNames[4] + ".";
```

Because Cartoons exists at index position 4 of the channelNames array, it can be broken down further:

```
displayText = "You are viewing Cartoons";
```

If the first part of the conditional statement is not satisfied (else), the local variable displayText is set with no value (or simply " "). The function ends by returning the value of displayText. But where does this value actually get returned to? We'll explain that in the next step. Because displayText has been specified as a local variable (using var), it's removed from memory as soon as its value is returned.

4. With the Actions panel still open, modify the **changeTheChannel()** function by inserting this code after the fifth line of the function definition:

```
cableBox_mc.cableDisplay_txt.text = displayCableText();
```

```
1  var tvPower:Boolean = false;
2  var numberOfChannels:Number = 6;
3  var channelNames:Array = ["", "News", "Classics", "Family", "Cartoons", "Horror", "Westerns"];
4  var currentChannel:Number;
5  function togglePower() {
6      if (tvPower) {
7          changeTheChannel(0);
8          tvPower = false;
9      } else {
10         tvPower = true;
11         changeTheChannel(1);
12     }
13 }
14 function changeTheChannel(newChannel:Number) {
15     if (tvPower) {
16         currentChannel = newChannel;
17         tv_mc.screen_mc.gotoAndStop(newChannel+1);
18         remote_mc.light_mc.play();
19         cableBox_mc.cableDisplay_txt.text = displayCableText();
20     }
21 }
```

You have modified changeTheChannel() so that each time a channel is changed and the changeChannel() function is called, the cableDisplay_txt text field (inside the cableBox_mc movie clip instance) is updated with the correct text. This line of ActionScript sets the value of the text field instance cableDisplay_txt (which is actually the dynamic text field in our cable box) using the returned value of the displayCableText() function. Thus, the displayCableText() function is called, goes to work, and comes up with a value. That value is inserted after the = sign. This is what's meant by a function *returning* a value. The value the function comes up with is returned to the line of script that called the function. This is also a great example of how using functions can be a real time-saver. We enhanced changeTheChannel() in a single location, but any script that calls the function automatically executes this enhancement as well—very efficient!

5. Choose Control > Test Movie. Select the Power button to turn the television on. Change the channel a few times.

Every time you select a button that changes the channel, the cable box is updated with the name of the channel you're watching. You have created a simple application that uses six functions to perform several tasks.

6. Close the test movie and save your work as *television4.fla*.

You're finished with this file. You'll apply what you've learned here in lessons to come.

What You Have Learned

In this lesson, you have:

- Created functions using various syntaxes (pages 39–43)
- Passed arguments into functions while calling them (pages 43–53)
- Used local variables (pages 53–54)
- Returned and used the results of calling a function (pages 54–60)

3 Conditional Logic

Every day we're confronted with all kinds of situations, large and small, that require us to make decisions about what actions we'll take. Although we might not be doing it consciously, we're constantly saying to ourselves, "If this is the case, I need to do that." If it's hot, wear shorts; if it's rainy, wear pants; and so on. This process of taking different actions based on current conditions (circumstances) is known as conditional logic, and it's something we all apply naturally.

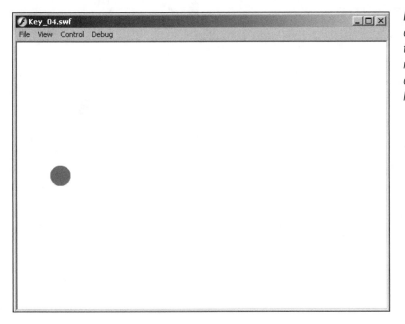

In this lesson we will create a simple project that will allow you to move a MovieClip onstage using the arrow keys on the keyboard.

Conditional logic is a critical component of interactivity. It allows you to program your project to react intelligently—to the movement or position of the mouse, to the current day of the week, and to many other dynamic conditions that exist as your movie plays. By employing conditional logic, you transform simple linear presentations and animations into dynamic projects that offer a unique experience each time they're viewed.

In this lesson, we'll introduce you to some of the ways in which you can use conditional logic to bring about graphical changes in your movies based on varying conditions.

What You Will Learn

In this lesson, you will:

- Learn how to use if, else, else if, and switch/case statements to control the flow of a script
- Explore the various operators used in conditional logic
- Script a project to react to various conditions and user interaction

Approximate Time

This lesson takes approximately forty-five minutes to complete.

Lesson Files

Media Files:
None

Starting Files:
Lesson03/Start/Key01.fla

Completed Project:
Lesson03/Completed/Key04.fla

Controlling a Script's Flow

Typically, actions in your scripts execute consecutively, from beginning to end—a sequence that represents your script's flow. Using *conditional logic*, you can control this flow by scripting specific actions to execute *only* when specific conditions are met or exist in your movie. By implementing conditional logic in your scripts, you give your movie the capability to make decisions and take action based on various conditions that you set, and your movie takes on more dimensions as a result. You'll use the *conditional statements* or phrases described in this lesson to implement conditional logic in your scripts.

if/else Statements

At the heart of conditional logic is the simple if/else statement. Here's an example:

```
if (moneySaved > 500) {
    buyStuff();
}
// next line of actions
```

The buyStuff() function is called only if the variable moneySaved has a value greater than 500. If moneySaved is equal to or less than 500, the buyStuff() function call is ignored and actions immediately below the if statement are executed.

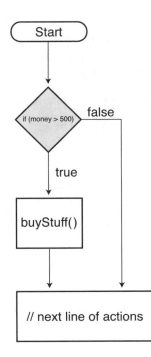

At its core, a conditional statement looks at a *circumstance* (placed within parentheses) and determines whether that circumstance is true or false. If the circumstance is true, actions within the statement are executed; if the circumstance is false, the actions are ignored. When you create an if statement, you essentially state the following:

```
if(true) {
    // do this
}
```

The data you place within parentheses represents the condition to be analyzed. The data within the curly braces ({}) represents the actions to be taken if the condition exists. If the curly braces are left out, only the next line will be executed if the condition is true. For example:

```
if(true)
    // do this
// additional actions
```

As in real life, sometimes an if statement needs to analyze multiple conditions before taking a single action or set of actions. For example:

```
if(moneySaved > 500 && billsPaid == true) {
    buyStuff();
}
```

The AND operator (&&) has been added to the statement so that now the buyStuff() function is called only if moneySaved is more than 500 *and* billsPaid has a value of true. If either condition is false, buyStuff() will not be called.

Using the OR operator (||) allows you to take a slightly different approach:

```
if(moneySaved > 500 || wonLottery == true) {
    buyStuff();
}
```

The buyStuff() function is called if *either* moneySaved has a value greater than 500 *or* wonLottery has a value of true. Both conditions need not be true for the buyStuff() function to be called, as was the case when using the AND operator (&&) in the earlier example.

You can mix the AND and OR operators to create sophisticated conditional statements like this one:

```
if((moneySaved > 500 && billsPaid == true) || wonLottery == true) {
    buyStuff();
}
```

In this script, the `buyStuff()` function is called only if `moneySaved` is more than 500 *and* `billsPaid` has a value of `true`, *or* `wonLottery` has a value of `true`. We wrapped the first condition in parenthesis to ensure it was evaluated first.

For Boolean (true/false) variables, you can make expressions more compact like this:

```
if((moneySaved > 500 && billsPaid) || wonLottery) {
    buyStuff();
}
```

You can also check for false values with the following expression:

```
if(!billsPaid) {
    payBills();
}
```

The `payBills()` function is called if the `billsPaid` variable is false.

The following table shows a list of the common operators (known as *comparison operators* because they're used to compare values) used in conditional logic, with brief descriptions and examples of how they're used.

Operator	Description	Example	Execute the function if...
==	Equality	if(name == "Derek")	name has a value of "Derek"
!=	Inequality	if(name != "Derek")	name has a value other than "Derek"
<	Less than	if(age < 30)	age has a value less than 30
>	Greater than	if(age > 30)	age has a value greater than 30
<=	Less than or equal to	if(age <= 30)	age has a value less than or equal to 30
>=	Greater than or equal to	if(age >= 30)	age has a value greater than or equal to 30
&&	Logical AND	if(day == "Friday" && pmTime > 5)	day has a value of "Friday" and pmTime has a value greater than 5
||	Logical OR	if(day == "Friday" || day == "Saturday")	day has a value of "Saturday" or "Sunday"

A common mistake when checking equality is to insert a single equals sign (=) where a double equals sign (==) belongs. Use a single equals sign to assign a value (for example, money = 300). Use a double equals sign to check for equality: money == 300 does not assign a value of 300 to money. Rather, it asks whether money has a value of 300.

Note *Although number comparisons are straightforward—after all, most of us understand that 50 is less than 100—text-value comparisons are less obvious. Derek doesn't equal derek even if the same letters are used. With string values, A has a lower value than Z, and lowercase letters have greater values than uppercase letters. Thus, if A has a value of 1, z has a value of 52 (ABCDEFGHIJKLMNOPQRSTUVWXYZabcdefghijklmnopqrstuvwxyz).*

if/else if Statements

An if/else if statement is similar to the basic if statement except that it enables your script to react to multiple conditions. Here's an example:

```
if(money > 500) {
    buyTV("35 inch");
}else if(money > 300) {
    buyTV("27 inch");
}
//next line of actions
```

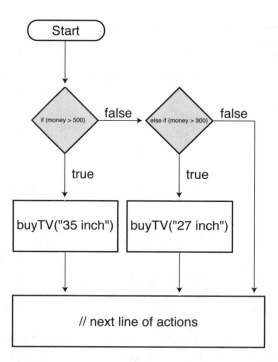

This script executes various actions depending on the value of money. If money has a value greater than 500, buy the 35-inch TV. If money has a value less than 500, this part of the script is ignored, and the next condition is examined. The next condition says that if money has a value greater than 300, buy the 27-inch TV. Thus, if money has a value of 450 when this script is executed, the first part of the statement is ignored (because 450 is not greater than 500), and the second part of the statement is executed (because a value of 450 *is* greater than 300). If money has a value less than 300, both parts of this statement are ignored.

You can create several lines of if/else if statements that react to dozens of conditions.

if/else Statements

An if/else statement allows your script to take action if no conditions in the statement are proven true. Consider this the fail-safe part of the statement.

```
if(money > 500) {
   buyTV("35 inch");
}else if(money > 300) {
   buyTV("27 inch");
}else {
   workOvertime();
}
//next line of actions
```

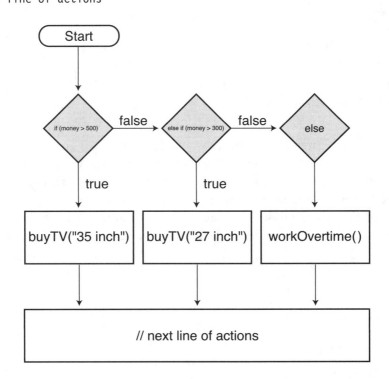

In this script, if money doesn't have a value of at least 300, neither of the conditions analyzed is true; as a result, neither of the actions that follow the conditions will be executed. Instead, the actions following the else part of the statement are executed—it's a bit like saying this:

```
If this is true
  Do this
otherwise, if this is true
  Do this
otherwise, if none of the conditions above are true
  Do this
```

switch/case Statements

A switch/case statement can be used to more efficiently replace some larger if/else if statements. It can be used if you want a script to take a specific set of actions when an exact value exists. For example:

```
switch(favoriteBand) {
  case "Beatles":
    gotoAndPlay("Beatles");
    break;
  case "U2":
    gotoAndPlay("U2");
    break;
  default:
    gotoAndPlay("Mozart");
}
```

A single expression in parentheses (usually a variable) is evaluated once. The value of the expression is compared with the values for each case in the structure. If a match exists, the block of code associated with that case is executed. If no match is found, the default statement at the end is executed. Each case can check string values (as shown in the example), numeric values, and Boolean values of true and false. We use the break command in each case to prevent the code from automatically running into the next case if a match has already been found. Removing the break statements allows for a way to handle OR conditions. For example:

```
switch(favoriteBand) {
  case "Beatles":
  case "U2":
    gotoAndPlay("Rock");
    break;
  case "Tim McGraw":
  case "Faith Hill":
    gotoAndPlay("County");
    break;
  default:
    gotoAndPlay("Classical");
}
```

The preceding statement says, if favorateBand equals "Beatles" or "U2", go to the frame labeled "Rock"; if favoriteBand equals "Tim McGraw" or "Faith Hill", go to the frame labeled "County"; if neither condition is met go to the frame labeled "Classical".

Because the expression in the switch statement is only evaluated once, there can be a significant performance improvement over a regular if/else if statement that requires each condition to be evaluated.

Conditional Operator

The *conditional (ternary) operator* (?:) is a shorthand version of an if/else statement. Here's an example:

```
var myMood:String = (money > 1000000) ? "Happy" : "Sad";
```

If the condition within the parentheses evaluates to true, the first expression ("Happy") is set as the value of myMood. If the condition evaluates to false, the second expression ("Sad") is used. This single line of ActionScript accomplishes the same thing as the following code:

```
if(money > 1000000) {
  myMood = "Happy";
}else {
  myMood = "Sad";
}
```

Reacting to Multiple Conditions

The best way to understand conditional logic is to examine it in the context of a simple application. We will use some of the concepts we've learned to script a project that reacts to user interaction.

In our project we will have a MovieClip in the center of the stage that will move based on the user pressing the arrow keys on the keyboard. It's a very simple idea that will clearly demonstrate conditional logic.

1. Open *Key01.fla* **in the Lesson03/Start folder.**

This FLA file contains a single frame with two layers, named according to their contents. Let's look at the various elements in the scene.

The Target layer contains one MovieClip placed on the center of the Stage with an instance name of target. This is the clip we will be moving as the user presses the arrow keys.

The Actions layer will contain all the scripts for this project. Let's begin.

2. With the Actions panel open, select Frame 1 of the Actions layer and add the following script:

```
this.onKeyDown = function() {
  if(Key.getCode() == Key.RIGHT) {
    trace("Move Right");
  }else if(Key.getCode() == Key.LEFT) {
    trace("Move Left");
  }else if(Key.getCode() == Key.UP) {
    trace("Move Up");
  }else if(Key.getCode() == Key.DOWN) {
    trace("Move Down");
  }
}
Key.addListener(this);
```

In this code block we have created an onKeyDown event handler for the Key class. We started by creating a function called onKeyDown. This function has an if/else if statement that checks for the key that has been pressed. To add this handler as a listener to the Key class we need to call the addListener method after we have defined the handler function. We're using the trace statement in this example to send a message to our output panel. This will help us determine which case is being caught.

Hopefully, looking at this conditional logic has given you an idea of how this could be done a little better. This is the perfect situation to use a switch/case statement. Let's go ahead and revise our event handler to use a switch statement now.

3. Replace the *onKeyDown* handler with this script; this is represented in *Key02.fla* in the Lesson03/Complete folder:

```
this.onKeyDown = function() {
  switch(Key.getCode()) {
    case Key.LEFT:
      trace("Move Left");
      break;
    case Key.RIGHT:
      trace("Move Right");
      break;
    case Key.UP:
      trace("Move Up");
      break;
    case Key.DOWN:
      trace("Move Down");
      break;
  }
}
```

As you can see from this code, a switch statement is much cleaner and easier to read. It's also more efficient because it will only evaluate the Key.getCode method once, and then switch based on its result.

4. Close and save your work as *Key02.fla*.

Reacting to User Interaction

So far, all we have done is output the user interaction using a simple trace command. Now we want to expand on that by calling a specific function for each type of user interaction. Specifically, we are going to move a ball around the stage based on the arrow key the user pressed.

1. Open *Key02.fla.*

We'll continue building on the file you worked with in the preceding exercise. The changes we will be making here are represented in the Key03.fla file in the Lesson03/Complete folder.

2. Replace the onKeyDown handler with this script:

```
this.onKeyDown = function() {
  switch(Key.getCode()) {
    case Key.LEFT:
      moveLeft();
      break;
    case Key.RIGHT:
      moveRight();
      break;
    case Key.UP:
      moveUp();
      break;
    case Key.DOWN:
      moveDown();
      break;
  }
}
```

In this new version of the onKeyDown event handler, we have replaced the trace output calls with calls to specific functions based on the type of user interaction. Now we will look at creating these functions.

3. Add this script at the end of the current script:

```
var SPEED:Number = 5;
function moveLeft():Void {
  target._x -= SPEED;
}
function moveRight():Void {
  target._x += SPEED;
}
```

```
function moveUp():Void {
   target._y -= SPEED;
}
function moveDown():Void {
   target._y += SPEED;
}
```

In the first line we are creating a constant variable that represents the number of pixels we will move the target clip each time the function is called.

Each function has specific logic in place to move the target clip. The moveLeft() function moves the target to the left, moveRight() moves it to the right, moveUp() moves it up, and moveDown() moves it down. The _x and _y properties of the movie clip class can be modified to move the clip along the x axis and the y axis. This is pretty straight forward logic.

4. Choose Control > Test Movie to test the project's functionality so far.

When the movie plays, you will see the red dot in the middle of the stage. When you press the arrow keys, the dot moves in the direction of the arrow you pressed.

5. Close the test environment to return to the authoring environment and save your work as *Key03.fla.*

We'll build on this file in the next exercise.

Detecting the Edge of the Stage

Now that we have our project working, we will add one final feature. You'll notice that in our current version of this project, the target clip keeps moving past the edge of the stage. Now we will add some conditional logic to our move functions so that they will detect the edge of the stage.

1. Open Key03.fla.

We'll continue building on the file you worked with in the preceding exercise. The changes we will be making here are represented in the Key04.fla file in the Lesson03/Completed folder.

2. Replace the move functions with the following script:

```
function moveLeft():Void {
  var leftWall:Number = 0;
  if(target._x > leftWall) {
    target._x -= SPEED;
  }else {
    target._x = leftWall;
  }
}
function moveRight():Void {
  var rightWall:Number = Stage.width - target._width;
  if(target._x < rightWall) {
    target._x += SPEED;
  }else {
    target._x = rightWall;
  }
}
function moveUp():Void {
  var topWall:Number = 0
  if(target._y > topWall) {
    target._y -= SPEED;
  }else {
    target._y = topWall;
  }
}
```

```
function moveDown():Void {
  var bottomWall:Number = Stage.height - target._height;
  if(target._y < bottomWall) {
    target._y += SPEED;
  }else {
    target._y = bottomWall;
  }
}
```

In each function, we are calculating the edge of our stage and making sure that the target clip hasn't gone too far. If it has, then we position it up against the edge. The edge values are represented by the topWall, bottomWall, leftWall, and rightWall properties. This is a simple example of an if/else statement.

3. Choose Control > Test Movie.

Now when the movie plays you can try and get the target off the stage. But as you can see, the target stops moving when it reaches the edge of the stage. Therefore, we have just created a boundary for our moving target.

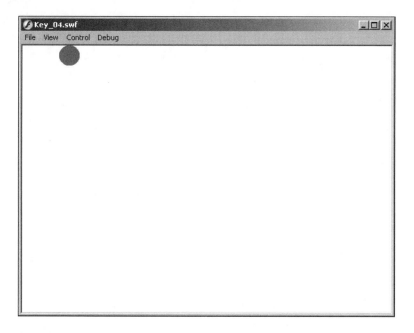

4. Close the test environment to return to the authoring environment, and save your work as *Key04.fla.*

This step completes the exercise and this lesson. By using conditional logic in your scripts, you can greatly increase your project's dynamism and provide a unique experience to every person who interacts with it.

What You Have Learned

In this lesson, you have:

- Learned how to use `if`, `else`, `else if`, and `switch/case` statements to control the flow of a script (pages 63–69)
- Learned about the operators used in conditional logic (pages 64–65)
- Programmed a project to react to user interaction (pages 70–73)
- Created a scripted boundary to restrict an object's movement (pages 74–75)

4 Arrays and Loops

We all have to perform repetitive tasks. Whether complicated or simple, a repetitive task requires performing at least one step in a process repeatedly. For example, if you were sending out 100 wedding invitations, repetitive tasks in that process could include folding papers, stuffing envelopes, sealing envelopes, and affixing stamps — you'd do each task 100 times. In ActionScript, performing a set of repeated steps (actions) multiple times is called *looping*. ActionScript lets you loop through a set of actions as many times as needed, which means that instead of writing an action (or set of actions) several times, you can write it once and loop through it any number of times. In this lesson, you'll learn how to use the three loop types that ActionScript offers.

The menu as well as the two-by-two grid of pictures in this application will be created dynamically by using loops.

What You Will Learn

In this lesson, you will:

- Discover the usefulness of loops
- Learn about the types of loops
- Examine loop exceptions
- Set loop conditions
- Create a nested loop

Approximate Time

This lesson takes approximately forty-five minutes to complete.

Lesson Files

Media Files:

None

Starting Files:

Lesson04/Start/pictureShow1.fla
Lesson04/Start/phoneNumberSearch1.fla

Completed Projects:

Lesson04/Completed/pictureShow3.fla
Lesson04/Completed/phoneNumberSearch2.fla

Why Loops Are Useful

Loops enable Flash to perform an action (or set of actions) repeatedly, which means that with just a few lines of ActionScript, you can force an action to be executed several thousand times. In ActionScript, you use loops for tasks that would be difficult or impossible without loops. For example:

- Creating dynamically generated drop-down lists
- Validating data
- Searching text
- Dynamically duplicating movie clips
- Copying the contents of one array to a new array

You can use loops to automate any number of tasks, such as dynamically creating MovieClip instances. Suppose that your project called for 100 evenly spaced instances of the same MovieClip. You could create a four- or five-line looping statement to attach a MovieClip from your library 100 times and position each clip on the Stage automatically—a great improvement over dragging 100 instances from the library and aligning each one manually.

Loops are also dynamic. Suppose that you scripted a loop to create a menu of 15 choices (buttons) dynamically. By altering the loop slightly, you could add and remove choices dynamically. This would be impossible to do without loops.

As you progress through this lesson (and the rest of the book), you'll see the value of using loops in your scripts.

Types of Loops

ActionScript can take advantage of three loop types, all of which repeat an action (or set of actions).

while Loop

The syntax for creating this common type of loop is as follows:

```
while(someNumber < 10) {
  // perform these actions
}
```

The expression someNumber < 10 is the condition that determines how long the loop will *iterate* (pass through the statement). The actions inside the loop are executed with each iteration. The logic that determines how the condition is evaluated (and how the loop is exited) is discussed shortly, in the section "Writing and Understanding Loop Conditions."

Here's an example of the while loop:

```
while(myClip._y < 0) {
    myClip._y += 3;
}
```

This script moves the myClip MovieClip instance along the *y* axis until its position is greater than or equal to 0.

You could also use a while loop to loop through an array like this:

```
var data:Array = ["one", "two", "three"];
var i:Number = 0;
while(i < data.length) {
    trace(data[i++]);
}
```

In the next section we will look at a more common way to iterate over predefined number of items, such as an array.

for Loop

The for loop is a compact, all-in-one looping solution for loops that rely on incrementing or decrementing a variable. The for loop lets you initialize a loop variable, set the loop condition, and increment or decrement that variable—all in one line of ActionScript. The for loop is typically used to perform an action or set of actions based on the value of an incremental variable—walking an array, for example, or applying actions to a list of movie clips. Here's the syntax of the for loop:

```
for(var someNumber:Number = 0; someNumber < 10; someNumber++) {
    // perform these actions
}
```

The three elements separated by semicolons within the parentheses are used to specify the number of iterations the loop will perform. In this example, the variable someNumber is created and assigned an initial value of 0. The script states next that as long as someNumber is less than 10, the loop executes the actions contained in the loop. The last element in the parentheses specifies that someNumber will be incremented by 1 with each loop iteration, eventually causing someNumber to have a value of 10, which means that the loop will cease after 10 iterations.

The for loop is structured to be used primarily to loop through a set of actions a specified number of times. Here's the same example given for the earlier while loop, but now using the for loop syntax:

```
var data:Array = ["one", "two", "three"];
for(var i:Number = 0; i < data.length ; i++) {
   trace(data[i]);
}
```

for...in Loop

This loop is used to iterate through all of an object's properties. Here's the syntax:

```
for(var key:String in someObject) {
   trace(key);
}
```

The key in the loop is a variable that temporarily stores the name of the property referenced by the variable with each loop iteration. The value of key can be used in the actions within the loop. For example, let's say you had the following car object in your application:

```
var car:Object = new Object();
car.color = "red";
car.make = "BMW";
car.doors = 2;
```

But there's a problem: You aren't aware of the properties the car object might have. This could be because your car object is dynamic, meaning the properties can be added at runtime. Therefore, you need a way to inspect the object and retrieve all the properties. The following script will iterate through the object and output the key and values for each property on the car object:

```
for(var key:String in car) {
   trace(key + ": " + car[key]);
}
```

On the first iteration of the loop, key has a String value of doors (because that was the name of the last property defined). During the first loop, the output looks like this:

```
"doors: 2";
```

car object

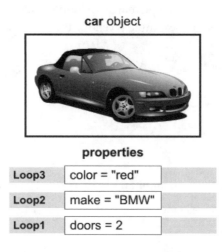

properties

Loop3	color = "red"
Loop2	make = "BMW"
Loop1	doors = 2

In the expression we trace the output; the variable key (without brackets) refers to the property *name* (such as doors, make, or color). Using car[key] (that is, placing key variable between brackets) is the same as writing car.doors and is a reference to that property's *value*.

When the loop is complete, the output panel has the following:

```
doors: 2
make: BMW
color: red
```

Because the car object has three properties, the for...in loop in this script will perform only three iterations.

> **Note** *In a regular array, elements are referenced by number, starting with 0. In contrast, elements in an associative array are referenced by name. The for...in loop in this section loops through the associative array that contains all of these references in a specific Timeline or object.*

Loop Exceptions

In general, a loop continues to perform iterations until its condition is no longer true. However, you can use two actions to change this behavior: continue and break.

With the continue action, you can stop the current iteration (that is, no further actions in that iteration will be executed) and jump straight to the next iteration in a loop. For example:

```
var total:Number = 0;
var i:Number = 0;
while(++i <= 20) {
  if(i == 10) {
    continue;
  }
  total += i;
}
```

The while statement in this script loops from 1 to 20, with each iteration adding the current value of i to a variable named total—until i equals 10. At that point, the continue action is invoked, which means that no more actions are executed on that iteration, and the loop skips to the eleventh iteration. This would create the following set of numbers:

1 2 3 4 5 6 7 8 9 11 12 13 14 15 16 17 18 19 20

Notice that there is no number 10, indicating that no action occurred on the tenth loop.

The break action is used to exit a loop, even if the condition that keeps the loop working remains true. For example:

```
var total:Number = 0;
var i:Number = 0;
while(++i <= 20) {
  total += i;
  if(total >= 10) {
    break;
  }
}
```

This script increases the value of a variable named total by 1 with each iteration. When the value of total is 10 or greater—as checked by an if statement—a break action occurs and the while statement halts, even though it's set to loop 20 times.

In practice, the break command is used more often than the continue command because programmers often use if statements rather than continue to bypass actions in a loop.

Creating a Search Application

In this example, we'll create a project that will search for a phone number from within an array based on the person's name.

1. Open *phoneNumberSearch1.fla* **in the Lesson04/Start folder.**

This file contains two layers: Actions and Search Assets. The Actions layer will contain the script for this project. The Search Assets layer contains the text fields, button, and graphics for this exercise.

In this exercise, you'll produce a simple application that lets you enter a name in a search field to return the phone number for that individual. Two text fields are on the screen: nameField will be used to enter the name to search; resultField will display the search result. An invisible MovieClip over the Search button graphic has an instance name of searchButton that will be used to call a search function.

2. With the Actions panel open, select the first frame in the Actions layer and add the following script:

```
var directory:Array = [{name:"John", phone:"919-555-5698"},¬
  {name:"Kelly", phone:"232-555-3333"},¬
  {name:"Ross", phone:"434-555-5655"}];
```

This script creates an array called directory containing three objects, each of which has two properties: name and phone.

To access the first name in this array, you use directory[0].name; the first phone number would be accessed using directory[0].phone. This syntax represents John's name and number. The syntax will play an important role in the search function we're about to script.

3. Add this function definition after the directory array:

```
function getPhoneByName(name:String):String {
  for(var i:Number = 0; i < directory.length; i++) {
    if(directory[i].name.toLowerCase() == name.toLowerCase()) {
      return directory[i].phone;
    }
  }
  return "No Match";
}
```

You just defined the function that will search the directory for a specific phone number. This function takes a name as a parameter and returns the result as a string. When this function is called, it will iterate over the directory until it finds a name that matches the name passed into the function.

The first thing we need to do in this function is create a for loop that loops as many times as there are items in the directory array.

Inside each loop we will create an if statement that compares the name property of the current object in the loop with the name passed into the function. We use the toLowerCase method of the String class on both strings in the statement to make the search case-insensitive.

If the condition evaluates to true, we return the value of the phone property of the current object in the loop.

If no match is found after the loop completes, we will return the string No Match.

4. Add this script after the getPhoneByName() function:

```
searchButton.onRelease = function() {
    resultField.text = getPhoneByName(nameField.text);
}
```

The script adds an onRelease event handler to the searchButton MovieClip. When the Search button is released, the resultField text property is set to the result of the getPhoneByName() function. We're passing in the value of the nameField as the parameter of our search function.

5. Chose Control > Test Movie. Enter *John*, *Kelly*, or *Ross* in the search field and then click the Search button. Enter any other name and click the Search button.

A phone number should appear when a name is valid, and "No Match" should appear when no match is found in the directory array.

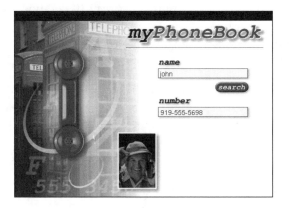

6. Close the test movie and save your work as *phoneNumberSearch2.fla.*

In this exercise, you used a simple loop to create a search routine.

Writing and Understanding Loop Conditions

For the rest of this lesson, we'll focus on the while loop. The actions within this type of loop are performed continuously—as long as the condition evaluates to true. For example:

```
var i:Number = 0;
while(i < 10) {
    // perform these actions
}
```

The condition in the loop is i < 10, so as long as the value of i is less than 10, the statement is true, and the actions within the loop are repeated. However, the looping statement is missing a key ingredient; it doesn't have a means by which the condition eventually becomes false. Without this functionality, the loop could continue forever, and in the real world endless loops cause applications to freeze. This is commonly known as an *infinite loop.* Flash can't do anything else until the looping statement completes its job. To prevent an endless loop in the example, the value of i must be incremented so that its value is eventually greater than or equal to 10; at which point the condition proves false, and the loop stops.

You can use the increment operator (++) to handle incrementing a variable. Here's an example:

```
var i:Number = 0;
while(i < 10) {
    i++;
    //perform these actions
}
```

Incrementing the value of i causes the loop to perform 10 iterations. The value of i is initially set to 0. However, with each loop, that value increases by 1. On the tenth loop, i = 10, which means that i < 10 is no longer true, and the loop halts. Here's a shortcut that accomplishes the same goal:

```
var i:Number = 0;
while(i++ < 10) {
    // perform these actions
}
```

This loop performs 10 iterations. The value of i is initially set to 0. However, that value is incremented by 1 within the conditional statement of the loop itself with each iteration. On the eleventh loop, i = 10, which means that i < 10 is no longer true, and the loop halts.

You can also use the decrement operator with a loop, which might look something like this:

```
var i:Number = 10;
while(i-- > 0) {
  // perform these actions
}
```

Alternatively, you can write this script using a for loop as follows:

```
for(var i:Number = 9; i >= 0; --i) {
  // perform these actions
}
```

The condition in a loop doesn't have to depend on an incremented value; it can be any sort of condition. It can also be the result of a function call that returns a value of true or false, like this:

```
while(someFunction()) {
  // perform these actions
}
```

In the following exercise, you create a photo grid list using a while loop. We will also be using what we have learned so far to implement for and for...in loops.

1. Open *pictureShow1.fla* in the Lesson04/Start folder.

The main Timeline includes two layers: Show Elements and Actions. The Actions layer contains all the ActionScript for this project. Not surprisingly, the Show Elements layer contains the project's graphic elements. All the other elements will be placed onto the Stage at runtime from the library.

The MenuItem is a MovieClip in our library with a linkage ID of MenuItem. The rest of the library assets that will be brought onto the Stage at runtime are bitmaps. To enable it we must set the linkage ID of our bitmaps. This is a new feature of Flash 8. In previous versions, MovieClip symbols were the only library items that could have attached at runtime. In the library we have a series of bitmaps placed in our Photos folder. By right-clicking on the bitmap in the library you can go to the properties for that item and view its linkage ID.

2. With the Actions panel open, select the frame in the Actions layer and add the following script:

```
var photoData:Object = new Object();
photoData["London"] = ["london1", "london2", "london3", "london4"];
photoData["New York"] = ["newyork1", "newyork2", "newyork3", "newyork4"];
photoData["Paris"] = ["paris1", "paris2", "paris3", "paris4"];
```

This script creates an associative array of arrays that will be used as our datasource for our simple photo viewer. The keys of the associative array represent each city and will be used as the display titles in our menu. Each second-level array contains the linkage IDs of the bitmaps that will be displayed when that item is selected from the menu.

3. Add this function after the script you just added in Step 2:

```
var menu:MovieClip = createEmptyMovieClip("menu", 0);
menu._x = 30;
menu._y = 80;
var i:Number = 0;
for(var city:String in photoData) {
    var menuItem:MovieClip = menu.attachMovie("MenuItem", city, i);
    menuItem._y = i * (menuItem._height + 2);
    menuItem.label.text = city;
    menuItem.photos = photoData[city];
    menuItem.onRelease = function() {
        populatePhotos(this.photos);
    }
    i++;
}
```

This script will create our menu from the data defined in Step 2. We first create a container for our menu items and put it in the correct position. This is simply an empty MovieClip named menu. Then we use a for...in loop to iterate over the items in our associative array. Each iteration will add an item to our menu by attaching the MenuItem symbol from our library.

Rather than positioning each menu item individually, we will use a container MovieClip and set each item's position relative to the container. Then we simply need to position the container to the desired location on the Stage. In the first line, we create our empty menu container and then we position it by setting its *x* and *y* properties.

Because this is a for...in loop we will need to track the number of iterations manually. Before the loop is defined, the script creates a local variable named i and assigns it the value 0. This variable will be manually incremented each time the loop is iterated.

Note *The letter i is commonly used as the name of an index variable in loops. For nested loops, the letter j is commonly used to define the inner loop's index value.*

We are using a for...in loop because we want to iterate through the keys in our photoData associative array. Each key value will represent the city name inside our loop.

The first thing we need to do inside our loop is attach the menu item to our menu container. Because this loop dynamically generates the menu items, we need to consider vertical spacing between the items in the menu. We determine this by multiplying the menu item's height by the current iteration count. We also add an additional two pixels for padding.

Inside each of our menu item clips is a text field named label. Once we have added the item, we will set the label field's text property to the name of the city. The city name is retrieved as the key in our associative array.

Rather than searching through the photoData object each time we want to retrieve the bitmap photos, we will simply set a reference to these photos inside the menu item instance. So when the item is clicked we can pass that data relative to the menu item.

Finally, we add an onRelease handler to the menu item. Inside this handler we call the populatePhotos() function and pass it the reference to the photo data for that city.

Before we end the loop we will increment our index (i) variable by 1.

4. Choose Control > Test Movie. Click the Menu button to test your script.

When the application launches you will see the menu populated with the cities defined in your photoData object.

5. Close the test movie and save your work as *pictureShow2.fla*.

You just created a dynamic menu using a loop. In the next exercise, you put this menu to work by making something happen when you click a menu item.

Nested Loops

Loops provide a great way of automating a set of scripting tasks. However, loops can accomplish more than the repetitive execution of a set of actions. A *nested loop*—that is, a loop placed inside another loop—can be useful for creating a looping sequence that executes a set of actions, changes a bit, executes those same actions again, changes a bit, and so on. Here's an example of a nested loop:

```
var i:Number = 0;
while(++i <= 10) {
   var j:Number = 0;
   while(++j <= 10) {
      // perform these actions
   }
}
```

The actions in the nested loop will be executed 100 times. Here's the underlying logic: the outer loop (which uses i) is set to loop 10 times. With each iteration of this outer loop, two things occur: the variable j is reset to 0, which then enables the inner loop (which uses j) to loop 10 times itself. In other words, on the first iteration of the outer loop, the inner loop will loop 10 times; on the second iteration, the inner loop will again loop 10 times; and so on.

Nested loops are great for breaking repetitive tasks into a hierarchical process. To help you understand this concept, think about writing a letter. A letter represents a nested-loop process in which you start on line 1 and write perhaps 100 characters, drop to line 2 and write 100 characters, and so on. If your letter is 25 lines long, a script to do the work might look something like this:

```
var i:Number = 0;
while (++i <= 25) {
   var j:Number = 0;
   while (++j <= 100) {
      // type a character
   }
   // drop down to the next line
}
```

Keep in mind that you aren't restricted to nesting just one loop inside another; you can use as many loops within loops as your project requires.

In the following exercise, you use nested loops to create a grid of images that appear when an item in the menu is selected.

1. Open *pictureShow2.fla.*

In each item of the photoData object there is an array of linkage IDs. Each ID points to a bitmap in your library. In this exercise, you will attach these bitmaps to the Stage (depending on which menu item is clicked) to form a grid of images.

2. With the Actions panel open, select Frame 1 in the Actions layer and add the following code after the current script on that frame:

```
import flash.display.BitmapData;
import flash.filters.DropShadowFilter;
function populatePhotos(photos:Array):Void {
  var photoGrid:MovieClip = createEmptyMovieClip("photoGrid", 1);
  photoGrid._x = 180;
  photoGrid._y = 20;
  var rowPosition:Number = 0;
  var i:Number = 0;
  while(i < photos.length) {
    for(var j:Number = 0; j < 2; j++) {
      if(i < photos.length) {
        var photo:MovieClip = photoGrid.createEmptyMovieClip(photos[i], i);
        photo._x = j * 180;
        photo._y = rowPosition;
        var photoBitmap:BitmapData = BitmapData.loadBitmap(photos[i]);
        photo.attachBitmap(photoBitmap, i);
        var dropShadow:DropShadowFilter = new DropShadowFilter(7, 45, 000000, ¬
          0.7, 7, 7, 1, 3);
        photo.filters = [dropShadow];
      }
      i++;
    }
    rowPosition += 130;
  }
}
```

We are using two built-in classes in this script that need to be imported. We will do that at the top of this script so we can reference them later in the script without using the full class paths. Those classes are flash.display.BitmapData and flash.filters.DropShadowFilter.

In the preceding exercise you set up the menu items to call this populatePhotos() function and pass it an array as a parameter value (photos). This array contains all the linkage IDs to the bitmap photos in your library. Our function basically loops through the items in that array and places them on the Stage. That's pretty straightforward, but it gets a little more interesting because we're placing those images into a two-by-two grid.

The first line inside our function will create a container MovieClip that will serve a task similar to our menu container. One additional advantage is that we can easily replace this clip when a different item is selected in the menu.

Because we are using a while loop we need to keep track of the index in the i variable much like we did with the menu loop. We will also keep track of our row position in a variable called rowPosition.

We're using a while loop because we want to loop as long as there are photos to be displayed. It will iterate until the index value (i) is no longer less than the length of the array passed into our function, which will ensure that all the photos are displayed regardless of the array length. Therefore, by design our code actually supports an infinite number of photos; however there is room on the Stage for only four.

Inside our while loop is a nested for loop. This loop iterates over the columns in our grid. For this example we will just have two columns, but this could easily be modified to a different column count, or it could even be dynamic, based on a condition like the width of the Stage.

Because it is possible to have an array of photos that wouldn't create a complete row, we could have more iterations than we have items in our photo array. Therefore, to check for this condition we will use an if statement inside our nested for loop that checks for the same condition as our outer while loop.

Now that we have verified that we should display a photo, we need to add it to the Stage in the correct position based on the column and row of our grid. Because our photos are bitmap symbols in the library, we need to create an empty MovieClip that we can attach our bitmap to.

We also need to position our empty MovieClip. We determine the proper x position by multiplying our inner loop's index (j) by the width of our columns. Based on our design our column width is 180 pixels. The y position is based on our rowPosition property. This value is initially set to 0, but with each iteration of the `while` loop, we increment its value by the height of our row. Based on our design, the row height is 130 pixels.

Our empty MovieClip is in the correct position, so now we need to attach the bitmap photo. The `attachBitmap` method is a new feature that has been added to the MovieClip class in Flash 8. This method enables us to attach bitmaps from the library based on the bitmap symbol's linkage ID.

The last thing we'll do is add a drop shadow to our photo using the new bitmap filter features in Flash 8. We do this by first creating an instance of the DropShadowFilter class. The parameters of the DropShadowFilter's constructor determine the display of our bitmap. To apply this filter to our photo we use a new property of MovieClip called `filters`. The `filters` property needs to be an array, so we add our filter to an array and assign it to our photo.

3. Choose Control > Test Movie to test your work.

As you click any of the menu items, the grid of images is created based on the value of photo `array` passed to the `populatePhotos()` function.

4. Close the test movie and save your work as *pictureShow3.fla*.

In this exercise, you used nested loops to create a grid of images on the Stage. Although you could have dragged and placed four movie clip instances on the Stage to accomplish the same goal, you used a nested loop to automate the entire process so that, with a couple of minor adjustments, the script can create a grid of any size—perhaps as large as 100 by 100 images. Using loops—especially nested loops—in this fashion not only helps you to automate processes that you might otherwise perform manually in the authoring environment but it also enables your projects to scale up or down dynamically based on conditions that exist while the project plays.

What You Have Learned

In this lesson, you have:

- Explored the usefulness of loops (page 79)
- Learned about the three loop types available in ActionScript (pages 79–82)
- Learned about the `continue` and `break` loop exceptions (page 83)
- Applied `for` and `while` loops to understand loop conditions (pages 84–89)
- Created and used a nested loop (pages 90–93)

5 Built-in Classes

Every day you use objects to perform any number of activities. You may have used Tupperware to store fresh cookies to prevent them from becoming stale, or the trash can to store a fruitcake from your Aunt Sally. Objects are items designed to meet specific needs. You can use them to perform tasks of their own (for example, a VCR playing or recording a movie) or you can employ them as simple storage devices.

Using Macromedia Flash, you can create objects that perform tasks or store something (such as data) in much the same way as real-world objects. A class is like a blueprint for a specific type of object. Using Flash's built-in classes, you can create objects to accomplish a variety of tasks. As a matter of fact, you'll probably be pleasantly surprised at how familiar Flash's classes seem after you understand basic concepts of how they

This Flash word processor is one of the projects you'll create in this lesson.

work. In addition to using the built-in classes, you can create your own custom classes. Creating custom classes is covered in Lesson 6, "Custom Classes." We'll discuss several of Flash's built-in classes and work with a few of them in this lesson on using built-in classes.

What You Will Learn

In this lesson, you will:

- Learn what classes are and why they are useful
- Get acquainted with several of the classes available in ActionScript
- Use the Color class
- Create a word processor using properties and methods of the String and Selection classes

Approximate Time

This lesson takes approximately forty-five minutes to complete.

Lesson Files

Media Files:

None

Starting Files:

Lesson05/Start/Clown1.fla
Lesson05/Start/wordProcessor1.fla

Completed Projects:

Lesson05/Completed/Clown2.fla
Lesson05/Completed/wordProcessor2.fla

What Classes Are and Why They're Useful

ActionScript classes allow you to perform all sorts of interactive tasks with Flash. They provide a means for you to work with text, sound, color, dates, and more in very dynamic ways.

As you'll soon learn, ActionScript classes, while intangible, are very much like objects in the real world. They have characteristics known as *properties*, which can be changed with a script, and they have abilities, known as *methods*, which allow them to perform various tasks. We'll discuss both of the aspects of objects in depth in a moment.

The primary benefit of using classes in ActionScript is that they allow you to program and manipulate data, colors, sound, dates, and so on in a context that makes sense to humans—we're all familiar with the idea of things having characteristics and abilities.

Understanding the Concept of Classes and Instances

At the introduction of this lesson, we introduced the term *class*. You are probably wondering what in the world it means. It's actually a simple yet important concept to understand in the world of object-oriented programming. We'll touch on it briefly here to acquaint you with its meaning. A more in-depth discussion can be found in Lesson 6, "Custom Classes," where you'll create your own custom classes.

Class is an organizational phrase used to denote sets of objects with similar characteristics and abilities. You've probably heard the terms *upper class*, *middle class*, or *working class* to describe groups of people that fit a certain mold due to their finances or capabilities. The same general idea applies to the concept of classes in ActionScript. Each object you use in ActionScript belongs to a specific class that defines the general characteristics and abilities of the objects in it. To help you grasp this concept in the realm of ActionScript, let's look at an example.

Perhaps you've noticed that all movie clip instances you place in your project have a _width or _alpha property (among a lot of other common properties), or that you can control every movie clip instance's Timeline using the gotoAndPlay() action (also known as a *method*). This is because Flash contains a MovieClip class (it's hidden from you, but it exists). This class defines the general capabilities of every movie clip instance you use in your project. Although each movie clip instance might look different, they all have the same basic properties and abilities. This is similar to how humans walk, talk, and sneeze (common abilities), but each human's way of doing it is unique. We are all part of the Human class, so to speak.

It's important to realize that when building your Flash projects, you create and use *instances* of various classes instead of placing the actual class in your project. It's a subtle but important distinction.

Classes of Objects

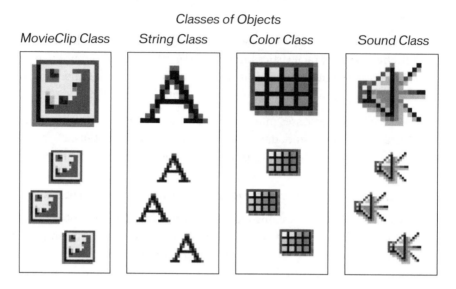

MovieClip Class   String Class   Color Class   Sound Class

For example, when you drag a movie clip onto the stage, you're actually creating an *instance* of the MovieClip class. When you create a dynamic text field, you're creating an instance of the TextField class. You will usually work with instances (also known simply as objects) in Flash, as opposed to the actual class (although this can be done, and you will learn how in Lesson 6, "Custom Classes"). A class is often referred to as a blueprint, whereas an instance of that class is thought of as the resulting usable object that you work with, based on that blueprint.

As we mentioned, classes of objects are defined by two primary characteristics: their *properties* and *methods*. Let's take an in-depth look at both.

Note *In the discussion that follows, the term* object *refers to an instance of a class. For example, if we mention an object named mySound, we are referring to an instance of the Sound class named mySound.*

Properties

Many but not all classes of objects have properties—values that represent characteristics belonging to instances of that class. In the real world, a car has properties such as color, make, model, and horsepower. If your project had a Car class and you had created an instance of it named myCar, you might access the value of its properties in this manner:

```
var carColor:String = myCar.color;
var carTopSpeed:Number = myCar.topSpeed;
```

Most classes in Flash have properties. For example, instances of the MovieClip class have property values that represent their transparency, visibility, horizontal position, vertical position, and rotation. Changes to any of these properties affect the movie clip instance's appearance or functionality, just as giving a car a paint job or changing its engine would alter the car. You can use property values of various objects in your scripts to set values elsewhere. Assume that a script in your project moves your car at a speed based on its horsepower. That line of script might look like this:

```
var speedFactor:Number = myCar.horsepower;
```

Here, the value of speedFactor is dependent on the value of the horsepower property of myCar.

Let's look at one more example of a property and how it's used in ActionScript.

The length of a string is a property of a String class. For example, the length of the term "Flash" is 5 because it contains five characters. In ActionScript, this would be written like this:

```
var name:String = "Flash";
var lengthOfName:Number = name.length;
```

The first line of code creates a variable called name whose value is the string "Flash". The second line creates a variable called lengthOfName whose value is that of the length property of the name object (5). Although property names associated with movie clips are *usually* preceded by an underscore (_alpha and _rotation, for example), the property names of most objects are *not* preceded by an underscore. MovieClip properties break from what is considered the norm because their properties were first introduced in Flash 4, when ActionScript had a much different form than it has today.

Methods

A method represents a task that instances of a class can perform. If you think of VCRs as a class, methods of that class would include the abilities to play, record, stop, rewind, fast forward, and pause. The syntax representing the methods of our VCR class would look like this:

```
play();
rewind();
record();
```

For an instance of the VCR class to invoke (use) a method of its class, the syntax requires that you first indicate the name of the VCR class instance, followed by a dot and the name of the method:

```
myVCR.record();
```

This tells the VCR instance named myVCR to start recording.

The parentheses included with the method sometimes allow you to invoke the method in a unique way by using a parameter or set of parameter values. Using the VCR example again, let's say you wanted to record a TV show on Channel 8 from 10:00 p.m. to 11:00 p.m. on September 9. The script required to perform this task might look like this:

```
myVCR.record("8", "10:00 pm", "11:00 pm", "September 9");
```

Commas separate the method parameters. Keep in mind that parameter values can be hard coded as shown, or they can be dynamic values such as variables. You can even use other methods as parameters. Although many ActionScript classes have methods that accept parameters, not all do. Some methods simply perform tasks that don't require special settings. For example, the stop() method of the MovieClip class allows you to stop the playback of a movie clip instance—nothing more, nothing less, thus additional parameters are unnecessary.

Each class has a unique set of methods, which makes sense because each has a specific function.

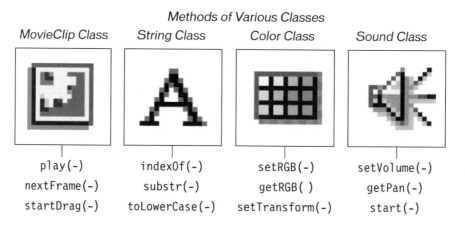

Methods of Various Classes

MovieClip Class	String Class	Color Class	Sound Class
play(-)	indexOf(-)	setRGB(-)	setVolume(-)
nextFrame(-)	substr(-)	getRGB( )	getPan(-)
startDrag(-)	toLowerCase(-)	setTransform(-)	start(-)

The various methods used by classes in ActionScript perform all sorts of tasks, including the following:

- Getting and setting values
- Doing conversions (for example, converting a negative number to a positive)

- Indicating whether something is true or false
- Activating or deactivating something
- Manipulating something (such as text or numbers)

We'll demonstrate some of these tasks in this lesson and many others throughout the book.

Built-in Classes

In this section, we'll briefly review many of the built-in classes that ActionScript provides, as well as some ways they are used. Before we do, however, it's important to discuss how to actually get instances of classes into your project in the first place, so you can begin to utilize their power and functionality.

You can create class instances in one of two ways. To create a new instance of the MovieClip, Button, or TextField class, you create it on the stage or drag it onto the stage from the library. However, only MovieClip, Button, and TextField instances can be created in this way. To create an instance of any other class, you must use a *constructor*—a simple line of code that tells Flash to create an instance of a particular class. A constructor looks like this:

```
var nameOfInstance:nameOfClass = new nameOfClass();
```

If you want to create an instance of the Sound class, the constructor will look like this:

```
var mySound:Sound = new Sound();
```

Whenever you create a class instance, you must give it a unique name. This allows you to change a property or invoke a method as it relates to that particular instance (remember, an instance gets all the properties and methods of the class to which it belongs). We'll demonstrate the concept in examples. As you gain programming experience, you'll begin to understand when you should use constructors.

Although instances of the MovieClip, TextField, and Button classes can be created on the stage manually by dragging them from the library, they can also be created dynamically using ActionScript.

Note   *Object names follow the same naming conventions as variables, which means they can't contain spaces, symbols, or a number as the first character.*

Some classes are known as *top-level classes*, and you can't create instances of them using the methods we've shown. What differentiates these classes from those of which you create instances? Top-level classes represent and control global functionalities within your project. Take, for example, the Mouse class, which controls cursor visibility (among other things). You have just one cursor, so it wouldn't make sense to be able to create instances of this class; instead, you use the methods available to it to do various things with the mouse. Look at this example:

```
Mouse.hide()
```

This line of script hides the cursor. Notice that the name of an instance is not referenced in relation to the hide() method. Instead, the *name of the top-level class* is referenced (in this case, Mouse), followed by the name of the method you wish to use. Similar syntax is used with any top-level class. As we go through the rest of this lesson, we'll introduce you to other top-level classes and the syntax required to use them.

In the Actions panel under the ActionScript 2.0 Classes book, you can access all of Flash's built-in classes, each of which is contained in one of the 12 subbooks. These four are the most commonly used:

- **Client/Server and XML.** These classes control the movement of information in and out of Flash.

- **Core.** These classes deal with information storage and manipulation, not including information that's being moved into or out of Flash itself.

- **Media.** These classes assist with manipulating sound and video in your Flash movie, such as playing sounds, gaining access to the system camera, and streaming video.

- **Movie.** These classes deal with visual content and system-related information such as movie clips, text fields, the stage, and accessibility.

The following describes many of the built-in classes available in ActionScript as well as where and how you might use them. We'll indicate whether a class is a top-level class (creating instances is not required) or not, in which case you must create individual instances.

Accessibility Class (Top-Level)

This class contains read-only information about the computer's capability to use a screen reader:

```
Accessibility.isActive();
```

This script returns a result of either true or false. If the result is true, the user's computer can employ a screen reader.

Array Class (Instances)

An array is a storage device for multiple pieces of information. Arrays store information that can be set and referenced using a numbering system. For example:

```
var cakeType:Array = new Array();
cakeType[0] = "Chocolate";
cakeType[1] = "Angel Food";
cakeType[2] = "Baked Alaska";
```

The first line creates a new instance of the Array class called cakeType using the Array constructor. The next lines place data inside that array.

The Array class contains many useful methods that will help you add, remove, and sort array items from instances of that class.

Note   *For more on arrays, see Lesson 4, "Arrays and Loops."*

Boolean Class (Instances)

Instances of the Boolean class store one of two values: true or false. You can create a Boolean class instance by using the Boolean constructor or by using the = assign operator. For example:

```
var toggle:Boolean = new Boolean(false);
```

and

```
var toggle:Boolean = false;
```

create identical instances.

Button Class (Instances)

When you place a button on the stage, you create an instance of the Button class. Only MovieClip and TextField class instances are created in a similar fashion—that is, by placing actual instances on the stage. The Button class contains properties and methods that allow you to control the appearance, tab order, functionality, and more of the button instances.

Capabilities Class (Top-Level)

This class contains information about the user's computer, such as screen resolution and whether it can play sounds. The following script places the horizontal resolution of the user's computer into myVariable:

```
var myVariable:Number = System.capabilities.screenResolutionX;
```

Note *Being able to access computer information allows you to create movies that tailor themselves to the capabilities of your user's computer. For example, you can determine whether a handheld computer is accessing the movie and, if so, redirect the user to a page designed expressly for handheld devices.*

Color Class (Instances)

You use an instance of this class to change a movie clip's color dynamically. When you create a Color class instance, you point it at a particular movie clip. Using the Color class's methods, you can alter your movie clip's color. You create a Color instance using the Color class constructor method:

```
var myColor:Color = new Color(pathToTimeline);
```

Later in this lesson you'll complete an exercise using an instance of the Color class.

ContextMenu Class (Instances)

The context menu is the menu seen in the Flash player when you right-click (Ctrl-click on the Macintosh). This class is used in conjunction with instances of the ContextMenuItems class (described shortly) to create customized context menus (with custom commands), which appear when the user right-clicks (or Ctrl-clicks) a visual element in the Flash player window. This class also allows you to enable most of the built-in context menu commands (such as Play, Stop, and Print), even as your movie plays.

This script creates a new ContextMenu instance named myCustomMenu:

```
var myCustomMenu:ContextMenu = new ContextMenu();
myCustomMenu.hideBuiltInItems();
myCustomMenu.builtInItems.print = true;
myMovieClip_mc.menu = myCustomMenu;
myButton_btn.menu = myCustomMenu;
myTextField_txt.menu = myCustomMenu;
```

The second line of the script uses the hideBuiltInItems() method to hide all the built-in menu commands, and the third line enables the Print command so that it will appear when the menu is opened. The last three lines assign the custom menu to a movie clip, button, and text field instance. Right-clicking (or Ctrl-clicking) any of these instances will cause the custom menu to appear.

ContextMenuItems Class (Instances)

This class is used in conjunction with the ContextMenu class (described previously) to create items that appear in a custom context menu. Your Flash project can be scripted to capture when a user clicks a custom menu item so that you can have a specific action or actions occur. For example, you can create a custom context menu that will allow a user to right-click in your project and choose to mute the volume.

Note You will see more on the ContextMenu and ContextMenuItems classes in Lesson 18, "Maximum-Strength SWF Files."

Date Class (Instances)

With this class you can access the current time as local time or Greenwich Mean Time (GMT), as well as easily determine the current day, week, month, or year. To create a new instance of the Date class, you use the Date class constructor method. This example demonstrates one use of the Date class:

```
var now:Date = new Date();
var largeNumber:Number = now.getTime();
```

The example creates a variable called largeNumber, whose value is the number of milliseconds since midnight January 1, 1970.

Error Class (Instances)

The Error class was introduced in Flash MX 2004 to help with managing errors in your projects. An error is whatever you define an error to be (a number was too large or too small, for example). When an error occurs, a new instance of the Error class is instantiated, which is known as "throwing" an error. With the Error class you can capture errors and write code to handle them so that your application behaves well, rather than acting in an unpredictable way.

Key Class (Top-Level)

You use the Key class to determine the state of the keys on the keyboard—for example, whether the Caps Lock key is toggled on, which key was pressed last, and which key or keys are currently pressed.

LoadVars Class (Instances)

Flash allows you to load data into a movie from an external source. Using the LoadVars class, Flash can load in variables from a specified URL (which can be a standard text file). For example:

```
var myObj:LoadVars = new LoadVars();
myObj.load("http://www.mysite.com/myFiles/file.txt");
```

In this example, all the loaded variables become properties of the myObj LoadVars instance.

Math Class (Top-Level)

With the Math class, you can perform many useful calculations and have the result returned. Here's one:

```
var positiveNumber:Number = Math.abs(-6);
```

The script uses the absolute value method of the Math class to convert the −6 to a positive number.

Mouse Class (Top-Level)

The Mouse class controls cursor visibility and allows you to set up Listeners to track mouse activity. Here is an example:

```
Mouse.hide();
```

The script hides the mouse from view. The mouse is still active, but it is not visible.

MovieClip Class (Instances)

You create instances of this most familiar class, either in the authoring environment (by placing them on the stage) or with ActionScript actions such as `createEmptyMovieClip()` and `duplicateMovieClip()`—*not* by using the constructor function. Movie clip instances have many properties and methods that are used frequently in an interactive project. Here's an example:

```
myClip_mc.gotoAndStop("Menu");
```

With this script, a movie clip with an instance name of `myClip_mc` will be sent to the frame labeled Menu.

MovieClipLoader Class (Instances)

This class provides a way for you to easily load and gain access to information during the load of a SWF or JPG file into a target movie clip or level. With an instance of the MovieClipLoader class, you know the file size of the external asset you are loading as well as how much of it has been loaded. By continually checking to see how much of the asset has been loaded, you can build a progress bar that indicates how far along an asset is in the loading process.

The MovieClipLoader class also provides a way for you to be informed of when the asset has finished loading.

Note   *This class will be used in Lesson 13, "External Data Connections."*

NetConnection Class (Instances)

The NetConnection class is used together with the NetStream class to play external Flash Video (FLV) files from an HTTP address or a hard drive.

NetStream Class (Instances)

The NetStream class provides methods and properties for controlling the playback of external Flash Video (FLV) files.

Note   *You will see more on the NetConnection and NetStream classes in Lesson 13.*

Number Class (Top-Level)

You can create a Number class instance by using its constructor method or by assigning a number as the value of a variable. For instance, the following:

```
var age:Number = new Number(26);
```

is equivalent to:

```
var age:Number = 26;
```

The new Number() constructor method is rarely used, however, because creating a new number without the constructor takes less effort and achieves the same result.

Object Class (Instances)

No, it's not a typo; there is an Object class! You can use this generic class—which is also known as ActionScript's root class (meaning that it's the highest in the class hierarchy) in various ways. By employing the properties and methods available to it, you can affect and modify other classes (such as those listed in this section). It also comes in handy for creating object instances that hold information about the current user, or instances that track chunks of related data (to name just a couple of uses).

The following is the syntax for creating a generic object:

```
var names:Object = new Object();
names.cat = "Hayes";
```

The first line of script creates a new object called names. The second line adds a variable (property) to the object called cat. The variable is considered a property of this object.

In Lesson 6, "Custom Classes," we'll show you how to create your own custom classes of objects (better than generic objects!) as well as how to create properties and methods for your custom class. After you know how to do this, you can create objects and classes that do precisely what you want.

PrintJob Class (Instances)

This class provides a great way to handle printing. With the PrintJob class you can dynamically specify frames from various timelines to print from a single Print dialog box.

Note *This class is used in Lesson 17, "Printing and Context Menus."*

Selection Class (Top-Level)

You use the Selection class to retrieve information or set characteristics relating to selected items in your movies, especially text in text fields. When the cursor is in an area of a text field, that field is said to be "in focus." You can employ the Selection class to set the focus to a specific text field, to find out which text field is currently in focus, or even to programmatically select specific chunks of text in a field so that it can be manipulated in some way. Here's an example of one use of the Selection class:

```
Selection.setFocus("firstName");
```

The script sets into focus the input text field with the instance name of firstName.

You'll complete an exercise using this class later in this lesson.

Sound Class (Instances)

You use instances of the Sound class to control sounds—for example, setting volume and adjusting left and right speaker pan settings. To learn more about this class, see Lesson 16, "Media in Flash."

Stage Class (Top-Level)

With the Stage class, you can control and get information about characteristics of the stage, such as alignment. For example:

```
Stage.height
```

The script returns the height of the stage in pixels.

String Class (Instances)

You use the String class to manipulate and get information about textual data. You can create a new string by using the String class constructor method or by putting quotes around a value when setting a variable. For example, the following:

```
var bird:String = new String("Robin");
```

is the same as this:

```
var bird:String = "Robin";
```

You'll use this class to complete an exercise later in this lesson.

StyleSheet Class (Instances)

The StyleSheet class is used to define a set of style rules for text. It can then be applied to a text field, which makes the text in that text field adhere to the style rules (such as font size and color). The StyleSheet class is useful because you can have several text fields use the same style. If you decide to change something about the style, such as the text color, all the text fields that use the style will be affected. In addition, external Cascading Style Sheet (CSS) files can be used, providing a way to achieve a uniform look to text content in your CSS-enhanced web pages and the Flash content embedded in them (because both can make use of a single style sheet definition). This script creates a new StyleSheet instance and then loads an external CSS file into that instance:

```
var myStyleSheet = new TextField.StyleSheet();
myStlyeSheet.load("externalStyleSheet.css");
```

System Class (Top-Level)

This class contains information about your user's computer system, such as the operating system, the language being used, and all the properties of the Capabilities class.

One of the System class's properties is a string called serverString, which contains a list of the system capabilities (concatenated into one string). You can send this list to the server so that you can store or use the information it contains. To access the string, use this:

```
System.capabilities.serverString
```

TextField Class (Instances)

Using this class, you can dynamically create a new text field and control most of its characteristics—for example, setting the format of the text field or the scrolling of text. Instances of this class are created when a text field is placed on the stage while you're authoring your movie, or created dynamically using the createTextField() method. We'll use this class later in this lesson.

TextFormat Class (Instances)

Instances of the TextFormat class are used to change the format/style of text displayed in text fields. After it's created, you apply the instance of the TextFormat class to a text field using the setTextFormat() or setNewTextFormat() methods:

```
nameOfTextField_txt.setTextFormat(nameOfFormatObject);
```

XML Class (Instances)

XML is one of the most popular standards for formatting data—it's no surprise when you consider that XML-formatted data lets all kinds of applications transfer information seamlessly. Using Flash, you can create an XML class instance (which is an instance of the XML class) to store an XML-formatted document that can then be sent from or loaded into XML instances. Here's one use of the XML class:

```
var myXML:XML = new XML();
myXML.load("myFile.xml");
```

The script creates a new XML instance and loads an XML-formatted file into that instance.

Note *In Lesson 14, "XML and Flash," you will learn more about using the XML class.*

XMLSocket Class (Instances)

Flash also allows you to set up a persistent connection with a *socket server*—an application that runs on a web server. The socket server waits for users to connect to it. Once connected, the socket server can transfer information between all connected users at very fast speeds, which is how most chat systems and multiplayer games are created. An XML socket is so named because it uses the XML format as the standard for transferred information.

You can create an XMLSocket class instance by using the XMLSocket class constructor method. The following is an example of one use of this type of class:

```
var mySocket:XMLSocket = new XMLSocket();
mySocket.connect("http://www.electro-server.com", 9875);
```

This script creates a new instance of the XMLSocket class and opens up a connection with a socket server. See Lesson 14, "XML and Flash," for a detailed description of socket servers and the XMLSocket class, as well as an exercise in creating your own chat application.

Covering every built-in class in detail would take a whole book. However, throughout the lessons we'll use many of these classes discussed here in various ways, and provide detailed instructions about how and why we're using them. The following exercises will concentrate on just a few of these classes to give you a general idea of how you can use them.

Using the Color Class

To use a Color class, you must first create an instance using the Color class constructor. Here's the syntax for creating a new instance of the Color class:

```
var myColor:Color = new Color(shirt_mc);
```

The script creates a new instance of the Color class named myColor and associates it with a movie clip instance named shirt_mc.

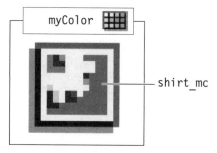

You can create the instance anywhere. The constructor accepts one parameter: the path to the movie clip it should modify. If you want to create the instance with ActionScript from within a movie clip that will reference itself, you would use this as the path. For example, the following script creates a new instance of the Color class on the movie clip instance that contains the script:

```
var myColor:Color = new Color(this);
```

Note   As with any class instance, you can create many instances of the Color class in a single project and associate them with various Timelines, providing you with dynamic control over the color of many instances simultaneously.

The most common Color class method is setRGB(), which changes the color of the movie clip instance specified as the parameter when the instance was created. Here's an example of one use of setRGB():

```
var myColor:Color = new Color(shirt_mc);
myColor.setRGB(0xFF3300);
```

The script creates a new Color class instance named myColor and then uses the setRGB() method to change the color of the shirt_mc movie clip instance to red. This method accepts a parameter (0x) followed by the hex value for a color. The 0x parameter is a reserved character combination that tells Flash that a hexadecimal number follows.

The number system that we're accustomed to using is called *base 10*, which means 10 numbers are used for all values (0 through 9). In other words, all other numbers (28; 6,403; 496; 300, 439; and so on) can be described using a combination of these 10. Hexadecimal numbers, in contrast, are *base 16*, which means their values are expressed using numbers *and* letters: 0 through 9 and A through F. Using this method, you can create hexadecimal values of 00 to FF, with 00 a base 10 value of 0, and FF a base 10 value of 255.

Base 10

10 numbers ⟶ 0 1 2 3 4 5 6 7 8 9
before repeating ⟶ 10 11 12 13 14 15 16 17 18 19

Base 16

16 numbers/letters ⟶ 00 01 02 03 04 05 06 07 08 09 0A 0B 0C 0D 0E 0F
before repeating ⟶ 10 11 12 13 14 15 16 17 18 19 1A 1B 1C 1D 1E 1F

However, you don't absolutely have to know hex values to describe certain colors when using the setRGB() method. Instead, if you know the RGB value of a color, you can convert it to a hexadecimal value dynamically using the Number class and the parseInt() function. We'll cover this topic in the next exercise (although we won't cover it in detail).

In this exercise you'll create a simple interactive scene in which you can change the color of a clown's hair using several buttons.

1. Open *Clown1.fla* in the Lesson05/Start folder.

The content has already been created and placed on the stage, so we can focus on the ActionScript involved in changing the color of a movie clip. The main Timeline has four layers: Actions, Background, Clown Hair, and Buttons.

The Clown Hair layer contains a movie clip instance named hair_mc. You will be changing the color of this instance with ActionScript.

The Buttons layer contains five circular, colored buttons. These buttons have instance names based on their respective colors: red_btn, green_btn, blue_btn, yellow_btn, and rainbow_btn. You'll be adding ActionScript to the first frame of the main Timeline, which will change the color of the hair_mc movie clip when any of the five buttons is clicked.

2. With the Actions panel open, select Frame 1 of the main Timeline and add the script:

```
red_btn.onRelease = function() {
  var hairColor:Color = new Color(hair_mc);
  hairColor.setRGB(0xCC0000);
};
```

This script assigns a callback function to the onRelease event of the red_btn instance.

The callback function (lines 2 and 3) tells Flash to create a new Color class instance named hairColor when this button is released and to associate that instance with the hair_mc movie clip instance. This function also uses the setRGB() method to change the color of the instance (hence the hair_mc movie clip instance) to CC0000, which is the hex value for the red in the middle of the button.

3. **On the same frame, below the script added in the preceding step, add this script:**

```
yellow_btn.onRelease = function() {
  var hairColor:Color = new Color(hair_mc);
  hairColor.setRGB(0xFFCC00);
};
```

This script is identical to the script used to assign the onRelease callback to the red button, except for the color value used in the setRGB() method, the value of which is the hex value for the yellow in the middle of the button. When a user clicks the yellow button, it will execute this callback, and the clown's hair will turn yellow.

4. **With Frame 1 still selected, add this script to the bottom of the current script:**

```
green_btn.onRelease = function() {
  var hairColor:Color = new Color(hair_mc);
  hairColor.setRGB(0x009900);
};
```

The hex value for green is 009900 and is used in the setRGB() method in the same manner as in the two preceding scripts.

5. **Add a similar script for the blue_btn instance:**

```
blue_btn.onRelease = function() {
  var hairColor:Color = new Color(hair_mc);
  hairColor.setRGB(0x336699);
};
```

As with the three other buttons, this script creates an instance of the Color class that it uses to change the color of the hair_mc movie clip instance.

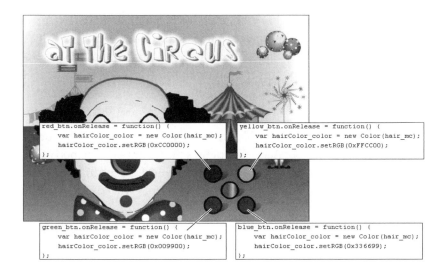

```
red_btn.onRelease = function() {
    var hairColor_color = new Color(hair_mc);
    hairColor_color.setRGB(0xCC0000);
};
```

```
yellow_btn.onRelease = function() {
    var hairColor_color = new Color(hair_mc);
    hairColor_color.setRGB(0xFFCC00);
};
```

```
green_btn.onRelease = function() {
    var hairColor_color = new Color(hair_mc);
    hairColor_color.setRGB(0x009900);
};
```

```
blue_btn.onRelease = function() {
    var hairColor_color = new Color(hair_mc);
    hairColor_color.setRGB(0x336699);
};
```

Now it's time to test your work.

6. Choose Control › Test Movie. Click the four buttons to view the color changes.

Every time you click one of these buttons, Flash creates a new Color class instance and associates it with the hair_mc movie clip instance. The setRGB() method available to Color class instances is then used to change the color of that instance.

Note *Although in this exercise a Color class is created on each button, an instance needs to be created only once—after which it exists as part of the Timeline. Any changes to that instance can be made by using methods available to that instance.*

Now let's use ActionScript to change the clown's hair color to a random color.

7. Close the test movie to return to the authoring environment. With the Actions panel open, select Frame 1 and add this script to the end of the current script:

```
rainbow_btn.onRelease = function() {
  var R:Number = random(256);
  var G:Number = random(256);
  var B:Number = random(256);
  var colorHexString:String = R.toString(16)+G.toString(16)+B.toString(16);
  var colorHex:Number = parseInt(colorHexString, 16);
  var hairColor:Color = new Color(hair_mc);
  hairColor.setRGB(colorHex);
};
```

There are two ways to describe a color programmatically: with its RGB (red, green, blue) value or with its hex value. There are three separate RGB values, each of which can have a numeric value between 0 and 255. The RGB value of red, for instance, is R=255, G=0, B=0. The corresponding hex value (for the same color of red) is FF0000. The idea behind the first five lines of this script is to generate a random RGB value, convert it to a hex value, and then use that value in the setRGB() method at the bottom of the script.

Lines 2, 3, and 4 of the script create variables R, G, and B, whose values are random numbers between 0 and 255. The next line of ActionScript uses the toString() method of the Number class to convert a base 10 number to a base 16 string value. Let's assume, for example, that when this script is executed, the following R, G, and B values will be generated:

```
R = 45
G = 202
B = 129
```

The next line of the script says to convert the value of R to a base 16 value, convert it to a string, and then do the same thing with G and B. Using the plus (+) operator to put the converted values together, the variable colorHexString will have a string value of "2DCA81". This needs to be converted to a hex number (the same value as the string value, without the quotes) to use the setRGB() method. To do this, you use the parseInt() function.

The last two lines of the script create a new Color instance pointing to the hair_mc movie clip instance and then change its color to the random value just created.

Note *This script can randomly generate more than 16 million possible colors.*

8. Choose Control > Test Movie and click the rainbow-colored button several times.

The hair_mc movie clip instance changes randomly. You can even modify this technique to randomly generate colors within a certain range.

9. Close the test movie and save your work as *Clown2.fla*.

You should now be able to easily change the color of any movie clip instance at any time.

Working with String and Selection Classes

As one of the most commonly used classes, the String class uses methods that can be helpful for modifying and building *strings*: quote-enclosed values that contain information (like the name "Jobe") that can be easily understood by humans.

```
var message:String = "No shoes, no service!";
```

The script creates a variable named `message` whose value is a string. In such cases, you can think of the variable itself as an instance of the String class—which means you can use String class methods to manipulate its value.

Let's look at a few examples.

The `toUpperCase()` method of the String class forces a string to become all uppercase letters:

```
message = message.toUpperCase();
```

The script modifies the variable `message` to contain `"NO SHOES, NO SERVICE!"` For the opposite effect—that is, to force the entire string to become all lowercase letters—you would apply `toLowerCase()` in the same fashion.

Note that the text value of a text field instance (the text within the field) is considered an instance of the String class. If `message` were the name of a text field instance, the previous script could be rewritten like this:

```
message.text = message.text.toUpperCase();
```

Although it is most common to create a String class the easy way (`var message:String = "Hello"`), it is also possible to create a String class instance by using the constructor of the String class.

```
var message:String = new String("Hello");
```

Is there any advantage of using one over the other? Not really: Every project is different, and you may find cases where one seems to be more appropriate than the other. To review, you can create an instance of the String class by doing the following:

- Using a constructor (for example, `var myNewStringObject:String = new String("Hello");`). The String class is identified as `myNewStringObject`.
- Assigning a string value to a variable (for example, `var myString:String = "Hello";`). The String class is identified as the name of the variable.
- Creating a text field using the text tool. The String class is identified as the text property of the field, as in `nameOfTextField.text`.

Another useful method of the String class—`indexOf()`—lets you find the first occurrence of a character or group of characters in a string. The result returned is a number corresponding to the *letter index* where the string starts. A letter index is the number of a character in relation to the whole string. The first character in a string has an index of 0, the second has an index of 1, and so on. If the `indexOf()` method finds no occurrences of the character or group of characters, it returns a value of -1. Here's an example of one use of the `indexOf()` method:

```
message_txt.text = "No shoes, no service!";
var firstS:Number = message_txt.text.indexOf("s");
```

The variable firstS will be assigned a value of 3 because that's the character number of the first s encountered (the first s in *shoes*).

string index values

"No shoes, no service!"

```
|   | | | | | | |
0   1 2 3 4 5 6 7
```

It can sometimes be useful to determine the number of characters in a string, which is easy to do because all instances of the string class have a length property. You can often use string length to validate user-input information in a text field. Perhaps you want a user to enter a valid zip code: You know that it must be five characters in length. By checking the length property of the zip code, you could create a simple validation script:

```
zipCode_txt.text = "27609";
var zipLength:Number = zipCode_txt.text.length
if (zipLength == 5) {
    // Correct length of zip code
} else {
    // Invalid zip code
}
```

The first line sets the text value shown in the zipCode_txt text field. (We assume that this is what the user has entered.) The next line creates a variable named zipLength and assigns it a value based on the length property of zipCode_txt.text. In this case, it is 5 because that's the number of characters the zipCode_txt field contains. The last part of the script uses an if statement to take one set of actions if zipLength equals 5 and another if it doesn't.

The Selection class allows you to control various aspects of the currently focused text field, including highlighting text, getting and setting the caret's (current insertion point) position, and more. A text field is considered focused if the user's cursor is placed there. Because only one text field can be focused at a time, there's no need to create an instance of the Selection class; you can use it directly (the Selection class is a top-level class). By clicking on a text field, the user dictates which one has focus. However, you can use the setFocus() method to override the user's current choice, which is important because you can only use other Selection class methods on the text field currently in focus. (As you'll see in the next exercise, you can't always rely on the user to select—and thus bring into focus—the proper text field.)

One last method of the Selection class allows you to highlight portions of text dynamically—without the user's help. The method Selection.setSelection(param1, param2) includes two parameters: the character index of where the selection starts and the character index of where the selection should end. For example, you have a text field that contains the text "Derek is the craziest person I know". To highlight the word *craziest* (assuming its text field is in focus), you would use this:

```
Selection.setSelection(13, 20);
```

"Derek is the craziest person I know"

13   20

In this exercise, you'll create a simple word processor using many of the String and Selection class methods we've discussed.

1. Open *wordProcessor1.fla* in the Lesson05/Start folder.

This file has three layers: Background, Buttons, and Actions. The Background layer contains the image of the word processor window as well as text fields. The Buttons layer contains the four buttons that appear at the top of the word processor window. Starting from the left, the buttons have these instance names: upper_btn, lower_btn, count_btn, and find_btn.

There are three text field instances on the stage. The largest one in the center represents the text document. It has an instance name of inputField_txt. The next text field, to the right of the Find button, is appropriately called findField_txt. When the movie is played, the user can enter a character or string of characters into this text field, which will be searched against the contents in the inputField_txt text field. The search results will be displayed in the third text field, at the bottom of the window, which is called status_txt. This text field is also used to display the results when counting the number of characters in the document.

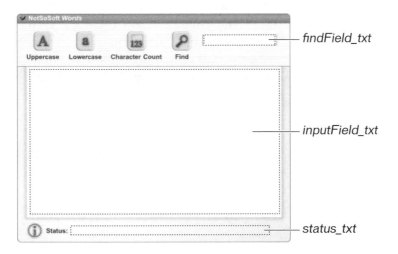

2. With the Actions panel open, select Frame 1 in the Actions layer and add the following script:

```
upper_btn.onRelease = function() {
   inputField_txt.text = inputField_txt.text.toUpperCase();
};
```

Flash interprets this script as saying, "On release of the button called upper_btn, make all letters in the inputField_txt text field uppercase." When the button is clicked, the contents of the inputField_txt text field are reassigned with uppercase letters.

3. Add this script to the same frame:

```
lower_btn.onRelease = function() {
   inputField_txt.text = inputField_txt.text.toLowerCase();
};
```

This script is similar to the one added in the preceding step. On release of the lower_btn button, the inputField_txt text field is reassigned with all lowercase characters.

4. Add this script, which counts the number of characters in the inputField_txt text field:

```
count_btn.onRelease = function() {
   status_txt.text = "There are "+inputField_txt.text.length+" characters ¬
      in the current document";
};
```

This script counts the number of characters in the inputField_txt text field and displays a message about the character count results in the status_txt text field. The length property of the inputField_txt text field is determined and inserted in the middle of the message. The message is built dynamically by adding, "There are" plus the value of the length property, plus the ending part of the message, "characters in the current document". If the document has 50 characters, the message will read, "There are 50 characters in the current document".

5. Add this script to search and highlight text:

```
find_btn.onRelease = function() {
    var result:Number = inputField_txt.text.indexOf(findField_txt.text);
    if (findField_txt.text != "" && result>=0) {
        status_txt.text = "The first instance of these characters occurs at ¬
            character "+result;
        Selection.setFocus("_root.inputField_txt");
        Selection.setSelection(result, result+findField_txt.text.length);
    } else {
        status_txt.text = "That string could not be found";
    }
};
```

This script is the most complex one in this exercise. The first line sets the value of the result variable using the indexOf() method of the String class. Here, we're asking the script to look in the inputField_txt text field and find the index number of the first occurrence of the character or group of characters entered into the findField_txt text field. In the end, result will have a value of –1 (no occurrence was found) or 0 to the string length (depending on how many characters are in the document). For example, if the first occurrence is found at index 13 (the fourteenth character), result will have a value of 13. This value plays an important part in the rest of the script.

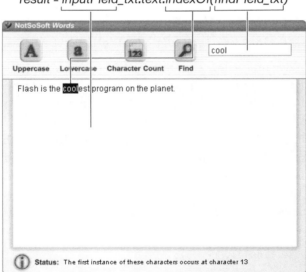

The next part of the script uses an `if` statement to carry out one of two sets of actions, depending on whether a couple of conditions prove true. The first part of the statement looks at the text values of findField_txt and the numeric value of result. It says that if findField_txt is not empty (this makes sure that the findField_txt text field has not been left blank) *and* the value of result is equal to or greater than 0 (which it will be if an occurrence of the characters entered is found), perform the following actions. The `else` part of the statement deals with what happens if neither of these conditions is met. In this case, nothing will happen except that the status_txt text field will display the text, "That string could not be found."

Assuming that both conditions are true, let's look at what the three actions under the first part of the `if` statement do. The first action will display a dynamic text message in the status_txt text field. The message is built dynamically by adding "The first instance of these characters occurs at character" plus the value of result. If result has a value of 7, the message will read, "The first instance of these characters occurs at character 7". The next two actions use methods of the Selection class to highlight the character or characters in the inputField_txt text field that were searched for and found. You'll remember that a text field must have focus before any of the Selection class methods can be used on the field. Because we want to highlight text in the inputField_txt text field, we use this line to ensure that this field has focus before the next Selection method is used on it:

```
Selection.setFocus("_root.inputField_txt");
```

The next line of script uses another Selection method to highlight text in the currently focused text field. This line reads as follows:

```
Selection.setSelection(result, result + findField_txt.text.length);
```

We used a couple of dynamic values with this method to determine where the selection begins and ends. Because we want the selection to start at the point where the first occurrence was found, we use the value of result as the starting point of the selection. The ending point of the selection is determined by adding the value of result to the value of the length property of the findField_txt text field. How does this work? Assume that you typed **I like my dog very much** in the inputField_txt text field. Next, in the findField_txt text field, you search for dog. When the script is executed, result will have a value of 10 (the first occurrence of dog is at the eleventh character), and findField_txt.text.length will be 3 (because the word dog is currently in this field, and it is three characters long). Using these values, the script could be written like this:

```
Selection.setSelection(11, 11 + 3);
```

or

```
Selection.setSelection(11, 14);
```

This will highlight characters 11 through 14, which is where "dog" appears in the inputField_txt text field.

6. Choose Control › Test Movie.

Type something into the inputField_txt text field and press the Uppercase and Lowercase buttons. Press the Count Characters button to determine how many characters the document contains. Finally, try out the search function by entering one or more characters into the findField_txt text field and pressing the button.

7. Close the test movie and save your work as *wordProcessor2.fla*.

You can see how easy it is to use the methods associated with the String and Selection classes—a good thing because you'll find yourself using the String class frequently to both validate and reformat data.

What You Have Learned

In this lesson, you have:

- Learned what classes are and why they are useful (pages 97–101)
- Become acquainted with the various built-in classes available in ActionScript (pages 101–111)
- Used the Color class (pages 111–116)
- Created a word processor using properties and methods of the String and Selection classes (pages 116–123)

6 Custom Classes

As an ActionScript programmer, you can create an unlimited variety of applications. The more experience you gain, the more you'll realize how often you end up writing code that performs certain custom tasks over and over again. For example, let's say that last month you created an address book application for a client. This month you learn that you need to create an employee directory for the same client. Immediately you'll notice that there are many similar features between an address book and an employee directory. In fact, an employee directory can have all the features of the address book, plus some extras. If you created an address book class for the address book application, you would be able to reuse it for the employee directory application.

In this lesson, you will create several custom classes whose functionality will be plugged into movie clips, allowing instances of those clips to perform customized tasks.

Creating custom classes helps promote code reusability and is essential for well-written object-oriented programming. In this lesson, you will be introduced to the syntax and concepts needed to create custom classes and you will gain experience writing your own classes.

What You Will Learn

In this lesson, you will:

- Learn class syntax and terminology
- Learn about class paths and how they're used
- Learn about private, public, and static members and how to use them
- Use inheritance to extend a class
- Use overriding
- Create custom object classes
- Associate a custom class with a movie clip in the library

Approximate Time

This lesson takes approximately two hours to complete.

Lesson Files

Media Files:

None

Starting Files:

Lesson06/Start/CurrencyConverter1.fla
Lesson06/Start/PetParade1.fla

Completed Projects:

Lesson06/Completed/CurrencyConverter.as
Lesson06/Completed/CurrencyConverter2.fla
Lesson06/Completed/PetParade2.fla
Lesson06/Completed/Animal.as
Lesson06/Completed/Dog.as
Lesson06/Completed/Cat.as

Understanding Classes, Top-Level Classes, and Instances

A *class* is a definition or blueprint of how an object is made up and how it should act. For example, an instance of the Array class (an Array object) can store multiple pieces of information in numerically indexed locations (myArray[0], myArray[1], myArray[2], and so on). How can the array do this? It knows how to do this because it was defined that way by the Array class, which has hidden logic and definitions (code) that work behind the scenes to define the way an Array object works and how it's used. Think of a class as a template from which objects are created. This is a vague description of a class, but as you progress through this lesson and are introduced to more concepts, terminology, and examples, you'll gain a better understanding of what a class really is.

A class exists to produce an instance of itself on demand. You create an instance of a class by invoking the *constructor method* of that class. For example:

```
var myArray:Array = new Array();
```

The action to the right of the equals sign, new Array() in this example, executes the constructor method of the Array class. You cannot use the Array class directly. You must create an instance of the class to use any of its properties and methods. When creating the array instance, the Array class creates an object and then populates it with properties and methods. In a sense, the Array class is similar to a factory for array objects. When asked, it creates and returns an Array object.

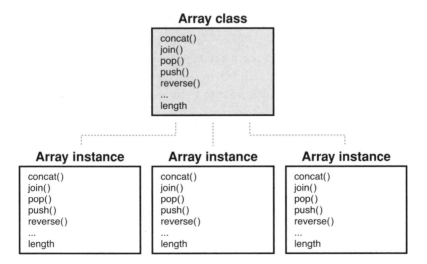

There also are classes that you can use without the need to create an instance because all the properties and methods are static. This type of a class is called a *top-level* class.

Examples of this type of class include the Math, Mouse, and Key classes. When you think about it, top-level classes make sense. Is there ever really a need to have more than one instance of the Mouse class or the Math class? With the Math class, you simply pass a number into a method, and a result is returned. The Math class doesn't store any of the information that you feed it, so only one copy is needed. On the other hand, arrays store unique data, so it wouldn't make sense to access the Array class directly because you would be able to have only one array.

Note   *Top-level classes are similar to classes that follow the Singleton design pattern. This pattern restricts a class to one instance and gives you global access to that instance.*

Creating a Class

The code for defining an ActionScript class exists in its own .as file (remember that the .as file extension stands for *Action Script*). Only one class can be defined per file. If you create 13 classes, you have to create 13 .as files. A class file is nothing more than a text file containing ActionScript code. The name of each class file is the name of the class followed by the .as file extension. For example, if you create a TestClass class, it has to exist in a file with this exact name: TestClass.as.

Note   *It's considered good coding practice to give classes a name with the first letter of each word capitalized. This notation is commonly referred to as camel-case.*

A class file can be created from within the Macromedia Flash authoring environment by opening the ActionScript editor (File > New > ActionScript File) or by using the text editor of your choice. There are many third-party ActionScript editors that offer many of the same features as the built-in editor offered in Flash. In fact, most ActionScript programmers use programs like PrimalScript, SEPY, or Eclipse to write their ActionScript classes.

Simply creating a text file with an .as extension doesn't automatically make it a functional class file. The contents of the file must be ActionScript whose syntax defines the class (including its methods and properties). For example, the following code, inside the TestClass.as file, is the beginning of a valid class:

```
class TestClass {
}
```

The statement class tells the compiler (the part of Flash that handles the creation of SWF files) that everything that follows in this file is considered part of a class definition (for defining the TestClass class). After the class statement is the name of the class being created: TestClass. The name of the class must be the same as the name of the .as file that contains the code defining the class; therefore, the TestClass class definition must be in a file named TestClass.as.

A class file defines characteristics about the class by creating properties and methods. The properties and methods of a class are referred to as *members*, and they are all defined within the outermost curly braces of the class. Consider the following example:

```
class Cube {
    var length:Number = 3;
    var height:Number = 2;
    var width:Number = 7;

    function getVolume():Number {
        return length * (height * width);
    }

}
```

In this example, the properties length, height, and width and the method getVolume() are all members of the Cube class.

To create a new instance of a class to use its functionality in your project, the class must have a constructor method. However, you don't have to define the constructor in your class. If you leave the constructor out, a default constructor will be added automatically. The constructor must have the same name as the class. Let's modify the Cube class we just created to contain a constructor method and accept parameters so that we can create a custom cube instance:

```
class Cube {
    var length:Number;
    var height:Number;
    var width:Number;

    function Cube(length:Number, height:Number, width:Number) {
        this.length = length;
        this.height = height;
        this.width = width;
    }

    function getVolume():Number {
        return length * (height * width);
    }

}
```

Note *Because our constructor's parameters have the same name as the private properties in our class, we must use the keyword this to explicitly reference the class properties and differentiate between the constructor's parameters.*

After coding the Cube class, you save it as an .as file named Cube.as in the same directory as your Flash authoring file. (Alternatively, you can place your .as class files elsewhere, which we'll discuss in a moment.) The name of the file must match the name of your class exactly. You would create a new instance of the Cube class on a frame in your Flash authoring file in the following way:

```
var myCube:Cube = new Cube(3, 2, 7);
```

You can then get the volume of the myCube object this way:

```
var volume:Number = myCube.getVolume();
```

By default, the properties and methods available to an instance of a class are fixed by the properties and methods defined in its class file. For example, the Cube class file defines three properties (length, height, and width) and one method (getVolume()). As a result, the myCube instance of the Cube class can access those particular properties and that method:

```
myCube.length //has a value of 3
myCube.height //has a value of 2
myCube.width //has a value of 7
myCube.getVolume() // returns a value of 42
```

The myCube properties can be set using the following syntax:

```
myCube.length = 6;
myCube.height = 4;
```

And so on. But if you attempt to add a property or method to the myCube instance that was not defined in its class file, such as the following, an error will result when you export your movie:

```
myCube.color = "red";
```

This principle helps you eliminate bugs in your code. Here's how. In your application, perhaps Cube instances shouldn't have color properties, and instead you meant to assign a color property to the myCup instance of the Cup class, which would have been acceptable. When you export your movie, Flash's compiler sees that you set the color property for an instance of the Cube class. It then looks at the Cube class definition to see whether the color property has been defined there. If not, Flash assumes that the code is wrong, and an error results. This setup helps you to script object instances in a nearly foolproof manner; no object instance is allowed to perform an action unless that action is explicitly permitted by the class definition.

Although this can be a great way to help you debug your applications—because Flash displays an error when you attempt to use an object in the wrong way—there might be times when you *do* want instances of a custom object class to be able to add or access properties and methods that were not defined in its class file. This is possible, too. You would simply need to add the dynamic class modifier to the class definition (notice the first line):

```
dynamic class Cube {
  var length:Number;
  var height:Number;
  var width:Number;

  function Cube(length:Number, height:Number, width:Number) {
    this.length = length;
    this.height = height;
    this.width = width;
  }

  function getVolume():Number {
    return length * height * width;
  }

}
```

With the addition of the dynamic modifier, all instances of the Cube class, including the myCube instance we created earlier, can add any property or method, regardless of whether that property or method was originally defined in the Cube class file.

Note *Some of Flash's built-in classes—for example, MovieClip, LoadVars, and SharedObject—are dynamic classes, which is why you can dynamically add properties and methods to instances of these classes. Other built-in classes— such as TextField and Sound—are not dynamic. If you attempt to add properties to instances of these classes, Flash displays errors when you export your movie.*

There are a couple of important points to note about classes and class members.

Although you're not required to use strong typing syntax (:Number, :Array, :String, and so forth) when creating a class, this strategy is highly recommended. Strong typing is useful because it explicitly tells the compiler what you're trying to do, and the compiler can then help you to debug your application.

You can create instances of a custom class from any Timeline or class within your project, in the same manner as you do with any of Flash's built-in classes; therefore, an instance of our custom Cube class can be created on the main Timeline or on any movie clip's Timeline.

Understanding the Classpath

So far you have been introduced to the basics of the class syntax and creating a class file. What you haven't yet learned is how class files relate to Flash authoring files—how they're used in tandem.

If you want to use a custom class in a Flash project to create instances of that class, Flash must know where to find its class file. This section explores how to instruct a Flash file to load and use a custom class. As with many things in Flash, there are several techniques.

When compiling a SWF file from a FLA file, Flash checks to see whether you created an instance of a custom class. If a custom class is being used, Flash attempts to load that custom class to include it inside the SWF file. The directories in which Flash searches for the class are called the *classpath*. If the class file is found within the classpath, the compiler includes the class in the SWF file. If the class file is not found, the compiler reports an error.

Two classpaths are recognized when authoring an FLA file: one classpath is global, and the other is at document level. The global classpath is the same no matter which FLA file you're authoring. The document-level classpath can be changed for a specific FLA file without affecting the classpaths seen by other FLA files.

Global Classpath

By default, the global classpath points to two separate directories. The first is the directory in which your current Flash document resides. For example, if you're editing a FLA file that's saved on your hard drive in a directory called MyTest, the MyTest directory is recognized as a global classpath for that FLA file. You can place class files used by your project in that directory, and Flash will find them. The global classpath also points to the directory that contains the class files and interfaces for Flash's built-in classes.

Note   *The global class directory can be found in the Flash 8 program folder. On Windows XP, it's in the following location:*

Documents and Settings\[user]\Local Settings\Application Data\Macromedia\ Flash 8\en\ Configuration\Classes

Class files placed in this directory are immediately available for use by any FLA you author.

To understand how the classpath works, let's consider an example. If you create an instance of a custom class in a FLA file, such as the following, during the compiling process (or when you select the Check Syntax option in the Actions panel), the global classpath will be searched for a file called AddressBook.as:

```
var addresses:AddressBook = new AddressBook();
```

If found, that file is loaded and included in the SWF file. If no such file is found, you get a compile error. You can enter multiple directories in your classpath and they will be searched in the order in which you entered them. After a match is found, the search is stopped, and that match is used.

You can edit the global classpath by adding or removing directories with the following process:

1. Select Edit > Preferences.
2. Click the ActionScript menu item.
3. Click the ActionScript 2.0 Settings button.
4. Use the options in this dialog box to add to or edit the list of directories in the classpath.

Document-Level Classpath

The document-level classpath is empty by default. You can add any number of directories to this classpath to make Flash search for necessary classes while compiling an authoring file to a SWF file. This classpath exists only for the current FLA file.

Editing the document-level classpath is a useful option when you want to specify a directory or list of directories that contain class files specific to the current application. If you added these directories to the global classpath, every FLA file or ActionScript file that you edited would include them in the search for the class files to add to a SWF file during compile.

To edit the document-level classpath, follow these steps:

1. Select File > Publish Settings.

2. Select the Flash tab.

3. Click the Settings button next to ActionScript 2.0.

4. Use the options in this dialog box to add to or edit the list of directories in the classpath.

Notice that a field called Export Frame For Classes in this dialog box was dimmed in the global classpath version. By default, all class files included in the compiled SWF file are initialized on Frame 1 of the movie. Including class files that beef up the SWF file size might cause a lag when loading the SWF file over the Internet because the data from the class files must be downloaded to the end user's computer before Frame 1 can be rendered.

In many cases, including the class files adds only a tiny amount to the total SWF file size because these files are relatively small. But if you run into a problem when loading this data before Frame 1, you can change the frame number in the Export Frame For Classes field. For example, this would allow you to include a two- or three-frame loading animation in the first few frames of the SWF file that loops while the data from the class files and the rest of the SWF file are loaded.

Using Packages and Importing Classes

You have learned that a classpath points to one or more directories. Each of these directories can contain class (.as) files. In addition to containing class files, a classpath directory can contain subdirectories. A subdirectory in a classpath directory is known as a *package* and it can contain class files and more packages.

Keeping classes in packages is a good way to keep them organized. You might have hundreds of class files after just a few months of programming with Flash. Saving these classes in a logical directory structure makes them easier to locate and can help you avoid class-name conflicts with multiple projects.

When you use packages, the class file syntax changes slightly and can complicate instantiating an instance of that class.

As shown earlier, this is the basic syntax used to create a class called TestClass:

```
class TestClass {
  function TestClass() {
    //Constructor
  }
}
```

The rule that we didn't mention earlier is that the name declaration of the class must contain the path to the class file from the root classpath directory in which the class resides. The TestClass class assumes that the class file is not in any package, but is sitting directly in a classpath directory. However, if we decided to create the TestClass class in a package called testpackage, the class definition would look like this:

```
class testpackage.TestClass {
  function TestClass() {
    //Constructor
  }
}
```

The text after the class keyword contains not only the name of the class (TestClass) but the overall path where it exists. In this case, TestClass exists inside the testpackage directory, which itself exists in a classpath directory.

Suppose you created an address book class for Macromedia. Because you're a very organized person, you created a logical package (directory) structure for your class file. The class definition might look like this:

```
class com.macromedia.AddressBook {
  function AddressBook() {
    //Constructor
  }
}
```

This class is contained in the macromedia directory, which is in the com directory, which is in a classpath directory.

Note *It's considered good coding practice to name packages with all lowercase letters. It's also becoming an industry standard to name your class structure based on the domain name. Therefore, a class built for macromedia.com would be placed somewhere inside the com.macromedia package. This follows a convention from Java.*

To create an instance of a class that's in a package, you must use the full package path. For example:

```
var myInstance:testpackage.TestClass = new testpackage.TestClass();
```

Notice that the data type and the constructor are referenced using the full path. As you can imagine, working with long class names such as this one can make for a lot of typing if you're creating many instances. But there's a way to use the abbreviated name of your class (the class name without package path): *import* the class. You can import a class by using the import statement followed by the path to the class. For example:

```
import testpackage.TestClass;
```

After the import statement, you can work with the class by using the abbreviated name. For example:

```
import testpackage.TestClass;
var myInstance:TestClass = new TestClass();
```

You can import all class files in a package by using an asterisk (*) in place of a class name. For example:

```
import testpackage.*
```

This line of ActionScript imports all classes found in the testpackage package. It doesn't import any classes from subpackages placed inside this package. Those must be imported separately.

The import statement allows you to use the abbreviated class name only within the frame on which the statement appeared. If you import testpackage on Frame 1, you cannot use the abbreviated name on Frame 2 unless Frame 2 also imports testpackage.

The same applies for other classes that import your class. You must import the class in each implementation inside another class.

You've been introduced to a lot of new concepts up to this point, and now it's time to get your hands dirty. In this exercise, you will create a simple custom class and use it in a Flash document.

1. Open Flash. Select File > New. Select ActionScript File from the list. Save the file as *CurrencyConverter.as*.

You have just created an empty ActionScript file that will contain a class called CurrencyConverter. This class will allow you to convert an amount of currency from U.S. dollars (USD) to Great Britain pounds (GBP) or vice versa.

Later in the exercise, you will add just a few lines of script to a FLA file to use the functionality of the CurrencyConverter class.

Note *When creating an ActionScript file, which in this case is a class file, Flash gives you a full-screen ActionScript window in which to type. You don't have access to the normal Flash user interface elements, such as the drawing tools or components.*

2. With the ActionScript file open, add the following line of ActionScript to start the class definition:

```
class CurrencyConverter {
```

The first word, class, tells Flash that what follows is a class definition. Not all ActionScript files contain a class, so this definition is necessary.

The text just after the class keyword is the name of the class. Remember that the name of the class must also contain the path to the class from a root classpath directory. The FLA file that will use this class (which we'll create in a moment) will be saved in the same directory as the class file (which is considered a global classpath); therefore, using just the name of the class is acceptable. If we decided to save this class file into a subdirectory called currency, we would name the class currency.CurrencyConverter.

The last character in the previous ActionScript is an opening curly brace ({). The last character that we will add in the class is the closing curly brace (}). Everything between these two braces defines the properties and methods of the class.

3. Add the following variable declaration on the next line:

```
var exchangeRate:Number;
```

The purpose of this class is to convert USD to GBP or GBP to USD. The exchangeRate variable stores the exchange rate ratio between GBP and USD. If the value of exchangeRate were 0.634731, for example, there would be 0.634731 GBP for one USD. This exchange rate will be used by a method of this class to convert the currency.

The value of the exchangeRate variable is set via the constructor method of the CurrencyConverter class, which we'll define next.

4. Add the following constructor method:

```
function CurrencyConverter(exchangeRate:Number) {
   this.exchangeRate = exchangeRate;
}
```

To use this class, you must be able to create an instance of it. A *constructor method* is a function that defines actions to take when creating a new instance of the class. It must have the same name as the class—but without the path to the class (if applicable).

This constructor method takes one parameter, exchangeRate, which is used to set the value of the class' exchangeRate when an instance is created.

The way the constructor method is set up allows us to create a new instance of the CurrencyConverter class in the following manner:

```
var myConverter:CurrencyConverter = new CurrencyConverter(0.54321);
```

5. Add the following methods, which will be used to convert the currency:

```
function convertToUSD(amount:Number):Number {
    return amount / exchangeRate;
}

function convertToGBP(amount:Number):Number {
    return amount * exchangeRate;
}
```

These method definitions are nothing more than functions. We call it a *method* simply to indicate that it's a function specifically designed to work with a particular class—in this case, our custom CurrencyConverter class. These methods accept one parameter—amount—and return a numeric value that represents the converted value. If the convertToUSD method is called, the amount is divided by the value of exchangeRate to arrive at a result. If the convertToGBP method is called, the amount is multiplied by the value of exchangeRate. The result of these calculations is returned to the callee.

6. Add a closing curly brace (}) on the last line of the class to close the definition. Save the file.

You have created a class file! The next thing that we need to do is create and use an instance of this class in a Flash movie.

7. Open *CurrencyConverter1.fla* in the Lesson06/Start directory.

Notice that this FLA file contains only one layer, called Actions, and one frame. The objective of this exercise is simply to create a custom class and then learn how to use it in a FLA file. Over the next three steps you'll add a few lines of ActionScript needed to accomplish this goal.

8. Select Frame 1, open the Actions panel, and create the following variable:

```
var rate:Number = 0.634731;
```

This is the exchange rate that we'll pass into the constructor method of the CurrencyConverter class when creating a new instance of it. When we invoke the convert() method, it will use this value to perform the conversions.

9. Create a new instance of the CurrencyConverter class by adding this code:

```
var converter:CurrencyConverter = new CurrencyConverter(rate);
```

The name of the instance that we're creating is converter. It has a data type of CurrencyConverter. By using the statement new CurrencyConverter(rate), we create a new instance of the CurrencyConverter class. The value of rate was passed in to set the exchange rate that this instance will use.

When the FLA file is compiled into a SWF file, the compiler sees that CurrencyConverter is used as if it were a class; therefore, the compiler searches the classpath directories for a class named CurrencyConverter. If the compiler finds the class, it adds the class to the SWF file. If the compiler doesn't find the class, a compile error is reported.

10. Add the following final two lines of ActionScript to convert some currency and to show the result:

```
trace(converter.convertToUSD(100));
trace(converter.convertToGBP(100));
```

The name of the CurrencyConverter instance created in Step 9 is converter. Here we call the convertToUSD and convertToGBP methods on the converter instance. In each case, we'll trace the result of the convert methods.

11. Select Control > Test Movie to test your work.

The Output window should pop up and display two numbers. When the SWF file was compiled, the compiler detected the use of a class called CurrencyConverter, searched the classpath directories for that class, and included the class in the SWF file. The ActionScript in the SWF file then created a new instance of the class and used it to perform two conversions.

12. Close the test movie and save your work as *CurrencyConverter2.fla*.

In this exercise, you created a class and then used it in a Flash movie. As this lesson progresses, you'll learn much more about classes and gain more experience working with them.

Using Getters and Setters

As you're well aware by now, when you create an instance of a class you're actually creating an object. Often these objects have properties, as defined by their class files. For example, look at this class definition:

```
class State {
  var population:Number;
  function State() {
    //Constructor
  }
}
```

This defines the State class. This class has a single property named population, which is used to hold the number of people in the state.

Creating an instance of this class would look like this:

```
var northCarolina:State = new State();
```

You can now set the value of the population property of the northCarolina instance in the following manner:

```
northCarolina.population = 8000000;
```

Although this might seem fine, problems can arise if you need to change the way in which the value of population is determined. Right now, population represents a number, so setting a new numeric value involves nothing more than entering the new number. But what if the instances of the State class need to be updated so that when setting the value of population, a growth percentage of five percent is factored in automatically? You could edit every script in every project that references this property to read similar to this:

```
northCarolina.population = 8000000 + (8000000 * .05);
```

But all that editing would take a lot of work. It's better to make your classes versatile enough to handle this kind of change simply by updating the class file. This is where *getters* and *setters* become useful. Look at the updated State class definition:

```
class State {
    var population:Number;
    function State() {
        //Constructor
    }
    function setPopulation(population:Number) {
        this.population = population + (population * .05);
    }
    function getPopulation():Number {
        return population;
    }
}
```

As defined by the class now, setting and getting the population property are handled by methods, which can be used in the following way:

```
northCarolina.setPopulation(8000000); //automatically adds a 5% growth ¬
    rate when set
northCarolina.getPopulation(); // returns a value of 8400000
```

Either of these getter or setter methods could be changed or enhanced as needed from within the class definition. As a result, all scripts in all projects that use the State class would automatically reflect the new functionality.

Because of the versatility of getters and setters, getting and setting property values directly is considered bad coding practice. Set up and use getter and setter methods instead.

Using Implicit get and set Methods

Now that you understand the power and efficiency of using getter and setter methods, it's time to introduce alternate syntax available in ActionScript 2.0. Look at the following updated State class definition:

```
class State {
  var statePopulation:Number;
  function State() {
    //Constructor
  }
  function set population(statePopulation:Number) {
    this.statePopulation = statePopulation + (statePopulation * .05);
  }
  function get population():Number {
    return statePopulation;
  }
}
```

Although it might not be obvious, the names of the setPopulation() and getPopulation() methods have been changed to set population and get population, respectively. This change converts the methods to what are known as *implicit* get and set methods. What does this mean? You get the best of both worlds—property values can be set or retrieved within the class file by using functions, but referencing them in a script is as easy as this:

```
northCarolina.population = 8000000;
```

Or this:

```
var myVariable:Number = northCarolina.population;
```

With this syntax, it seems as if we're once again referencing the population property directly, but we're actually calling either the set population or get population method (depending on the task) to take care of the state's population. Notice that we changed the name of the population property to statePopulation. If we hadn't done this, using the following syntax would result in an error:

```
northCarolina.population = 8000000;
```

Flash wouldn't know whether we were attempting to set the property named population or invoking the set population set method because doing either requires the same syntax. Changing the population property name to statePopulation solves this problem.

> **Note** *Using implicit get and set methods offers no technical advantages over using the getter and setter methods described in the previous section, other than saving a few keystrokes.*

Defining Members

Not all class members are created equal. Using special keywords, members can be configured in various ways, allowing you to specify how the member is accessed and the scope of its influence. Next, we'll discuss what this means and how you can use this functionality when creating class members.

Public and Private Members

By default, all members of a class (its properties and methods) are public. This means that the property or methods of that class can be accessed by instances of that class. Look again at our State class definition:

```
class State {
  var statePopulation:Number;
  function State() {
    //Constructor
  }
  function setPopulation(num:Number) {
    statePopulation = num + (num * .05);
  }
  function getPopulation():Number {
    return statePopulation;
  }
}
```

The members in this class, statePopulation, setPopulation(), and getPopulation(), are all publicly accessible by instances of the class. For example, the following script shows us setting the value of statePopulation directly:

```
northCarolina.statePopulation = 8000000;
```

As mentioned in the preceding section, although this property is used to hold a numeric value representing the state's population, it's better to use getter and setter methods to get and set the value, which our class definition has been set up to do. In other words, statePopulation should be a variable that cannot be directly accessed from outside the class definition. To make this change, you use the private and public keywords to indicate each member's access in a class:

```
class State {
   private var statePopulation:Number;
   public function State() {
     //Constructor
   }
   public function setPopulation(num:Number) {
     statePopulation = num + (num * .05);
   }
   public function getPopulation():Number {
     return statePopulation;
   }
}
```

The statePopulation property has been declared as a private member of the class. As a result, only code within the class definition itself, such as the setPopulation() and getPopulation() methods, can access it directly. Attempting to access it from an instance in the following way results in an error:

```
northCarolina.statePopulation = 8000000;
```

Any property or method can be declared private or public, as you see fit.

Why would you want to hide some members in this way? Because a robust class definition often has many properties and methods that are used to take care of tasks internally; they have functionality built into them that should not be exposed for use outside the class. Let's look at a real-world example.

When most people use a computer, all they want to know is how to turn it on and off, and how to interact with it via the keyboard and mouse. Most people aren't interested in knowing how it works internally (information about how the hardware is sending data through the circuits or the way the hard drive is reading and writing data—the internal workings of the computer that are important, but that don't affect how it's used). In the same sense, it's not necessary to open all the functionalities of a class to direct access from an instance of that class. A class might have 10 properties and 15 methods internally that affect how instances of that class work, but maybe only 3 or 4 methods that should be directly referenced from an instance.

In the long run, setting member access helps prevent bugs because, as mentioned earlier, it prevents you from scripting an object in a way that you shouldn't. If you attempt to use an object in the wrong way (attempting to use or access a private class member that should only be used internally within the class), Flash displays an error and lets you know that you need to reexamine your code.

Static Members

By default, every member of a class is duplicated within an instance whenever that instance is created. Consider the State class example that we used a few times in this lesson. For every new instance of that class, a copy of the statePopulation property is created within the instance. This makes sense because every state has its own population. In other words, although every instance of the State class has a statePopulation property, the value of that property might differ for each instance.

There might be times, however, when you need a property that is not only accessible by every instance of a class, but has a universal value across all instances. This is the functionality that *static* properties provide.

If a property is static, it's created in memory only once. All instances of the class see the same copy of this member. If any instance of the class edits the value of the property, all instances of the class see the new value.

Take the following class as an example:

```
class Star {
  static private var starsInTheSky:Number = 1000000000;
  public function Star() {
    //Constructor
  }
  public function setTotalStars(num:Number) {
    starsInTheSky = num;
  }
  public function getTotalStars():Number {
    return starsInTheSky;
  }
}
```

The property starsInTheSky has been specified as static and is used to store the total number of stars that can be seen in the sky. If we were to create several instances of this class, as follows:

```
var star1:Star = new Star();
var star2:Star = new Star();
var star3:Star = new Star();
```

referencing the starsInTheSky property from any one of these instances would result in the same value:

```
star1.getTotalStars(); //has a value of 1000000000
star2.getTotalStars(); //has a value of 1000000000
star3.getTotalStars(); //has a value of 1000000000
```

If a star goes supernova or another star is born, the setTotalStars() method can be executed to change the value of starsInTheSky. When the value is changed to 1000000037, all Star class instances see the following new value:

```
star1.getTotalStars(); //has a value of 1000000037
star2.getTotalStars(); //has a value of 1000000037
star3.getTotalStars(); //has a value of 1000000037
```

When would this kind of functionality be useful? Imagine having a class in which each instance has to load data from the same URL. If the URL was created as a static property of the class, it could be changed at a later time, and all the instances would automatically load from the new URL.

Methods can be static, too. Take a look at the following example:

```
class Sky {
  static private var starsInTheSky:Number = 1000000000;
  static public function setTotalStars(num:Number) {
    starsInTheSky = num;
  }
  static public function getTotalStars():Number {
    return starsInTheSky;
  }
}
```

This class has the starsInTheSky static property and two static methods: setTotalStars() and getTotalStars().

Similar to static properties, static methods have a universal functionality. These methods can be called from any instance to update and return the value of starsInTheSky.

An interesting aspect about static methods (and properties) is that they can be accessed simply by referencing the class name, followed by the name of the method, such as the following:

```
Sky.setTotalStars(999999999); //One star died
var numStars:Number = Sky.getTotalStars();
```

In this example, we used the class name (Sky) instead of an instance name to invoke both the setTotalStars() and getTotalStars() methods. This makes sense due to the class-wide functionality of static methods and properties. You used similar syntax when invoking methods of the Math class, which has several static methods:

```
Math.round();
Math.random();
Math.floor();
Math.ceil();
```

Note *A static method can change the value of a static property, but a static method cannot change the value of an instance-based (nonstatic) property.*

Understanding Inheritance

A class can gain (inherit) all members from another class. This is called *inheritance*. The class that's gaining the members is called a *subclass*, and the class from which it inherits is called the *superclass*. If B is a subclass of A, B is said to *extend* A.

Inheritance promotes code reusability. It allows you to give functionality to other classes without having to rewrite code that would be redundant. This concept will be much clearer by the end of this lesson.

Imagine for a moment that you're writing the ActionScript for a game. This game has a hero, controlled by the user, and lots of simple enemy characters. The enemies are not the same as the hero, but they share a number of similarities, such as the ability to walk, get hurt, heal, and die. If you program-separate Hero and Enemy classes, you end up rewriting much of the same code to handle these common capabilities. So it makes sense to create a general class that programs these common capabilities—let's call it the Character class—and then create additional classes (Hero and Enemy) that inherit all the functionality of the Character class as well as extend that functionality, each in unique ways. The Hero class might extend the Character class with the capability to be controlled via a user interface and the capability to wield many types of weapons. The Enemy class might extend the Character class with the capability to use an artificial intelligence algorithm to govern its movement.

In this example, the base superclass (Character) is written once, and two subclasses (Hero and Enemy) extend the functionality of the base class to make new and unique classes. Let's look at how this is done.

Let's assume that a Character class has already been created, given properties and methods, and saved as Character.as. A subclass of the Character class (we'll use the Hero class) is created by using the keyword extends in the class definition. For example:

```
class Hero extends Character {
  public function Hero() {
    //Constructor
  }
}
```

The first word, class, says that what follows is a class definition. The next word, Hero, gives a name to the class. Next you see extends Character. This statement gives the Hero class all the methods and properties found in the Character class (the Hero class *inherits* from the Character class). In addition to inheriting from the Character class, the Hero class can also be given functionality (properties and methods) unique to itself.

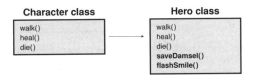

A class can only extend (inherit from) one other class. For example, if Hero extends Character, it cannot extend any other class; however, Hero can extend Character and then MyHero can extend Hero, and so on.

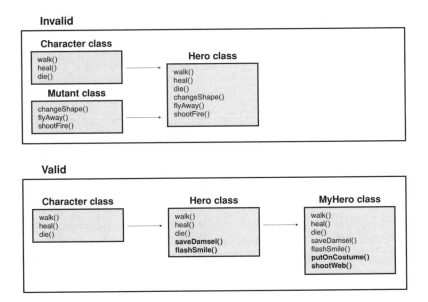

When a class extends another class, the resulting subclass gains all the properties and methods of the superclass; however, those properties and methods can still be changed or enhanced. Replacing a property value or method of the superclass with a new one in the subclass is called *overriding*. Let's look again at the Character class example to help you get a better understanding of this concept.

Let's say that both the Hero and Enemy classes extend the Character class, and the Character class has a die() method. As a result of inheritance, both the Hero and Enemy classes inherit the functionality of the die() method, as well as all the other members of the Character class. But let's say you want heroes and enemies to die in a different manner than the inherited die() method allows. In this case, you would simply define a new die() method in the Hero and Enemy classes. Creating a method in a subclass with the same name as an inherited method from its superclass causes the functionality of the subclasses' method to take precedence over the inherited method.

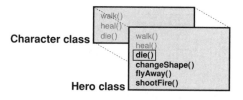

Being able to override properties and methods in this way is useful for creating object-oriented code.

You can explicitly call a method in the base superclass by using the super keyword like this:

```
super.die();
```

You can explicitly call the constructor of the base superclass like this:

```
super();
```

In the following exercise, you'll put into practice most of the concepts you learned in this lesson so far. You'll create a class called Animal and program the Animal class with several capabilities, including running and stopping, as most animals can do. You'll also create a Cat class that extends Animal by giving Cat animals the capability to meow. (Because the Cat class extends the Animal class, the Cat class inherits the functionality of the Animal class; Cat animals automatically can run and stop.) In addition, you'll create a Dog class that extends the Animal class in a manner similar to that of the Cat class, except that Dog animals will be able to bark. When you finish scripting these classes, you'll associate the Cat and Dog classes with different movie clips in the library. As a result of this association, each instance of one of those clips that you drag into your project will take on the characteristics of the class with which it's associated.

In this exercise, you'll gain experience creating classes, extending a class, overriding methods and properties, and working with instances of custom-made classes. Let's get started!

1. Open *PetParade1.fla* from the Lesson06/Start folder.

The first order of business is to become familiar with the contents of this FLA file. There are three layers in this project file. The Background layer holds the background graphics; the Assets layer currently contains six buttons named dogRun, dogStop, dogSound, catRun, catStop, and catSound. The Actions layer is currently empty, but will eventually contain script.

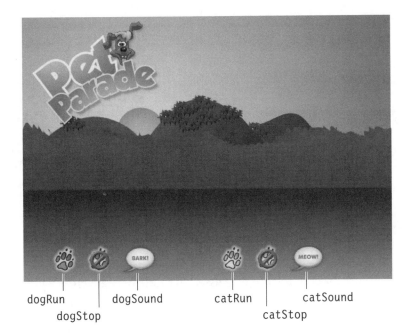

For this exercise, it's also important to understand the assets in the library because they will play an integral role in how the final application works.

2. Choose Window > Library to open the Library panel.

The library contains a folder, two sound clips, and three movie clips. The Interface Elements folder contains miscellaneous elements that you're free to examine, but you won't work with them directly in this exercise.

The three movie clips are named Dog, Cat, and Balloon. Dog and Cat are the graphical and interactive representations of the Dog class and Cat class. This is important to understand; things that we program the Dog and Cat classes to do will be graphically and interactively carried out by instances of the Dog and Cat movie clips. The Balloon movie clip will be used and explained later in the exercise.

The two sound clips, Meow.mp3 and Bark.mp3, represent the sounds that our Cat and Dog animals will make. If you right-click (Ctrl-click on a Macintosh) either of these sounds and then choose Linkage from the menu that appears, you see that the Meow.mp3 sound has been given an identifier of Meow, and the Bark.mp3 sound has been given an identifier of Bark. Steps 9 and 11 in this exercise will explain how these sounds are used.

Now that you're familiar with the project's assets, it's time to begin creating the class files that it will use.

Note *You will be creating and working with several files in this exercise. As we progress through the steps, keep all the files open. You will be instructed when to switch between the files.*

3. Create a new ActionScript file called *Animal.as* in the Lesson06/Start folder. Add the following script to the *Animal.as* file:

```
class Animal extends MovieClip {
  private var speed:Number;
  public function Animal() {
    speed = 5
  }
}
```

The first line gives the class a name, Animal, and then specifies that this class extends the MovieClip class. This means that instances of the Animal class inherit all the functionalities (properties and methods) of movie clips—properties such as _x and _name, as well as methods such as gotoAndPlay() and loadMovie(). This is your first experience creating a new class that inherits from another class. You can think of this technique as taking the basic functionality of movie clips and extending it in a way that's appropriate for programming how Animals work. This will become clearer as we progress through the steps.

Note *Any of Flash's built-in classes can be extended in this way. With this capability, for example, you can create an enhanced Sound, TextField, or Array class to fit your needs exactly.*

The line following the class declaration defines a private variable named speed that will used by the class. Remember that private variables can only be accessed and used by scripts within the class definition—not directly by instances of the class. The speed variable will be used by a method named run() that we'll create in a moment. This method will be used to move a movie clip based on the value of speed.

The final three lines of the ActionScript in this step define the constructor method for the Animal class. Remember that scripts within the constructor are executed at the moment when an instance of the class is created. Because the Dog and Cat classes inherit from the Animal class, any scripts placed here will be executed when an instance of the Dog class or Cat class is created. The only action here is to set the value of speed for the class. In other words, whenever an instance of the Animal class is created, that instance is given an initial speed value of 5. We'll add more scripts to the Animal class constructor later in the exercise.

4. After the class constructor, add the following script to handle making an animal run:

```
public function run():Void {
  onEnterFrame = function() {
    _x += speed;
  }
}
```

The run() method is used to put instances of the Animal class into motion. When an instance of the Animal class invokes this method, an onEnterFrame event is attached to that instance. The action within the event moves the instance along its x axis by the value of the speed variable. Remember that in Step 3 we set the initial value of speed in the constructor method to 5. When an instance of the Animal class invokes this method, it will begin moving 5 pixels at a time, 24 times per second (the frame rate of our movie). The instance will continue to move until stopped with the `stop()` method.

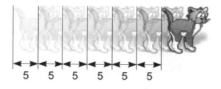

5. Next, add the following `stop()` method:

```
public function stop():Void {
   delete onEnterFrame;
}
```

This method stops the instance from moving, simply by deleting the `onEnterFrame` event from the instance.

6. End the definition of the Animal class with a closing curly brace (**}**); then choose File > Save to save the class file.

You created the Animal class. Next you'll create the two subclasses (Dog and Cat) that extend Animal.

7. In the same directory as *Animal.as*, create a new ActionScript file named *Cat.as*. Start the class definition with the following script:

```
class Cat extends Animal {
```

The first two words tell Flash that you're creating a new class called Cat. The next two words, `extends Animal`, tell Flash that this class inherits every method and property of the Animal class, including `run()` and `stop()`. We used similar syntax when defining the Animal class; it extended the MovieClip class. As a result, not only does the Cat class get all the capabilities of the Animal class, but those of the MovieClip class as well. Inheritance trickles down like this as long as you continue extending classes.

In the following steps, we'll program the Cat class to deal with functionalities unique to cats. Running and stopping is something that most animals can do; that's why those functionalities were defined in the more general Animal class, from which the Cat class inherits. The great thing about object-oriented inheritance is that we could create 50 more classes (based on different animals) that all extend the Animal class, but to change the way in which each class handles running we would simply edit the `run()` method in the Animal class file. We'll demonstrate this principle later in the exercise.

Let's set up the unique features of the Cat class.

8. Create the following constructor method for the Cat class:

```
public function Cat() {
    speed = 1;
}
```

When a new instance of the Cat class is created, its speed property is given a value of 1. In Step 3, we created a variable named speed in the Animal class constructor method and gave it an initial value of 5. Because the Cat class inherits from the Animal class, it automatically inherited that property and its value. You might be wondering why we're setting it again here. Instances of the Animal class will still have a speed value of 5, but instances of the Cat class will have a speed value of 1. We're *overriding* the inherited value with a value specific to cats.

Overriding an inherited property value involves nothing more than using the name of the property you want to override—the speed property in this case—and assigning it a new value. As a result, when an instance of the Cat class is created, its speed property is set to 1.

Properties and methods defined in a class always have precedence over properties and methods inherited from another class with the same name; therefore, instances of the Cat class will see and use the speed value of 1 as opposed to a value of 5.

The run() and stop() methods of the Animal class are still inherited and still work with instances of the Cat class as they were defined in the Animal class file because we haven't overridden them with methods of the same name in the Cat class (we won't override those methods in this exercise).

9. Create a method called meow() that plays a meowing sound when called:

```
public function meow():Void {
    var sound:Sound = new Sound(this);
    sound.attachSound("Meow");
    sound.start();
}
```

When called, this method creates a new sound object. This object has the sound in the library with a linkage identifier of Meow attached to it. The sound is played by calling the start() method of the sound object. Because this method is defined in the Cat class, only instances of the Cat class can call it.

10. End the definition of the Cat class by adding the closing curly brace (}); then choose File > Save to save the class file.

You have completed the first subclass of Animal. Next you'll create another subclass of Animal, the Dog class.

11. In the same directory as *Animal.as*, create a new ActionScript file called *Dog.as*. Define this class as follows:

```
class Dog extends Animal {
  public function Dog() {
    speed = 2;
  }
  public function bark():Void {
    var sound:Sound = new Sound(this);
    sound.attachSound("Bark");
    sound.start();
  }
}
```

This class is similar to the Cat class. The first line of ActionScript names the class Dog and extends the Animal class.

Next, the constructor method sets the value of speed to 2, overriding the value of the property with the same name in the Animal class; instances of the Dog class will all have a speed property with a value of 2.

Similar to the meow() method discussed in Step 9, the bark() method creates a new sound object. The method attaches the sound with the linkage identifier of Bark and then plays the sound.

In the end, Dogs and Cats both run() and stop(), as most Animals do, but Dogs run at a speed of 2 and Bark, while Cats run at a speed of 1 and Meow.

12. Choose File > Save to save the Dog class file.

For the moment, our class files are complete. We'll return to the Animal class file shortly, but it's time to open the actual project file to plug in these class files and their functionality.

13. *PetParade1.fla* should already be open in the authoring environment. Click its tab to make *PetParade1.fla* the active window.

The first order of business is to associate our Dog and Cat classes with the Dog Clip and Cat Clip movie clips in the library.

14. With the Library panel open, right-click (Ctrl-click on a Macintosh) the Cat movie clip and choose Linkage from the menu that appears. In the Linkage Properties dialog box, select the Export For ActionScript option; then enter *cat* in the Identifier field and *Cat* (the first letter must be uppercase) in the AS 2.0 Class field. Click OK.

Although you configured several settings in this step, the one you need to focus on is the AS 2.0 Class field. By entering a value of Cat in this field, you're associating the Cat movie clip in the library to the Cat class you created. This means that all instances of the Cat movie clip you place in your project will take on the functionality defined in the Cat class file. As a result, these instances can run(), stop(), and meow(), as you will soon see.

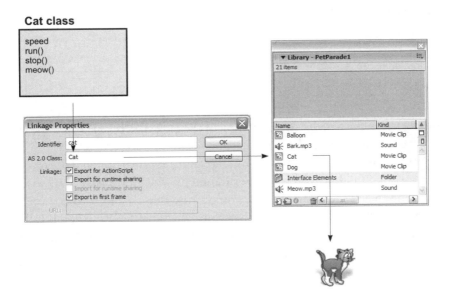

15. Right-click (Ctrl-click on a Macintosh) the Dog movie clip and choose Linkage from the menu that appears. In the Linkage Properties dialog box, select the Export For ActionScript option; then enter *dog* in the Identifier field and *Dog* (the first letter must be uppercase) in the AS 2.0 Class field. Click OK.

This step associates the Dog movie clip with the Dog class. As a result, all instances of the Dog movie clip you place in your project can run(), stop(), and bark(). This is a great feature of Flash that allows you to create highly interactive class-based movie clips. You simply create a custom class and then associate that class with a movie clip; you instantly have a custom movie clip.

> **Note** *To use this feature, the associating class (which in this case is Dog) must inherit from the MovieClip class somewhere up the line.*

16. Click and drag instances of the Dog and Cat movie clips onto the stage. Give the Dog instance the name *dog* and give the Cat instance the name *cat*.

Next, we'll add scripts to cause these instances to perform the actions that cats and dogs do, based on what we programmed into our custom class files.

17. With the Actions panel open, select Frame 1 of the Actions layer and add the following button events to control the **dog** movie clip instance:

```
dogRun.onRelease = function() {
    dog.run();
}
dogStop.onRelease = function() {
    dog.stop();
}
dogSound.onRelease = function() {
    dog.bark();
}
```

When the dogRun is clicked, the run() method of the Dog class is called, and the dog instance starts moving. Remember that the Dog class inherits the run() method from the Animal class. The method is set up to move the calling instance horizontally by using an onEnterFrame event (added in Step 4). The amount by which the instance is moved is based on its internal speed value. We programmed the Dog class to set this value to 2 for all instances created from the Dog class; therefore, when the run() method is called in relation to the dog movie clip instance, that instance will move 2 pixels at 24 times per second.

dogStop() calls the stop() method to stop the dog from moving, and the dogSound instance makes the dog bark. When clicked, it calls the bark() method.

18. Add the following button events to control the **cat** movie clip instance:

```
catRun.onRelease = function() {
    cat.run();
}
catStop.onRelease = function() {
    cat.stop();
}
catSound.onRelease = function() {
    cat.meow();
}
```

As with the buttons that control the dog instance, these buttons will make the cat instance run, stop running, and make a sound. The cat's sound is a meow, so the meow() method is called when the catSound instance is clicked.

Whew! It's finally time to test your work.

19. **Select Control › Test Movie. When the movie appears, click the buttons at the bottom of the stage to see the results. Then close the test movie to return to the authoring environment, but leave the Library panel open for the next exercise.**

As the movie is being exported, Flash pulls in code from the external Animal, Dog, and Cat class files as it detects the references to these classes in our project. The dog and cat can both run, stop, and make sounds, all based on the code in our class files.

Updating an Inheritance-Based Project

We're not finished quite yet. To help solidify your understanding of inheritance, we'll make a few enhancements to the Animal class so you can see how easy it is to update an object-oriented/inheritance-based project.

1. **The Library panel should still be open from the preceding exercise. Double-click the *Balloon* movie clip to edit its Timeline.**

This movie clip's Timeline is simple. It contains a transparent white box and a text field instance called name. The name of this field is important to remember.

2. **Return to the main Timeline. In the library, right-click (Ctrl-click on a Macintosh) the Balloon movie and select Linkage from the menu that appears. In the Linkage Properties dialog box, give this movie clip an identifier of *balloon*; then click OK.**

This identifier will be used in a moment to dynamically attach this movie clip to our animal movie clip instances when the mouse rolls over them.

3. ***Animal.as* should still be open. Click its tab to make *Animal.as* the active window.**

Over the next several steps we'll add functionality to this class; by extension, that new functionality will filter down into the Dog and Cat classes because they inherit from this class.

4. **Insert the following script just below `private var speed:Number;`:**

```
private var balloon:MovieClip;
private var name:String;
```

This step creates two new private properties called balloon and name in the Animal class. The name property eventually will be used to hold the name we give to instances of the

Animal class, or, by extension, the Dog and Cat classes. The `balloon` property will hold a reference to the movie clip that will be used to show the name of the animal on stage.

5. Insert the following method just below the end of the `stop()` method definition:

```
public function setName(name:String):Void {
  this.name = name;
}
```

This step creates a setter method called `setName()` that accepts a single parameter, name. The parameter value that's passed in is used to set the name property of an instance. For example, the following will set dog's name property to have a value of `"Fido"`:

```
dog.setName("Fido");
```

In a moment, we'll add script that will invoke the `setName()` method to set the name properties of both the dog and cat instances. First we'll add several lines of script to the Animal constructor function.

6. Insert the following line of script into the Animal constructor method, just below `this.speed = 5`:

```
name = "Animal";
```

Remember that the script inside the constructor function is executed as soon as an instance of the class is created. In our project, because the Dog and Cat classes inherit from Animal, and the Dog and Cat movie clips in the library are associated with the Dog and Cat classes, when an instance of either clip appears in the movie this constructor function is executed in relation to the instance.

With the line of script in this step, we give a default name value to instances of the Animal class as well as the Dog and Cat classes. So when dog and cat first appear in the movie, each will have a default name value of `Animal`. This value can be changed as a result of the `setName()` method we added in Step 5, which we'll use shortly.

7. Add the following method to the animal class:

```
private function onRollOver():Void {
  useHandCursor = false;
  balloon = attachMovie("balloon", "balloon", 0);
  balloon._x = _xmouse;
  balloon._y = _ymouse - 50;
  balloon.name.text = name;
}
```

This method overrides the onRollOver method of the MovieClip class. This script executes when the dog or cat instance appears on the stage and the user rolls the mouse over the instance. The purpose of this script is to display the value of the instance's name property in a little window based on the Balloon clip in the library (we discussed the Balloon clip in Step 1).

The first line of the function sets the instance's useHandCursor property to false; therefore, the hand cursor won't appear when the instance is rolled over. The next line attaches the movie clip with the *balloon* identifier in the library. The attached instance is given a name of balloon and a depth of 0. The next two lines position the newly attached instance so that it appears at the same *x* position as the mouse, but 50 pixels less than the *y* position of the mouse; therefore, the balloon will appear slightly offset from the mouse cursor.

Remember that the Balloon movie clip has a text field instance called name on its Timeline. When you attach that clip and give it an instance name of balloon, you can set the text displayed in that field by referencing it as follows:

```
balloon.name.text
```

The last line of the script uses this reference to display the name property of the instance in the text field.

Let's create the functionality that will remove the balloon when the user rolls away from the instance.

8. Add the following method to the animal class:

```
private function onRollOut():Void {
   balloon.removeMovieClip();
}
```

This script removes the balloon movie clip instance when the user rolls away.

9. Choose File > Save to save the Animal class file with its new functionality.

The Animal class is now complete. All that's left to do is to return to the FLA file for this project and add a couple of lines of script.

10. *PetParade1.fla* should already be open in the authoring environment. Click its tab to make *PetParade1.fla* the active window. With the Actions panel open, select Frame 1 of the Actions layer and add the following script at the end of the current script:

```
dog.setName("Fido");
cat.setName("Fluffy");
```

These two lines of script utilize the new setName() method created in the Animal class file in Step 5. The name property of the dog instance is set to "Fido" and the name property of the cat instance is set to "Fluffy". These new values override the default name value for Animal instances, discussed in Step 6.

This property value will appear in a balloon when the instance is rolled over. Let's do one final test.

11. Choose Control › Test Movie.

When the movie appears, you can move the mouse over either the dog or cat, and the animal's name will appear in a balloon. The important thing to realize about this new functionality is that it was set up in a single file: the Animal class. All instances that inherited from this class automatically inherited this new behavior when the class file was updated. We hope that you can now appreciate the power of inheritance and how it allows you to create more manageable projects.

12. Close the test movie and save your work as *PetParade2.fla*.

Due to page constraints, most of the projects in the remainder of the book will not use a class-based object-oriented structure. However, the concepts you learned here can be applied in class-based projects you create on your own.

What You Have Learned

In this lesson, you have:

- Explored the terminology and syntax of classes (pages 127–132)
- Learned how to use classpaths (pages 132–139)
- Used getters and setters (pages 139–142)
- Learned about private, public, and static members, and how to use them (pages 142–146)
- Used inheritance to extend a class (pages 146–147)
- Become familiar with overriding (pages 148–149)
- Created custom object classes (pages 149–154)
- Associated a custom class with a movie clip in the library (pages 154–160)

7 Events, Listeners, and Callbacks

We push buttons, we push people, and we even push people's buttons, all with a single purpose: to elicit a response. The Macromedia Flash way of saying this is with events.

Events are actions that happen in Flash. These actions could range from the user clicking a button to data loading into the application. By responding to these events you can make your project much more dynamic. Events are like an engine that moves an application along and makes our Flash projects interactive.

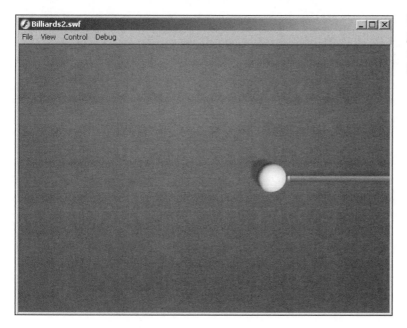

We'll create a Billiard project in this lesson that will use events to respond the user interaction.

What You Will Learn

In this lesson, you will:

- Learn what events do
- Learn about the types of events in Flash
- Learn how event handlers are used
- Use movie clip event handlers in a project
- Learn how listeners are used
- Use listeners in a project

Approximate Time

This lesson takes approximately thirty minutes to complete.

Lesson Files

Media Files:

None

Starting Files:

Lesson07/Start/Billiards1.fla
Lesson07/Start/MouseKeyboardHistory1.fla

Completed Projects:

Lesson07/Completed/Billiards2.fla
Lesson07/Completed/MouseKeyboardHistory2.fla

What Events Do

Many computer programs allow users to accomplish tasks by dragging and dropping items on the screen, resizing windows, making adjustments with sliders, and creating artistic masterpieces using "virtual" art tools—all modes of interaction determined by the way in which the software has been programmed to deal with various events (mouse presses, mouse movements, keyboard input, and so on).

Responding to events lets you orchestrate your movies' interactivity by controlling when scripts are triggered. They provide a "when" to a script so that it executes only when something specific occurs.

The better you understand events, the more control you'll have over the user experience. By responding to events properly, you can create immersive environments the user will enjoy.

Types of Events in Flash

In a Flash environment there are three ways to work with events: using clip events, event handlers, and listeners. The first type of event, the clip event, is a way of placing code directly on a movie clip or button and having that code respond to an event. The following is an example:

```
on(press) {
  // do something
}
```

We will not be covering clip events in this lesson because they involve placing code directly on an object. This is considered bad practice and therefore clip events should be avoided. It's considered bad practice because your code is all over the place. Best practice is to place your code in external class files or designate a layer called Actions. In our examples, we will use an Actions layer, and all our code will be placed on frames in that layer. Because there are many different ways to handle events in Flash, you will always have a better option than using a clip event.

The second way to work with events in Flash is by using an event handler. The responses that come from pushing, holding, moving, entering, and leaving a movie clip are triggered by event handlers. Event handlers represent the first step in getting your movie to do anything interactive—which is why a thorough understanding of them is vital. Handlers, sometimes referred to as callbacks, are also used in other classes besides the MovieClip. The LoadVars and XML classes use event handlers to trigger the onLoad events that occur when data has finished loading.

The third way to work with events is through listeners. The Key and Mouse classes use the listener model to handle events. Listeners have some distinct advantages over callbacks. We will cover those later in the lesson.

Event Handlers

Event handlers are the most common way to work with events in Flash. Event handlers are nothing more than methods on objects. For example, the XML class has an event handler named onLoad. This onLoad event handler is actually a method of the XML class. When we create an instance of the XML class we can handle the onLoad event by overriding the onLoad method of that class. Overriding is a term used in object-oriented programming for when you replace one method with another. The following is an example that loads in an XML document:

```
var xml:XML = new XML();
xml.onLoad = function() {
  // Do Something
}
xml.load("http://www.dannypatterson.com/XML/rss.xml");
```

When we created the XML object, it already had an onLoad method that didn't do anything. Sometimes these are known as abstract methods. An abstract method is designed to be overridden and is how events are handled in most of the built-in Flash objects.

One thing to remember about this method of event handling is that you must deal with scope issues. The XML example is a good way to demonstrate this. Let's assume that the following code is on your main Timeline. The code inside the onLoad method will be run in the scope of the XML object. Therefore, the keyword this references the XML object. You can demonstrate this by using the trace command inside the event handler like this:

```
var xml:XML = new XML();
xml.onLoad = function() {
  trace(this);
}
xml.load("http://www.dannypatterson.com/XML/rss.xml");
```

You'll see in this example that this actually outputs the XML object. This isn't always the desired behavior. What if you wanted the event handler to execute in the scope of your main Timeline? One approach is to create a function and assign it to the event handler like the following example:

```
this.onXMLLoad = function() {
  trace(this);
}
var xml:XML = new XML();
xml.onLoad = this.onXMLLoad;
xml.load("http://www.dannypatterson.com/XML/rss.xml");
```

If you execute this code you might expect the output of this to be a reference to your main Timeline. But it isn't. It still references your XML object because the assignment of your onXMLLoad() function to the onLoad method was just a function reference. To get your onXMLLoad method to be called in the scope of the object it belongs to, you must use a utility class provided by Macromedia. The utility class is called Delegate and comes shipped with Flash 8. The following example shows you how to use it:

```
import mx.util.Delegate;
this.onXMLLoad = function() {
  trace(this);
}
var xml:XML = new XML();
xml.onLoad = Delegate.create(this, onXMLLoad);
xml.load("http://www.dannypatterson.com/XML/rss.xml");
```

Now when you run this code you will see that your trace statement outputs a reference to your main Timeline. The Delegate class has fixed our scoping issue.

There are many built-in classes that use event handlers, or callbacks. The following is a list of the classes and their callback methods:

Class	Callback Method	Class	Callback Method
Button	onDragOut	Camera	onActivity
	onDragOver		onStatus
	onKeyDown	ContextMenu	onSelect
	onKeyUp	ContextMenuItem	onSelect
	onKillFocus	LoadVars	onData
	onPress		onHTTPStatus
	onRelease		onLoad
	onRollOut	LocalConnection	onStatus
	onRollOver	Microphone	onActivity
	onSetFocus		onStatus

continues on next page

Class	Callback Method	Class	Callback Method
MovieClip	onData	SharedObject	allowDomain
	onDragOut		allowInsecureDomain
	onDragOver		onStatus
	onEnterFrame	Sound	onID3
	onKeyDown		onLoad
	onKeyUp		onSoundComplete
	onKillFocus	StyleSheet	onLoad
	onLoad	System	onStatus
	onMouseDown	TextField	onChanged
	onMouseMove		onKillFocus
	onMouseUp		onScroller
	onPress		onSetFocus
	onRelease	XML	onData
	onReleaseOutside		onHTTPStatus
	onRollOut		onLoad
	onRollOver	XMLSocket	onClose
	onSetFocus		onConnect
	onUnload		onData
NetConnection	onStatus		onXML
NetStream	onCuePoint		
	onMetaData		
	onStatus		

There is one major limitation to this method of event handling. It is a one-to-one event communication. What if you had two objects that needed to respond to the XML onLoad event? You would need to create a handler that notified both those objects individually. This is a difficult work around. The real solution is listeners. We'll discuss those in more detail later in this lesson.

Creating a Project Using Event Handlers

In this project we will create a simple Billiards application in which the user can hit a ball with a stick. It's a very simple demonstration of how to use event handlers in a project.

1. Open *Billiards1.fla* in the Lesson07/Start folder.

This FLA file has the following four layers: Actions, Ball, Stick and Background. The Actions layer is where we will place all the actions for this project. The Ball layer contains a MovieClip with an instance named `ball`, and the Stick layer contains a MovieClip with an instance named `stick`. The Background layer contains our green billiards table background image.

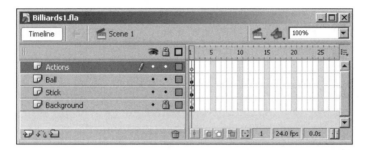

After our project is done, the user can drag the stick to the right and let up to hit the ball. Then the ball will roll a distance as determined by the distance the stick was pulled back, which simulates the action of hitting the ball with the stick.

2. With the Actions panel open, select Frame 1 of the Actions layer and add the following script:

```
var stickStart:Number = stick._x;
var stickStop:Number = stick._x + 100;
var ballStart:Number = ball._x;
var ballStop:Number = ball._x - 350;
var isBallRolling:Boolean = false;
var rollDistance:Number = 0;
```

In this script we set some initial variables that we'll be using from inside our event handlers. The first four variables will help us track the positioning of the stick and ball. The first variable, named `stickStart`, represents the initial position of the `stick` MovieClip on the x axis. The second variable, named `stickStop`, represents the maximum position the stick can be moved on the x axis. The third variable, named `ballStart`, represents the initial position of the ball on the x axis. The fourth variable, named `ballStop`, represents the maximum distance the ball can move on the x axis.

The fifth variable, named isBallRolling, is a Boolean value that represents whether the ball is currently rolling or moving. It is initially set to false, but after we hit the ball it is set to true until it has completed its move.

The final variable, named rollDistance, is set when the ball is initially hit. As the ball moves, this value is reduced until it is less than or equal to zero. When it reaches that point, we know the move is complete.

3. Add the following event handler after the script you added in Step 2:

```
stick.onPress = function() {
  if(!isBallRolling) {
    ball._x = ballStart;
    this.startDrag(false, stickStart, this._y, stickStop, this._y);
  }
}
```

This first event handler is added to the stick MovieClip and enables us to drag the stick away from the ball. We want the code in this event handler to execute only if the ball is *not* currently rolling, so we place it inside an if statement. Inside the if statement, we reset the ball position and then start the drag.

However, if you run this script, you'll notice that the drag doesn't stop because we need to stop the drag manually when the stick's onRelease event is fired.

4. Add the following event handler after the script you added in Step 3:

```
stick.onRelease = function() {
  if(!isBallRolling) {
    this.stopDrag();
    var power:Number = Math.round(this._x - stickStart) / 100;
    rollDistance = Math.round((ballStart - ballStop) * power);
    this._x = stickStart;
    isBallRolling = true;
  }
}
```

This event handler is also added to the stick MovieClip. When the mouse is released, this event is fired. Once again, we want this code to run only if the ball is *not* currently rolling, so we again place our code inside an if statement.

Inside the if statement we first want to stop the drag. Then we need to calculate the distance we want the ball to travel based on the distance the stick was pulled back.

We start this calculation by determining the percent the stick was pulled back. We store this value in a function-level variable named power. Then we need to set the initial value of the rollDistance variable using our ballStart, ballStop, and power variables.

Then we reset the position of the stick to the start position and set the isBallRolling variable to true. In our next script you'll see that by setting this variable to true, our ball will begin moving.

5. Add the following event handler after the script you added in Step 4:

```
ball.onEnterFrame = function() {
  if(isBallRolling) {
    this._x -= 5;
    rollDistance -= 5;
    if(rollDistance <= 0) {
      isBallRolling = false;
    }
  }
}
```

```
Actions - Frame
Actions   Help

1  var stickStart:Number = stick._x;
2  var stickStop:Number = stick._x + 100;
3  var ballStart:Number = ball._x;
4  var ballStop:Number = ball._x - 350;
5  var isBallRolling:Boolean = false;
6  var rollDistance:Number = 0;
7
8  stick.onPress = function() {
9      if(!isBallRolling) {
10         ball._x = ballStart;
11         this.startDrag(false, stickStart, this._y, stickStop, this._y);
12     }
13 }
14 stick.onRelease = function() {
15     if(!isBallRolling) {
16         this.stopDrag();
17         var power:Number = Math.round(this._x - stickStart) / 100;
18         rollDistance = Math.round((ballStart - ballStop) * power);
19         this._x = stickStart;
20         isBallRolling = true;
21     }
22 }
23
24 ball.onEnterFrame = function() {
25     if(isBallRolling) {
26         this._x -= 5;
27         rollDistance -= 5;
28         if(rollDistance <= 0) {
29             isBallRolling = false;
30         }
31     }
32 }
```

This event handler will be added to the `ball` MovieClip instance. The `onEnterFrame` event handler is called each time the frame is rendered and is executed at the same rate as your Movie's frame rate. Our Movie's frame rate value is set to 24 frames per second (fps). Therefore, our `onEnterFrame` event will be fired 24 times per second.

Because we want to execute the code inside this event handler only if the ball is currently rolling, we will wrap the code in an `if` statement. We will start subtracting 5 from the values of the ball's `_x` property and the `rollDistance` variable. This will move the ball five pixels to the left each time the `onEnterFrame` event is fired. We then check whether the `rollDistance` variable is less than or equal to 0. If it is, we set the `isBallRolling` variable to `false`, which stops the ball from rolling any farther and enables another shot to be made.

6. From the menu, choose Control › Test Movie to see the movie in action.

Interact with the project by clicking the stick MovieClip, dragging it to the right, and then releasing it. You should see the ball move to the left, and the distance should be proportionate to the distance you pull the stick back.

7. Close the test movie to return to the authoring environment. Save your project as *Billiards2.fla*.

This completes the exercise. You should now have a basic understanding of event handlers and the ways you can use them to enhance your projects.

Listeners

Listeners are a different kind of event handler. Instead of overriding a method of the object, listeners "register" themselves with the object. Then when the event occurs, the object is responsible for notifying all the registered listeners by calling specific methods on the listener objects.

The main advantage of listeners over traditional event handlers is that more than one object can listen for a specific event. It supports the idea of "broadcasting" the event—one object trigging an event handler on multiple listening objects.

Many of the built-in classes support listeners such as the following: Key, Mouse, Stage, MovieClipLoader, FileReference, and so on.

In the following example, we will listen for an onResize event on the Stage class:

```
function onResize() {
    trace(Stage.width + " x " + Stage.height);
}
Stage.addListener(this);
```

In this simple example we are creating a function on our main Timeline called onResize. This is the name of the method the Stage class will attempt to call on all registered listeners whenever the stage size is changed.

Inside this listener function we are simply outputting the new dimensions of the stage using the trace command.

The final thing we do is register our Timeline as a listener to the Stage class using the addListener method. If we want to unregister our Timeline, we could use the removeListener method. In the following example, we will remove the listener after the first resize of the stage, which ensures that the stage is resized only once:

```
function onResize() {
    trace(Stage.width + " x " + Stage.height);
    Stage.removeListener(this);
}
Stage.addListener(this);
```

There are many built-in classes that use listeners. The following is a list of all those classes in Flash 8:

Class	Listeners
flash.net.FileReference	onCancel
	onComplete
	onIOError
	onHTTPError
	onOpen
	onProgress
	onSecurityError
	onSelect
flash.net.FileReferenceList	onCancel
	onSelect
System.IME	onIMEComposition
Key	onKeyDown
	onKeyUp
Mouse	onMouseDown
	onMouseMove
	onMouseUp
	onMouseWheel
MovieClipLoader	onLoadComplete
	onLoadError
	onLoadInt
	onLoadProgress
	onLoadStart
Selection	onSetFocus
Stage	onResize
TextField	onChanged
	onScroller

Creating a Project Using Listeners

In this project, we will create a simple History application that will output each time the user clicks the mouse or presses a key on the keyboard. This example will demonstrate how to use listeners in a project.

1. Open *MouseKeyboardHistory1.fla* in the Lesson07/Start folder.

This FLA file has two layers: Actions and Output. The Actions layer is where we'll place the actions for this project. The Output layer contains a TextField object with an instance name of output.

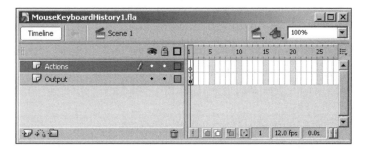

2. With the Actions panel open, select Frame 1 of the Actions layer and add the script:

```
var history:Object = new Object();
```

The first step is to create an empty Object called history, which will act as our listener target. We will then add our specific listener methods to this object.

3. Add the following event handler after the script you added in Step 2:

```
Key.addListener(history);
```

To register our history Object with the Key class, we simply need to call the addListener method. Now, whenever a Key event happens, our history object will be notified. So let's go ahead and handle one of those events.

4. Add the following event handler after the script you added in Step 3:

```
history.onKeyDown = function() {
  var action:String = "[KEY] " + chr(Key.getAscii());
  output.text = action + newline + output.text;
}
```

The onKeyDown method is called on all registered listener objects whenever one of the keys on the keyboard it pressed. In our example, we'll create a string to add to the output TextField. To determine which key was pressed, we can use either the static getAscii or getCode methods of the Key class. For our example, we want a string representing that key, so we'll use the getAscii method and convert that to a string using the built-in chr method.

5. Add the following event handler after the script you added in Step 4:

```
Mouse.addListener(history);
```

We will also register our history Object with the Mouse class. This syntax is the same as what was used to register with the Key class and is consistent with all the built-in classes in Flash that use listeners.

6. Add the following event handler after the script you added in Step 5:

```
history.onMouseDown = function() {
    var action:String = "[MOUSE] " + _level0._xmouse + " x " + ¬
      _level0._ymouse;
    output.text = action + newline + output.text;
}
```

```
▼ Actions - Frame

 Actions    Help

  ⇪ ⌕ ⊕ ✔ ☰ ⍰ ℘                                    Script Assist  ⑦

   1  var history:Object = new Object();
   2
   3  Key.addListener(history);
   4
   5  history.onKeyDown = function() {
   6      var action:String = "[KEY] " + chr(Key.getAscii());
   7      output.text = action + newline + output.text;
   8  }
   9
  10  Mouse.addListener(history);
  11
  12  history.onMouseDown = function() {
  13      var action:String = "[MOUSE] " + _level0._xmouse + " x " + _level0._ymouse;
  14      output.text = action + newline + output.text;
  15  }

  ● Actions : 1
```

Now that our history Object is also listening for Mouse events, we'll create a method to be called when the mouse is pressed. This event is called onMouseDown and has the same goal as our Key listener. We want to output a string that represents that click, so we'll output the *x* and *y* coordinates of the mouse position at the time of the click using the _xmouse and _ymouse properties of _level0.

7. From the menu, choose Control > Test Movie to see the movie in action.

Verify that your code is working by clicking the mouse anywhere on the stage and pressing random keys on the keyboard. Notice the history text appearing in the TextField.

```
MouseKeyboardHistory2.swf                        _ □ x
File   View   Control   Debug

[MOUSE] 152 x 237
[MOUSE] 480 x 251
[MOUSE] 438 x 347
[MOUSE] 225 x 210
[MOUSE] 46 x 162
[MOUSE] 78 x 278
[MOUSE] 239 x 169
[MOUSE] 470 x 41
[KEY] d
[KEY] l
[KEY] r
[KEY] o
[KEY] w
[KEY] o
[KEY] l
[KEY] l
[KEY] e
[KEY] h
[MOUSE] 456 x 187
[MOUSE] 28 x 209
[MOUSE] 107 x 307
[MOUSE] 439 x 105
```

8. Close the test movie to return to the authoring environment. Save your project as *MouseKeyboardHistory2.fla*.

This completes the exercise. You should now have a basic understanding of listeners and the ways you can use them in your Flash projects.

What You Have Learned

In this lesson, you have:

- Learned what events do (page 163)
- Learned the types of events in Flash (page 163)
- Learned how event handlers are used (pages 164–166)
- Used movie clip event handlers in a project (pages 167–170)
- Learned how listeners are used (pages 171–172)
- Used mouse and key listeners in a project (pages 173–175)

8 Dynamically Creating Assets

Although you might be familiar with adding assets to the stage at authoring time, there are programmatic ways to add assets at runtime as well. Adding assets such as movie clips and text lets you build more dynamic applications. You can even draw programmatically, as you'll see in this lesson. Adding assets programmatically requires more code than adding them at authoring time. However, the benefits of adding assets programmatically are numerous and far-reaching. For example, by adding assets programmatically you can display images at random. By adding text programmatically you can assign

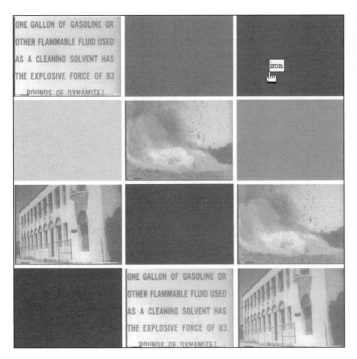

Adding assets programmatically lets you build dynamic applications such as the memory game you'll build in this lesson.

labels to the random images. You can programmatically draw frames around the random images. With just this one simple example you can already see how much flexibility programmatic asset creation offers. In this lesson you'll learn more about this topic, and you'll build a sample application using what you've learned.

What You Will Learn

In this lesson you will:

- Attach movie clips with code
- Add new empty movie clips programmatically
- Draw programmatically
- Add text fields with code
- Apply formatting to text fields

Approximate Time

This lesson takes approximately an hour to complete.

Lesson Files

Media Files:

None

Starting Files:

Lesson08/Start/memory1.fla

Completed Projects:

Lesson08/Completed/memory6.fla

Attaching Movie Clips

When you start building Flash applications it is most common to initially add all movie clips to the stage at authoring time by dragging instances of symbols from the library to the stage. That method is appropriate in many cases. However, there are many cases when it is more appropriate, and perhaps even necessary, to add movie clips programmatically. For example, you might want to build a game such as Tetris. When building something that is interactive and dynamic, such as a game like Tetris, it would be nearly impossible to add all the necessary movie clips to the stage at authoring time. Instead, it's necessary to add the movie clips (the tetragram game pieces) to the stage at runtime using ActionScript. The new movie clips can thus get added in a manner that is dynamic and dependent upon the user or completely random.

The MovieClip class defines a method called `attachMovie()` that enables you to programmatically add new movie clip instances to the stage at runtime. However, for `attachMovie()` to work you must notify Flash which symbol or symbols you want to be able to add programmatically. You can accomplish it by applying linkage settings to the symbol.

You can apply linkage settings by way of the Linkage Properties dialog box. You can open the Linkage Properties dialog box by selecting the symbol in the library and selecting Linkage from the context menu or from the library menu. By default, the Linkage Properties dialog box has no selected options. If you want to enable a movie clip symbol so that you can attach an instance programmatically you must select the Export For ActionScript option. When you select the Export For ActionScript option, Flash automatically selects the Export In First Frame option as well. You can generally let Flash apply that setting. After you select the Export For ActionScript option, the Linkage identifier field is enabled. The default value is the symbol name, which is generally okay. There is no requirement that the linkage identifier be the same as the symbol name. However, generally it's most appropriate to use the same value. The only time that's not appropriate is when you're already exporting a movie clip in the same library with the same linkage identifier. Every linkage identifier must be unique within a library.

After you apply the Export For ActionScript option to a movie clip symbol you can use the `attachMovie()` method to add an instance of the symbol programmatically. The `attachMovie()` method adds a new instance of the specified symbol as a nested movie clip of the object from which the method is called. For example, if you called `attachMovie()` from `exampleClip`, the new movie clip is a nested instance within `exampleClip`.

The attachMovie() method requires three parameters:

- Linkage identifier—The linkage identifier of the symbol you want to attach
- New instance name—The name you want to assign to the new movie clip instance
- Depth—An integer specifying the z-index of the new object

Depth is an important concept that applies to every MovieClip, Button, TextField, Video, and BitmapData object. An object's depth specifies the stacking order along the z-axis. Depths are always integers, and the higher the number, the nearer the object appears. For example, an object with a depth of 2 appears in front of an object with a depth of 1. Every movie clip has its own set of depths. For example, if aClip is at depth 1 and bClip is at depth 2 (both on the main Timeline), the contents of bClip always appear in front of aClip, regardless of the depths of the contents of each.

Typically, programmatic depths ought to start with 1 and increment from there. Negative depths are permissible, but they are generally reserved for authoring time instances. Only one object can exist per depth. If you add an object to a depth already occupied by an existing object, the new object overwrites the old. If you want to add new objects to the stage without deleting existing objects, you must use unique depths. You can write custom code to keep track of the depths used by existing objects. However, the simplest way to ensure that you are using a unique depth is to use the getNextHighestDepth() method of the MovieClip class. The getNextHighestDepth() method returns the next unoccupied depth within the movie clip from which it is called. The following code illustrates how you can use attachMovie() and getNextHighestDepth() to add a new movie clip instance. The following code assumes that there is a movie clip symbol that is set to export with a linkage identifier of Example.

```
this.attachMovie("Example", "exampleClip", ¬
  this.getNextHighestDepth());
```

The attachMovie() method returns a reference to the new movie clip. That is particularly useful when adding new movie clip instances with dynamic instance names. For example, the following code adds 10 new instances of Example, each with an instance name that is dynamically determined using the index variable from the for statement:

```
for(var i:Number = 0; i < 10; i++) {
  this.attachMovie("Example", "exampleClip" + i, ¬
    this.getNextHighestDepth());
}
```

That code works well until you want to reference the new movie clip. For example, you might want to add an onPress() method to the new instances as soon as they are added. If you assign the new movie clip reference to a variable, the task becomes much easier:

```
var newClip:MovieClip;
for(var i:Number = 0; i < 10; i++) {
  newClip = this.attachMovie("Example", exampleClip", + i, ¬
    this.getNextHighestDepth());
  newClip.onPress = function():Void {
    trace(this);
  };
}
```

When you call the attachMovie() method you also have the option of passing it a fourth parameter that acts as an initialization object. The initialization object is an object with properties corresponding to any valid properties of the new instance. When the new instance is attached, those properties are automatically set. For example, you can use the initialization object to assign values to the _x and _y properties, as the following example illustrates:

```
this.attachMovie("Example", "exampleClip", this.getNextHighestDepth(),¬
  {_x: 100, _y: 400});
```

In this next task you'll start to build a memory game. The first step is simply to add movie clips to the stage with the attachMovie() method.

1. Open *memory1.fla* from the Lesson08/Start directory.

The Flash document contains all the elements to build the memory game. The library contains two folders, one of which (MovieClips) has six movie clips that you can attach with attachMovie(). You'll add two instances of each movie clip in a random order.

2. For each movie clip symbol in the MovieClips folder in the library, set the symbol to export for ActionScript with the default linkage identifier.

To add instances of the movie clips they must be set to export for ActionScript.

3. Select the first keyframe of the main Timeline, and open the Actions panel. Then add the following code that defines an array of linkage identifiers:

```
var linkageArr:Array = ["A", "B", "C", "D", "E", "F", "A", "B", "C",¬
  "D", "E", "F"];
```

The linkageArr array has elements that correspond to each of the movie clip symbols' linkage identifiers. There are two elements for each linkage identifier because you'll want to add two instances of each symbol.

4. Next, add the following code to sort the array:

```
linkageArr.sort(sort);
function sort(a:Object, b:Object):Number {
  return (Math.random() < .5) ? -1 : 1;
}
```

It's necessary to sort the array in a random order so that the cards are in a different order each time. The sort() method allows you to specify a sorting function, which is automatically passed two parameters representing two elements of the array to compare. In this case you want to sort in a random order. Therefore, the sorting function returns either 1 or -1 randomly.

5. Define an initialize() function that adds the movie clip instances to the stage. Then call the initialize() function.

```
initialize();

function initialize():Void {
  var depth:Number;
  var clip:MovieClip;
  var x:Number = 10;
  var y:Number = 10;
  for(var i:Number = 0; i < linkageArr.length; i++) {
    depth = this.getNextHighestDepth();
    clip = this.attachMovie(linkageArr[i], "clip" + depth, ¬
      depth, {_x: x, _y: y});
    if((i + 1) % 3 != 0) {
      x += clip._width + 5;
    }
    else {
      x = 10;
      y += clip._height + 5;
    }
  }
}
```

The initialize() function loops through each element of the linkageArr array, and it adds a new movie clip instance based on the current element. It uses an initialization object to set the _x and _y properties of the movie clip, and then updates the values of the x and y variables so that the movie clips are arranged in a grid.

6. Test the movie.

When you test the movie you ought to see a grid of movie clips. Each time you test the movie, the movie clips are in a different random order.

Adding Empty Movie Clips

Aside from adding movie clip instances of exported movie clip symbols, you can also programmatically add movie clip instances that have no symbol. The `createEmptyMovieClip()` method, as the name implies, adds a new empty movie clip instance. The benefit of an empty movie clip instance might not be immediately apparent. However, there are many cases in which it can be useful. Remember that movie clips can contain nested movie clips. If you move the parent movie clip, for example, the nested movie clips are also moved. So if you attach movie clips within an empty movie clip, the parent movie clip is a convenient way to group nested instances. Additionally, as you'll read in the next section, you can draw programmatically within a movie clip. That means that you can add a new empty movie clip and then you can draw content within that instance.

Regardless of how you intend to work with the new empty movie clip instance, you can create it the same way. The `createEmptyMovieClip()` method is a method of the MovieClip class, and it adds a new empty movie clip instance nested within the object from which it is called. The method requires two parameters: the new instance name and the depth at which to add the instance. The following code adds a new movie clip instance called `exampleClip`:

```
this.createEmptyMovieClip("exampleClip", this.getNextHighestDepth());
```

As with the `attachMovie()` method, the `createEmptyMovieClip()` method returns a reference to the new movie clip.

Drawing Programmatically

The MovieClip class defines a set of methods for drawing programmatically. The set of methods are frequently called the Drawing API. The basic methods are fairly simple and they enable you to set a line style, draw line segments, draw curves, and apply fills.

Each movie clip has its own line style. By default the line style is undefined, so before you can draw anything you must set the line style by way of the `lineStyle()` method, which requires at least one parameter specifying the line thickness in pixels. A value of 0 means that the line style is a hairline. A value of 1 or greater means that the line style has a thickness of the specified number of pixels. The maximum thickness of a line style is 255. The following code tells Flash to use a hairline for `exampleClip`:

```
exampleClip.lineStyle(0);
```

In addition to the one required parameter for `lineStyle()` you can also specify parameters for the following:

- **color:** A number to use for the color. The default is 0x000000 (black).
- **alpha:** A number to use for the alpha. The default is 100.
- **pixelHinting:** By default no pixelHinting is applied. If a value of `true` is specified, Flash snaps points to whole pixels.
- **noScale:** A string specifying how the line thickness scales when the movie clip scales. The default is `normal`, which means that the line scales. A value of `none` means that the line doesn't scale. A value of `vertical` means the line scales only when the movie clip is scaled vertically. A value of `horizontal` means the line scales only when the movie clip is scaled horizontally.
- **capsStyle:** A string specifying the line cap style. The default is `round`. You can also specify `none` and `square`.
- **jointStyle:** A string specifying the join style. The default is `round`. You can also specify `miter` and `bevel`.
- **miterLimit:** If a miter join style is applied, you can specify the miter limit.

After you set a line style, you can start to draw. By default, the drawing point starts at 0,0. If you want to start drawing from a different point, you can use the `moveTo()` method to move the drawing point without drawing a line. The `moveTo()` method requires two parameters specifying the x and y coordinates to which you want to move the drawing point.

```
exampleClip.moveTo(100, 400);
```

The `lineTo()` method works just like the `moveTo()` method, except that it draws the line to the new point.

```
exampleClip.lineTo(200, 200);
```

The `curveTo()` method is slightly more complex because you have to specify not only the new endpoint but also the control point that determines the curve. The control point is a point that forms a tangent to the curve from both endpoints. The following code draws a curve from 100,100 to 200,100 with a control point at 150, 0.

```
exampleClip.moveTo(100, 100);
exampleClip.curveTo(150, 0, 200, 100);
```

Aside from drawing lines, you can also apply fills using the `beginFill()` and `endFill()` methods. When you call the `beginFill()` method, Flash applies the specified fill to any closed shape that is formed by `lineTo()` and `curveTo()` methods following the method call until you call `endFill()`. The `beginFill()` method requires at least one parameter specifying the fill color. You can also specify a second parameter to control the alpha of the fill. The following code applies a blue fill to a rectangle.

```
exampleClip.lineStyle(0);
exampleClip.beginFill(0x0000FF);
exampleClip.lineTo(550, 0);
exampleClip.lineTo(550, 400);
exampleClip.lineTo(0, 400);
exampleClip.lineTo(0, 0);
exampleClip.endFill();
```

The next task uses the Drawing API to draw movie clips corresponding to each of the movie clips attached in the preceding task.

1. Open the Flash document you completed in the previous task. Optionally, you can open *memory2.fla* from the Lesson08/Completed directory.

The Flash document has all the elements to build this stage of the application.

2. Select the first keyframe of the main Timeline and open the Actions panel. Then add the following code:

```
var clips:Object = new Object();
```

The clips object is an associative array that keeps track of which drawn movie clips correspond to which image movie clips.

3. Within the `initialize()` function add the following code just after declaring the clip variable:

```
var card:MovieClip;
```

The card variable is used to store a reference to the new movie clips.

4. Next, within the `for` statement, just after attaching the movie clip instance, add the following code.

```
card = drawRectangle(Math.random() * 0xFFFFFF, clip._width, ¬
    clip._height, x, y);
clips[card._name] = {id: linkageArr[i], clip: clip};
```

The `drawRectangle()` function is a custom function defined in the next step. It adds a new movie clip and it draws a rectangle in the new movie clip. Then, use the card movie clip's instance name as the key for the clips associative array and assign to that element an object that contains the corresponding linkage identifier of the image movie clip and a reference to the image movie clip. That way, you can retrieve the corresponding image movie clip and linkage identifier when the user clicks on the rectangle card clip.

5. Define the `drawRectangle()` function.

```
function drawRectangle(color:Number, width:Number, ¬
    height:Number, x:Number, y:Number):MovieClip {
    var depth:Number = this.getNextHighestDepth();
    var clip:MovieClip;
    clip = this.createEmptyMovieClip("clip" + depth, depth);
    clip.lineStyle(0, 0, 0);
    clip.beginFill(color);
    clip.lineTo(width, 0);
    clip.lineTo(width, height);
    clip.lineTo(0, height);
    clip.lineTo(0, 0);
    clip.endFill();
    clip._x = x;
    clip._y = y;
    return clip;
}
```

The drawRectangle() function simply adds a new empty movie clip and then it draws a rectangle and returns a reference to the new object.

6. Test the movie.

When you test the movie you'll see randomly colored rectangles in front of each of the image movie clips.

Working with Movie Clips as Buttons

Movie clips dispatch the same events as buttons, so you can work with movie clips in the same ways you work with buttons. You can define onPress(), onRelease(), onRollOver(), onRollOut(), and so on, for movie clips, and the methods are automatically called when the corresponding events occur. The following example illustrates how to define an onPress() method for a movie clip called exampleClip. When the user clicks on the instance it writes the instance path to the Output panel.

```
exampleClip.onPress = function():Void {
  trace(this);
};
```

In the next task you'll add an event handler method to the rectangle movie clips so that when the user clicks on them they will temporarily turn invisible so you can see the image movie clip they obscure.

1. Open the Flash document you completed in the previous task. Optionally, you can open memory3.fla from Lesson08/Completed.

The Flash document has all the elements to build this stage of the application.

2. Select the first keyframe of the main Timeline and open the Actions panel. Add the following code following the declaration of the clip variable:

```
var selected:MovieClip = null;
var correct:Number = 0;
```

The selected movie clip stores references to movie clips as the user clicks them. The correct variable stores the number of correct cards the user has selected.

3. In the `initialize()` function, add the following code just after assigning the value to the card:

```
card.onPress = function():Void {
   onCardClick(this);
};
```

When the user clicks a card, tell Flash to call the `onCardClick()` function. Pass the function a reference to the card the user clicked. You'll define `onCardClick()` in the next step.

4. Define `onCardClick()`:

```
function onCardClick(cardClip:MovieClip):Void {
   cardClip._visible = false;
   if(selected == null) {
      selected = cardClip;
   }
   else {
      if(clips[cardClip._name].id == clips[selected._name].id) {
         correct += 2;
         clips[cardClip._name].clip._alpha = 50;
         clips[selected._name].clip._alpha = 50;
         selected = null;
         if(correct == linkageArr.length) {
            trace("you win");
         }
      }
      else {
         setTimeout(resetclips, 1000, cardClip, selected);
         selected = null;
      }
   }
}
```

The onCardClick() function first tests whether selected is null. If so, it assigns a reference to the card that was clicked to selected. However, if selected is not null, it means that the user already clicked a card. In that case, the code tests whether the corresponding linkage IDs are equal for the card referenced by selected and the card that was just clicked. If they are, it means that the user has correctly selected two cards. In that case, the code adds 2 to the score, sets the _alpha property of the two cards to 50, and resets selected to null. If the correct variable is equal to the number of elements in linkageArr, the user has won. In the event that the IDs aren't equal, use setTimeout to reset the cards in one second.

5. Define resetclips():

```
function resetclips(a:MovieClip, b:MovieClip):Void {
    a._visible = true;
    b._visible = true;
}
```

The resetclips() function simply sets the visibility of the two movie clips.

6. Test the movie.

When you test the movie you can click on the cards.

Adding Text Fields Programmatically

You can add text fields programmatically with the createTextField() method. Like the attachMovie() and createEmptyMovieClip() methods, the createTextField() method is a MovieClip method, and it adds the new instance nested within the object from which the method is called. The createTextField() method requires six parameters:

- **instanceName:** The instance name of the new text field
- **depth:** The depth of the new text field
- **x:** The x coordinate
- **y:** The y coordinate
- **width:** The width of the new text field
- **height:** The height of the new text field

The following code adds a new text field called exampleField:

```
this.createTextField("exampleField",¬
    this.getNextHighestDepth(), 0, 0, 100, 25);
```

Like attachMovie() and createEmptyMovieClip(), the createTextField() method returns a reference to the new object.

When you add text fields you don't necessarily always know the dimensions before you apply the text. However, you always have to specify some value for the width and height properties of the createTextField() method. In the event that you want the text field to have the same dimensions of the text, you can use the autoSize property with the text field and set the initial dimensions to 0. The following example illustrates how that works:

```
var exampleField:TextField = this.createTextField("exampleField",¬
    this.getNextHighestDepth(), 0, 0, 0, 0);
exampleField.autoSize = "left";
exampleField.text = "Example Text";
```

In the following task you'll add hints to the memory game.

1. Open the Flash document you completed in the previous task. Optionally, you can open *memory4.fla* from the Lesson08/Completed directory.

The Flash document contains all the necessary assets and code as the starting point for this task.

2. Select the first keyframe of the main Timeline and open the Actions panel. Then add the following code following the variable declaration for correct:

```
var hints:Object = new Object();
hints.A = "explosion";
hints.B = "iron";
hints.C = "buttons";
hints.D = "text";
hints.E = "building";
hints.F = "fire";
var currentHint:MovieClip;
var hintInterval:Number;
```

The hints object is an associative array that stores the hint text for each of the movie clips using the linkage identifier as the key. The currentHint variable stores a reference to the current hints object, and the hintInterval variable stores the interval ID that adds the hint after a slight delay.

3. Define onRollOver() and onRollOut() methods for the card movie clip. Add the following code within the initialize() method following the onPress() method definition:

```
card.onRollOver = function():Void {
   startHintInterval(hints[clips[this._name].id]);
};
card.onRollOut = function():Void {
   currentHint.removeMovieClip();
   clearInterval(hintInterval);
};
```

When the user moves the mouse over a card, call the startHintInterval() function (defined in the next step.) When the user moves the mouse off of a card, remove the current hint and clear the interval set by startHintInterval().

4. Define startHintInterval():

```
function startHintInterval(hintText:String):Void {
   hintInterval = setInterval(this, "addHint", 1000, hintText);
}
```

The startHintInterval() function sets an interval so that Flash calls addHint() in one second. That way there's a delay before the hint appears.

5. Define `addHint()`:

```
function addHint(hintText:String):Void {
  currentHint.removeMovieClip();
  var depth:Number = this.getNextHighestDepth();
  var hintClip:MovieClip = this.createEmptyMovieClip("clip" + depth, depth);
  var hint:TextField = hintClip.createTextField("hint",¬
    hintClip.getNextHighestDepth(), 0, 0, 0, 0);
  hint.autoSize = "left";
  hint.background = true;
  hint.border = true;
  hint.text = hintText;
  hint.selectable = false;
  hintClip._x = _xmouse;
  hintClip._y = _ymouse - hint._height;
  currentHint = hintClip;
}
```

The `addHint()` function adds a new empty movie clip that contains a text field. Then it sets some properties of the text field and moves the movie clip to the location of the mouse.

6. Test the movie.

When you move the mouse over a card and pause for a second, a hint will appear.

Formatting Text

You can apply formatting to text using the TextFormat class, which defines many properties that allow you to set everything from font family and font size to kerning and color. The Flash Help documentation lists all the properties of the TextFormat class, and it is an excellent reference for details of each setting. However, regardless of which properties you want to set, you'll construct the new TextFormat and apply it in the same ways.

When you want to construct a TextFormat object, you can use the constructor as part of a new statement, as the following code illustrates:

```
var formatter:TextFormat = new TextFormat();
```

After you construct a TextFormat object, you can apply settings. The following sets the font and size properties:

```
formatter.font = "_sans";
formatter.size = 20;
```

After you set the properties, you can apply the formatting to a text field with the setTextFormat() method of the TextField class. The method allows you to apply a TextFormat object to the entire text field. The following code illustrates by applying a TextFormat object called formatter to the text of a text field called exampleField:

```
exampleField.setTextFormat(formatter);
```

When you apply formatting to a text field with the setTextFormat() method, it applies the current TextFormat settings to the current text of the text field. If you update the text after applying the formatting, you'll have to reapply the formatting. And if you change the settings of the TextFormat object, you'll have to reapply it if you want it to change the formatting of the text field.

You can optionally apply the formatting to just a specific substring of the text by specifying the starting and stopping indices of that substring as parameters for the setTextFormat() method.

```
exampleField.setTextFormat(formatter, 10, 20);
```

In the next task, you'll add a message when the user wins the game. The message uses a TextFormat object.

1. Open the Flash document you completed in the previous task. Optionally, you can open *memory5.fla* from the Lesson08/Completed directory.

The Flash document contains all the necessary assets and code as the starting point for this task.

2. Select the first keyframe of the main Timeline and open the Actions panel. Add the following code in place of the **trace()** statement currently within the code:

```
var youWin:TextField = this.createTextField("youWin",¬
   this.getNextHighestDepth(), 275, 250, 0, 0);
youWin.autoSize = "center";
youWin.text = "You Win";
youWin.background = true;
youWin.border = true;
youWin.selectable = false;
var formatter:TextFormat = new TextFormat();
formatter.size = 100;
formatter.color = 0xFF0000;
formatter.font = "_sans";
formatter.bold = true;
youWin.setTextFormat(formatter);
```

The preceding code adds a new text field that uses TextFormat to apply formatting to a You Win message.

3. Test the movie.

When you win the game, a message will display.

What You Have Learned

In this lesson you have:

- Added new movie clips programmatically from library symbols (pages 179–183)
- Added new empty movie clips programmatically (page 183)
- Drawn with the Drawing API (pages 183–187)
- Used events with movie clips (pages 187–189)
- Added text fields programmatically (pages 190–192)
- Applied formatting to text fields (pages 193–194)

9 Bitmap Features

Macromedia Flash 8 introduces many new bitmap features not previously available to Flash Player. You can apply runtime filter effects such as realistic drop shadows and bevels. You can also optimize animations by caching bitmap surfaces of complex vectors. And perhaps the neatest new feature in Flash is the Bitmap API, which enables you to work with images pixel by pixel.

90

By using new bitmap features, you can apply runtime filter effects such as bevels and glow effects.

What You Will Learn

In this lesson you will:

- Learn about bitmap surface caching
- Apply filter effects to movie clips
- Apply blends to movie clips
- Use the BitmapData class to add bitmap symbol instance programmatically
- Copy bitmap data from movie clips
- Use flood fill functionality with BitmapData objects
- Retrieve and set the pixel values in a BitmapData object

Approximate Time

This lesson takes approximately an hour and a half to complete

Lesson Files

Media Files:

Lesson09/Assets/message.txt
Lesson09/Assets/Tree.gif

Starting Files:

Lesson09/Start/snowflake1.fla
Lesson09/Start/spaceship1.fla
Lesson09/Start/message1.fla
Lesson09/Start/coloringPage1.fla

Completed Projects:

Lesson09/Completed/snowflake2.fla
Lesson09/Completed/spaceship4.fla
Lesson09/Completed/message2.fla
Lesson09/Completed/coloringPage4.fla

Using Bitmap Surface Caching

Flash Player has its humble beginnings in the world of vector animations. And although it has added a lot of new functionality over the years, vector animations remain one of its strengths. Vectors generally require significantly less data than rasterized bitmaps. The latter requires data for each pixel, whereas the former only requires data for things such as line segment end points and fill color. That means that vectors are typically much more compact than bitmaps (except in the case of extremely complex vector artwork). Additionally, although bitmaps don't scale well, vectors do.

Although vectors have many advantages, there are some potential drawbacks. In particular, we want to discuss issues related to translating complex vector artwork within Flash Player. Translating means moving the object in the x and y coordinate space. Every time a movie clip with vector artwork tweens across the Stage, Flash Player has to re-plot each line segment within the vector artwork. For the majority of vector shapes, that is still a relatively inexpensive operation. However, the more complex the vector artwork, the more points Flash Player has to re-plot. The result is that in some cases Flash Player maxes out on its use of system resources attempting to re-plot each point within the vector and it starts to run more slowly. Animations can then become noticeably slower and/or choppier.

Contrast that with how Flash Player translates bitmaps. Flash Player treats bitmaps as single units. It does not attempt to shift the bitmap one pixel at a time. It simply translates the entire bitmap unit, which makes bitmap translation an inexpensive operation compared with complex vector artwork translation.

Wouldn't it be nice if there were some way in which you could tell Flash Player to treat movie clips containing complex vector artwork as though they contained bitmaps? Starting with Flash Player 8, the MovieClip class enables that very functionality with the cacheAsBitmap property. The cacheAsBitmap property lets you tell Flash Player to take a snapshot of the vector artwork and use that snapshot as a bitmap surface for the movie clip. Flash Player then translates the movie clip as though it contained a bitmap. The result can potentially be smoother animations.

The cacheAsBitmap property expects a Boolean value. The default value is false, so no bitmap surface is used. A value of true tells Flash Player to use a bitmap surface.

```
exampleClip.cacheAsBitmap = true;
```

Although caching bitmap surfaces is a useful solution in some cases, it is not a catch-all to use with every movie clip. Caching bitmap surfaces is not without some cost. When a movie clip has a cached bitmap surface, it must redraw the surface whenever the following events occur:

- The contents of the movie clip change (for example, the movie clip contains a nested movie clip that tweens)
- The movie clip rotates
- The movie clip scales

If any of the preceding events occur with the frequency of a movie clip, caching a bitmap surface can be more detrimental than helpful. For example, if a movie clip rotates while translating, as long as cacheAsBitmap is true it is even more expensive than previously. In such a case, the movie clip has to rotate, translate, and then redraw the bitmap surface.

Caching bitmap surfaces is a useful feature when used correctly. Use the feature only when you notice that it is required. For example, if you have complex vector artwork that tweens across the Stage and you notice that the animation slows down at that point, you can set the movie clip or movie clips containing the artwork to use a cached bitmap surface.

In this next task, you'll make a snowfall scene animation using bitmap caching to optimize the animation of the snowflakes. The snowflakes are each movie clips containing complex vector artwork. As you'll see in Step 7, the animation can start to run slowly. So as a solution you'll set each movie clip to use a cached bitmap surface.

1. Open *snowflake1.fla* from the Lesson09/Start directory.

The snowflake1.fla document contains the necessary elements. Specifically, it contains a movie clip symbol called Snowflake.

2. Select the Snowflake movie clip symbol in the library, and open the Linkage Properties dialog box. Check the Export For ActionScript option. Use the default linkage identifier of Snowflake. Click OK.

To add instances of the symbol programmatically, you'll need to adjust the linkage properties for the movie clip. You can do so from the Linkage Properties dialog box. You can access the dialog box either by way of the library menu (select Linkage) or from the right-click/Ctrl-click context menu for the library symbol (select Linkage).

Set the symbol to Export For ActionScript so that you can attach instances using `attachMovie()`.

Linkage Properties		☒
Identifier:	Snowflake	OK
AS 2.0 class:		Cancel
Linkage:	☑ Export for ActionScript	
	☐ Export for runtime sharing	
	☑ Export in first frame	
	☐ Import for runtime sharing	
URL:		

3. Select the first keyframe on the Actions layer from the main Timeline, and open the Actions panel by pressing F9. Then add an import statement to import the Tween class.

```
import mx.transitions.Tween;
```

You'll use the Tween class to animate the snowflakes. The Tween class is installed in the global Flash classpath with the default installation of Flash 8. However, it's in a package called mx.transitions. To reference the class simply as Tween throughout the rest of the code, you can use the import statement at the beginning of the code.

4. Following the import statement, add the following line of code:

```
setInterval(this, "addSnowflake", 250);
```

The setInterval() function tells Flash Player to call a function at a specified interval. In this case, you're telling Flash Player to call the addSnowflake() function every 250 milliseconds.

5. Define the `addSnowflake()` function following the preceding code.

```
function addSnowflake():Void {
    // Add each snowflake to a unique depth.
    var depth:Number = this.getNextHighestDepth();
    var snowflakeClip:MovieClip = this.attachMovie("Snowflake", ¬
        "snowflakeClip" + depth, depth);

    // Make a random scale factor from 20 to 100. Then set the
    // _xscale and _yscale properties of the snowflake movie clip
    // to that scale factor so that the snowflakes have different
    // sizes.
    var scaleFactor:Number = Math.random() * 80 + 20;
    snowflakeClip._xscale = scaleFactor;
    snowflakeClip._yscale = scaleFactor;

    // Set the x coordinate of the snowflake to a random number
    // between 0 and 550.
    snowflakeClip._x = Math.random() * 550;

    // Use a Tween object to animate the snowflake such that it
    // falls from the top of the stage to the bottom of the stage.
    // Add a listener so that Flash Player gets notified when the
    // animation has completed.
    var snowflakeTween:Tween = new Tween(snowflakeClip, "_y", ¬
        null, 0, 400, Math.random() * 50 + 100);
    snowflakeTween.addListener(this);
}
```

The inline comments provide the detailed description of the preceding code. Generally, the addSnowflake() function adds a new instance of the Snowflake symbol to the Stage. It scales the instance to a random value between 20 and 80 percent, and it places the instance at a random *x* coordinate along the top of the Stage. It then uses a Tween object to start an animation that causes the snowflake to fall from the top to the bottom of the Stage.

6. Define the `onMotionFinished()` function following the `addSnowflake()` function.

```
function onMotionFinished(tweenObject:Tween):Void {
    tweenObject.obj.removeMovieClip();
}
```

Because the main Timeline is the listener object for each Tween object, Flash Player automatically calls a function named onMotionFinished() when each tween completes. The function gets passed a reference to the Tween object that just completed the animation.

Within the onMotionFinished() function you can tell Flash Player to delete the corresponding movie clip using removeMovieClip(). Note that each Tween object has an obj property that references the targeted movie clip.

7. Test the movie.

When you test the movie you'll see snowflakes falling. Initially the animation ought to playback smoothly. However, as more snowflakes are added to the scene you'll likely notice that the animation slows significantly.

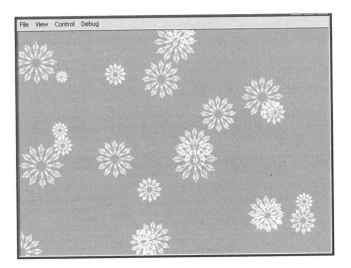

8. Edit the ActionScript code by adding the bolded line of code to the addSnowflake() function.

```
function addSnowflake():Void {
    var depth:Number = this.getNextHighestDepth();
    var snowflakeClip:MovieClip = this.attachMovie("Snowflake", ¬
        "snowflakeClip" + depth, depth);
    var scaleFactor:Number = Math.random() * 80 + 20;
    snowflakeClip._xscale = scaleFactor;
    snowflakeClip._yscale = scaleFactor;
    snowflakeClip._x = Math.random() * 550;
    snowflakeClip.cacheAsBitmap = true;
    var snowflakeTween:Tween = new Tween(snowflakeClip, "_y", ¬
        null, 0, 400, Math.random() * 50 + 100);
    snowflakeTween.addListener(this);
}
```

The cacheAsBitmap property is false by default. By setting the property to true you're telling Flash Player to use a cached bitmap surface for the snowflake movie clip. That means Flash Player can translate the movie clips as bitmaps rather than as vectors.

9. Test the movie again.

When you test the movie this time, you'll likely notice that the animation plays without slowing. The bitmap caching enables Flash Player to translate the snowflake movie clips as efficiently as possible.

Applying Filters

Flash Player 8 has built-in runtime effects called filters that you can apply to movie clips, buttons, and text fields. You can apply any combination of the following filter types:

- BevelFilter
- BlurFilter
- ColorMatrixFilter
- ConvolutionFilter
- DisplacementMapFilter
- DropShadowFilter
- GlowFilter
- GradientBevelFilter
- GradientGlowFilter

Filters represent a major advance in the sort of effects that you can apply to Flash movie content. Each of the filter types is configurable. For example, the BlurFilter allows you to specify parameters such as the number of pixels to blur in the x direction and the number of pixels to blur in the y direction. You can adjust those values at runtime as well. That means that you can create animated filter effects. The potential with filters is limitless. So let's take a look at how to start working with filters.

Constructing Filters

To apply a filter, you must first construct an instance of the corresponding class. For example, if you want to apply a drop shadow effect, you need to construct a DropShadowFilter instance. Each of the filter classes is in the flash.filters package. To simplify working with filter classes, it's recommended that you import the class or classes with which you plan to work. For example, if you want to apply drop shadow effects, you can import the flash.filters.DropShadowFilter class as follows.

```
import flash.filters.DropShadowFilter;
```

If you intend to work with many or all of the filter classes, you can use the * wildcard as follows.

```
import flash.filters.*;
```

After you import the class or classes, you can construct instances using the constructor and a new statement. The following constructs a new DropShadowFilter object and assigns it to a variable called dropShadow:

```
var dropShadow:DropShadowFilter = new DropShadowFilter();
```

Each filter class has different parameter lists for the constructor. You can quickly reference that information in the Flash Help documentation. Many of the basic filters—such as BevelFilter, BlurFilter, DropShadowFilter, and GlowFilter—have default values, so the parameters are optional. For example, the preceding code constructs a DropShadowFilter object with the default values. However, the following code makes a DropShadowFilter instance with an offset of 10 pixels, an angle of 0, a blue color, 50% transparency, and blurred 10 pixels in both the *x* and *y* directions.

```
var dropShadow:DropShadowFilter = new DropShadowFilter(10, 0, ¬
    0x0000FF, 50, 10, 10);
```

Assigning Filters to Objects

After you construct a filter, you can apply it to a movie clip, button, or text field using the filters property of the assignee. The filters property expects an array of filter objects. Even if you want to assign only one filter to the object, you still must place it within an array before you can assign it to the filters property of that object. The following code assigns a DropShadowFilter instance called dropShadow to a movie clip called exampleClip.

```
exampleClip.filters = [dropShadow];
```

If you assign more than one filter to an object, the filters are applied cumulatively in the order in which they appear in the filters array. For example, the following code applies a DropShadowFilter and a GlowFilter (called glow) to exampleClip.

```
exampleClip.filters = [dropShadow, glow];
```

Because dropShadow appears first in the array, it is applied first. The glow is then applied to the result of the dropShadow application. That means that the glow won't appear around the outline of the original artwork within exampleClip. It will appear around the outline of the original artwork combined with the drop shadow.

Building a Spaceship Game

In this next task, you'll build the first stage of a spaceship game. When the game is completed, it will allow the user to move a spaceship with the arrow keys to try to stay out of the path of meteors. Several filter effects are used to make the spaceship and game play more interesting. In this first stage, you'll add a bevel filter to the spaceship, and you'll add the code that makes the spaceship move when the arrow keys are pressed.

1. Open *spaceship1.fla* located in Lesson09/Start.

The spaceship1.fla document contains all the elements necessary for building the game. You'll note that two movie clip instances and one text field are already on the Stage. On the Background layer is a movie clip instance with an instance name of backgroundClip. On the Spaceship layer is a movie clip with an instance name of shipClip. And on the Score layer is a text field with an instance name of scoreField.

2. Select the keyframe on the Actions layer and open the Actions panel by pressing F9. Then add the following import statement to the script pane.

```
import flash.filters.BevelFilter;
```

The game eventually uses the BevelFilter class to apply effects to the spaceship. To simplify working with the class, import it to start.

3. Define a variable (collisionClip) that is used throughout the rest of the code.

```
var collisionClip:MovieClip;
```

The collisionClip variable is used to determine whether or not a collision occurred. You'll use the variable in the remainder of the code.

4. Apply a bevel to the spaceship using the following code.

```
var bevelArr:Array = [new BevelFilter()];
shipClip.filters = bevelArr;
```

The bevel makes the spaceship appear more three-dimensional.

5. Make the main Timeline a listener for keyboard events by registering it with the Key class.

```
Key.addListener(this);
```

For the spaceship to move when the user presses the arrow keys you must tell Flash Player how to handle keyboard events. You can do that by registering a listener object. When a key is pressed, the onKeyDown() method of the listener gets called. And when the key is released, the onKeyUp() method of the listener gets called. In this case you're registering the main Timeline as the listener object, so you'll define the onKeyDown() and onKeyUp() methods as functions on the main Timeline.

6. Define the **onKeyDown()** function as follows:

```
function onKeyDown():Void {
  if(Key.getCode() == Key.RIGHT) {
    shipClip.onEnterFrame = function():Void {
      this._x += 20;
    };
  }
  else if(Key.getCode() == Key.LEFT) {
    shipClip.onEnterFrame = function():Void {
      this._x -= 20;
    };
  }
  else if(Key.getCode() == Key.UP) {
    shipClip.onEnterFrame = function():Void {
      this._y -= 20;
    };
  }
  else if(Key.getCode() == Key.DOWN) {
    shipClip.onEnterFrame = function():Void {
      this._y += 20;
    };
  }
}
```

The preceding code might appear rather complex, but if you look at it closely, you'll see that it repeats similar blocks of code. As previously mentioned, the onKeyDown() function gets called when a key is pressed on the keyboard. The function uses a series of if and else if statements to determine which key was pressed. If the user has pressed one of the arrow keys, the code defines an onEnterFrame() method for shipClip. The onEnterFrame() method increments or decrements the _x or _y property of shipClip. Which property and whether to increment or decrement the value is determined by which key was pressed. The result is that the spaceship moves when one of the arrow keys is pressed.

7. Define the **onKeyUp()** function as follows:

```
function onKeyUp():Void {
    delete shipClip.onEnterFrame;
}
```

The onKeyUp() function is very simple in comparison with the onKeyDown() function. When the user releases a key, you want the spaceship to stop moving. You can accomplish that by deleting the onEnterFrame() method definition for shipClip.

8. Test the movie

When you test the movie you'll see that the spaceship has a bevel applied to it programmatically. If you press the arrow keys, the spaceship moves in the corresponding direction.

Retrieving Filters

You can read from the filters property of a movie clip, button, or text field to retrieve an array of filters already applied to the object. For example, the following retrieves an array of filters already applied to exampleClip:

```
var filtersArr:Array = exampleClip.filters;
```

However, it's important to note that when you read from the filters property it returns an array of copies of the filters already applied to the object. It's an important distinction, and it has several repercussions as you'll read in the next few sections.

Appending Filters

As noted in the preceding section, the filters property returns a copy of the array of filters applied to an object. So if you want to append filters to the list of filters already applied to an object, you cannot go about it in some of the ways you might expect. For example, the following will not work to append a new BevelFilter to exampleClip:

```
exampleClip.filters.push(new BevelFilter());
```

If you want to append a filter to an existing list of filters, you must first retrieve the copy of the array of existing filters.

```
var filtersArr:Array = exampleClip.filters;
```

Then, you can append the new filter to that array.

```
filtersArr.push(new BevelFilter());
```

After the new array contains the correct list of filters, you can assign it to the filters property of the object.

```
exampleClip.filters = filtersArr;
```

Deleting Filters

If you want to delete filters from an object, the same rules apply as when appending. If you want to delete one or more filters, but leave one or more applied, you must retrieve the copy array, modify the copy, and reassign it to the object's filters property.

If you want to delete all the filters applied to an object, you can simply assign null to the filters property.

```
exampleClip.filters = null;
```

Updating Filters

If you want to update a filter applied to an object, you must first retrieve a copy of the filter via the filters property. You can then update the properties of that filter object and then reapply the filter. The following code assumes that exampleClip has a DropShadowFilter instance applied as the first filter in the filters array. It retrieves the current filters array, updates the alpha property of the DropShadowFilter in the first element of the array, and then reassigns the array to the filters property of exampleClip.

```
var filtersArr:Array = exampleClip.filters;
filtersArr[0].alpha++;
exampleClip.filters = filtersArr;
```

Continuing the Spaceship Game

In this task you'll continue building the spaceship game. In this second stage, you'll add a blur to the spaceship when it moves.

1. Open the Flash document you completed from the previous task. Or optionally open *spaceship2.fla* from Lesson09/Completed.

The Flash document has the necessary assets as well as the ActionScript code from stage 1. It is the starting point for stage 2.

2. Select the keyframe on the Actions layer, open the Actions panel, and add the following import statement immediately following the existing import statement:

```
import flash.filters.BlurFilter;
```

In this task you're adding a blur to the spaceship when it moves. That requires the BlurFilter class. To simplify working with the class, import it to start.

3. Edit the **onKeyDown()** function by adding a BlurFilter object to the **shipClip filters** array each time an arrow key is pressed. The updated code is as follows:

```
function onKeyDown():Void {
    if(Key.getCode() == Key.RIGHT) {
        shipClip.filters = bevelArr.concat(new BlurFilter(50));
        shipClip.onEnterFrame = function():Void {
            this._x += 20;
        };
    }
    else if(Key.getCode() == Key.LEFT) {
        shipClip.filters = bevelArr.concat(new BlurFilter(50));
        shipClip.onEnterFrame = function():Void {
            this._x -= 20;
        };
    }
    else if(Key.getCode() == Key.UP) {
        shipClip.filters = bevelArr.concat(new BlurFilter(0, 50));
        shipClip.onEnterFrame = function():Void {
            this._y -= 20;
        };
    }
    else if(Key.getCode() == Key.DOWN) {
        shipClip.filters = bevelArr.concat(new BlurFilter(0, 50));
        shipClip.onEnterFrame = function():Void {
            this._y += 20;
        };
    }
}
```

When the user presses either the right or left arrow keys, the code applies a BlurFilter object to the spaceship with a 50-pixel blur in the *x* direction. When the user presses either the up or down arrow keys, the code applies a BlurFilter object with a 50-pixel blur in the *y* direction. The effect is that when the user presses the right or left keys the spaceship appears to have a motion blur applied from right to left, and when the user presses the up or down keys the spaceship appears to have a motion blur applied from top to bottom.

However, notice that the code does not merely apply the blur in place of the bevel. It applies a new array with two elements: the bevel and the blur. The bevelArr array contains the BevelFilter object. The concat() method returns a new array with two elements.

4. Edit the **onKeyUp()** function so that it clears the blur filter. The updated function is as follows:

```
function onKeyUp():Void {
  shipClip.filters = bevelArr;
  delete shipClip.onEnterFrame;
}
```

While the spaceship is moving, you want the blur applied. However, after the spaceship stops you want to remove the blur, which you can accomplish by assigning bevelArr to the filters property of shipClip.

5. Test the movie.

When you move the spaceship with the arrow keys you ought to see a blur applied in addition to the bevel. When the spaceship stops, the blur is removed, but the bevel remains.

Completing the Spaceship Game

In this next task, you'll complete the spaceship game. In this stage you'll add meteors that animate across the Stage. If a meteor collides with the spaceship, it will deduct 10 points and it will add a glow effect to the spaceship to indicate that it was hit.

1. Open the completed Flash document from the preceding stage. Optionally, open *spaceship3.fla* from Lesson09/Completed.

The Flash document has all the assets to complete the game.

2. Select the Meteor symbol in the library and open the Linkage Properties dialog box. Check the Export For ActionScript option and use the default linkage identifier of Meteor.

The Meteor symbol is used for the meteors that animate across the Stage. Because you'll be adding instance programmatically, you need to set the symbol to export.

3. Select the keyframe in the Actions layer and open the Actions panel. Add the following import statements immediately following the existing import statements:

```
import flash.filters.GlowFilter;
import mx.transitions.Tween;
```

You'll use the GlowFilter class to add the glow effect to the spaceship. The Tween class is utilized by the meteors. It animates them across the Stage. In both cases, you can import the classes to start to simplify working with them through the code.

4. Set an interval calling a function called **addMeteor()** every five seconds. Add the following code immediately following the line of code that registers the listener with the **Key** class:

```
setInterval(this, "addMeteor", 5000);
```

The setInterval() function tells Flash Player to call a function at a frequency determined in milliseconds. In this case, it's telling Flash Player to call addMeteor() every 5000 milliseconds, or 5 seconds.

5. Define the **addMeteor()** function as follows. Place the function just after the **onKeyUp()** function.

```
function addMeteor():Void {
  this.attachMovie("Meteor", "meteorClip", this.getNextHighestDepth());
  var angle:Number = Math.random() * 2 * Math.PI;
  meteorClip._x = Math.cos(angle) * 600 + backgroundClip._x;
  meteorClip._y = Math.sin(angle) * 600 + backgroundClip._y;
  angle += Math.PI;
  new Tween(meteorClip, "_x", null, meteorClip._x, ¬
    Math.cos(angle) * 600 + backgroundClip._x, 40);
  var meteorTween:Tween = new Tween(meteorClip, "_y", ¬
    null, meteorClip._y, Math.sin(angle) * 600 + backgroundClip._y, 40);
  meteorTween.addListener(this);
}
```

The addMeteor() function adds a new instance of the Meteor symbol using the attachMovie() method. It then determines where to place the instance using trigonometry. The trigonometry is required so that each meteor is placed randomly along a circle that is concentric with the middle of the background. Then, using a Tween object, the code animates the meteor to the opposite side of the circle. It registers the main Timeline as the listener object for the Tween object so that it gets notified when the tween has completed.

6. Define the **onMotionFinished()** function as follows (add the code after the **addMeteor()** function):

```
function onMotionFinished(tweenInstance:Tween):Void {
  tweenInstance.obj.removeMovieClip();
  collisionClip = null;
}
```

The onMotionFinished() gets called each time a meteor completes its animation to the opposite side of the circle. The function removes the movie clip instance. It also sets collisionClip to null. The collisionClip variable is used during collision detection. After the meteor completes moving across the Stage, you want to reset collisionClip.

7. Set an interval to check for collisions. Add the following code following the setInterval() code from Step 4:

```
setInterval(this, "checkCollision", 100);
```

The game needs to see whether the meteors have collided with the spaceship. To accomplish that, use an interval that calls checkCollision() every 100 milliseconds.

8. Define checkCollision() as follows (add the code following the onMotionFinished() function):

```
function checkCollision():Void {
  if(collisionClip == meteorClip) {
    return;
  }
  if(shipClip.hitTest(meteorClip)) {
    collisionClip = meteorClip;
    shipClip.filters = shipClip.filters.concat(new ¬
      GlowFilter(0xFF0000, 50, 20, 20));
    setTimeout(this, "resetFilters", 1000);
    scoreField.text = parseInt(scoreField.text) - 10;
  }
}
```

The checkCollision() function uses the hitTest() method to see whether shipClip and meteorClip have collided. If so, it appends a GlowFilter instance to the filters array for shipClip. It then uses setTimeout() in order to call resetFilters() in one second. It decrements the score by 10.

You'll also notice that checkCollision() uses collisionClip, the variable defined in an earlier stage. It's possible that checkCollision() could get called more than once during one collision between a meteor and the spaceship. However, you want the collision to get registered just once per meteor. When a collision is detected, collisionClip is assigned a reference to meteorClip. Then, if checkCollision() is called again during the same collision the if statement evaluates to true, and it exits the function. As you saw in Step 6, the collisionClip variable is reset to null after the meteor moves across the Stage.

9. Define the `resetFilters()` function as follows. Place the code so it follows the `checkCollision()` function.

```
function resetFilters():Void {
  var filtersArr:Array = shipClip.filters;
  if(filtersArr[filtersArr.length - 1] instanceof GlowFilter) {
    filtersArr.pop();
  }
  shipClip.filters = filtersArr;
}
```

The `resetFilters()` function simply resets the filters applied to the spaceship to whatever they were before the glow was applied.

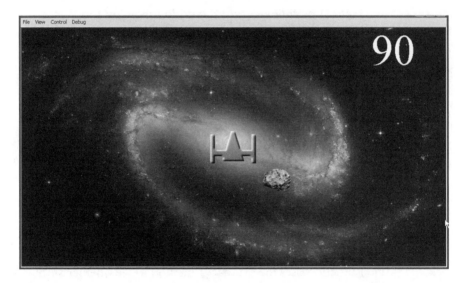

Applying Blend Modes Programmatically

Blend modes are yet another feature new to Flash Player 8. Blend modes are applied at runtime using native player-level functionality. Blend modes enable you to instruct Flash Player to mathematically combine the pixels of a movie clip with the pixels of what is beneath it. For example, if you use the lighten mode, Flash will compare each pixel of a movie clip with the pixels that are beneath it. It will then select the pixel color value that is lightest, and it will use that value in the movie clip to which the blend mode is applied. Or, if you apply the add blend mode, Flash Player adds the pixel color values and uses that value for the corresponding pixel in the movie clip to which the blend mode is applied. Blend modes enable effects where movie clips appear to merge with what is underneath it.

You can programmatically manage blend modes for movie clips using the `blendMode` property. The default value for the `blendMode` property is the string `normal`. Common `blendMode` values are as follows: `multiply`, `screen`, `lighten`, `darken`, `difference`, `add`, `subtract`, `invert`, `overlay`, `hardlight`. The Flash Help describes each blend mode in detail. You can refer to that documentation for detailed descriptions.

In this next task, you'll build an application that has a hidden message. The user can read the message by clicking a sequence of movie clips. Each of the movie clips, as well as the message, has blend modes applied to them to make interesting effects.

1. Open *message1.fla* from the Lesson09/Start directory.

The message1.fla Flash document has all the assets necessary to complete the task. On the main Timeline you'll see there are four layers: Actions, Click Areas, Message, and Background. On the Click Areas layer there are four movie clips with instance names of `clickArea1Clip`, `clickArea2Clip`, `clickArea3Clip`, and `clickArea4Clip`. Those movie clips will function as the clickable regions that are necessary to display the message.

On the Message layer is a movie clip with an instance name of `messageClip`. Within `messageClip` is a text field called `messageField`. The text field will display the message after the clickable regions are clicked in order. The text field is placed within a movie clip so that a blend mode can be applied to the text by way of the parent movie clip.

2. Select the keyframe on the Actions layer, and open the Actions panel by pressing F9. Add the following code to the script pane to make the clickable regions invisible to start:

```
clickArea1Clip._visible = false;
clickArea2Clip._visible = false;
clickArea3Clip._visible = false;
clickArea4Clip._visible = false;
```

To start each of the clickable regions needs to be invisible. After the message text has loaded from a text file, the first clickable region is made visible, and then each of the remaining regions is made visible in sequence as each is clicked.

3. Assign blend modes to each of the clickable regions using the following code:

```
clickArea1Clip.blendMode = "overlay";
clickArea2Clip.blendMode = "multiply";
clickArea3Clip.blendMode = "hardlight";
clickArea4Clip.blendMode = "difference";
```

Each of the clickable regions has a different blend mode in this example.

4. Make the message movie clip invisible and assign a blend mode to it as well using the following code:

```
messageClip._visible = false;
messageClip.blendMode = "difference";
```

The message movie clip also remains invisible until the clickable regions have been clicked in sequence. After the message movie clip is made visible, it ought to have a blend mode applied so that it combines with the background.

5. Assign button event handler methods to the clickable regions with the following code:

```
clickArea1Clip.onPress = function():Void {
   this._visible = false;
   clickArea2Clip._visible = true;
};

clickArea2Clip.onPress = function():Void {
   this._visible = false;
   clickArea3Clip._visible = true;
};

clickArea3Clip.onPress = function():Void {
   this._visible = false;
   clickArea4Clip._visible = true;
};

clickArea4Clip.onPress = function():Void {
   this._visible = false;
   messageClip._visible = true;
};
```

The preceding code is not nearly as difficult as it might look at first. Each of the onPress() event handler methods are very similar. Each makes the clickable region invisible after it is clicked, and it makes the next movie clip in the sequence visible. After clickArea4Clip is clicked, it causes the message movie clip to display.

6. Use a LoadVars object to load the message from *message.txt* (also located in Lesson09/Assets) with the following code:

```
var messageLv:LoadVars = new LoadVars();
messageLv.onData = function(messageText:String):Void {
  messageClip.messageField.text = messageText;
  clickArea1Clip._visible = true;
};
messageLv.load("message.txt");
```

The LoadVars object loads the text from message.txt. After the text loads the onData() method is called and passed a parameter with the context of the file. Assign the text to the messageField text field. When the text has loaded into the player, it's okay to make the first clickable region visible.

7. Test the movie.

When you test the movie, the first clickable region will display within a second or so depending on how much text is in the text file and whether you're loading the content locally or over the Internet. After the clickable region has appeared, click each region as prompted. After the fourth region, the message will display.

Introducing the Bitmap API

Flash Player 8 has a new class called BitmapData that you can use to work with bitmap data in many ways that were not possible with previous versions of Flash Player. For example, in this lesson you'll build an application that applies flood fills to a bitmap in order to make a coloring page program. You can also use BitmapData objects to get and set the values of each pixel, which you'll use in order to add a flexible color palette to the coloring page program.

The BitmapData class comprises what is often called the Bitmap API. The Bitmap API has quite an array of functionality. In this lesson we'll look at some of the more common features as well as how to get started.

The BitmapData class is in the flash.display package. That means that either you have to use the fully qualified class name when referencing the class or you need to import the class before using it. Using an import statement is often simpler and clearer than using the fully qualified class name every time you reference the class. Throughout the rest of this lesson we'll assume in every example that the following import statement precedes the example code:

```
import flash.display.BitmapData;
```

Constructing BitmapData Objects

There are two basic ways in which you can construct a BitmapData object. You can use the constructor method in a new statement, or you can use the static loadBitmap() method. Let's take a look at each of the two options, how they work, and when you'd use each option.

> **Tip** *In addition to the constructor method and the loadBitmap() method, you can also construct a new BitmapData object that is a duplicate of an existing object using the clone() method.*

The BitmapData constructor method requires, at minimum, two parameters specifying the width and height of the new BitmapData object. The following constructs a new object that is 200 pixels wide and 400 pixels high:

```
var exampleBmp:BitmapData = new BitmapData(200, 400);
```

The constructor accepts two additional parameters that specify whether the object supports transparency and what background color to use. By default, BitmapData objects support transparency, but the background is set to 0xFFFFFFFF, which is a 32-bit integer in the form of 0xAARRGGBB specifying a white, fully opaque background color. So although the object supports transparency, it has a white background. If you want to make the object truly transparent, set the background color to 0x00000000.

```
var exampleBmp.BitmapData = new BitmapData(200, 400, true, 0x00000000);
```

Use the BitmapData constructor when you want to build a new object for the purposes of adding content programmatically (adding noise, rectangular fills, copying content from movie clips, and so on). If you want to make a BitmapData object from a bitmap symbol in the library, however, you can simply use the static loadBitmap() method of the BitmapData class.

The loadBitmap() method requires just one parameter—a string specifying the linkage identifier of the bitmap symbol from which you want to make the new object. That means that you must set the bitmap symbol to Export For ActionScript and assign it a linkage identifier in the symbol's linkage properties. You can accomplish that much as you would for a movie clip symbol. Select the bitmap symbol in the library, open either the library menu or the symbol's context menu, and select Linkage. Then click the Export For ActionScript option and specify a linkage identifier. The following code makes a new BitmapData object from a bitmap symbol exported with a linkage identifier of Example:

```
var exampleBmp:BitmapData = BitmapData.loadBitmap("Example");
```

Displaying BitmapData Content

BitmapData objects aren't displayed by default. If you want to display the content from a BitmapData object, you have to use a movie clip object. You can call the attachBitmap() method from any movie clip object to add the content from a BitmapData within the movie clip. The method requires, at minimum, two parameters specifying the BitmapData object and the depth at which you want to attach the content within the movie clip. The following adds the content from exampleBmp to a movie clip called exampleClip:

```
exampleClip.attachBitmap(exampleBmp, exampleClip.getNextHighestDepth());
```

You can specify two additional parameters that determine how the content snaps to pixels and whether smoothing is applied. By default, bitmap content snaps to whole pixel values unless the content is scaled or rotated. That means that if a movie clip containing bitmap content is placed so that its x coordinate is at 40.1 on the Stage, the bitmap content will snap to 40. The default value for the snapping parameter is the string auto. You can also specify always if you want the bitmap content to snap to whole pixels regardless of whether it's scaled or rotated and you can specify never if you don't want the content to snap to pixels. The smoothing setting is false by default. That means that as the bitmap is scaled, it can appear pixelated. If smoothing is set to true, the pixelated appearance of scaled bitmap content is smoothed. The following code attaches bitmap content to exampleClip, specifying that it ought to always snap to whole pixels and that smoothing is enabled.

```
exampleClip.attachBitmap(exampleBmp, exampleClip.getNextHighestDepth(), ¬
"always", true);
```

Building a Coloring Page Program

In this next task you'll start building a coloring page program. The program displays line art to the user and it enables the user to select a color from a color palette and apply the color to a section of the page. To start, however, you'll simply attach the bitmaps from the library.

1. Open *coloringPage1.fla* from the Lesson09/Start directory.

The Flash document contains all the assets you'll need to get started with the program. You'll notice that there's nothing on the Stage. However, if you look in the library you'll see that there are several symbols that you'll be able to attach programmatically.

2. Set the ColorPalette, ColorSelector, and ColoringPage symbols to export for ActionScript. Use the default linkage identifiers of ColorPalette, ColorSelector, and ColoringPage.

You'll attach each of the symbols programmatically—ColorPalette using attachMovie(), and ColorSelector and ColoringPage using loadBitmap().

3. Select the keyframe on the Actions layer of the main Timeline and open the Actions panel by pressing F9. Add the following import statements to the script pane:

```
import flash.display.BitmapData;
import flash.filters.DropShadowFilter;
```

The program uses BitmapData for most of the functionality, so you'll want to import the class to simplify working with it. In addition, you'll add a drop shadow to the color palette, so import the DropShadowFilter class.

4. Load the bitmaps using the following code:

```
var coloringPageBmp:BitmapData = ¬
  BitmapData.loadBitmap("ColoringPage");
var colorSelectorBmp:BitmapData = ¬
  BitmapData.loadBitmap("ColorSelector");
```

The preceding code loads the ColoringPage and ColorSelector bitmaps into two new BitmapData objects. Remember, the bitmaps don't get displayed by default. For that you'll have to add the bitmap content to movie clips.

5. Add the coloring page bitmap content to a movie clip using the following code:

```
var coloringPageClip:MovieClip = ¬
  this.createEmptyMovieClip("coloringPageClip", ¬
  this.getNextHighestDepth());
coloringPageClip.attachBitmap(coloringPageBmp, ¬
  coloringPageClip.getNextHighestDepth());
```

The preceding code makes a new movie clip object called coloringPageClip. It then attaches the bitmap content from coloringPageBmp to the new movie clip so that it gets displayed. If you were to test the movie at this point you'd see the coloring page.

6. Add the color palette, and attach the color selector to it using the following code:

```
var colorPaletteClip:MovieClip = this.attachMovie("ColorPalette", ¬
  "colorPaletteClip", this.getNextHighestDepth());
colorPaletteClip.createEmptyMovieClip("selectorClip", ¬
  colorPaletteClip.getNextHighestDepth());
colorPaletteClip.selectorClip.attachBitmap(colorSelectorBmp, ¬
  colorPaletteClip.selectorClip.getNextHighestDepth());
colorPaletteClip.selectorClip._y = 40;
colorPaletteClip.selectorClip._x = colorPaletteClip._width / 2 - ¬
  colorPaletteClip.selectorClip._width / 2;
colorPaletteClip.filters = [new DropShadowFilter(10, 45, 0x000000, 50, 10, 10)];
```

The preceding code attaches an instance of the ColorPalette movie clip symbol and calls it colorPaletteClip. It then creates a new movie clip within colorPaletteClip and it attaches the bitmap content from colorSelectorBmp to the nested movie clip. The nested movie clip is necessary to center the bitmap content within the color palette. When attaching bitmap content to a movie clip, there is no option to translate the content. Because you want the color selector to appear centered within the color palette you need to add it to a nested movie clip which can be moved.

The color selector movie clip is placed just below the palette title bar, and it is centered horizontally. Then you add a drop shadow to the entire palette.

7. Test the movie.

When you test the movie, you'll see the coloring page as well as the color palette with the nested color selector.

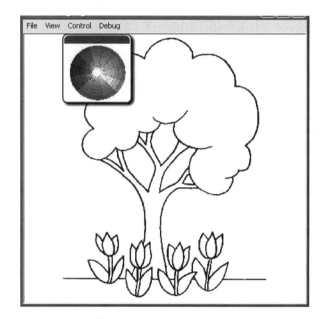

Applying Flood Fills

Flood fills are fills in which Flash Player applies a solid color to a contiguous region within a bitmap. A region is determined by specifying a pixel, and Flash Player then selects that pixel and every adjacent pixel with the same color value. You can apply flood fills to BitmapData objects using the floodFill() method. The method requires three parameters:

the *x* coordinate, the *y* coordinate, and the fill color in the form of 0xRRGGBB. For example, the following code applies a red fill to the contiguous region specified by the point 100,100 within exampleBmp.

```
exampleBmp.floodFill(100, 100, 0xFF0000);
```

Working with Pixels

You can get and set pixel values within BitmapData objects using the getPixel(), setPixel(), getPixel32(), and setPixel32() methods. The getPixel() and setPixel() methods use 24-bit integer values in the form of 0xRRGGBB. The getPixel32() and setPixel32() methods use 32-bit integer values in the form of 0xAARRGGBB. Otherwise, the two sets of methods work identically.

The getPixel() and getPixel32() methods require two parameters, specifying the *x* and *y* coordinates of the pixel within the bitmap content for which you want to retrieve the pixel value. The following code retrieves the 24-bit color value for the pixel at 100,400 within exampleBmp:

```
var pixelValue:Number = exampleBmp.getPixel(100, 400);
```

The setPixel() and setPixel32() methods require three parameters, specifying the *x* coordinate, the *y* coordinate, and the new pixel value. The following code sets the pixel at 100, 400 to red:

```
exampleBmp.setPixel(100, 400, 0xFF0000);
```

Continuing the Coloring Page Program

In this next task you'll add the coloring functionality to the coloring page program.

1. Open the Flash document completed from the previous task. Optionally, open *coloringPage2.fla* from Lesson09/Completed.

The Flash document contains all the necessary elements to complete the task.

2. Select the keyframe on the Actions layer of the main Timeline and open the Actions panel by pressing F9. Then, following the existing code, declare a new variable called selectedColor as follows:

```
var selectedColor:Number;
```

You'll use the selectedColor variable to store the color value that the user selects from the color selector.

3. Add an `onPress()` event handler method to `colorPaletteClip.selectorClip` so that it gets the pixel value from the color selector where the user clicks and assigns it to `selectedColor`.

```
colorPaletteClip.selectorClip.onPress = function():Void {
  selectedColor = colorSelectorBmp.getPixel(colorPaletteClip._xmouse - ¬
    colorPaletteClip.selectorClip._x, colorPaletteClip._ymouse - ¬
    colorPaletteClip.selectorClip._y);
};
```

The preceding code is fairly straightforward except that the x and y coordinates specified for `getPixel()` might not seem immediately clear. The x and y coordinates that you specify for `getPixel()` must be relative to the upper-right corner of the bitmap. In the case of the color selector, the x and y coordinates can be determined by the x and y coordinates of the mouse within `colorPaletteClip`. However, because `selectorClip` is translated within `colorPaletteClip` you have to subtract the x and y coordinates of `selectorClip` from the `_xmouse` and `_ymouse` values.

4. Make the color palette draggable with the following code:

```
colorPaletteClip.titleBarClip.onPress = function():Void {
  this._parent.startDrag();
};
colorPaletteClip.titleBarClip.onRelease = function():Void {
  this._parent.stopDrag();
};
colorPaletteClip.titleBarClip.onReleaseOutside = ¬
  colorPaletteClip.titleBarClip.onRelease;
```

The preceding code makes `colorPaletteClip` draggable when the user clicks and drags the nested title bar. Making the palette draggable is useful so that the user can move it around in order to color areas of the page that are covered by the palette.

5. Add the following code so that the selected color is applied as a flood fill to the color page when the user clicks it:

```
coloringPageClip.onPress = function():Void {
  if(coloringPageBmp.getPixel(_xmouse, _ymouse) == 0x000000) {
    return;
  }
  coloringPageBmp.floodFill(_xmouse, _ymouse, selectedColor);
};
```

The code initially checks to see whether the pixels at the point at which the user clicks are black. If so, Flash exits the function without applying the flood fill so the user doesn't inadvertently apply a color to the black outlines. Assuming that the user doesn't click the black outlines, the code uses floodFill() to apply the selected color to the coloring page.

6. Test the movie.

Drag the color palette around, select colors, and apply them to the coloring page.

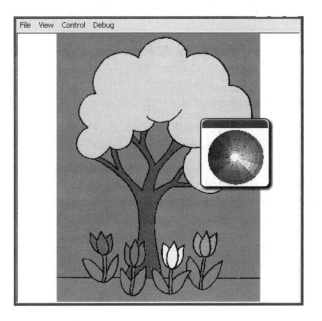

Copying Content

You can copy content from any BitmapData object, movie clip, or even video object to a BitmapData object using the draw() method. The draw() method requires at minimum two parameters that specify the object from which you want to copy the contents and a transform matrix to use when copying the content. To apply no transforms when copying the content, you can specify a flash.geom.Matrix object with the default values. The following code copies the content from the movie clip imageClip to exampleBmp (the code assumes that the flash.geom.Matrix class has been imported previously):

```
exampleBmp.draw(imageClip, new Matrix());
```

Copying content is particularly useful when you want to make a BitmapData object from an image loaded at runtime, as you'll see in the next task.

Completing the Coloring Page Program

In this task you'll complete the coloring page program so that it loads an image from a file at runtime, which makes it simple to update the line art without having to recompile the SWF file.

1. Open the Flash document you completed from the previous task. Optionally, open *coloringPage3.fla* **from the Lesson09/Completed directory.**

The document contains all the assets necessary to complete the program.

2. Select the keyframe on the Actions layer and open the Actions panel by pressing F9. Then add the following import statement immediately following the existing import statements:

```
import flash.geom.Matrix;
```

You'll use the Matrix class when copying the loaded image to a BitmapData object, so import it to simplify working with it.

3. Change the line of code in which you previously constructed the `coloringPageBmp` object. Declare the variable, but don't construct the object.

```
var coloringPageBmp:BitmapData;
```

In this task you're no longer loading the bitmap from the library. Instead you're loading it from a file at runtime. So you'll use `draw()` to copy the image to the BitmapData object and you can't construct the object until the image has loaded.

4. Add the following code to load the image from *Tree.gif* **(add the code just following the declaration of colorPaletteBmp):**

```
var imageTemporaryClip:MovieClip = ¬
   this.createEmptyMovieClip("imageTemporaryClip", ¬
   this.getNextHighestDepth());
var imageLoader:MovieClipLoader = new MovieClipLoader();
imageLoader.addListener(this);
imageLoader.loadClip("Tree.gif", imageTemporaryClip);
```

You'll use a MovieClipLoader object to load the image into an empty movie clip called imageTemporaryClip. Add the main Timeline as a listener object so it gets notified when the image loads.

5. Delete the line of code in which you previously attached the bitmap contents from `coloringPageBmp` to `coloringPageClip`.

Because the bitmap data doesn't exist until the image has loaded, you'll need to defer attaching the bitmap content to the movie clip until that point.

6. Add an `onLoadInit()` function that draws the image to the BitmapData object and attaches it to the movie clip.

```
function onLoadInit(imageClip:MovieClip):Void {
  coloringPageBmp = new BitmapData(imageClip._width, ¬
    imageClip._height, false, 0xFFFFFFFF);
  coloringPageBmp.draw(imageTemporaryClip, new Matrix());
  imageTemporaryClip._visible = false;
  coloringPageClip.attachBitmap(coloringPageBmp, 1);
}
```

The first step in the function is to construct the BitmapData object that has the same dimensions as the loaded image. Set the transparency to false so that even if the background of the loaded image is transparent, the background of the BitmapData object won't be transparent. After the object is constructed, use the `draw()` method to copy the contents of the movie clip containing the image. At that point, the `imageTemporaryClip` movie clip object doesn't need to be visible any longer.

7. Test the movie.

When you test the movie it ought to look and function much as it did in the previous version. However, this time the color page image is loaded from a file at runtime. So for the program to work properly, you'll have to make sure that Tree.gif (from Lesson09/Assets) is located in the same directory as the SWF file.

What You Have Learned

In this lesson you have:

- Used bitmap surface caching to optimize animation of complex vector artwork (pages 199–204)
- Used filters to add effects to a game causing three-dimensional beveling of objects, motion blurs, and collision effects (pages 204–214)
- Added blend modes to movie clips to make interesting effects (pages 214–217)
- Made a coloring page program using the Bitmap API (pages 218–227)

10 UI Components

Look at nearly any computer program, whether it's used for creating and managing a database or drawing illustrations, and you'll notice a number of interface elements common to those applications. You'll see similarities in buttons, scroll bars, drop-down boxes, sliders, and so on. These elements can be found in most applications because they are accepted and time-tested tools for allowing the user to interact with and receive information from the interface.

In most application development environments, such as Visual Studio .NET, the interface elements are preassembled, meaning that developers can simply drag an element such as a slider from a palette, drop it into the application being developed, and add some code to make the new element do something useful.

Of course, developers could create their own interface elements from scratch; however, many of these prebuilt elements are not only highly functional but also contain a number

Using components, we'll create a fairly sophisticated URL manager that dynamically responds to user interaction.

of inherently powerful capabilities that can easily be accessed with a relatively minimal amount of programming.

The Macromedia Flash authoring environment comes with its own prebuilt interface elements, called components. There are buttons, sliders, alert boxes, scrollable windows, menus, check boxes, and more. Components allow you to quickly and easily drag and drop complex interactive elements into your project. After you have the interface elements where you want them, you can use ActionScript to control the elements in a number of useful ways.

In this lesson, we'll use components extensively to create an application with a highly interactive user interface. Creating this application from scratch would take many days. Using components and ActionScript, however, you can put together the application in a fraction of that time.

What You Will Learn

In this lesson, you will:

- Learn how to set and get component property values
- Use component events to trigger scripts
- Use component methods to insert data dynamically
- Work with the FocusManager component to make a more usable application
- Style component instances individually and globally using ActionScript

Approximate Time

This lesson takes approximately two hours to complete.

Lesson Files

Media Files:

None

Starting File:

Lesson10/Start/Components1.fla

Completed Project:

Lesson10/Completed/Components6.fla

Components: A Scripting Primer

Because the focus of this book is ActionScript, our discussion in this lesson largely centers on how to work with and use Flash components from a scripting standpoint. For a more thorough overview of components, consult the documentation that comes with Flash.

A component is nothing more than a precompiled movie clip with some built-in functionality. Components can be customized using ActionScript in two ways:

- You add components to a project manually by dragging them onto the Stage within Flash's authoring environment via the Property inspector or Component inspector.
- You add components to a project dynamically using ActionScript while the movie plays.

When a component is added by either technique, you're actually placing an instance of that component type/class into your project. For example, if you drag and drop a CheckBox component onto the Stage in the authoring environment, that object is considered to be a CheckBox component instance. As when using other instances, you assign names to component instances; the instance name can be used in your scripts to communicate with that component instance.

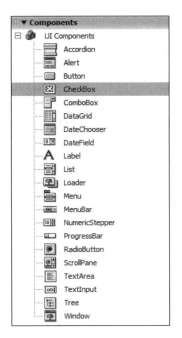

A number of *user interface components* ship with Flash. These components allow you to create forms and menus, or to display information and visual content in interactive ways.

Flash also ships with data components and media components. *Data components* provide a relatively easy way of working with the data in your application, especially sending and retrieving external data. *Media components* enable you to display and control the playback of media elements such as video and MP3 files. The primary focus of this lesson involves using and working with user interface components. You'll learn about media element component types in later lessons.

As you'll learn throughout this lesson, most components share some common functionalities and capabilities. As a result, the common ActionScript syntax works in the same way no matter what component instance you're scripting. At the same time, each type of component is built to be used for a specific purpose; thus, each type of component has some unique ActionScript commands.

Using ActionScript, you can do any of the following:

- Configure a component instance while your movie plays
- Tell the component instance to react to a specific event
- Retrieve data from a component instance
- Change the appearance of a component instance

In the exercises in this lesson, you'll implement each of these types of interactivity in the creation of a URL manager, which is used as a minidatabase for web, FTP, and email addresses. The result will be a highly interactive application, requiring relatively little scripting to make it work.

Configuring Component Properties

As you're well aware by now, most graphical elements used in a Flash application have configurable *properties* that ActionScript can access and change while the application is running. For example, movie clip instances have properties that allow you to change their position, rotation, and transparency. Because components are usually nothing more than enhanced movie clips, it's obvious that they, too, have configurable properties that can be accessed and changed while a movie plays; however, due to their enhanced nature, working with component properties is slightly different from working with standard movie clip instance properties.

Component properties can be categorized into two groups: properties that are common to all component instances (to Macromedia-based components, at least) and properties that are unique to each type of component. Let's look at both.

Note *You may have installed some third-party components that don't abide by the following guidelines. This discussion focuses on the use and capabilities of the components that come preinstalled with Flash.*

Common Properties

In Lesson 6, "Custom Classes," you learned about object-oriented programming. In this lesson, you put that information to use. How? Well, as already mentioned, most component instances have a set of common properties because most components inherit properties from the UIComponent class, which itself inherits properties from the UIObject class. Both of these classes are automatically and invisibly added to your project whenever you add a component instance. Let's break down this concept by looking at the Button component.

First, UIObject is a class that defines a number of properties:

```
UIObject.bottom
UIObject.left
UIObject.right
UIObject.scaleX
UIObject.scaleY
UIObject.top
UIObject.visible
UIObject.width
UIObject.x
UIObject.y
```

The programming that gives these properties meaning exists within the UIObject class definition.

Next, the UIComponent class is set up to extend (inherit) all the functionalities of the UIObject class. This means that any properties of the UIObject class become available as properties of the UIComponent class. But the UIComponent class doesn't just inherit all the properties of the UIObject class; it also defines some of its own:

```
UIComponent.enabled
UIComponent.tabIndex
```

As a final step, most component classes (CheckBox, Alert, RadioButton, and so on) inherit or extend the UIComponent class. This means that most component classes not only inherit the enabled and tabIndex properties of the UIComponent class, but also *all* of the properties of the UIObject class, because the UIComponent class extends the UIObject class. In the end, this means that most component instances you place in your project have the properties x, y, visible, top, bottom, enabled, tabIndex, and so on. Again, this entire inheritance process occurs invisibly whenever you place a component instance in a project.

Because most component instances share these common properties, it's easy to affect any component instance using a common syntax, as the following example demonstrates:

```
myButton_pb.enabled = false;
myRadioButton_rb.enabled = false;
myListBox_lb.enabled = false;
```

No matter what kind of component instance you're scripting—Button, RadioButton, or some other component instance—the enabled property is used in the same way and affects the component instance in the same manner across the board.

Component properties let you control various aspects of a component instance, including its size, position, and visibility; or they can be used to access property information pertaining to a particular component instance. For example, the following script assigns a value to myVariable based on the rightmost position of the component instance named myButton_pb:

```
var myVariable:Number = myButton_pb.right;
```

Component-Specific Properties

In addition to common properties, each component class has its own set of unique properties that allow you to work with an instance of that component class in specific ways. For example, the NumericStepper component class has properties named maximum, minimum, and stepSize. These properties have meaning only in the context of scripting NumericStepper instances. Attempting to use the stepSize property in relation to a RadioButton instance is an exercise in futility. It just won't do anything.

| Note | *There are too many component-specific properties to list here. For a complete listing of the properties of a component class, look up its entry in the ActionScript dictionary. Component-specific properties can also be found under each component listing in the Actions Toolbox section of the Actions panel.* |

Using ActionScript in the following exercise, you'll set the initial property settings for most of the components in an application.

1. Open *Components1.fla* in the Lesson10/Start folder.

This project contains three layers: Background, Components, and Actions. The Background layer contains all the noncomponent content in the project. This includes a static image of the URL manager's interface as well as two movie clip instances named currentWin_mc and newWin_mc. The Components layer contains all the components used in the project. A TextInput component instance named inputURL_ti accepts text input from the user; a List component instance named listURL_lb displays a list of items; three Button component instances, named addURL_pb, deleteURL_pb, and openURL_pb work similarly to buttons; and a couple of RadioButton component instances named currentWin_rb and newWin_rb work in the same manner as HTML radio buttons.

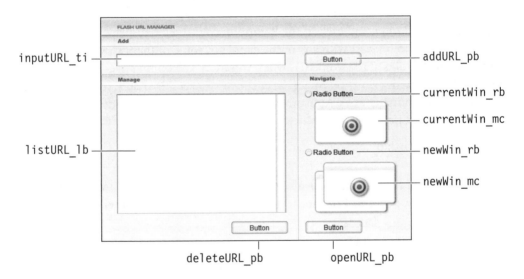

Although certain component instance properties can be configured within the authoring environment by using either the Component inspector or the Property inspector, the component instances in this project have been given only instance names. We'll use ActionScript to completely configure these instances, including their initial properties. Before you begin scripting, it's important for you to have a general idea of how this application will work.

When the application is finished and played within a browser window, the user can enter a URL (*www*, *ftp*, or *mailto*) into the inputURL_ti component instance and then click the addURL_pb component instance, which displays the URL in the listURL_lb component instance. All added URLs appear in the listURL_lb component instance. When the user selects a URL from the listURL_lb component instance, he or she has two choices: clicking the openURL_pb component instance opens the URL in either the current browser window or a new one (depending on whether the currentWin_rb or newWin_rb radio button is selected); clicking the deleteURL_pb component instance deletes the selected URL from the list. As the user interacts with the application, these various component instances are enabled and disabled dynamically, depending on the task the user is trying to accomplish. The finished application will have a few more capabilities, as you'll discover the further we progress.

To help you see how an unscripted version of the project looks and feels, let's do a quick test.

2. Choose Control > Test Movie.

Within the testing environment, notice that the application doesn't look any different now than it did in the authoring environment. All the Button component instances display the word *Button*, and each of the RadioButton instances displays the words *Radio Button*. If you try to interact with any of the elements, some of them glow green (dubbed haloGreen by the folks at Macromedia) when you move the pointer over the element or click it; otherwise, they don't do much. Over the next several exercises, this application will come to life in many ways. Along the way, you'll also be swapping the green glow effect for another effect.

We have a lot of work to do, so let's get started.

3. Close the test movie and return to the authoring environment. With the Actions panel open, select Frame 1 of the Actions layer and add the following script:

```
addURL_pb.label = "Add";
addURL_pb.enabled = false;
```

These two lines of script set the label and enabled properties of the addURL_pb Button component instance. The label property controls the text displayed on the button. Setting the enabled property to false *disables* the button. You can't interact with the button in this state; it appears dimmed, indicating to the user that the button is disabled, much like operating system interface elements appear in a disabled state.

The reason we're disabling this button initially is because it has no use until the user types a URL into the inputURL_ti TextInput component instance. When the movie first plays, that instance is devoid of any text; therefore, it makes sense that the addURL_pb instance should be disabled. Later, we'll add scripts that enable and disable this instance, depending on how the user interacts with the interface.

4. Add the following script at the end of the current script:

```
listURL_lb.enabled = false;
deleteURL_pb.label = "Delete";
deleteURL_pb.enabled = false;
openURL_pb.label = "Open";
openURL_pb.enabled = false;
```

These five lines of script do nearly the same thing as the two lines of script in Step 3 of this exercise. The first line disables the listURL_lb List component instance; the remaining four lines set the label values for and disable the deleteURL_pb and openURL_pb Button component instances, respectively.

5. Add the following script at the end of the current script:

```
newWin_rb.groupName = "windowOption";
currentWin_rb.groupName = "windowOption";
newWin_rb.label = "New Window";
newWin_rb.data = "_blank";
currentWin_rb.label = "Current Window";
currentWin_rb.data = "_self";
windowOption.enabled = false;
```

These seven lines of script set the initial properties of the two radio buttons named newWin_rb and currentWin_rb.

> **Note** *You may have noticed that the script in Step 5 sets the New Window button before setting the Current Window button, yet they appear in the opposite order in the application, with the Current Window button on top. Scripting is an abstract process that really has little to do with the way things are positioned on the stage.*

The first two lines set the groupName property for each radio button instance. Radio buttons in most programming environments (including Flash) are designed to work within groups. Clicking a particular radio button in the group automatically deselects the previously selected button in the group, thus allowing only a single radio button in the group to be selected at any time. To facilitate this functionality, each radio button must be associated with a group. The groupName property sets the association. Both of our application's RadioButton component instances are assigned to the windowOption group. This group didn't exist before and is created by using this script. As a result of associating the two RadioButton instances to the same group, only one can be selected at any time. The purpose of these instances is to allow the user to choose whether to open a URL in the current browser window or open a new window. This is important to remember as we discuss the remaining lines of the script.

Note By default, all RadioButton instances added to a project belong to the same group (named radioGroup). Therefore, the RadioButton component instances in our project initially had the single-selection functionality that we just discussed.

The next four lines set the `label` and `data` properties for the `newWin_rb` and `currentWin_rb` instances. Similar to the `label` property for Button component instances, the `label` property for RadioButton instances allows you to set the text that appears next to the instance. The `data` property lets you assign a value to the instance. This value is assigned to the group of which the instance is part whenever that instance is selected. This can be a tricky concept to understand, so let's look at it a bit more closely.

Remember that both of the RadioButton component instances are assigned to the `windowOption` group. Because the `newWin_rb` instance is given a `data` property value of "`_blank`", selecting that instance assigns that value as the `windowOption` group value. Thus, the following script assigns a value of "`_blank`" to `myVariable`:

```
var myVariable:String = windowOption.getValue();
```

The significance of this fact will be explained later in this lesson.

The last line in the script disables both the radio button instances. We could have disabled each instance individually using the following syntax, but we can easily disable all instances belonging to our group with a single line of code because they're both part of the `windowOption` group:

```
newWin_rb.enabled = false;
currentWin_rb.enabled = false;
```

As a result of the code we added so far, all the component instances within our project, except for `inputURL_ti`, will initially be disabled. The only interface elements left to disable are the two movie clip instances named `newWin_mc` and `currentWin_mc`, which are graphical elements associated with our radio buttons. We want these movie clip instances to always appear in the same state (enabled or disabled) as our radio buttons. Because they're movie clip instances and not component instances, they don't have built-in `enabled` properties that can be set. We can get around this limitation, however, with a function.

6. Add the following function definition at the end of the current script:

```
function enableWindowGraphics(mode:Boolean){
  if(mode){
    currentWin_mc._alpha = 100;
    newWin_mc._alpha = 100;
  }else{
    currentWin_mc._alpha = 30;
    newWin_mc._alpha = 30;
  }
}
```

This function, named enableWindowGraphics(), accepts a single parameter value of true or false. A conditional statement within the function checks this value when the function is called and makes the movie clip instances completely opaque if the function is true, but nearly transparent if it's false (which will cause the movie clip instances to appear dimmed, similar to a disabled component instance). This function is an acceptable substitute for the missing inherent enable property.

7. Add the following function call at the end of the current script:

```
enableWindowGraphics(false);
```

```
▼ Actions - Frame
1  addURL_pb.label = "Add";
2  addURL_pb.enabled = false;
3  listURL_lb.enabled = false;
4  deleteURL_pb.label = "Delete";
5  deleteURL_pb.enabled = false;
6  openURL_pb.label = "Open";
7  openURL_pb.enabled = false;
8  newWin_rb.groupName = "windowOption";
9  currentWin_rb.groupName = "windowOption";
10 newWin_rb.label = "New Window";
11 newWin_rb.data = "_blank";
12 currentWin_rb.label = "Current Window";
13 currentWin_rb.data = "_self";
14 windowOption.enabled = false;
15 function enableWindowGraphics(mode:Boolean){
16     if(mode){
17         currentWin_mc._alpha = 100;
18         newWin_mc._alpha = 100;
19     }else{
20         currentWin_mc._alpha = 30;
21         newWin_mc._alpha = 30;
22     }
23 }
24 enableWindowGraphics(false);
```

Actions : 1

Line 24 of 24, Col 29

This function call will cause our two movie clip instances to initially appear disabled, similar to the component instances we scripted in Steps 3–5.

Let's test our project up to this point.

8. Choose Control > Test Movie.

Several things occur as soon as the movie begins to play. Most of the interface elements are disabled initially, and the various component instances with `label` properties display the text labels we assigned to them.

As you can see from this exercise, working with properties of component instances is simple and straightforward.

9. Close the test movie and save your file as *Components2.fla*.

We'll continue building on this file in the exercises that follow.

Triggering Scripts Using Component Events

Users can interact with components in many ways. Depending on the component, users can type text into the component, click the component, select an item, and more. As with any interactivity such as this, it's important for your application to react according to what the user is doing. For example, if the user clicks a radio button, you might want your application to react to that selection by updating a variable's value or you might want to change the appearance of your application's interface. Fortunately, most components have several built-in events that can be used to trigger a script's execution, providing you with the flexibility to easily create highly interactive applications.

Similar to component properties, component *events* can be categorized into two groups: events that are common to most component instances and events that are unique to each type of component.

Common Events

As mentioned in our discussion of properties, most components inherit from the UIObject and UIComponent classes. Not only do those classes define properties that are available to most component instances but they also specify a number of events that as a result of inheritance are available to all component instances. Some of these common events include (but are not limited to) the following:

- move—Triggered when a component instance's *x* or *y* coordinates change
- focusIn—Triggered when a user interacts with a component instance in any way
- focusOut—Triggered when a user leaves a component instance and interacts with something else

Later in this lesson, you'll see how these events are used.

Component-Specific Events

In addition to the common events just discussed, most components have events relating to their specific functionality. Let's look at a couple of simple examples.

Button and RadioButton component instances react to click events, in addition to the common events previously discussed. A click event is fired when a Button component instance is pressed and released, or when a RadioButton instance is selected. When you think about it, these are not complex components; having such a simple event associated with them makes sense.

A component such as a ComboBox is a totally different story because it's designed to be interacted with in many ways. ComboBox component instances react to the following events:

- change—Triggered when the user selects a new item within the combo box
- close—Triggered when the drop-down box within the combo box begins to close
- open—Triggered when the drop-down box within the combo box is opened
- enter—Triggered when the user presses Enter after entering a value into the combo box
- scroll—Triggered when the list of items within the combo box is scrolled
- itemRollOver—Triggered when the user rolls the mouse over a list item
- itemRollOut—Triggered when the user rolls the mouse away from a list item

With such a wide range of available events, component instances become powerful tools in the creation of your applications.

Note *There are too many component-specific events to list here. For a complete listing of the events of a component class, look up its entry in the ActionScript dictionary. Component-specific events can be found under each component listing in the Actions Toolbox section of the Actions panel.*

Handling Events

There are a couple of ways to use component events in your scripts. You can use the on() handler, and you can also create Listener objects, as you learned about in Lesson 7, "Events, Listeners, and Callbacks." Let's first look at using the on() handler.

The on() handler allows you to script events directly on a component instance, much in the same way that you add scripts directly to button and movie clip instances. For example, if you select a ComboBox instance and open the Actions panel, you can attach the following script to that instance:

```
on (open) {
    trace("A ComboBox instance has been opened");
}
on (scroll) {
    trace("A ComboBox instance has been scrolled");
}
```

If you use the term this in this type of script, it's a reference to the component instance to which the script is attached. Look at the following example:

```
on (focusOut) {
    this._alpha = 50;
}
```

Assuming that this script is attached to a NumericStepper component instance, for example, its transparency will be set to 50% when the focusOut event occurs.

The preferred way of handling component events is to use Listener objects. Let's convert our previous sample scripts to the Listener model syntax:

```
var myComboBoxListener:Object = new Object();
myComboBoxListener.open = function(){
    trace("A ComboBox instance has been opened");
}
myComboBoxListener.scroll = function(){
    trace("A ComboBox instance has been scrolled");
}
```

These several lines of code create an object named myComboBoxListener and then script it to react to the open and scroll events. Now we have to register this Listener object with a particular ComboBox component instance. If we have a ComboBox instance named myCB_cb, the syntax would look similar to the following:

```
myCB_cb.addEventListener("open", myComboBoxListener);
myCB_cb.addEventListener("scroll", myComboBoxListener);
```

When myCB_cb is opened or scrolled, the open() or scroll() function of our Listener object is fired.

Note *A single Listener object can be registered to listen to any number of component instance events.*

Another way of scripting for component events involves using functions as Listeners. For example, suppose that you created the following function:

```
function myFunction(eventObj:Object){
   trace ("I'm a Listener too!");
}
```

You could script this function to be called whenever a particular event was fired by a particular component instance:

```
myCB_cb.addEventListener("open", myFunction);
```

Whenever the myCB_cb component instance triggers an open event, myFunction() is called and thus executed.

As mentioned in the discussion of the on() handler, use of the term this in either Listener object syntax or the syntax of functions that are used as Listener objects is a reference to the component instance that triggers the event.

You probably noticed within the parentheses of the myFunction Listener example the use of the syntax eventObj:Object.

When you use a Listener object or a function as a Listener, an *Event object* is passed to the specified handler script. This object usually contains two properties: type and target. The type property is a string reference to the event that was triggered; the target is a string reference to the target path of the component instance that fired the event. Using our previous ComboBox example, here's how an Event object is used.

Let's say we defined a Listener function and registered it to listen for open events triggered by myCB_cb, as shown here:

```
function myFunction(eventObj:Object){
    trace(eventObj.target);
    trace(eventObj.type);
}
myCB_cb.addEventListener("open", myFunction);
```

If the myCB_cb instance triggers an open event, the Output panel will open and display the following:

```
_level0.myCB_cb
open
```

Information provided by the Event object can be used in a conditional statement within the function to take appropriate action, depending on the event that has been triggered and the instance that triggered it, as the following example shows:

```
function myFunction(eventObj:Object){
    if(eventObj.target == "_level0.myCB_cb"){
        //actions
    }else if(eventObj.name == "_level0.myRadioButton_rb"){
        //actions
    }
    if(eventObj.type == "click"){
        //actions
    }
}
```

As you can see, using the properties of the Event object allows you to set up a single function to handle several events from several different component instances.

> **Note**   Some components, such as the MenuBar component, generate Event
> objects containing properties in addition to *target* and *name*. We'll discuss some
> of these properties in later lessons.

In the following exercise, we'll create several Listener objects and script them to listen to various events that are triggered by components in our project.

1. Open *Components2.fla*.

This project continues from where we left off in the preceding exercise.

We'll add all the scripts for this exercise to Frame 1 of the Timeline. The focus for this exercise is to create the framework for using component events via Listener objects. The Listener objects won't actually be scripted to do anything until the next exercise.

2. With the Actions panel open and Frame 1 selected, add the following script at the end of the current script:

```
var inputURL_tiListener:Object = new Object ();
inputURL_tiListener.focusIn = function () {
};
inputURL_ti.addEventListener ("focusIn", inputURL_tiListener);
```

The first line of this script creates an object named `inputURL_tiListener`. We'll use this object to listen for events generated by the TextInput component instance named `inputURL_ti`, which will be used in the application as an input field for new URLs.

The next two lines of script create a handler for the `focusIn` event. This handler will be scripted in the next exercise.

The last line of the script in this step registers the Listener object with the `inputURL_ti` instance. Any time this instance generates the `focusIn` event, our Listener object will be notified and will execute its handler for that event.

3. Add the following script at the end of the current script:

```
var addURL_pbListener:Object = new Object ();
addURL_pbListener.click = function () {
};
addURL_pb.addEventListener ("click", addURL_pbListener);
```

This script creates a Listener object for the addURL_pb PushButton component instance and sets it up to listen for any `click` events generated by that instance. The Listener object is registered with the addURL_pb instance.

4. Add the following script at the end of the current script:

```
var listURL_lbListener:Object = new Object ();
listURL_lbListener.focusIn = function () {
};
listURL_lb.addEventListener ("focusIn", listURL_lbListener);
var openURL_pbListener:Object = new Object ();
openURL_pbListener.click = function () {
};
```

continues on next page

```
openURL_pb.addEventListener ("click", openURL_pbListener);
var deleteURL_pbListener:Object = new Object ();
deleteURL_pbListener.click = function () {
};
deleteURL_pb.addEventListener ("click", deleteURL_pbListener);
```

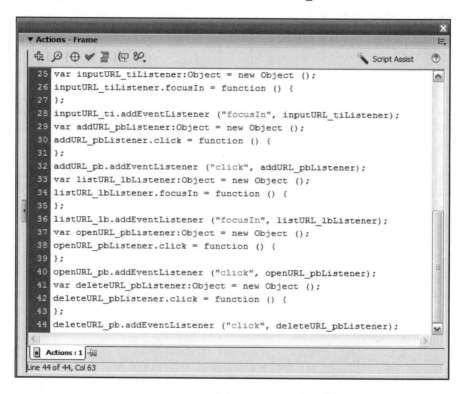

This creates three more Listener objects, which are registered to the listURL_lb, openURL_pb, and deleteURL_pb instances, respectively. Make a note of the events the objects are set up to handle because they are important for the next exercise.

5. Save this file as *Components3.fla*.

In this exercise, we created five Listener objects and registered them to listen for events generated by various component instances in our project. At this point, the event handlers attached to our Listener objects are not scripted to do anything, but we'll take of that in the next exercise.

Using Component Methods

As should be obvious by now, both the UIObject and UIComponent classes have methods that are inherited by all component instances. In addition, different component types have methods that are unique to themselves. For brevity, we'll mention only a few examples here before moving on to the exercise for this section.

Common Methods

The following methods are common to all component instances:

- move(x, y) moves a component instance to the specified *x* and *y* coordinates. For example: myButton_pb.move(100, 200);

- setSize(width, height) resizes a component instance to the specified width and height values. For example: myButton_pb.setSize(250, 150);

- getFocus() returns a value of the current object that has focus. For example, var myVariable:String = myButton_pb.getFocus(); assigns myVariable, a string value representing the name of the component instance that currently has focus.

- setFocus() sets the focus to a particular component instance. For example, myButton_pb.setFocus() gives focus to the myButton_pb instance.

> **Note** *For more information on what focus means and how it's used, see "Using the FocusManager Component" later in this lesson.*

There are other methods that are inherited by all instances, but these are the most common.

Component-Specific Methods

Although most components have methods specific to themselves, most of these methods are used to do one of the following:

- Add something to a component instance, such as a piece of data or a graphic

- Get (return) information about a component instance; for example, what item is currently selected in a combo box

- Tell (set) the component instance to do something such as scroll up or down, or highlight a specific piece of data

- Sort the component's data in a specific manner

> **Note** *There are too many component-specific methods to list here. For a complete listing of the methods of a component class, look up its entry in the ActionScript dictionary. Component-specific methods can be found under each component listing in the Actions Toolbox section of the Actions panel.*

In the following exercise, we'll use component methods to dynamically insert, delete, and manipulate the data within our List component as well as to dynamically insert icon graphics. In addition, we'll use component methods to control and communicate with several other component instances.

1. Open *Components3.fla*.

In the preceding exercise, we set up the framework for using component events via Listener objects; however, we didn't script our Listener objects to do anything when events were triggered. In this exercise, we'll insert scripts that cause the application to perform an action when these events occur.

2. With the Actions panel open and Frame 1 selected, insert the following script just below `inputURL_tiListener.focusIn = function () {`:

```
deleteURL_pb.enabled = false;
openURL_pb.enabled = false;
windowOption.enabled = false;
enableWindowGraphics(false);
addURL_pb.enabled = true;
```

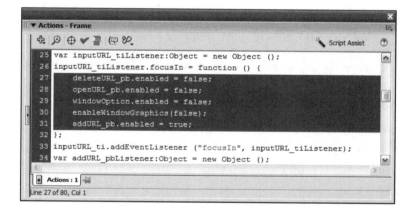

In the preceding exercise, we registered the `inputURL_tiListener` object to listen for the `focusIn` event in relation to the `inputURL_ti` component instance. The script we just inserted tells the Listener object what to do when this event occurs in relation to that instance. When the user clicks inside the `inputURL_ti` instance (gives it focus), this script will execute.

The purpose of this script is to reset various elements to their initial state. The `deleteURL_pb` and `openURL_pb` Button instances are disabled, the radio buttons within the `windowOption` group are disabled, the enableWindowGraphics() function is called (making the graphics associated with the radio buttons transparent), and the addURL_pb instance is enabled.

We're resetting these various elements to their initial states. Other scripts we'll add shortly will change these states as the user interacts with the application; this script places these elements into the appropriate state for inputting a new URL. This will become clearer as we progress.

It's important to understand that the addURL_pb button is enabled (as shown in the last line of the script) when the inputURL_ti instance is given focus for inputting a new URL. This occurs because the two instances work in tandem. When typing a URL, the user adds it to the list by clicking the addURL_pb button, requiring that instance to be enabled. We'll script the functionality that adds the URL in a moment, but first let's take a look at some of the items in the library that play an important role in one of the following steps.

3. Choose Window › Library to open the Library panel.

You'll find two folders within the library that contain movie elements, as well as four additional movie clips not contained within a folder. These movie clips represent icon graphics. Here's how they'll be used by our application.

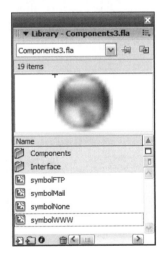

When the user enters a URL containing *www*, not only will that URL be added to the listURL_lb instance but our application will also be scripted to detect that a *www* address has been entered. The appropriate icon graphic will be shown next to the URL in the list, which in this case would be the movie clip named *symbolWWW*. If the user enters a URL containing *ftp*, the *symbolFTP* movie clip will be used. Entering *mailto* causes *symbolMail* to be used. If none of the aforementioned URL types is entered, our app will assume that an errant URL has been added, and the *symbolNone* movie clip will be shown next to that URL.

This functionality is made possible as the result of the capability of List component instances to dynamically attach icon graphics, which are nothing more than movie clips that have been given linkage identifier names. Let's look at how one of these movie clips is set up.

4. Right-click (Ctrl-click on a Macintosh) the symbolWWW movie clip in the library and choose Linkage from the menu that appears.

This opens the Linkage Properties dialog box, which shows that this movie clip has been given a linkage name of symbolWWW. (Yes, it's the same name as the movie clip itself; it was done this way for simplicity.)

The remaining three movie clips have also been given identifier names representative of their movie clip names. Giving movie clips identifier names allows us to dynamically insert them into our project as it plays, which is something we'll script next.

5. Click OK to close the Linkage Properties dialog box. With the Actions panel open, insert the following script just below `addURL_pbListener.click = function () {`:

```
listURL_lb.enabled = true;
listURL_lb.addItemAt (0, inputURL_ti.text);
listURL_lb.selectedIndex = 0;
listURL_lb.iconFunction = function (item:Object):String {
  var tempString:String = item.label;
  if (tempString.indexOf ("www.") >= 0) {
    return "symbolWWW";
  } else if (tempString.indexOf ("mailto:") >= 0) {
    return "symbolMail";
  } else if (tempString.indexOf ("ftp.") >= 0) {
    return "symbolFTP";
  } else {
    return "symbolNone";
  }
};
inputURL_ti.text = "";
```

Because this script is inserted within the click handler of the addURL_pbListener object, it gets executed when the addURL_pb instance is clicked. Let's look at how this script works.

The first line enables the listURL_lb instance, just in case it has been disabled (such as when the application is initially opened). The next line of script uses the addItemAt() method, which is available to List component instances. This method adds an item (line of information) to the specified List component instance, which in this case is the one named listURL_lb.

| Note | A disabled component cannot be manipulated by the user or via ActionScript.

To understand how this method works, you need to understand that each item displayed in a List component instance is actually an object with two properties named label and data. The label property holds a value representing the text displayed for the item; the data property is a hidden value associated with that label. For example, if you had a List component that displayed computer parts, the label property could be used to hold a text description of the piece of hardware, whereas the associated data property could be used to hold the associated part number (hidden from the user) like this:

```
label: Monitor data: Mon359a4
label: Keyboard data: Key4e94f
```

And so on.

If the user later selected one of these items from the list, you could use a script to retrieve either the label or data value of the selected item. The data item is the preferred choice because it contains more specific information; the label property is used mostly for readability. With this understanding, let's look at the syntax for using the addItemAt() method:

```
nameOfListInstance.addItemAt(index, label, data);
```

The index parameter indicates where in the list to add the new item, with 0 being the top of the list. The label parameter represents the text you want to display for the new item. The data parameter represents any hidden value you want to associate with the new item. The data parameter is optional, and omitting it will cause the label and data properties of the newly added item to contain the same value.

As you can see in the script we inserted, the method is set up to add a new item to index 0 (which again is the topmost position on the list), and the value assigned to the label property of this newly added item is the text currently displayed in the inputURL_ti instance (what the user has entered). Because we're not using the optional third parameter in the method call, the label and data properties contain the same value when the item is added to the list.

Tip *Items shown in List component instances have index numbers (beginning with 0), indicating their position in the list. Thus, the first item in the list has an index of 0, the second has an index value of 1, and so on.*

The third line of the script assigns a value to the selectedIndex property of the listURL_1b instance. This will set and highlight the item at index 0, which will always be any newly added item.

The next several lines of script set the iconFunction property of the listURL_1b instance. The value of this property specifies a function to execute when a new item is added to the list. This function is used to add an icon to the newly added item by returning a string value, representative of the identifier name of the icon to use (as discussed in Step 3). Let's look at how this function works.

When this function is executed, it's passed an object that we named item. This object has two properties named label and data. The values of these properties are the same as the label and data properties, as defined in the addItemAt() method call we just discussed. If our method call looked similar to the following, the object passed to iconFunction would have a label property value of "fruit" and a data property value of 47:

```
myList.addItemAt(0, "fruit", 47);
```

The value of one or both of these passed properties is used by the function to determine the name of the icon to attach.

The function's first action creates a variable named tempString. This variable is assigned a value based on the label property of the object passed to the function. If the user is adding the URL *www.derekfranklin.com*, for example, tempString will be assigned that URL as its value. Next, a series of conditional statements is used to determine whether the value contained in tempString includes *www.*, *mailto:*, *ftp.*, or none of these. As a result, the function will return a string value representing the linkage identifier name of the movie clip in the library to use.

```
var tempString:String = "www.derekfranklin.com"
if (tempString.indexOf ("www") >=0){
    return "symbolWWW";
}else if (tempString.indexOf ("mailto") >=0){
    return "symbolMail";
}else if (tempString.indexOf ("ftp") >=0){
    return "symbolFTP";
}else {
    return "symbolNone";
}
```

www.derekfranklin.com

The last line in the script clears the inputURL_ti instance of the URL the user has entered, allowing the user to quickly add another URL.

Let's test our project.

6. **Choose Control > Test Movie.**

When the application appears, click inside the inputURL_ti instance. Notice that the addURL_pb instance immediately becomes enabled, as scripted in Step 2. Enter a URL and click the Add button to enable the listURL_lb URL and add it to the list. The URL is highlighted, the appropriate icon is attached, and the inputURL_ti instance is cleared of text and ready for the next entry, as we scripted in Step 5.

Let's return to the authoring environment to add a few more scripts.

7. **Close the test movie to return to the authoring environment. With the Actions panel open and Frame 1 selected, insert the following script just below listURL_lbListener.focusIn = function () {:**

```
addURL_pb.enabled = false;
deleteURL_pb.enabled = true;
openURL_pb.enabled = true;
windowOption.enabled = true;
enableWindowGraphics(true);
```

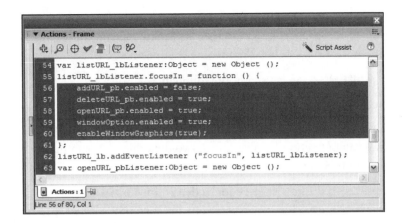

Because this script is inserted within the focusIn handler of the listURL_lbListener object, it gets executed when the listURL_lb instance is given focus (the user interacts with it). This script does nothing more than disable the addURL_pb instance while enabling the other elements specified within the script. The bottom half of our app comes to life as a result. These elements are enabled because they have a purpose when the user gives focus to the listURL_lb instance (selects a URL from it).

Let's test this functionality.

8. Choose Control > Test Movie.

When the application appears, enter a URL and then click the Add button to add the URL to the list. Next, click the URL you just entered in the list. When you do, all the elements in the bottom half of the application become enabled as a result of the script we added in Step 7. These enabled elements don't do anything yet, but that will change in a moment. If you click inside the inputURL_ti instance at this point to add another URL, the script we added in Step 2 is executed, resulting in the Add button being enabled and the elements in the bottom half of the application becoming disabled.

This interactivity is all being managed through component events that make creating a responsive application simple and straightforward.

Let's return to the authoring environment to script the Delete and Open buttons and wrap up this exercise.

9. Close the test movie to return to the authoring environment. With the Actions panel open and Frame 1 selected, insert the following script just below openURL_pbListener.click = function () {:

```
getURL (listURL_lb.value, windowOption.getValue ());
```

Because this script is inserted within the click handler of the openURL_pbListener object, it gets executed when the openURL_pb instance is clicked. As you can see, the getURL() action is used to perform a single task: opening the specified URL.

Typically, the getURL() action is used in the following manner:

```
getURL("http://www.derekfranklin.com", "_blank");
```

The first parameter specifies the URL to open; the second specifies the HTML target. Our use of the getURL() action involves using two dynamic values in place of hard-coded values, as shown in this sample script.

The URL parameter of the getURL() action is determined by looking at the current value of the listURL_lb instance. This property reflects the currently selected item in the instance. If the currently selected item is *http://www.electrotank.com*, that's considered the value of the instance.

The value of the second parameter of the getURL() action is derived by getting the current value of the windowOption radio button group. You'll remember that in the first exercise of this lesson, we assigned data values to both of the radio button instances in our application, with the top radio button instance being given a data value of _self and the other instance a data value of _blank. We then assigned both of those radio buttons to the windowOption group. Depending on which radio button is currently selected when this getURL() action is executed, the method call of windowOption.getValue() will return a value of either _self or _blank. This determines whether the specified URL is opened in the current browser window or a new one.

Note *URLs entered containing www must be preceded by http:// for the getURL() action to work properly.*

10. Insert the following script just below deleteURL_pbListener.click = function () {:

```
listURL_lb.removeItemAt (listURL_lb.selectedIndex);
listURL_lb.selectedIndex = listURL_lb.length - 1;
if (listURL_lb.length == 0) {
  deleteURL_pb.enabled = false;
  openURL_pb.enabled = false;
  windowOption.enabled = false;
  enableWindowGraphics(false);
  listURL_lb.enabled = false;
}
```

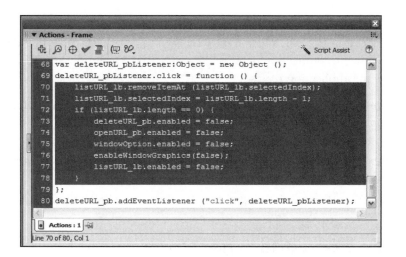

```
68  var deleteURL_pbListener:Object = new Object ();
69  deleteURL_pbListener.click = function () {
70      listURL_lb.removeItemAt (listURL_lb.selectedIndex);
71      listURL_lb.selectedIndex = listURL_lb.length - 1;
72      if (listURL_lb.length == 0) {
73          deleteURL_pb.enabled = false;
74          openURL_pb.enabled = false;
75          windowOption.enabled = false;
76          enableWindowGraphics(false);
77          listURL_lb.enabled = false;
78      }
79  };
80  deleteURL_pb.addEventListener ("click", deleteURL_pbListener);
```

Actions : 1

Line 70 of 80, Col 1

Because this script is inserted within the click handler of the deleteURL_pbListener object, it gets executed when the deleteURL_pb instance is clicked and takes care of deleting items from the list.

The first line of the script uses the removeItemAt() method to remove an item from the list contained in the listURL_lb instance. This method accepts a single parameter, representing the index number of the item to be deleted. In our use of this method, this index value is dynamically determined by retrieving the index of the currently selected item in the list. If the currently selected item in the list is fourth from the top, it will have an index value of 3. As a result, item 3 on the list is deleted.

The next line of the script sets the selectedIndex property of the listURL_lb instance to select and highlight the last item in the list after a deletion occurs. The value of this property is dynamically assigned by determining the length of the listURL_lb (how many items it contains) minus 1. If the instance contains 5 items, for example, after the deleted item is removed the instance length property will be 5 and the item selected will have an index of 4. The extra step of subtracting 1 is done because although the length property is determined with a count starting at 1 (one item in the list means a length of 1), index values start from 0 (the first item in the list has an index of 0). This functionality is added simply from a usability standpoint, allowing the user to continue clicking the Delete button, removing the last item in the list automatically.

The last part of this script uses a conditional statement to react in the event that all items in the list have been deleted. If this occurs, the actions within the statement again disable the elements in the application used for managing and navigating URLs because they have no meaning when no URLs exist.

Let's do one final test.

11. Choose Control › Test Movie.

When the application appears, add some URLs; then select a URL and either delete it or open it to see how the application handles these activities. Delete all the URLs from the list to see how the application reacts.

Component properties, events, and methods allow you to quickly create useful and responsive applications.

12. Close the test movie to return to the authoring environment. Save this file as *Components4.fla*.

In the sections that follow, we'll tweak the application's usability and appearance.

Using the FocusManager Component

One of the main goals of any good application is to make the user's experience as pleasant and straightforward as possible. A large part of accomplishing this goal involves anticipating the user's needs and making sure that your application allows users to accomplish tasks with minimal effort. For example, look at the process of doing a search on Google. When you navigate to Google's homepage, your cursor is automatically inserted in the Search box because they believe that your main purpose for visiting their site is to do a search. It's a simple thing, but it allows you to begin typing keywords as soon as the page loads, without having to first drag your mouse to place the cursor in the Search box manually.

What happens when you press Enter/Return? Because you've typed keywords into the Search box, pressing Enter/Return should submit your keywords to Google's search engine. Fortunately, it does. Imagine how awful it would be if pressing Enter/Return took you to their Help page. This would make using Google a real pain.

These kinds of simple anticipatory behaviors within an application are deliberately programmed by the developer as a way of making the application easier to use. Besides Google's homepage, you probably experienced similar functionality in other applications— especially those with dialog boxes in which pressing the Tab key allows you to quickly navigate from one field to the next.

Within Flash, these types of interactions are handled by the *FocusManager* component. Why is this component special? Because you never see it physically, unlike Button or CheckBox component instances. You can only see its effects—an invisible instance of the FocusManager component is automatically added to your project whenever you add a regular component instance. The FocusManager component takes care of managing focus-related tasks via ActionScript.

> **Note** | *Because the FocusManager component is invisible, it can't be configured using the Component inspector or Property inspector, as other component instances can. It can be configured and worked with only by using ActionScript.*

The term *focus* is simply a computer geek term meaning the object that's currently being manipulated. Type text into TextInput component instance, and it's said to have focus. Click a button; it has focus. Select a check box, and it has focus. Only a single item at a time in an application can have focus.

As you can see, what's considered as having focus in an application is constantly in flux. Normally, the user controls what has focus at any particular time due to the way he or she is interacting with the application. However, the FocusManager component gives you some control over the focus. Why would having control over the focus aspects of your application be helpful? Consider these scenarios.

Scenario 1

The user clicks a check box in your application, indicating that he or she wants to receive email about special offers. The FocusManager component enables you to automatically give focus to the TextInput instance, allowing the user to immediately begin typing an email address after selecting the check box—without having to manually move the cursor to the textbox. If the TextInput instance is named myTextInput_ti, it would be given focus using the following syntax:

```
focusManager.setFocus(myTextInput_ti);
```

Scenario 2

You want users to be able to press Enter/Return at any time, depending on the task they're trying to accomplish, and have Enter/Return simulate clicking the appropriate button. Because our sample application allows the user to enter an email address, chances are that there's a button on the interface that when clicked, will submit the address. Instead of making the user click the button, you can set the FocusManager's setDefaultButton property like this:

```
focusManager.defaultPushButton = mySubmitButton_pb;
```

As a result, the click event for the Button component instance mySubmitButton_pb will be triggered when the Enter/Return button on the keyboard is pressed. Any objects registered to listen for this event will be notified that it has occurred, thus executing any scripts set up to execute as a result of the event.

In the following exercise, we'll use the functionality that the FocusManager provides to make our application a bit more user-friendly in several ways, which we'll explain as we go along.

1. Open *Components4.fla*.

This project continues from where we left off in the preceding exercise. We'll insert several lines of code throughout the existing code on Frame 1.

2. With the Actions panel open and Frame 1 selected, insert the following line of script as the last line of the function that begins `inputURL_tiListener.focusIn = function () {`:

```
focusManager.defaultPushButton = addURL_pb;
```

Remember that this function handles what happens when the `inputURL_ti` instance is given focus. As a result of placing this line of script within this function definition, when the `inputURL_ti` instance is given focus the `addURL_pb` button becomes the default button when the Enter/Return key is pressed. This means that pressing the Enter/Return key triggers a `click` event, just as if the `addURL_pb` were actually clicked. The Listener object we have set up to listen for this event is notified that the event has occurred and takes action accordingly.

Let's do a test.

3. Choose Control › Test Movie.

When the application appears, click inside the `inputURL_ti` instance. The Add button (`addURL_pb`) will become highlighted, indicating that it's the default button. Type a URL, press the Return/Enter key, and the resukt is the same effect as manually clicking the Add button.

4. Close the test movie to return to the authoring environment. With the Actions panel open and Frame 1 selected, insert the following line of script as the last line *within* the conditional statement that's part of the function beginning `deleteURL_pbListener.click = function () {`:

```
focusManager.setFocus(inputURL_ti);
```

```
     ▼ Actions - Frame

     ⊕ ⊅ ⊕ ✔ ☰ (⊜ 80,                              ✎ Script Assist    ⑦

  69  var deleteURL_pbListener:Object = new Object ();
  70  deleteURL_pbListener.click = function () {
  71      listURL_lb.removeItemAt (listURL_lb.selectedIndex);
  72      listURL_lb.selectedIndex = listURL_lb.length - 1;
  73      if (listURL_lb.length == 0) {
  74          deleteURL_pb.enabled = false;
  75          openURL_pb.enabled = false;
  76          windowOption.enabled = false;
  77          enableWindowGraphics(false);
  78          listURL_lb.enabled = false;
  79          focusManager.setFocus(inputURL_ti);
  80      }
  81  };
  82  deleteURL_pb.addEventListener ("click", deleteURL_pbListener);

     ◉ Actions : 1 ⊣⋈
  Line 79 of 82, Col 1
```

When the `deleteURL_pb` instance is clicked for the purpose of deleting a URL from the list, the function to which we added this line of script is executed. The conditional part of the statement is executed only when the *last* URL in the list is deleted. Because this line of script was inserted within that conditional statement, it also is executed only when the last URL is deleted from the list. When the last URL is deleted from the list, the `inputURL_ti` instance is given focus, allowing the user to immediately begin entering new URLs without manually placing the cursor first.

5. Choose Control › Test Movie.

When the application appears, add some URLs; then begin deleting them. As soon as you delete the last one, the `inputURL_ti` instance is automatically given focus, allowing you to immediately add new URLs again.

> **Note** *The FocusManager component has additional functionality that can be explored by looking up its entry in the ActionScript dictionary.*

6. **Close the test movie to return to the authoring environment. Save this file as** *Components5.fla.*

Our application needs a bit of final visual tweaking, and we'll take care of it next.

Customizing UI Components with ActionScript

Let's face it—most coders couldn't care less about the design aspects of an application. They just want to see it work. However, there's no getting around the fact that in the real world, a great-looking application is just as important as a properly functioning one.

Because user interface components are visual elements, their appearance must fit in well with the overall design of your application. Fortunately, they have the built-in capability to be styled and customized in various ways using ActionScript. This allows you to easily change visual features such as colors, fonts, margins, and more.

> **Note** *The look of components can also be changed in more dramatic ways by using Flash's drawing tools to tinker with the graphical elements that make up a component. Because the focus of this book is ActionScript, in this section we'll look only at visual aspects that can be changed using a script.*

Following are some of the visual aspects of components that can be changed:

```
borderColor
fontSize
fontStyle
fontWeight
marginLeft
marginRight
textAlign
textDecoration
```

For a complete listing and definitions of style properties that can be changed, look for "Supported Styles" in Flash's Help documentation.

Components can be styled on several different levels, including individually and globally. Components can also be styled as a class (such as RadioButton, CheckBox, or Button) so that all instances of that class share the same attributes. Although this strategy might be useful in some cases, individual and global styling are likely to be more commonly used, so we'll focus on those techniques.

When an individual component instance is styled a certain way, only that instance's appearance changes. When components are styled globally, all component instances are affected.

Note *Individual styling changes applied to an instance will override global styling changes in relation to that instance.*

To set a style property for an individual component instance such as `fontSize`, you use the following syntax:

```
myComponentInstance.setStyle("fontSize", 14);
```

To set its border color, you use the following syntax:

```
myComponentInstance.setStyle("borderColor", 0x006633);
```

When setting color styles, which would include any style property whose name ends with *Color*, there is the built-in capability to use color names instead of hexadecimal values:

```
myComponentInstance.setStyle("borderColor", "green");
```

Note *Most common color names (black, red, green, blue, and so on) can be used. For greater versatility, use hex values. For more information about hex values, see Lesson 5, "Built-in Classes."*

Scripting global styling changes is similar to scripting individual components; however, instead of naming the individual component instance, you reference the global `style` object:

```
_global.style.setStyle("fontSize", 14);
```

This script will cause all component instances to use a font size of 14.

In the following exercise, we'll use both individual and global styling to give our application its final beautiful appearance.

1. Open *Components5.fla*.

This project continues from where we left off in the preceding exercise. We'll insert several lines of code at the end of the existing code on Frame 1.

2. With the Actions panel open and Frame 1 selected, add the following script at the end of the current script:

```
listURL_lb.setStyle("fontStyle", "italic");
listURL_lb.setStyle("color", 0x006699);
```

These two lines of script set the fontStyle and color properties of the listURL_lb instance. Setting the fontStyle property to italic causes text in the component to appear italicized; the color property determines the color of the text. Yes, it seems as though the property for changing the font color should be called fontColor, but it's not. It's simply color.

> **Note** For items in a List component instance, the color property refers to the color of text when the item is not selected.

3. Add this script at the end of the current script:

```
deleteURL_pb.setStyle("color", 0x990000);
openURL_pb.setStyle("fontWeight", "bold");
```

The first line causes the text on the Delete button to appear red, as a proper Delete button should. The next line boldfaces the text on the Open button.

One more global change and our application will be finished.

4. Add the following line of script at the end of the current script:

```
_global.style.setStyle("themeColor", "haloOrange");
```

```
68  openURL_pb.addEventListener ("click", openURL_pbListener);
69  var deleteURL_pbListener:Object = new Object ();
70  deleteURL_pbListener.click = function () {
71      listURL_lb.removeItemAt (listURL_lb.selectedIndex);
72      listURL_lb.selectedIndex = listURL_lb.length - 1;
73      if (listURL_lb.length == 0) {
74          deleteURL_pb.enabled = false;
75          openURL_pb.enabled = false;
76          windowOption.enabled = false;
77          enableWindowGraphics (false);
78          listURL_lb.enabled = false;
79          focusManager.setFocus (inputURL_ti);
80      }
81  };
82  deleteURL_pb.addEventListener ("click", deleteURL_pbListener);
83  listURL_lb.setStyle("fontStyle", "italic");
84  listURL_lb.setStyle("color", 0x006699);
85  deleteURL_pb.setStyle("color", 0x990000);
86  openURL_pb.setStyle("fontWeight", "bold");
87  _global.style.setStyle("themeColor", "haloOrange");
```

Actions : 1

Line 87 of 88, Col 1

As you probably noticed during the testing phases of this project, all the component instances are highlighted in a greenish tint whenever you interact with them. This tint is known as haloGreen. With this line of script, we set the global themeColor property of all component instances to haloOrange, causing them to take on an orange tint when you interact with them.

Tip *A third possible value for this property is haloBlue.*

Time for one final test.

5. Choose Control › Test Movie.

When the application appears, you'll notice that the Add button glows orange when manipulated. Add some URLs. As you interact with the other elements, they also glow orange. In addition, the word Delete appears on the Delete button in red, and the word Open appears bold on the Open button. Items in the URL list appear italicized at all times, in addition to appearing blue when not selected.

This is just a small sampling of the dozens of style changes that can be made using ActionScript.

6. Close the test movie to return to the authoring environment. Save this file as Components6.fla.

This step completes this exercise and the lesson.

What You Have Learned

In this lesson, you have:

- Learned how to set and get component property values (pages 231–240)
- Used component events to trigger scripts (pages 240–246)
- Used component methods to insert data dynamically (pages 247–258)
- Worked with the FocusManager component to make a more usable application (pages 258–262)
- Styled components instances individually and globally using ActionScript (pages 262–265)

11 Advanced Object-Oriented Design

Basic object-oriented design requires that you learn the basic syntax of a class. You learned how to write a class in Lesson 6, "Custom Classes." However, learning just the basic syntax is just the start. After you start building applications with classes, you'll likely run into some common pitfalls such as incorrect scope or how to notify objects when an event occurs. In this lesson, you'll learn how to work with practical object-oriented design solutions.

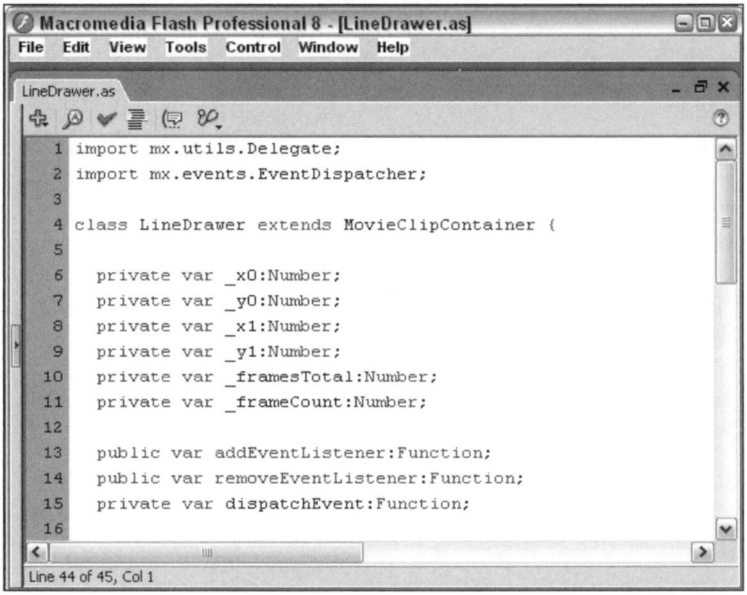

```
🎬 Macromedia Flash Professional 8 - [LineDrawer.as]          _ □ ✕
File   Edit   View   Tools   Control   Window   Help

LineDrawer.as                                                _ ⊟ ✕
⊕ �🔎 ✔ ≣ (⊟ 𝒮.                                                 ⑦
  1  import mx.utils.Delegate;
  2  import mx.events.EventDispatcher;
  3
  4  class LineDrawer extends MovieClipContainer {
  5
  6      private var _x0:Number;
  7      private var _y0:Number;
  8      private var _x1:Number;
  9      private var _y1:Number;
 10      private var _framesTotal:Number;
 11      private var _frameCount:Number;
 12
 13      public var addEventListener:Function;
 14      public var removeEventListener:Function;
 15      private var dispatchEvent:Function;
 16

Line 44 of 45, Col 1
```

Learn to build classes using delegation, inheritance, composition, and event dispatching

What You Will Learn

In this lesson you will:

- Learn how to correct scope issues that occur in classes
- Write classes that use encapsulation
- Work with composition
- Dispatch events

Approximate Time

This lesson takes approximately an hour to complete.

Lesson Files

Media Files:

Lesson11/Assets/lorem.txt

Starting Files:

Lesson11/Start/textLoader1.fla

Completed Projects:

Lesson11/Completed/textLoader2.fla
Lesson11/Completed/TextLoader.as
Lesson11/Completed/rectangle1.fla
Lesson11/Completed/rectangle2.fla
Lesson11/Completed/Rectangle.as
Lesson11/Completed/MovieClipContainer.as
Lesson11/Completed/DraggableRectangle.as
Lesson11/Completed/lineDrawer1.fla
Lesson11/Completed/lineDrawer2.fla
Lesson11/Completed/LineDrawer.as

Correcting Scope Errors with Delegate

There are many classes in ActionScript that use the callback event handler method style. For example, MovieClip uses callback methods such as onPress() and onRelease() to handle mouse events, and LoadVars uses onLoad() and onData() to get notifications when the data has loaded. When you use an instance of such a class as a property of a custom class, it is quite likely that you'll run into scope issues. Let's look at an example.

Consider the following class that defines a LoadVars object as a property. It adds an onData() method to the LoadVars instance so that it can get a notification when the data loads. When the data loads, it attempts to assign the text to a private property of the class.

```
class Example {
  private var _textLoader:LoadVars;
  private var _text:String;

  public function get text():String {
    return _text;
  }

  public function Example() {
    _textLoader = new LoadVars();
    _textLoader.onData = function(data:String):Void {
      _text = data;
    };
    _textLoader.load("file.txt");
  }

}
```

Although the preceding code might seem logical, it does not work as intended. When the data loads, Macromedia Flash will call the onData() method of the LoadVars property. However, within the onData() method it attempts to reference _text, which is declared as a property of the Example class. Because the onData() method is a method of _textLoader, it is scoped to _textLoader, not to the instance of the Example class. That means that when onData() gets called, it doesn't know what _text is, so it won't correctly assign the data to the private property of the Example instance.

The most obvious solution is to define the onData() method as a method of the Example class. The following code illustrates how that might look:

```
class Example {
  private var _textLoader:LoadVars;
  private var _text:String;

  public function get text():String {
    return _text;
  }

  public function Example() {
    _textLoader = new LoadVars();
    _textLoader.onData = onText;
    _textLoader.load("file.txt");
  }

  private function onText(data:String):Void {
    _text = data;
  }
}
```

Although the preceding rewrite appears to be different from the first example, it works in exactly the same way. ActionScript 2.0 is a prototype-based language, so when a function reference is assigned to a callback for an object, the function is always called as a method of the object to which the reference was assigned. Even though onText() is defined as a method of Example, when it gets called as a callback of _textLoader it is called as a method of that object, and the same scope issue exists as previously.

The solution is to use a class called mx.utils.Delegate. The Delegate class defines a static method, create(), which returns a function that will call a specified function with the correct scope. The create() method requires two parameters: the object to which you want the function call scoped and the function. The following code rewrites the Example class with the Delegate.create() method so that when onText() is called, it is called as a method of the Example instance:

```
import mx.utils.Delegate;

class Example {
  private var _textLoader:LoadVars;
  private var _text:String;

  public function get text():String {
    return _text;
  }
```

```
public function Example() {
  _textLoader = new LoadVars();
  _textLoader.onData = Delegate.create(this, onText);
  _textLoader.load("file.txt");
}
private function onText(data:String):Void {
  _text = data;
}
}
```

You can use the Delegate.create() method to correct scope issues with any callback method. For example, you can assign the return value from Delegate.create() to the onPress() method of a movie clip. You can even use Delegate.create() when registering listeners to component instances via the addEventListener() method.

In this task you'll build a text loader component that uses Delegate.create().

1. Open *textLoader1.fla* from the Lesson11/Start directory.

The Flash document has a movie clip symbol called TextLoader, which has a nested TextArea instance with an instance name of _textArea. There's an instance of TextLoader on the stage. Initially, the TextLoader instance merely displays the TextArea instance. However, after you complete the following steps, it will load text from a text file and display it in the TextArea.

2. Open a new ActionScript file and add the following class declaration:

```
class TextLoader extends MovieClip {

}
```

Because the TextLoader class is to be associated with a movie clip symbol, it needs to subclass MovieClip.

3. Add two import statements to the top of the code to import the mx.controls.TextArea and mx.utils.Delegate classes.

```
import mx.controls.TextArea;
import mx.utils.Delegate;
```

The class needs to reference the nested TextArea instance, so it needs to import the TextArea class. And it needs to import Delegate so that it can call the create() method.

4. Define the following private properties for the class.

```
private var _textArea:TextArea;
private var _textUrl:String;
private var _loadVars:LoadVars;
```

The _textArea property references the nested TextArea. The _textUrl property is to store the URL to the text file. The _loadVars property is to reference the LoadVars object that loads the text.

5. Define an inspectable setter method called **textUrl** that sets the value of _textUrl.

```
[Inspectable]
public function set textUrl(url:String):Void {
  _textUrl = url;
}
```

The textUrl setter method simply assigns a value to the _textUrl property.

6. Define the constructor so that when the object is constructed it instantiates a new LoadVars object, adds an **onData()** callback, and loads the data from the URL specified by _textUrl.

```
public function TextLoader() {
  _loadVars = new LoadVars();
  _loadVars.onData = Delegate.create(this, onText);
  _loadVars.load(_textUrl);
}
```

The constructor loads the text from the URL specified by _textUrl, and it tells Flash to call onText() when the data loads.

7. Define the **onText()** method such that when the data is loaded it is assigned to the TextArea.

```
private function onText(data:String):Void {
  _textArea.text = data;
}
```

When the data loads and the onText() method is called, assign the loaded text to the TextArea.

8. Save the ActionScript file as *TextLoader.as* in the same directory as the Flash document.

The class needs to be in a directory that's part of the classpath so that Flash can locate it.

9. Open the library in the Flash document and open the Linkage Properties dialog box for the TextLoader symbol. Select the Export For ActionScript option, and assign TextLoader to the AS 2.0 Class field. Then click OK.

The Linkage Properties dialog box lets you associate an ActionScript class with a symbol. In this case, you're associating the TextLoader class with the TextLoader symbol. So when an instance is placed on stage, the TextLoader constructor is automatically called.

10. Open the Component Definition dialog box for the TextLoader symbol. Set the AS 2.0 Class field to TextLoader, and click OK.

The Component Definition dialog box lets you tell Flash what ActionScript class to use for the inspectable properties. In this case the TextLoader class defines one inspectable property: textUrl.

11. If necessary, copy *lorem.txt* from the Lesson11/Assets directory to the directory in which you saved the Flash document. Then select the TextLoader instance on the stage, and from the Component inspector panel, set the textUrl parameter to *lorem.txt*.

The lorex.txt document contains text that you can use to test the class. When you set the textUrl parameter to lorem.txt, it will attempt to load the text from that file when you test the movie.

12. Test the movie.

You'll see the text loaded into the TextArea instance.

File View Control Debug

Lorem ipsum dolor sit amet, consectetuer adipiscing elit. Etiam nunc est, dignissim nec, varius eu, commodo sit amet, quam. Donec pulvinar, enim egestas dignissim sagittis, dolor tellus rhoncus felis, ac facilisis elit est vitae tellus. Sed lectus ligula, convallis vel, dictum ut, sollicitudin vitae, elit. Class aptent taciti sociosqu ad litora torquent per conubia nostra, per inceptos hymenaeos. Pellentesque leo. Integer posuere venenatis ante. Ut placerat rutrum magna. Class aptent taciti sociosqu ad litora torquent per conubia nostra, per inceptos hymenaeos. Proin massa. Aliquam sapien pede, tempor a, adipiscing eu, fringilla vel, quam. Morbi vel turpis.

Curabitur ut neque. Fusce et eros. Phasellus aliquet. Vivamus eu erat. Morbi quis pede quis pede sollicitudin venenatis. In convallis molestie odio. In consequat leo quis mi. Morbi eget magna laoreet ligula rhoncus gravida. Vestibulum arcu urna, dapibus in, ornare sit amet, feugiat id, urna. Etiam fringilla pellentesque neque. Mauris id velit.

Understanding Encapsulation

A basic principle of object-oriented design is encapsulation, which means that a class hides the internals while providing a robust and flexible public API (meaning properties and methods) by which it can interact. The benefit of good encapsulation is flexibility and scalability. When one class can peer into and interface directly with the code of a different class, it makes for very rigid designs. If any part of a class's internal code changes, it could potentially break the entire application in such a scenario. However, when all classes interface only by way of a public API, as long as the public API remains the same, the internal code of the classes can change without necessarily breaking anything. That means greater flexibility.

Although the basic principles of good encapsulation are fairly obvious and even intuitive, there are some common errors that programmers make with regard to encapsulation. Those common errors generally involve absolute references within the class such as _root or _global. Although there are exceptions, it is very unlikely that _root or _global should appear within a class.

Applying Composition

The relationship that classes have can be generally grouped into "is a" and "has a" categories. When a class has an "is a" relationship with another class, we call that inheritance. (Inheritance is discussed in Lesson 6.) Inheritance is appropriate in many cases. For example, to use the ever-popular car example, a car is a vehicle. Therefore, if a Vehicle class exists, it would be appropriate for a Car class to subclass it. However, inheritance is frequently used when inappropriate. To continue with the car example, a car has a wheel. It would be an obvious mistake to say that a car is a wheel. Yet a frequent programming mistake is to try to define inheritance relationships when they are not appropriate. When a class has an instance of another class, we call that composition. Therefore, in a composition relationship, a Car class has a Wheel (or four) property. As you can likely see, inheritance and composition are not necessarily at odds with one another. For example, a Car class can have an inheritance relationship with a Vehicle class and a composition relationship with the Wheel class.

Some composition relationships are obvious. Some composition relationships are established because they are necessary given the way that Flash and ActionScript work. One such example is necessary because of the way in which the MovieClip class works. There are many scenarios in which you want to write a class that would seem to have an "is a" inheritance relationship with MovieClip. However, when you want to subclass MovieClip, you have to associate the class with a symbol in the library. Then you cannot construct an instance of the class with the constructor. Instead, you have to use `attachMovie()` to add an instance of the symbol. In some cases, that is okay, but in some cases that presents some obstacles to good workflow and design. Instead, it can be beneficial to write a class that uses composition rather than inheritance. In such cases the class has a MovieClip instance property. In this task, you'll see an example of that.

There are many cases in which you'll potentially want to draw a rectangle within an empty movie clip. This scenario presents a perfect case for using composition. If you wanted to use inheritance you'd have to have an empty movie clip symbol with which to associate the class. You'd then have to add instances of the class with `attachMovie()`. A much more intuitive API would be once in which you can simply call the class constructor. Composition makes that possible. In this task, you'll write a Rectangle class that draws a rectangle in a new movie clip.

1. Open a new ActionScript file, save it as *Rectangle.as*, and add the following class declaration:

```
class Rectangle {

}
```

Notice that the Rectangle class does not subclass MovieClip because it uses composition rather than inheritance.

2. Define a private MovieClip property called _target.

```
private var _target:MovieClip;
```

The MovieClip property is the movie clip that the Rectangle wraps.

3. Define the constructor so it constructs a new empty movie clip.

```
public function Rectangle(parent:MovieClip, width:Number, ¬
  height:Number, color:Number) {
  var depth:Number = parent.getNextHighestDepth();
  _target = parent.createEmptyMovieClip("clip" + depth, depth);
}
```

The Rectangle constructor accepts four parameters. The `parent` parameter is the movie clip within which to construct the target empty movie clip. The `width`, `height`, and `color` parameters determine how to draw the rectangle (see the next step.) Then use `createEmptyMovieClip()` to add the new empty movie clip.

4. Draw a rectangle using the Drawing API.

```
public function Rectangle(parent:MovieClip, width:Number, ¬
    height:Number, color:Number) {
  var depth:Number = parent.getNextHighestDepth();
  _target = parent.createEmptyMovieClip("clip" + depth, depth);
  _target.lineStyle(0, 0, 0);
  _target.beginFill(color, 100);
  _target.lineTo(width, 0);
  _target.lineTo(width, height);
  _target.lineTo(0, height);
  _target.lineTo(0, 0);
  _target.endFill();
}
```

Draw the rectangle using the width, height, and color specified by the parameters.

5. Open a new Flash document and save it as *rectangle1.fla* in the same directory as *Rectangle.as*.

This is the Flash document you'll use to test the Rectangle class.

6. Select the first keyframe and open the Actions panel. Then add the following code to the Script pane:

```
var rectangle:Rectangle = new Rectangle(this, 550, 400, 0x00FFFF);
```

The preceding code constructs a new Rectangle class that adds a movie clip nested within the main movie clip (this) that is 550 pixels by 400 pixels with a cyan color.

7. Test the movie.

You'll see a cyan rectangle that fills the stage.

Using Composition and Inheritance Together

Inheritance and composition aren't in opposition; they can work together. In this next task, you'll build a more generic superclass, MovieClipContainer, which wraps much of the MovieClip class API. Then, you'll rewrite Rectangle to extend MovieClipContainer. Additionally, you'll write a DraggableRectangle class that subclasses Rectangle.

1. Open a new ActionScript document and save it as *MovieClipContainer.as* in the same directory as *Rectangle.as*. Then add the following class declaration:

```
class MovieClipContainer {

}
```

You'll abstract some of the basic functionality from Rectangle and move it to MovieClipContainer. As with Rectangle, note that MovieClipContainer does not subclass MovieClip.

2. Define a private MovieClip property called _target.

```
private var _target:MovieClip;
```

The MovieClip property is the movie clip that the MovieClipContainer wraps.

3. Define the constructor so that it constructs a new empty movie clip.

```
public function MovieClipContainer(parent:MovieClip) {
  var depth:Number = parent.getNextHighestDepth();
  _target = parent.createEmptyMovieClip("clip" + depth, depth);
}
```

The MovieClipContainer constructor consists of some of the code that was defined in Rectangle. Specifically, when you construct a MovieClipContainer instance, it adds a new empty movie clip to the specified parent.

4. Define getters and setters for some of the basic properties normally defined by the MovieClip class. For each, simply proxy the requests to the corresponding property of the _target property.

```
public function get _x():Number {
  return _target._x;
}

public function set _x(x:Number):Void {
  _target._x = x;
}

public function get _y():Number {
  return _target._y;
}
```

continues on next page

```
  public function set _y(y:Number):Void {
    _target._y = y;
  }
  public function get _alpha():Number {
    return _target._alpha;
  }
  public function set _alpha(alpha:Number):Void {
    _target._alpha = alpha;
  }
    public function get _rotation():Number {
    return _target._rotation;
  }
  public function set _rotation(rotation:Number):Void {
    _target._rotation = rotation;
  }
  public function get _width():Number {
    return _target._width;
  }
  public function set width(width:Number):Void {
    _target._width = width;
  }
  public function get _height():Number {
    return _target._height;
  }
  public function set _height(height:Number):Void {
    _target._height = height;
  }
```

Each of the getters and setters corresponds to basic properties from the MovieClip class. When you call a getter or setter for an instance of the MovieClipContainer class, it proxies the request to the corresponding property for the target movie clip. For example, when you set _x for a MovieClipContainer, it proxies that to the _x property of the target movie clip.

5. Edit *Rectangle.as*, make it subclass MovieClipContainer, delete the _target property declaration, and replace the first two lines of code in the constructor with a call to the superclass constructor. The new Rectangle class looks like the following:

```
class Rectangle extends MovieClipContainer {

    public function Rectangle(parent:MovieClip, width:Number, height:Number, ¬
        color:Number) {
        super(parent);
        _target.lineStyle(0, 0, 0);
        _target.beginFill(color, 100);
        _target.lineTo(width, 0);
        _target.lineTo(width, height);
        _target.lineTo(0, height);
        _target.lineTo(0, 0);
        _target.endFill();
    }

}
```

Now that Rectangle subclasses MovieClipContainer, it no longer needs to have a _target property or add the new empty movie clip because the superclass takes care of those things.

6. Open a new ActionScript file, and save it as *DraggableRectangle.as* in the same directory as *Rectangle.as* and *MovieClipContainer.as*. Add the following class declaration:

```
class DraggableRectangle extends Rectangle {

}
```

DraggableRectangle subclasses Rectangle so it inherits from both Rectangle and MovieClipContainer.

7. Add the following import statement to the top of the class:

```
import mx.utils.Delegate;
```

To correct scope issues you'll want to use Delegate.

8. Define the constructor.

```
public function DraggableRectangle(parent:MovieClip, width:Number, ¬
    height:Number, color:Number) {
    super(parent, width, height, color);
}
```

DraggableRectangle needs to call the superclass constructor to create the empty movie clip and draw the rectangle.

9. Within the constructor, define the `onPress()`, `onRelease()`, and `onReleaseOutside()` event handler methods for `_target` so that they call methods of the DraggableRectangle class.

```
public function DraggableRectangle(parent:MovieClip, width:Number, ¬
    height:Number, color:Number) {
    super(parent, width, height, color);
    _target.onPress = Delegate.create(this, onPress);
    _target.onRelease = Delegate.create(this, onRelease);
    _target.onReleaseOutside = _target.onRelease;
}
```

When the user clicks on the target movie clip, call the `onPress()` method of DraggableRectangle. When the user releases the mouse, call the `onRelease()` method of DraggableRectangle.

10. Define `onPress()` and `onRelease()` methods so they call `startDrag()` and `stopDrag()` for `_target`.

```
private function onPress():Void {
    _target.startDrag();
}

private function onRelease():Void {
    _target.stopDrag();
}
```

When the user clicks on the target movie clip, make it draggable.

11. Open *rectangle1.fla* and add the following code after the existing line of code:

```
var block:DraggableRectangle;

for(var i:Number = 0; i < 10; i++) {
    block = new DraggableRectangle(this, 25, 25, 0xFFFF00);
    block._x = Math.random() * 550;
    block._y = Math.random() * 400;
}
```

Draw 10 draggable rectangles and place them at random coordinates on the stage.

12. Test the movie.

When you test the movie, you'll see 10 yellow rectangles placed in random locations. You can click and drag any of the yellow rectangles.

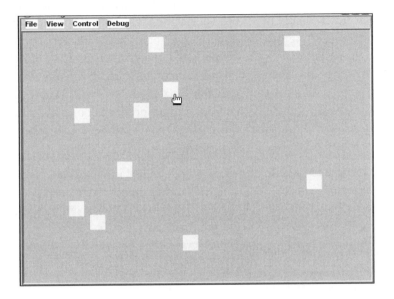

Dispatching Events

There are lots of ways to design an application. Each has relative advantages and disadvantages. Yet there are general principles that can help to make designs more flexible and manageable. One such principle states that loosely coupled systems are more flexible than tightly coupled systems. A tightly coupled system is one in which the elements have specific rigid interfaces in which they interact. For example, A can interact with B only if it knows a specific method to call on B—that is a tightly coupled system. A loosely coupled system is one in which the elements know little to nothing about one another. Instead, elements can send out notifications when states have changed, and any element that happens to be listening for that notification can respond. That way, A doesn't have to know anything about B, and B doesn't have to know anything about A. Instead, B can listen for a notification from A, and when A sends the notification, B can respond.

We call the notifications events, and when an object listens for an event, we call it a listener. If you've worked with the user interface (UI) components in Flash 8, you're already familiar with basic event dispatching. For example, a Button component dispatches a click event when the user clicks it with the mouse. The Button instance sends the event, and any listener that happens to have registered for notifications for the click event will respond.

The event-dispatching system that the UI components use is accessible to you to use within your classes as well. The event-dispatching system is built in a class called mx.events.EventDisatcher. The EventDispatcher class uses a methodology that is unique to prototype-based languages such as ActionScript. The class is known as a mix-in class because it injects functionality into a class at runtime. The concept of a mix-in class is not familiar to most people because prototype-based languages are not very common and because although ActionScript is prototype-based, the prototype nature of ActionScript is hidden in ActionScript 2.0. Therefore, if you aren't familiar with the way prototypes work, you needn't concern yourself with exactly how mix-in classes work. Simply know that mix-in classes are capable of adding methods and properties to objects at runtime. In the case of EventDispatcher, it adds the addEventListener(), removeEventListener(), and dispatchEvent() methods to a class at runtime.

You can add the event dispatching functionality to an instance of a class by calling the static EventDispatcher.initialize() method and passing it a reference to the instance of the class. Typically, you'll want to call the initialize() method from the constructor. The following example adds event dispatching to the Example class:

```
import mx.events.EventDispatcher;
class Example {
  public function Example() {
    EventDispatcher.initialize(this);
  }
}
```

Although the initialize() method adds the methods at runtime, you'll want to reference the methods from your code. Because you aren't defining the methods in the class the Flash compiler will throw an error. For example, if you construct an instance of Example, and you try to call addEventListener(), the compiler will thrown an error because as far as it can tell there is no addEventListener() method. The method is getting added at runtime, but you have to tell the compiler about that. You can effectively communicate to the compiler that the methods will exist by declaring properties with the method names as in the following.

```
public var addEventListener:Function;
public var removeEventListener:Function;
private var dispatchEvent:Function;
```

The addEventListener() and removeEventListener() methods are likely already familiar to you because they are identical to the methods you use with UI components. The dispatchEvent() method is probably not familiar to you, however. It is a method that you use within the class to dispatch an event. The method requires one parameter. The parameter must be an object with a type property specifying the name of the event to dispatch. For example, if you want to dispatch an event called exampleEvent, the dispatchEvent() method call might look like the following:

```
dispatchEvent({type: "exampleEvent"});
```

The event object is passed to any listeners. Therefore, any additional values you want to pass to the listener can be passed as properties of the event object. By convention, the event object generally also has a target property that references the object dispatching the event.

```
dispatchEvent({type: "exampleEvent", target: this});
```

In this task, you'll build a class that animates the drawing of lines. When each line segment is drawn, it will dispatch an event. In this particular case, once the event is dispatched a listener will get notified, and it will draw the next segment from an array.

1. Open a new ActionScript file and save it as *LineDrawer.as* in the same directory as *MovieClipContainer.as*. Then add the following class declaration:

```
class LineDrawer extends MovieClipContainer {

}
```

The LineDrawer class subclasses MovieClipContainer so that it automatically inherits the functionality that adds the new empty movie clip.

2. Next add the following import statement to the top of the code:

```
import mx.utils.Delegate;
```

You'll use Delegate to correct scope issues so that Flash will call a method of LineDrawer at the frame interval of the Flash file.

3. Declare the following properties:

```
private var _x0:Number;
private var _y0:Number;
private var _x1:Number;
private var _y1:Number;
private var _framesTotal:Number;
private var _frameCount:Number;
```

The properties store settings specifying the endpoints of the line segment as well as the number of frames over which to draw the line segment.

4. Declare the constructor so it expects a MovieClip parameter and passes that to the superclass constructor.

```
public function LineDrawer(parent:MovieClip) {
   super(parent);
}
```

The `LineDrawer()` constructor needs to call the superclass constructor to add the new empty movie clip.

5. Define a *drawLine()* method as follows.

```
public function drawLine(thickness:Number, color:Number, ¬
    x0:Number, y0:Number, ¬
    x1:Number, y1:Number, ¬
    frames:Number):Void {
    _target.lineStyle(thickness, color);
    _target.moveTo(x0, y0);
    _target.onEnterFrame = Delegate.create(this, draw);
    _x0 = x0;
    _y0 = y0;
    _x1 = x1;
    _y1 = y1;
    _frameCount = 0;
    _framesTotal = frames;
}
```

When the `drawLine()` method is called, it tells Flash to start calling the `draw()` method (see Step 6) at the frame interval of the Flash file. It sets the values of the private properties so that Flash can keep track of what to draw and for how long.

6. Define the draw() method as follows.

```
private function draw():Void {
    _frameCount++;
    var x:Number = _frameCount * (_x1 - _x0) / _framesTotal + _x0;
    var y:Number = _frameCount * (_y1 - _y0) / _framesTotal + _y0;
    _target.lineTo(x, y);
    if(_frameCount == _framesTotal) {
        delete _target.onEnterFrame;
    }
}
```

Each time draw() is called, it draws part of the line segment. It draws for the duration of the specified frame count. After it's drawn for the specified number of frames, it stops drawing by deleting the onEnterFrame assignment.

7. Open a new Flash document and save it as *lineDrawer1.fla* in the same directory as *LineDrawer.as*.

You'll use the Flash document to test the LineDrawer class.

8. Select the first keyframe, open the Actions panel, and add the following code:

```
var lineDrawer:LineDrawer = new LineDrawer(this);
var lineSegments:Array = [[100, 100], [200, 100], [200, 200], ¬
  [100, 200], [100, 100]];
var index:Number = 0;
drawNext();

function drawNext():Void {
  if(lineSegments[index + 1] == undefined) {
    return;
  }
  var vertex0:Array = lineSegments[index];
  var vertex1:Array = lineSegments[index + 1];
  lineDrawer.drawLine(1, 0x000000, vertex0[0], vertex0[1], vertex1[0], ¬
    vertex1[1], 10);
  index++;
}
```

The preceding code defines an array of vertices that form a square. The drawNext() function tells the LineDrawer instance to draw the next line segment defined by the array.

9. Test the movie.

You'll see one line segment draw over the course of 10 frames. The remaining line segments aren't drawn yet because nothing is notifying Flash to draw the next line segment.

10. Edit *LineDrawer.as* and add the following import statement:

```
import mx.events.EventDispatcher;
```

Import the EventDispatcher class so you can call the initialize() method.

11. Add the following property declarations:

```
public var addEventListener:Function;
public var removeEventListener:Function;
private var dispatchEvent:Function;
```

Declare the properties so that the compiler knows the methods will exist.

12. Call the `initialize()` method from the constructor.

```
public function LineDrawer(parent:MovieClip) {
  super(parent);
  EventDispatcher.initialize(this);
}
```

The `EventDispatcher.initialize()` method call tells the EventDispatcher class to add the event dispatching functionality to the instance of the LineDrawer class.

13. Dispatch a complete event when the line is completely drawn.

```
private function draw():Void {
  _frameCount++;
  var x:Number = _frameCount * (_x1 - _x0) / _framesTotal + _x0;
  var y:Number = _frameCount * (_y1 - _y0) / _framesTotal + _y0;
  _target.lineTo(x, y);
  if(_frameCount == _framesTotal) {
    delete _target.onEnterFrame;
    dispatchEvent({type: "complete", target: this});
  }
}
```

When the line segment is completely drawn, the LineDrawer class now dispatches an event to notify any listeners.

14. Edit the code in *lineDrawer1.fla* so that it listens for a complete event from the LineDrawer instance. When the complete event is dispatched, have it call `drawNext()`.

```
var lineDrawer:LineDrawer = new LineDrawer(this);
var lineSegments:Array = [[100, 100], [200, 100], [200, 200], ¬
  [100, 200], [100, 100]];
var index:Number = 0;
lineDrawer.addEventListener("complete", drawNext);
drawNext();
```

Now each time a line segment is drawn, Flash will listen for the event and it will call drawNext().

15. Test the movie.

This time, you'll see four line segments drawn in succession. The following figure shows the animation in progress.

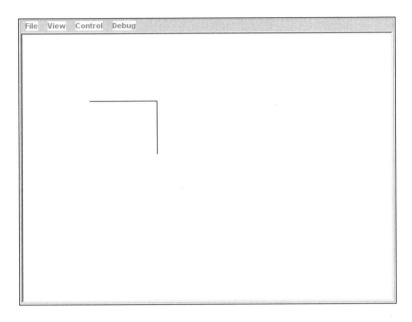

What You Have Learned

In this lesson you have:

- Learned that when you work with event handlers of class properties you frequently run into issues of incorrect scope (pages 269–270)
- Discovered that you can correct scope issues with the Delegate.create() method (pages 270–273)
- Learned that good encapsulation means that classes are self-contained and don't reference global objects such as _root and _global (page 274)
- Used composition to define a "has a" relationship between classes (pages 274–276)
- Enabled classes that act like movie clips but for which you don't have to have symbols (pages 276–281)
- Used event dispatching to design flexible applications (pages 281–287)

12 Data Validation

Many applications collect information from users — phone numbers, email addresses, and so on — for later use, or to send to a database where the data can be stored and retrieved as needed. However, if an application trusted users to enter properly formatted, error-free information, the application probably wouldn't function properly — or your database would quickly fill with useless data. The fact is that users often enter data incorrectly, which is why it's a good idea to validate data before it's used or processed. Validating data usually entails writing a script to check the way data was entered against a set of guidelines or rules. If data-entry errors are found, the user can be prompted to reenter the data; or in some cases, the script can make the needed adjustments without further input from the user.

Our fictional product contains a product registration form that allows us to collect data from the user, validate it, and display any errors found.

In this lesson, we'll create an application that includes a form requiring user-input data that needs to be validated. After our application validates this information, the app will display a custom confirmation page and then send the data to a server for processing.

What You Will Learn

In this lesson, you will:

- Learn why validation is important
- Define validation requirements
- Set up a mechanism to handle errors found in the validation process
- Create functions for validating strings, sequences, and numbers
- Send data from a validated form to a server for processing

Approximate Time

This lesson takes approximately one and one half hours to complete.

Lesson Files

Media Files:

None

Starting Files:

Lesson12/Start/validate1.fla

Completed Project:

Lesson12/Completed/validate7.fla

The Logic Behind Validating Data

We validate things every day—from words in a sentence (to make sure they make sense) to change received from purchases. The concept of validation is a natural and easy one for us to understand. For example, examine the following (U.S.) phone number: 555-34567. Chances are you quickly recognized the phone number to be invalid. How? Your brain analyzed the phone number and noted that it contained eight digits. After comparing this fact to the rule that defines valid local phone numbers as those that include seven digits, your brain made a determination of true (the number was valid) or false (it was invalid). If you determine that the number is valid, you can place the phone call. If the number is invalid, however, your brain will log an error message—something similar to "That number is wrong. I need to get the correct number and then try to call."

If we were to break down the validation process, it would look similar to the following:

1. Define criteria for valid data.

2. Analyze submitted data.

3. Compare this data against defined criteria.

4. Continue if data is valid; determine and note error if data is invalid; resolve and then try again.

In Macromedia ActionScript, this process of analyzing information—comparing it to a set of rules and then determining the data's validity—is known as a *validation routine*. Just as your brain analyzes data instantaneously, an ActionScript validation routine takes a split second to complete.

You usually need to validate data within a Flash application whenever you require the user to enter information into an input text field—for example, on forms (name, address, phone number, and so on) and quizzes (to verify answers) and in e-commerce shopping carts (quantities, sizes, colors, and so on).

Using Validation Routines

You can think of a validation routine as a mini-scripting machine within your project that validates the data it receives and then acts accordingly, based on whether that data is valid or invalid. As such, most validation routines comprise functions composed primarily of conditional (if) statements.

It's typical to split validation routines into separate functions, one for each type of data to be validated, such as one function for validating strings, another for numbers, and so on. This allows you to script a function once and then use it anywhere in your project, as opposed to writing the validation routine repeatedly whenever a certain type of data needs to be validated.

```
function validateEmail()          function validateState()
   function validateName()           function validateZip()
```

You can create two main types of validation routines (functions that validate data):

- Those that don't receive parameters but work in a specific way
- Those that receive parameters to provide additional functionality to your application

Let's take a look at each type.

With a validation routine that is not sent parameters, you define the function to work in a specific way, usually to validate a specific piece of data. Imagine that you want to create a routine to validate a seven-digit telephone number that includes eight characters in all—

seven digits and one hyphen (-) that the user enters into a text field named telephone_txt.
The structure of that function would look similar to the following:

```
function validateTelephone () {
  if (telephone_txt.length == 8) {
    // number is valid, so do these specific actions
  } else {
    // number is invalid, so do these specific actions
  }
}
```

This routine can validate only the data in the telephone_txt text field because that's the
field defined in the script. Let's now look at how versatile we can make this function by
allowing it to accept a couple of parameters:

```
function validateTelephone (lookForAreaCode:Boolean, pNumber:String) {
  if (lookForAreaCode == true && pNumber.length == 12) {
    message_txt.text = "That is a valid 10-digit telephone number";
  } else if (lookForAreaCode == false && pNumber.length == 8) {
    message_txt.text = "That is a valid 7-digit telephone number";
  } else {
    message_txt.text = "That is not a valid telephone number";
  }
}
```

When called, this validation function receives two parameters: lookForAreaCode, a true or
false value that indicates whether to look for an area code in the number to be validated,
and a pNumber that represents the number to be validated. If lookForAreaCode is true when
called, the number (pNumber) sent to the function is valid only if it contains 10 digits. If
lookForAreaCode is false, the number sent to the function is valid only if it contains seven
digits (and a hyphen).

A call to this validation routine would look similar to the following:

```
validateTelephone(true, 812-555-1234);
```

After processing this call, the function would display the following in the message_txt text
field: "That is a valid 10-digit telephone number."

> **Note** You'll remember from previous lessons that the values sent to a function
> can actually be variables; therefore, you could use the validation function to
> validate the text in any text field by referencing that field's name and text property
> (textField_txt.text) in the second parameter of the function call.

By creating a validation routine that accepts parameters and validates data accordingly, you increase the routine's usefulness because you can employ it to validate similar data in various ways.

Conditional statements play an important role in validating data because that process entails nothing more than evaluating various conditions to determine whether user-input data is valid. The rules that define valid data are considered *validation points*. To define validation points, you must consider the following:

- **Length.** Does the data contain the correct number of characters? A typical zip code, for example, contains five digits. If a user-entered zip code includes fewer than five digits, this is an error. Or imagine a name: Because most names include more than one character, you would have an error if the length of the data entered were 1. (A length of 0 means that nothing has been entered. If you require something to be entered, this would be an error.)

- **Value.** Is the value of the entered data more, less, or equal to what is considered valid? If you were asking for someone's age, you might define a lower limit of 18 and an upper limit of 100. If the value entered were more than 100 or less than 18, this would be an error.

- **Type.** Is the data entered a number when it should be a string, or vice versa? If the user specifies a garment size on an order, "pizza" would be an error when a number is required.

- **Sequence.** Is the data properly formatted? Some data needs to contain numbers, letters, and other characters, all placed in a specific sequence—for example, phone numbers (123-4567), dates (01/23/45), account numbers (1-2345-67-890), and so on. Missing or misplaced hyphens, slashes, or other characters represent errors.

Validation Points

Length	Value	Type	Sequence
• Must contain 5 characters	• Must equal "Macromedia"	• Must be a number	• Must be in this format xx/xx/xxxx
Fred ⊘	Micromidia ⊘	Three ⊘	12/30/1956 ✓
7271966 ⊘	Macromedia ✓	3 ✓	072/7/1966 ⊘
Hello ✓	Puppy ⊘	Thirty7 ⊘	10-03-83 ⊘

Most validation routines contain conditional statements that are used to validate data based on multiple validation points. We will use and discuss each of these validation points in more detail in the exercises that follow.

Handling Errors

Different projects require varying solutions for handling the errors that the validation process brings to light. In some cases, you may want to provide a graphical indicator such as a red *X* next to the field containing the error; in others, a text message may suffice.

The conditional statement within the validation routine usually determines how to handle any error that it detects. Take, for example, the following:

```
if (dataValid) {
  // Perform these actions
} else {
  // Execute action to denote an error
}
```

Because error handling plays a major role in the validation process, you should think about how you want to handle errors in a particular project or situation before you script anything else.

In this exercise, we'll lay the foundation for the error-handling process in our project.

1. Open *validate1.fla* in the Lesson12/Start folder.

This project contains two frame labels: Registration and Confirm. We'll work on the Confirm label in a later exercise; for now, we'll concentrate on the Registration label, which includes a form that the user must fill out, and thus data that needs to be validated. The Timeline contains six layers named according to their content:

- The Background layer contains the project's static graphical content.
- The Text Components layer contains four TextInput component instances (named name_ti, email_ti, state_ti, and zip_ti) and a List component instance (named errorLog_lb). The TextInput instances allow the user to input name, email address, and so forth. The List component instance will be used to display any error messages generated during the form's validation process.
- The Button Components layer contains two button component instances named clear_pb and submit_pb—the former will be used to clear all form fields of data; the latter will be used to submit the form, thus initiating our application's form validation process.
- The Confirm Field layer contains a text field that we'll discuss in a later exercise.
- The Actions layer will contain all the scripts for this application.

- The Labels layer contains two frame labels (Registration and Confirm) to represent the application's two states: one containing the registration form, the other containing a "thank you" message. All the scripting for this project will take place at the Registration label. In a later exercise, we'll script the application to move to the Confirm label when the user has completed the registration form accurately.

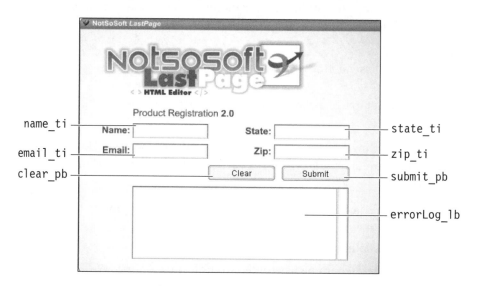

2. With the Actions panel open, select Frame 1 on the Actions layer and add the following script:

```
stop();
var errors:Array = new Array();
```

The first action prevents the Timeline from moving beyond Frame 1 until we instruct it to do so.

The second action creates an array named errors that will hold error messages to be displayed as the result of the validation process. (We'll explain this in more detail as we move forward.)

3. Add the following function definition at the end of the current script:

```
function clearForm() {
    name_ti.text = "";
    email_ti.text = "";
    state_ti.text = "";
```

```
   zip_ti.text = "";
   errorLog_lb.removeAll();
   errors.length = 0;
   errorLog_lb.alternatingRowColors = null;
}
```

When called, this function resets the value of the scene elements. First, we remove any text that has been entered into the four TextInput instances. The next line uses the removeAll() method of the List component to remove any error messages displayed in the errorLog_lb instance. The next line removes any error messages stored in the errors array. The last line sets the alternatingRowColors property of the errorLog_lb instance to null. What does this do, and why are we doing it?

Setting the alternatingRowColors property of a List component instance allows you to configure the instance to display items shown in the list with alternating row colors. This is done by creating an array with two or more color values and then setting that array as the value of the alternatingRowColors property, such as the following:

```
var myArray:Array = new Array(0xFFCC00, 0xCC9900, 0x003366);
myList_lb.alternatingRowColor = myArray;
```

Later in this lesson we will script the errorLog_lb instance to display error messages using alternating row colors. When the form is cleared using this function, we want the errorLog_lb instance to revert back to its original all-white row colors. Setting the alternatingRowColors property to null, as this function does, takes care of that requirement.

```
var myColors:Array = new Array(0xCCCCCC, 0x999999);
errorLog_lb.alternatingRowColors = myColors;
```

```
errorLog_lb.alternatingRowColors = null;
```

In the end, the scene will be reset to its original state.

4. With the Actions panel still open, add the following script:

```
clear_pb.addEventListener("click", clearForm);
```

This script calls the `clearForm()` function when the `clear_pb` instance is clicked.

5. Save this file as *validate2.fla*.

We'll build on this file throughout this lesson. The most important aspect of this exercise was the creation of the `errors` array, which will play a major role in the way our application handles any errors it detects in the validation process.

Validating Strings

As mentioned earlier in this lesson, when validating different types of data (names, phone numbers, email addresses, and so on) it's best to break the process into specialized functions or validation routines. We will begin that process in this exercise.

The first type of data our form asks for is the user's name. For our form, the data entered must meet two requirements:

- **Length.** The name must be at least two characters long.
- **Type.** Text must be used; a number cannot be accepted as a valid name.

Note   *We could define other validation points, such as a maximum length or even that the name should begin with a D, but the ones we have chosen are sufficient for our purposes.*

In this exercise, we'll create a function for validating the name entered into our project's registration form.

1. Open *validate2.fla*.

We'll build on the project from the last exercise.

2. With the Actions panel open, select Frame 1 on the Actions layer and add the following function definition at the end of the current script:

```
function validateName() {
    if (name_ti.text.length < 2 || isNaN(name_ti.text) == false) {
        errors.push("Please enter a valid name.");
        name_ti.setStyle("color", 0x990000);
    }
}
```

```
 1  stop ();
 2  var errors:Array = new Array();
 3  function clearForm() {
 4      name_ti.text = "";
 5      email_ti.text = "";
 6      state_ti.text = "";
 7      zip_ti.text = "";
 8      errorLog_lb.removeAll();
 9      errors.length = 0;
10      errorLog_lb.alternatingRowColors = null;
11  }
12  clear_pb.addEventListener("click", clearForm);
13  function validateName() {
14      if (name_ti.text.length < 2 || isNaN(name_ti.text) == false) {
15          errors.push("Please enter a valid name.");
16          name_ti.setStyle("color", 0x990000);
17      }
18  }
```

Script Assist

Actions : 1

Line 18 of 18, Col 2

When called, this function checks the data entered in the name_ti instance for two conditions: length and type (the validation points we defined at the beginning of this exercise). The conditional statement here says that if the name_ti instance contains fewer than two characters or is a number (which would be considered an error), the string "Please enter a valid name." should be pushed into the errors array. In addition, we use the setStyle() method to change the color of text in the name_ti instance to red to make the location of the error a little more noticeable. Although we used the length property in other scripts, some of this syntax is new and thus requires explanation.

One of the validation points we defined for the name_ti instance is that a number entered into it would be considered an error (of course, a name containing a number, such as derek66, would be acceptable). To determine whether data is a number or text string, we would use the isNaN() function. This built-in function verifies that the argument passed to it (within the parentheses) is not a number (hence the name isNaN, or *is Not a Number*). Take a look at the following examples:

isNaN("Box") returns a value of true because the value of "Box" is a string, meaning it's true that it's not a number.

isNaN(465) returns a value of false because 465 is a number—that is, it's false to state that 465 is not a number.

Thus, isNaN(name_ti.text) == false is the same as saying, "If what name_ti contains is a number..."

If either of the conditions in the statement exists, data has been input improperly. As a result, the actions within the if statement are executed. The first action within the statement uses the push() method of the Array instance to add an element to the end of the errors array. (This element is what's enclosed in the parentheses.) If you think of the errors array as a book, using the push() method is like adding a page to the end of the book, with the string within the parentheses representing the text on that page. The page number of this page would be its index position within the array.

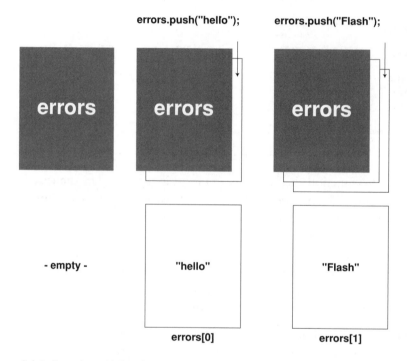

In the case of this function, if the data in the name_ti instance is invalid, the text "Please enter a valid name" is pushed into the errors array.

Next, we'll create a function to retrieve this error from the array (if name_ti doesn't contain a valid entry and an error is pushed into the array) and display it in the errorLog_lb List component instance.

3. With the Actions panel still open, add the following function definition at the end of the current script:

```
function validateForm() {
  errorLog_lb.removeAll();
  errors.length = 0;
  validateName();
  if (errors.length > 0) {
    errorLog_lb.defaultIcon = "errorIcon";
    var altColorArray:Array = new Array(0xF9F2F2, 0xECD9D9);
    errorLog_lb.alternatingRowColors = altColorArray;
    errorLog_lb.rollOverColor = 0xFFFFFF;
    errorLog_lb.selectionColor = 0xFFFFFF;
    errorLog_lb.dataProvider = errors;
  } else {
    gotoAndStop ("Confirm");
  }
}
```

In Step 2, we created a validation function to check the data entered into the name_ti instance. As we progress through this lesson, we'll create several more validation functions to validate the data entered into our other TextInput instances. The function created in this step—validateForm()—is really the mother of all these other functions; eventually it will be used to call all the individual validation functions and then finalize the validation process, including outputting error messages to the errorLog_lb List component instance. Take special note of the sequence of actions in this function: This flow plays an important role in how the function works.

The first two actions in this function clear the errorLog_lb instance of any displayed errors as well as any messages that might exist in the errors array. Obviously, the first time the form is validated, these actions are worthless because both begin empty. Any subsequent validation of the entered data will require that the errorLog_lb instance begin the validation process empty of any displayed items, and that any error messages in the errors array be erased.

The next line contains a function call to the validateName() function we defined in Step 2. This will cause that function to execute and validate the data in the name_ti instance. As a result, an error message is pushed into the errors array if data is invalid.

Note *We will add more function calls as we define them in the following exercises.*

The next action in this function is an `if` statement, which is evaluated only after the `validateName()` function has completed its job. This is where the sequence of actions becomes important. If an error message is pushed into the `errors` array as a result of calling the `validateName()` function, the `length` property of the `errors` array is changed to 1, indicating that it contains one error message. This `if` statement then looks at the `length` property of the `errors` array and then acts accordingly. If the `length` property has a value greater than 0 (indicating error messages within the array), the resulting actions output those messages to the `errorLog_lb` List component instance. If `errors.length` is 0, this means there are no error messages and the data is valid; therefore, a `gotoAndStop()` action sends the Timeline to the frame labeled Confirm.

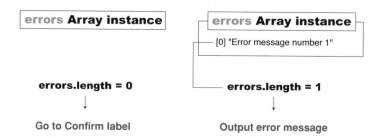

The actions used to output the error messages are fairly straightforward. The first action sets the `defaultIcon` property of the `errorLog_lb` instance. The value of this property is the identifier name of a movie clip in the library that will appear next to every item shown in the list. We've set the value of this property to `"errorIcon"`. This is the identifier name of a movie clip in the library that looks like a round circle with an *X* in the middle.

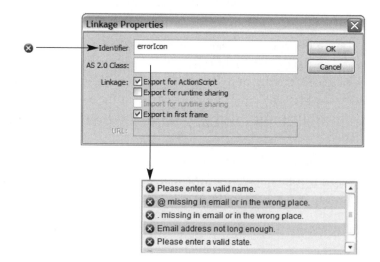

The next two lines of script set the alternatingRowColors property of the errorLog_lb instance. As explained in Step 3 of the preceding exercise, an array is created that holds two or more color values (in this case, altColorArray). That array is then set as the alternatingRowColors property of the errorLog_lb instance. As a result, the rows in that instance will alternate between the colors listed in the altColorArray array.

The next two lines of the script set the color values used when items in the errorLog_lb instance are rolled over or selected.

Finally, the last line sets the dataProvider property of the errorLog_lb instance. As you can see, we set the errors array as the value of this property. As a result, any error messages contained in that array will show up as individual items in the list.

4. **With the Actions panel still open, add the following script at the end of the current script:**

```
submit_pb.addEventListener("click", validateForm);
```

This script calls the validateForm() function when the submit_pb instance is clicked, causing the actions within that function to be executed when the button is released.

5. **Choose Control > Test Movie to test the project up to this point.**

Enter an invalid name into the name_ti instance to see what the validation process turns up. Click the Clear button to reset the scene's visual and data elements.

6. **Close the test movie to return to the authoring environment, and save this file as *validate3.fla*.**

We'll build on this file in the following exercise.

Validating Sequences

A *sequence* is a string of characters (letters, numbers, and special characters) placed in a specific order or formatted in a special way. Following are some sample sequences:

- Telephone number (xxx-xxxx)
- Credit card number (xxxx xxxx xxxx xxxx)
- Date (xx/xx/xxxx)
- URL (http://www.xxxxxx.xxx)

Although the characters within sequences can change, they must still follow certain formatting rules. Sequence validation is typically a bit more involved than other types of data validation, primarily because there are numerous validation points to check. By breaking down the process, you can more readily understand how it works. The following are some validation points for a typical email address:

- It cannot contain more than one @ symbol.
- It must include at least one period (separating the actual domain name from the domain extension, such as in *mydomain.com* or *mydomain.net*).
- The last period must fall somewhere after the @ symbol, but it can't be either of the last two characters.
- The @ symbol cannot be the first or second character.
- There must be at least two characters between the @ symbol and the first period that precedes it.
- The email address must include at least eight characters (aa@bb.cc).

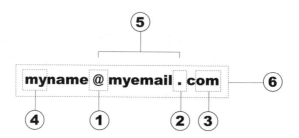

Note *If an email address has been checked for the six points listed previously, you performed a reasonable validation. Although we could add many more validation points (for example, characters following the last period must be com, net, org, or something similar), your code would become extremely long and you would need to update it frequently to keep pace with changing Internet standards. It's crucial to determine the most important validation points and check for them.*

In this exercise, we'll check only the following three validation points for text entered into the email_ti instance of our registration form:

- The @ symbol must be included somewhere after the second character.
- The email address must include a period at least two characters after the @ symbol.
- The email address must consist of at least eight characters.

Note *Be sure to provide users with clear instructions about how to format data. It's common practice to provide an example of correctly formatted data either above or below the text box where it's to be entered, providing a quick reference for the user.*

Phone:	_____
	(e.g., 123-456-7890)
Date:	_____
	(e.g., 07/27/1966)
SS#:	_____
	(e.g., 123-45-6789)

1. Open *validate3.fla*.

We will continue building on the project from the last exercise.

2. With the Actions panel open, select Frame 1 on the Actions layer and add the following function definition at the end of the current script:

```
function validateEmail() {
  if (email_ti.text.indexOf("@") < 2) {
    errors.push("@ missing in email or in the wrong place.");
    email_ti.setStyle("color", 0x990000);
  }
  if (email_ti.text.lastIndexOf(".") <= (email_ti.text.indexOf("@") + 2)) {
    errors.push(". missing in email or in the wrong place.");
    email_ti.setStyle("color", 0x990000);
  }
  if (email_ti.text.length < 8) {
    errors.push("Email address not long enough.");
    email_ti.setStyle("color", 0x990000);
  }
}
```

The validateEmail() function validates the text entered into the email_ti instance and is made up of three conditional statements, each of which checks one of the individual validation points we outlined at the beginning of this exercise. Because these are separate if statements, rather than if/else, if/else if groupings, all of them will be evaluated. Let's look at each one in depth. The first statement reads as follows:

```
if (email_ti.text.indexOf("@") < 2) {
  errors.push("@ missing in email or in the wrong place.");
  email_ti.setStyle("color", 0x990000);
}
```

You'll remember from Lesson 5, "Built-in Classes," that the indexOf() method returns the position (character number) where the value in the parentheses is first found in a string.

Using this method, the previous statement determines whether the first @ symbol appears before the third character in the email_ti instance. Because the first character in a string has an index number of 0, this statement evaluates to true, and an error message is pushed into the errors array if the @ symbol is found at position 0 or 1. If the @ symbol doesn't occur anywhere within the email_ti instance, this statement returns a value of -1, which is still less than 2; this result causes the statement to evaluate to true and the error message to be pushed into the array. In addition to an error message being pushed into the errors array whenever this error occurs, the text in the email_ti is styled as red, which is helpful for emphasizing the location of the error.

> **Note** *Using the indexOf() method, you can also check for the existence of strings longer than one character. For example, you can check for http:// in a string by using something similar to the following syntax: string.indexOf("http://"). The number returned is the character number of the first letter in the string.*

Let's look at the second statement in this function, which reads as follows:

```
if (email_ti.text.lastIndexOf(".") <= (email_ti.text.indexOf("@") + 2)) {
    errors.push(". missing in email or in the wrong place.");
    email_ti.setStyle("color", 0x990000);
}
```

This statement uses the lastIndexOf() method—similar to the indexOf() method except that it returns the character number of the last occurrence of the character in the parentheses. The following example returns 28:

```
email_ti.text = "derek.franklin@derekfranklin.com",¬
    email_ti.text.lastIndexOf(".")
```

Using this method, the statement looks at the position of the last period in relation to the @ symbol. If the period is less than two characters to the right of the @ symbol, this statement proves true, and an error message is pushed into the errors array. Again, if this error occurs, the text in the email_ti instance is styled in red, indicating the location of the error.

m	y	e	m	a	i	l	@	d	.	c	o	m
0	1	2	3	4	5	6	7	8	9	10	11	12

```
if (email.text.lastIndexOf(".") <= (email.text.indexOf("@")+2))
                            ↓
                  if (9 <= (7+2))
                            ↓
                  if (9 <= 9)
                            ↓
                       true
```

The third statement in this function is the easiest one to comprehend. It reads as follows:

```
if (email_ti.text.length < 8) {
  errors.push("Email address not long enough.");
  email_ti.setStyle("color", 0x990000);
}
```

The smallest reasonable email address is *aa@bb.cc*—eight characters, including the @ symbol and the period. If the length of the text entered into the email_ti instance is fewer than eight characters, an error message stating that the email address is too short is pushed into the error array and the text in the email_ti instance is styled as red.

After all these statements have been evaluated, you might find that the information entered into the email_ti instance is invalid on all counts. In this case, three different error messages would be pushed into the errors array.

3. Add the following function call just below the **validateName()** function call in the **validateForm()** function definition:

```
validateEmail();
```

This is a call to the function we just defined. Placing this function call here adds email validation capability to the main validateForm() function. This function call is placed just

above the statement that checks the length of the errors array because the validateEmail()
function can push error messages into the array, thus affecting its length and the way the
statement is evaluated. In the end, if either the validateName() or validateEmail() function
finds errors, the corresponding messages will be displayed in the errorLog_lb instance.

> **Note** *The Submit button already calls the validateForm() function when clicked;
> therefore, any new functionality we add to that function (as we have just done) is
> automatically executed when the button is released.*

4. Choose Control > Test Movie to test the project up to this point.

Enter an invalid email address into the email_ti instance or an invalid name into the
name_ti instance to see what the validation process turns up. Clicking the Clear button
resets the visual and data elements in the scene.

5. Close the test movie to return to the authoring environment, and save this file
as *validate4.fla.*

We will build on this file in the following exercise.

Validating Against a List of Choices

There are times when a value entered into a form must match one of several choices. For
example, if a form asks the user to enter a specific color—red, yellow, or blue—and the
user accidentally enters *rod* or *yullow* instead, it's important to be able to detect that error
when validating the form.

If you'll compare data entered against a list of choices, obviously you must define that
list first. In ActionScript, an array can include a list of choices. The validation process
is simply a matter of comparing the entered data against the values in the array to see
whether there's a match.

In this exercise, we'll create another validation routine—this one to compare what's
entered in the state_ti instance against an array of state names.

> **Note** *It's best to have users do as little manual data entry as possible. Instead of
> requiring the user to input data that matches one of several choices, you would be
> better off providing a drop-down list from which the user could choose a value—
> a method that eliminates the need for data validation. In some applications, however,
> this is impossible—for example, in a quiz application that contains a list of answers
> you don't want users to be able to access. In such cases, there's no way to avoid
> manual validation.*

Method 1

State: [Indianer|]

Method 2

State: [Indiana   ]
       [Illinois   ]
       [Kentucky   ]

1. Open *validate4.fla.*

We will continue building on the project from the last exercise.

2. With the Actions panel open, select Frame 1 on the Actions layer and add the following function definition at the end of the current script:

```
function validateState() {
    var states:Array = ["California", "Indiana", "North Carolina", "Oklahoma"];
    var matchFound:Boolean = false;
    for (var i = 0; i <= states.length; ++i) {
        if (state_ti.text == states[i]) {
            matchFound = true;
            break;
        }
    }
    if (!matchFound) {
        errors.push("Please enter a valid state.");
        state_ti.setStyle("color", 0x990000);
    }
}
```

The validateState() function validates the data entered into the state_ti instance.

The first action in this function creates an array named states, which will hold all the possible choices. To keep this as short as possible, we included only four state names, although you could easily add all 50.

The next action creates a variable named matchFound and assigns it an initial value of false. The importance of this variable will become evident in a moment.

The next several lines in this function are part of a looping statement, which is used to loop through all the values in the states array, comparing each to the value entered in the `state_ti` instance. If a match is found, `matchFound` is set to `true`. If no match is found, the value of this variable remains `false` (its initial state), indicating an error.

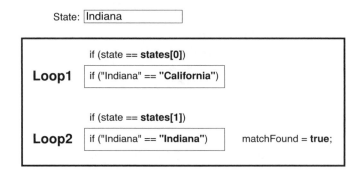

The last part of the function contains an `if` statement that's executed after the looping statement has completed its job. It says that if `matchFound` is `false` (which it will be if no match is found), an appropriate error message should be pushed into the `errors` array, and the `state_ti` instance's text should be styled as red (as in the other functions we created thus far).

3. Add the following function call just below the `validateEmail()` function call in the `validateForm()` function definition:

```
validateState();
```

This is a call to the `validateState()` function we just defined. Placing this function call here adds state-name validation capability to the main `validateForm()` function. This function call is placed just above the conditional statement that checks the `length` of the `errors` array because that function can push error messages into the array, thus affecting its length and the way the statement is evaluated. In the end, if `validateName()`, `validateEmail()`, or `validateState()` finds errors, the corresponding messages will be displayed in the `errorLog_lb` List component instance.

4. Choose Control > Test Movie to test your project thus far.

Enter an invalid state name (anything other than the four state names in the array) into the `state_ti` instance to see what the validation process turns up. Click the Clear button to reset the visual and data elements in the scene.

5. Close the test movie to return to the authoring environment, and save this file as *validate5.fla*.

We will build on this file in the following exercise.

Validating Numbers

Validating numbers is not much different from validating strings, which we've already discussed.

In this exercise, we'll create one last validation function to validate the data entered into the zip_ti instance. To be a valid five-digit zip code, the entered data must meet the following two requirements:

- **Length.** The data must include exactly five characters.
- **Type.** The data must contain numbers; text is invalid.

> **Note** *When validating numbers, you might need to call for the number entered to be more or less in value than another number—which by now you should be able to do easily!*

1. Open *validate5.fla*.

We will continue building on the project from the last exercise.

2. With the Actions panel open, select Frame 1 on the Actions layer and add the following function definition at the end of the current script:

```
function validateZip() {
    if (zip_ti.text.length != 5 || isNaN(zip_ti.text) == true) {
        errors.push("Please enter a valid zip.");
        zip_ti.setStyle("color", 0x990000);
    }
}
```

When called, this function checks that the data entered into the zip_ti instance meets two conditions regarding length and type—the validation points we defined at the beginning of this exercise. The conditional statement here states that if the zip_ti instance does not contain five characters, or if it consists of text (rather than numbers), the text in the zip_ti instance should be styled as red, and the following text string should be pushed into the errors array: "Please enter a valid zip."

> **Note** *If you need to refresh your understanding of isNaN(), review the information in the "Validating Strings" exercise earlier in this lesson.*

3. Add the following function call just below the `validateState()` function call in the `validateForm()` function:

```
validateZip();
```

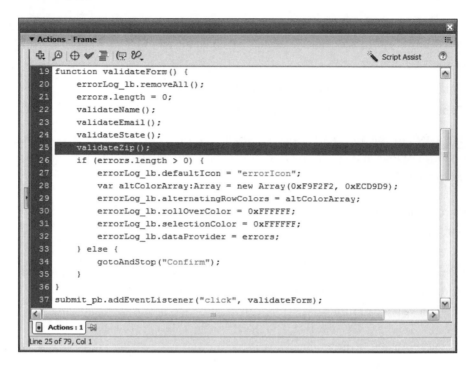

This is a call to the function we just defined. Placing this function call here adds zip code validation capability to the main `validateForm()` function. This function call is placed just above the statement that checks the length of the `errors` array because that function can push error messages into the array, thus affecting its length and the way this statement is evaluated. In the end, if `validateName()`, `validateEmail()`, `validateState()`, or `validateZip()` finds errors, the corresponding messages will be displayed in the `errorLog_lb` instance.

4. Choose Control > Test Movie to test the project up to this point.

Enter an invalid zip code in the `zip_ti` instance to see what the validation process turns up. Clicking the Clear button resets the visual and data elements in the scene.

As you've probably noticed when testing the application, the text in the TextInput instances remains red from the point at which an error is found in a particular instance until the application is shut down or moves to the Confirm label as the result of an error-free form submission. In addition, the haloGreen color used by the components just doesn't suit our design.

In the next couple of steps, we'll add some cosmetic improvements to our application so that a TextInput instance that contains red text (as the result of an error found there) is updated to contain black text whenever the user subsequently clicks inside the text box. We'll also change the theme color of components to a light blue.

5. **Close the test movie to return to the authoring environment. With the Actions panel open, select Frame 1 of the Actions layer and add the following script:**

```
function resetColor(eventObj:Object){
  eventObj.target.setStyle("color", 0x000000);
}
name_ti.addEventListener("focusIn", resetColor);
email_ti.addEventListener("focusIn", resetColor);
state_ti.addEventListener("focusIn", resetColor);
zip_ti.addEventListener("focusIn", resetColor);
```

The first part of the script contains a function named resetColor(). The remaining lines set up the TextInput instances in our application to call the resetColor() function when any of the text boxes is given focus.

As you learned in Lesson 10, "UI Components," when a function is called as the result of being registered as an event listener, the function is passed an Event object containing two properties: target and type. The target property identifies the target path of the component instance that calls the function. As a result of this script, when the user clicks in the email_ti instance, it is given focus and the resetColor() function is called. The single action inside the function uses the target property of the Event object (which in this case would have a value of _level0.email_ti) to reference the component instance that calls the function and the setStyle() method to set that instance's text color to black.

6. **Add the following script at the end of the current script:**

```
_global.style.setStyle("themeColor", 0xBDDDEB);
```

This sets the overall theme color of all component instances in our application to light blue.

7. **Choose Control > Test Movie to test our cosmetic improvements to the project.**

As you interact with the interface, you'll see how the last two scripts we added improve the overall look of our application.

8. Close the test movie to return to the authoring environment, and save this file as *validate6.fla.*

We'll build on this file in the following exercise.

Processing Validated Data

The last task for our application is to send all the validated data to a server for processing. We'll use a LoadVars instance to accomplish this goal.

1. Open *validate6.fla.*

We'll continue building on the project from the preceding exercise.

2. With the Actions panel open, select Frame 1 of the Actions layer and add the following script at the top of the current script, just below the stop() action:

```
var registrationData:LoadVars = new LoadVars();
```

This creates a new LoadVars instance named registrationData. In the next step we will add a script that places our validated data into this instance and sends it to the server.

3. Add the following script to the else leg of the validateForm() function:

```
registrationData.name = name_ti.text;
registrationData.email = email_ti.text;
registrationData.state = state_ti.text;
registrationData.zip = zip_ti.text;
registrationData.sendAndLoad("http://www.myDomain.com/registration.php",¬
   registrationData, "POST");
```

When all the data entered into the form is valid, the actions in the else part of the validateForm() function—including this section of script—are executed.

The first four lines of the script place the data in the various TextInput instances into the registrationData instance. The last line sends this data to a server-side script.

> **Note**   *For the last line of script, you should insert the URL to a script on your server for processing the data.*

The else part of this script already had an action that would send the application to the Confirm label automatically when all the data entered was valid. Because the application is now set up to send data to a server, let's change this functionality a bit so that the application only moves to that frame label after a response has been received from the server, indicating that the submitted data has been received and processed.

4. Remove the line of script in the `else` leg of the `validateForm()` function that reads `gotoAndStop("Confirm")` and then insert the following script just above the `sendAndLoad()` method call:

```
registrationData.onLoad = function(){
    gotoAndStop("Confirm");
}
```

This script will move the application to the Confirm label when a server response has been sent back to the `registrationData` instance. Let's do one final test.

Note *Before testing, make sure that the URL specified in the sendAndLoad() method discussed in Step 3 contains a server-side script for handling the incoming data.*

5. Choose Control > Test Movie.

If you enter valid data into the form fields and click the Submit button, the application should send the data to the specified server-side script for processing, and eventually move the application's Timeline to the Confirm label after a response has been received from the server.

6. Close the test movie to return to the authoring environment, and save this file as *validate7.fla.*

This step completes the exercise and this lesson. The great thing about the way we set up this project's validation process is that it's dynamic. To analyze additional rules or validation points for any of the text fields, all you have to do is add more conditional statements to the appropriate function. The validation process can grow as your needs grow.

What You Have Learned

In this lesson, you have:

- Learned why validation is important (page 291)
- Defined validation requirements and used them to create conditional statements (pages 292–294)
- Set up a mechanism to handle errors detected in the validation process (pages 295–298)
- Created several functions for validating strings, sequences, and numbers (pages 298–314)
- Sent data from a validated form to a server for processing (pages 314–316)

13 External Data Connections

One of Macromedia Flash's most useful features is its capability to communicate with external sources, sending data to and receiving data from other locations. This makes Flash a powerful application development tool: It enables you to perform tasks such as loading news dynamically, facilitating user login and registration, and building Flash chat applications.

In this lesson, we'll show you various ways in which Flash can send and receive data. You'll use this knowledge to build a simple Flash polling application that enables you to vote for a movie and displays the poll results, a journal that saves entries to your hard drive, and a Web services application that helps you to translate English text into several other languages.

You will build this language translator application, which demonstrates how easy it is to plug into a Web service to send data to and retrieve data from a third-party source.

What You Will Learn

In this lesson, you will:

- Discover the data formats that Flash can load
- Learn about the objects designed for data transfer
- Send and receive data from a server
- Learn about policy files and how to use them
- Save data to your hard drive using shared objects
- Communicate with a Web service

Approximate Time

This lesson takes approximately one and one half hours to complete.

Lesson Files

Media Files:

Lesson13/Assets/Poll.asp
Lesson13/Assets/Poll.mdb

Starting Files:

Lesson13/Start/poll1.fla
Lesson13/Start/journal1.fla
Lesson13/Start/Translator1.fla

Completed Projects:

Lesson13/Completed/poll2.fla
Lesson13/Completed/journal2.fla
Lesson13/Completed/Translator2.fla

Understanding Data Sources and Data Formats

A *data source* is a place from which Flash can load *external data* (that is, data not directly programmed into the movie). For example, Flash can load data from a simple text file, and that text file is considered a data source. *Data transfer* is the act of retrieving data from a source or sending data from Flash to another application. In this section, you'll learn about the different types of data sources as well as the Flash objects and methods used to communicate with these sources in the data-transfer process.

Any data that you plan to load into Flash from an external source must be structured (formatted) in a specific way. Flash supports the following formats:

- **URL string.** In this type of name/value pair formatting, variables and their values are defined as a string of text. For example, the following text string defines three variables (`name`, `website`, `hairColor`) and their respective values (`Jobe`, `http://www.electrotank.com`, `brown`):

  ```
  name=Jobe&website= http://www.electrotank.com&hairColor=brown
  ```

  After this text string has been loaded, Flash automatically breaks it into its respective variable names/values, making them available for use just as any other variables. An equals sign (=) is used to associate a variable name with its value, and an ampersand (&) marks the end of one variable and the beginning of another. You will use this format in an exercise later in this lesson. The format supports an unlimited number of variables. Only simple variables can be stored in URL string format; data contained in objects, arrays, or any other data type is not supported by a string of text.

- **XML.** This popular formatting standard allows data to be stored in a logical structure. For example:

  ```
  <States>
    <State>
      <Name>North Carolina</Name>
      <Capital>Raleigh</Capital>
    </State>
    <State>
      <Name>Virginia</Name>
      <Capital>Richmond</Capital>
    </State>
  </States>
  ```

After an XML document is loaded into Flash, a script that you write is used to extract information from the XML document.

Note See Lesson 14, "XML and Flash," for more information on the XML format.

- **Shared objects.** Although they will be discussed later in this lesson, understand for now that shared objects are similar to cookies: Shared objects allow you to store objects (data) locally on the user's hard drive. This means that after a user views and exits a Flash movie (as a projector or online), the data created while the movie was playing (user's name, last section visited, and so on) is saved. This data can be retrieved the next time the user plays the movie on the same computer. By using shared objects, you can store not only variables and their values but also *any* kind of data object, including arrays, XML objects—even custom objects. You can make this process of saving data transparent to users, or you can provide buttons for them to initiate the action. You can also have multiple shared-object data files on a single computer because each movie usually creates its own data file.

Now that you're familiar with the various data formats that Flash supports, let's review the sources from which Flash can load data:

- **Text files.** Flash can load text files (*.txt) containing data formatted using the URL string format mentioned earlier in this lesson. Text files can be loaded using loadVariables() or the load() method of the LoadVars class, both of which we'll discuss later in this lesson. You can easily create these types of data sources using Windows Notepad or Apple Simple Text.

- **Server-side scripts.** Server-side scripts are files that contain code and are executed by the server. Examples that you've probably heard of are ASP, .Net, CFML, CGI, or JSP pages. Although invisible to the user, the scripted page actually generates formatted data (HTML, XML, and so on) that's sent back to the requesting source. For example, imagine visiting a page called news.asp that contains a server-side script and probably no real content. The script, which is executed when a user visits the page, is used to dynamically generate and send to the user's browser an HTML-formatted page containing the latest news (probably extracted from a database). Server-side scripts can return data in both the XML and URL string formats. This means that by communicating with a page containing a server-side script, Flash can load dynamic data created on the fly.

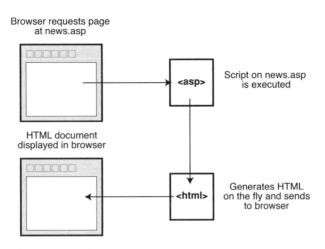

Browser requests page
at news.asp

HTML document
displayed in browser

Script on news.asp
is executed

<asp>

<html>

Generates HTML
on the fly and sends
to browser

- **XML files.** An XML file is simply a text file that contains XML-formatted data; such files usually include an xml extension.

- **XML socket servers.** Socket servers are applications that run on a server and connect several users to one another simultaneously. Flash can send or receive information via the socket using the XML format. (You'll learn more about socket servers—including how to build a chat application with them—in Lesson 14.)

- **Shared objects.** Shared objects are used to create data files that store information on a user's hard drive. You can then retrieve these files for use with a movie, as you will see in the last exercise in this lesson.

GET versus POST

There are two ways to transfer data between the server and Flash when working with server-side scripts: via GET or via POST. These two techniques for sending variables and their associated values are used in regular HTML pages and in Flash whenever data entered into a form is sent to a server to be processed. (We'll discuss the specific methods in the following exercises.)

When you send variables using GET, you're simply concatenating variable name/value pairs onto the URL itself. For example, if you want to use GET to send my name and email address to a script located on the register.asp page, you'd specify the URL as follows:

http://www.somedomain.com/register.asp?name=jobe&email=jobe@electrotank.com.

The question mark (?) tells the script and server that everything that follows comprises variables. Although GET is easier to use than POST, it won't work for every situation because it has a 1024-character limit.

Now let's take a look at how POST is used. When variable data is sent using POST, that data is contained within the header of the HTTP request, which means you cannot see it being transferred. This gives you an added layer of security because the variables are not easily read. Because POST doesn't have a character limit, it provides a slightly more versatile way of sending variable data.

Using GET

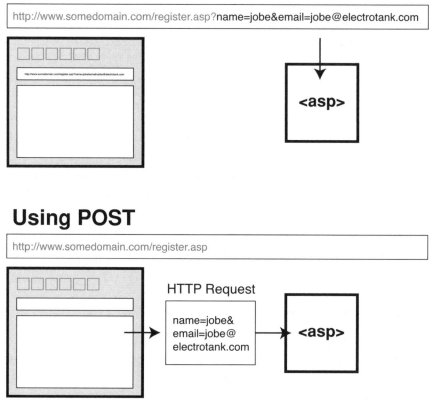

Using POST

We'll return to the topic of GET and POST in the exercise that accompanies the next section, "Using the LoadVars Class."

> **Note** *Because GET and POST are not always easily interchangeable, most server-side scripts are programmed to accept variables via either GET or POST, but usually not both.*

Using the LoadVars Class

You use the LoadVars class when working with data in the URL string format. This class enables you to load variable data from a text file, or to send and load variable data to and from a server-side script.

Note *Although variable data contained in a text file can be loaded into Flash, Flash cannot save data to a text file directly; you must use a server-side script to do that.*

Creating a LoadVars instance in Flash is simple. Look at the following example:

```
var container:LoadVars = new LoadVars();
```

This creates a new LoadVars instance named `container`. To load variables from a URL into a LoadVars instance, use the `load()` method:

```
container.load("http://www.myDomain.com/myFile.txt");
```

Note *You can get the total number of bytes loaded so far or the total bytes that will be loaded by using the getBytesLoaded() and getBytesTotal() methods of the LoadVars class.*

When data has been loaded into a LoadVars instance, you can access it by referencing the name of the particular instance that contains the data you want, followed by the variable name of that piece of data. For example, if you were to load the following string into an instance named `myData`:

```
name=Jobe&age=28&wife=Kelly
```

these variable values could be referenced as follows:

```
myData.name
myData.age
myData.wife
```

For example:

```
userAge = myData.age;
```

Here, `userAge` would have a value of 28. In the same manner, a variable value in a LoadVars instance can be set from within a script in Flash like this:

```
myData.age = 45;
```

Therefore, a variable value inside a LoadVars instance can be set not only by loading external data into the object but also by setting the value internally (using a script inside the movie).

Note *When loading variables into a LoadVars instance, Flash will overwrite existing variable values in the object or append new variable values.*

If you want to send the variables in a LoadVars instance to a server-side script for processing, use the send() method. That syntax is as follows:

```
myLoadVarsObject.send("http://www.mydomain.com/process.asp");
```

No response is sent back to Flash when you use this method, so you would use it only to send variable data to the server for processing.

The sendAndLoad() method allows you to specify a LoadVars instance whose contents you want to send and the LoadVars instance in which you want the response to load:

```
myLoadVarsObject.sendAndLoad("http://mydomain.com/process.asp", ¬
    receivingLoadVarsObject);
```

In this case, the variables in myLoadVarsObject are sent to the specified URL for processing. The server sends data back to Flash, and that data is loaded into receivingLoadVarsObject. At that point, you can work with the receivingLoadVarsObject to extract the data that the server sent back. If you want to send variables in a LoadVars instance and have that same instance receive the data that the server sends back, simply use the load() method described in the following exercise.

Using the toString() method of the LoadVars class, you can create a URL-formatted string that represents the variables/values contained in the object.

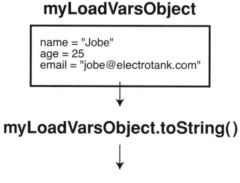

myLoadVarsObject

name = "Jobe"
age = 25
email = "jobe@electrotank.com"

myLoadVarsObject.toString()

name=Jobe&age=25&email=jobe@electrotank.com

The LoadVars class has two properties: contentType and loaded. The contentType property can be changed before sending out variables, simply giving you the mime type specified in the HTTP header of the loaded document. The loaded property returns true if data has finished loading into the object, `false` if it has not, and undefined if a `load()` method has not yet been invoked.

There is only one event available to the LoadVars class: onLoad. Use this event to call a function when data has finished loading into the instance. Each time data is loaded into the instance, this event is fired again.

To load variables from a specified URL into a LoadVars instance and then call a function when loading is complete, you must do the following:

1. Define a function.

2. Create a new LoadVars instance using the new LoadVars constructor.

3. Specify the function to be called when the loading has completed.

4. Invoke the `load()` method of the LoadVars instance.

For example:

```
function myFunction(){
  trace("Data is loaded");
}
var container:LoadVars = new LoadVars();
container.onLoad = myFunction;
container.load("http://www.somedomain.com/myFile.asp");
```

In this example, myFunction() is called when a string of data from the specified URL has been completely loaded into the container LoadVars instance.

In the following exercise, you'll create a simple polling system using a LoadVars instance. This instance will send data to and load data from an ASP page in the URL string format. The ASP page contains a server-side script that enables it to read and write to a Microsoft Access database. When variable data is *sent* to the ASP page, the page interprets the data and updates the values in the database accordingly. When a LoadVars instance requests that data be *loaded* into it from the ASP page, the page is set up so that it gets the data from the various fields in the database, encodes that data into the URL string format, and sends that data to the LoadVars instance.

You will find this scripted page (Poll.asp) and the accompanying database (Poll.mdb) in the Lesson13/Assets folder on your CD-ROM. To complete this lesson successfully, you will need access to a Windows server running IIS so that the server-side script on the ASP page can be executed. Before you begin this exercise, upload Poll.asp and Poll.mdb to a Windows server and make a note of their location (URL).

Note *The database that you are uploading to the server will be written to by the* Poll.asp *script. To allow this to occur, you must set the permissions on the database to allow it to be written to. Please contact your web host or your server administrator for help doing this.*

1. Open *poll1.fla* in the Lesson 13/Start folder.

We already created the layers, frames, frame labels, and movie clips you'll need so that you can focus on the ActionScript.

With the Timeline at Frame 1, you'll notice the text, "What was the best movie of 2005?" Below this text is some space and a Submit button. You will place four Radio Button components in the empty space between these two elements. These radio buttons will represent the selection method for your choice of the best movie of 2005. When a user presses the Submit button, the movie will execute a script, sending data to the server (based on which radio button is selected) and at the same time move the playhead to Frame 3, Waiting, in which it will wait for a response from the server. When a response is received (data is loaded into a LoadVars instance), the movie will move to the frame labeled Display. This frame will contain a script used to interpret the response from the server (data will be extracted from the LoadVars instance). The data will be used to determine the percentage of the total number of votes that each of the four movies has received. Each movie's overall percentage value will then be displayed in a text field as well as graphically by using simple bar graphs.

2. Move the playhead to Frame 1, and select the frame in the layer called Text and Buttons.

You will add four instances of the Radio Button component to this layer (beneath the question but above the Submit button).

3. Open the Components panel. Locate the Radio Button component and drag four instances of it onto the Stage. Align these four components in a vertical column under the question on the screen.

You have just added four Radio Button components to the Stage. If you select one of them and look at the Property inspector, you'll see a list of the component's properties/parameters, all of which are editable.

Note   *Although the Property inspector lists what you see as parameters, from an ActionScript standpoint they represent properties of the component. Because this is an ActionScript book, we identify them as properties.*

The first property, data, should be blank. The data property associates a data value with the selected radio button instance. When the radio button instance is selected by the user as the movie plays, this value can be used by a script to perform a task based on that value.

The next property shown on the Property inspector is groupName. As you learned in Lesson 10, "UI Components," radio button instances are designed to work in groups, allowing only a single radio button within a group to be selected at any time. This property setting enables you to assign the instance to a particular radio button group. You'll use the radioGroup default value for this property; therefore, the four radio button instances we dragged onto the Stage belong to the radioGroup group.

The label property represents the text displayed next to the radio button instance.

Next is the labelPlacement property. You can click the value of this property to display a drop-down list of label placement options. Each option specifies where the label text should be placed relative to the button itself. The default setting is right, which means that the text is shown to the right of the button.

The final property in the Property inspector is selected. This is a Boolean value that determines whether a radio button should start off with a dot, indicating that the button is selected. By default, all radio button instances start with a selected value of false, meaning that the button is not selected. If you want one of your radio buttons to start off selected, you would change the value here to true.

4. Select the top radio button and change its label property to *War of the Worlds*. Change the label properties of the next three radio buttons to *March of the Penguins*, *Star Wars: Episode III*, and *Wedding Crashers*, respectively.

As you change the label names of the radio buttons (from top to bottom on the screen), you should see the text updated in the component itself.

Note *If the text in the component isn't updated, choose Control > Enable Live Preview.*

You may need to resize a couple of instances horizontally to avoid truncating the appearance of the label text.

5. Change the `data` property of the four radio buttons to *1, 2, 3,* and *4,* from top to bottom.

When the movie is published and a radio button is selected, its `data` property value is set as the data value of the `radioGroup`. You retrieve this data value for use at any time by accessing the `selectedData` property of the RadioButtonGroup class. For example, if a radio button with a `data` property value of 3 were selected, and this radio button were part of a group of radio buttons with a group name of `radioGroup`, the following syntax would assign a value of 3 to `myValue`:

```
var myValue:Number = radioGroup.selectedData;
```

6. With the Actions panel open, select Frame 1 in the Actions layer and add `stop();`.

This `stop()` action prevents the movie from playing past Frame 1 until you instruct it to do so.

7. With Frame 1 still selected, add the following line of script:

```
var pollURL:String = "http://www.myDomain.com/poll.asp";
```

This creates a variable named `pollURL` and assigns it a value that represents the location (URL) of the `Poll.asp` page you uploaded to your server at the beginning of this exercise. (The URL shown should be replaced with the actual location where `Poll.asp` resides on your server.)

8. Add the following line of script:

```
var poll:LoadVars = new LoadVars();
```

This creates a new LoadVars instance. With this instance, we can load data from a remote location and make use of the convenient methods and properties described earlier in this lesson.

9. Define the `pollLoaded()` function by adding the following script at the end of the current script:

```
function pollLoaded() {
  gotoAndStop("Display");
}
```

This function is used to move the playhead to the frame labeled Display. (The next step explains when this function gets called.)

10. To associate the function we just defined with the onLoad event of the poll LoadVars instance, add the following line of ActionScript:

```
poll.onLoad = pollLoaded;
```

This script says that when the last byte of data is completely loaded into the poll LoadVars instance, the pollLoaded() function will be called; therefore, when the data has finished loading, the Timeline will move to the frame labeled Display, as set up in Step 9. In a moment, we'll add a script at the Display label that will use the loaded data to display the results in several bar graphs.

11. Add the following function definition just below the last line of script:

```
function submitChoice() {
  var choice:Number = radioGroup.selectedData;
  poll.load(pollURL + "?choice=" + choice);
  gotoAndStop("Waiting");
}
```

This function, which is used to submit the user's choice for best movie of 2005, is called when the Submit button is clicked.

The first line of the function definition creates a local variable named choice. This variable is assigned the current data value of the radioGroup group of radio buttons by accessing the selectedData property of the RadioButtonGroup class. If the user selected the second radio button, choice would have a value of 2.

The next line of ActionScript invokes the load() method of the poll LoadVars instance. Using an expression, the URL of the Poll.asp page is specified (pollURL), and the variable choice is added to the end of the string to send this to the server using the GET method of transferring variable data. If the user clicked the third radio button, this argument would look something like this:

```
"http://www.mydomain.com/poll.asp?choice=3"
```

Remember, everything after the question mark in the argument is a variable. In this case, we're sending a vote (choice=3) to the Poll.asp page. That page will then update the values in the database based on this vote and load the results into the poll LoadVars instance. Those results are used in the actions described in Step 14.

http://www.mydomain.com/poll.asp?choice=3

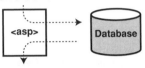

poll LoadVars Object

```
totalVotes = 65
item1total = 27
item2total = 15
item3total = 9
item4total = 14
```

The final line of script in this function tells Flash to go to the frame labeled Waiting. The movie will stay on this frame until the data is loaded back into Flash from the server. At that point, the pollLoaded() function will be called (as described in Step 10), moving the Timeline to the frame labeled Display.

12. Add the following **onRelease** event handler for the **Submit** button at the end of Frame 1:

```
submit_btn.onRelease = function() {
   submitChoice();
};
```

The submitChoice() function defined in Step 11 is executed when the Submit button is clicked.

13. Move the playhead to the frame labeled Display.

On this frame are four movie clip instances with horizontal bars—one bar graph for each movie on which the user is voting. All are instances of the same movie clip: Their instance names are barGraph1_mc, barGraph2_mc, barGraph3_mc, and barGraph4_mc. Notice that all these instance names include numbers. These numbers are used to associate one bar graph movie clip for each movie in the poll. Each of these instances also includes two text fields— topPercent_txt and bottomPercent_txt—that are used to display a textual representation of the percent. Both of these text fields display the same text; bottomPercent_txt is simply there to provide a slight shadow effect behind topPercent_txt. This movie clip also contains a horizontal bar with an instance name of bar_mc. It will be scaled horizontally based on the percentage value.

14. Select the frame in the Actions layer and add the following loop:

```
for (var i:Number = 1; i <= 4; ++i) {
    var graphName:String = "barGraph" + i + "_mc";
    var votes:Number = poll["item" + i + "total"];
    var totalVotes:Number = poll.totalVotes;
    var percent:Number = Math.round((votes / totalVotes) * 100);
    this[graphName].bar_mc._xscale = percent;
}
```

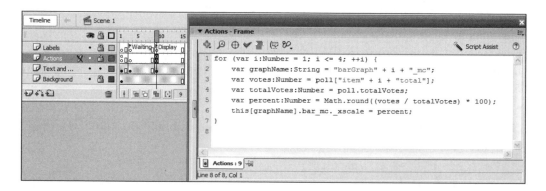

When the playhead has made it to this frame label (Display), the user has submitted his or her choice and the server has accepted it, added it to the current results, and loaded the resulting data into the poll LoadVars instance. Remember that in Steps 9 and 10 we scripted our movie so that it would move to this frame label only after the resulting data from the server had been loaded completely into the poll LoadVars instance. The script on this frame will now use that data. The variables loaded from the remote script into the LoadVars instance are named totalVotes, item1total, item2total, item3total, and item4total. Obviously, totalVotes has a numeric value representing the total number of all votes submitted, and will be used to figure percentage values. The other variables hold the number of individual votes that each of the movies received. Because these variables have been loaded into the poll LoadVars instance, you can access their values by using the following syntax:

```
poll.totalVotes
poll.item1total
poll.item2total
poll.item3total
poll.item4total
```

The loop calculates the percentage of votes received by each movie and scales the bar in the appropriate movie clip instance based on that number. The first line of script in the loop defines the variable graphName. Because the value of this variable is based on the concatenation of the string "barGraph" with the current value of i and the string "_mc", it's actually a reference to the name of the movie clip instance that will be used during the current loop (barGraph1_mc, barGraph2_mc, and so on). Again, using the value of i, the next action in the loop sets a variable called votes equal to the total number of votes for the current item (poll.item1total, poll.item2total, and so on). A variable called totalVotes is then assigned a value that represents the total number of votes cast for all of the movies. Next, the percent variable is calculated by dividing the current item's number of votes by the total votes and multiplying by 100. This is rounded using the Math.round() method of the Math class. Finally, the bar_mc clip in the current movie clip (as referenced by the current value of graphName) is scaled to match the percent value. This loop will repeat these actions four times, scaling each of the bar graphs in the process.

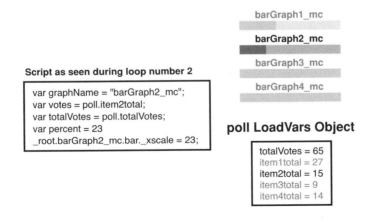

Script as seen during loop number 2

```
var graphName = "barGraph2_mc";
var votes = poll.item2total;
var totalVotes = poll.totalVotes;
var percent = 23
_root.barGraph2_mc.bar._xscale = 23;
```

barGraph1_mc

barGraph2_mc

barGraph3_mc

barGraph4_mc

poll LoadVars Object

```
totalVotes = 65
item1total = 27
item2total = 15
item3total = 9
item4total = 14
```

Note *For more information about loops, see Lesson 4, "Arrays and Loops."*

15. Add the following two lines of ActionScript at the end of the loop but *within* the loop:

```
this[graphName].topPercent_txt.text = percent + "%";
this[graphName].bottomPercent_txt.text = percent + "%";
```

The text to be displayed in the topPercent_txt and bottomPercent_txt text fields, above the scaled bar_mc movie clip instance, is set using the value of the percent variable and concatenating "%" at the end.

16. Choose Control › Test Movie to test your work. Select a movie radio button and click the Submit button.

When you click the Submit button, your choice is sent to the Poll.asp page, which updates the database and returns the results of the poll to the poll LoadVars instance. Your movie then moves to the frame labeled Display and shows you the results.

17. Close the test movie and save your work as *poll2.fla*.

You have just completed a basic application that uses the LoadVars class to talk to external scripts. You can now use this knowledge to build more complex and useful applications.

Policy Files

In this section, you will learn about the Flash Player security restrictions as they apply to loading external data, and how the restrictions can be bypassed.

By default, a SWF file can load external data only from the domain on which it resides. In other words, a SWF file running within the Web page at *www.electrotank.com/addressbook.html* could not load the XML file at *www.derekfranklin.com/addresses.xml* because the running SWF file and the file it's attempting to load are not on the same domain. However, the domain *derekfranklin.com* can give permission to SWF files that exist on *electrotank.com* by using a policy file, allowing those SWF files to load and use content from the *derekfranklin.com* domain. You will learn more about policy files later in this lesson, but you should understand what the Flash Player considers to be a different domain.

The Flash Player uses *exact domain matching* to determine whether a Flash file and external data source are on the same domain. A subdomain of a domain is not considered the same domain as its parent. For example, *store.electrotank.com* is not considered the same domain as *games.electrotank.com*, and *www.electrotank.com* is not the same as *electrotank.com*. If the two domain names don't look exactly alike, letter for letter, they're mismatched, and data exchange is not permitted without being granted access via a policy file.

A *policy file* is an XML-formatted file that usually sits in the root directory of a domain. When a SWF file attempts to load data from another domain, the Flash Player checks the destination domain for a policy file. If a policy file exists, the Flash Player loads it and checks whether the origin domain is granted access. If the origin domain is granted access, the Flash Player loads the requested data; otherwise, it doesn't.

> **Note** *The loading of the policy file is transparent to the user. It happens in the background without any special ActionScript coding.*

The following is the format of a policy file:

```
<cross-domain-policy>
<allow-access-from domain="www.derekfranklin.com" />
<allow-access-from domain="www.electrotank.com" />
<allow-access-from domain="63.74.114.215" />
</cross-domain-policy>
```

If the XML were saved to a file called *crossdomain.xml* and uploaded to the root directory of *www.gamebook.net*, Flash files on *www.derekfranklin.com*, Flash files on *www.electrotank.com*, and the IP *63.74.114.215* would be granted access to load data from *gamebook.net*.

> **Note** *A policy file for a domain must always be named* crossdomain.xml *and must exist in the root directory of the domain.*

The *crossdomain.xml* file would not grant access to an SWF file on *store.electrotank.com* because it doesn't exactly match the authorized domain.

The *crossdomain.xml* file supports wildcards. If you wanted your policy file to allow all subdomains of *electrotank.com*, you would use an asterisk in the policy file code as follows:

```
<cross-domain-policy>
  <allow-access-from domain="*.electrotank.com" />
</cross-domain-policy>
```

If you wanted to grant access to all domains everywhere, here is how you would set up the policy file:

```
<cross-domain-policy>
  <allow-access-from domain="*" />
</cross-domain-policy>
```

Policy files don't have to be located in the server root directory; they can exist in a custom location. When a policy file is in a custom location, the Flash Player will not automatically look for it because it does not know where to look. To load a policy file from a custom location, the following line of ActionScript is needed:

```
System.security.loadPolicyFile("http://www.myDomain.com/dir1/dir2/ ¬
    crossdomain.xml");
```

Using Shared Objects

A SWF file can save data (variables as well as array, XML, and other data objects) to a user's hard drive using *shared objects*—similar to but more powerful than the cookies used by web browsers. You can use shared objects to store information generated by the user while viewing your movie (name, last frame visited, music preference, and so on). Shared objects can be used by movies played in a web browser as well as those turned into standalone projectors.

The following is an example of a script you might use to create a shared object:

```
var myObject:SharedObject = SharedObject.getLocal("stuff_I_saved");
```

If the shared object stuff_I_saved already exists on the user's hard drive, its data is loaded instantly into myObject. If stuff_I_saved does not yet exist, it's created and still referenced by myObject. In the latter case, myObject would be empty—that is, it would contain no data.

> **Note** If used as just mentioned, the getLocal() method will create a shared object if none exists, or will retrieve data from an existing shared object.

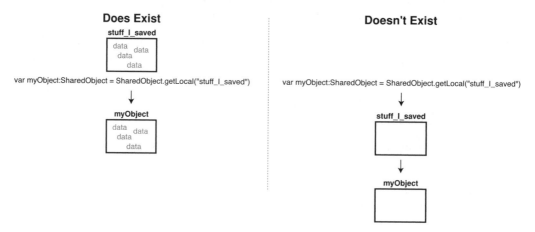

As you can see from the previous syntax, the shared object's name is actually "stuff_I_saved"; however, in ActionScript you can't reference the shared object directly using that name. Therefore, a reference to the shared object is created using myObject.

This means that whenever you reference myObject in a script, you're actually referencing the shared object named "stuff_I_saved"—a tricky concept but essential to understanding how ActionScript deals with shared objects.

Data is saved to a shared object using the data property. Take a look at the following example:

```
myObject.data.userName = userName_txt.text;
```

This would save the userName variable (and its value, the text in the userName_txt text field) in the shared object. You can save entire objects as well. For example, if you wanted to save an array contained by your project, you would use the following syntax:

```
myObject.data.savedArray = nameOfArray;
```

A single shared object can contain multiple bits of data simultaneously:

```
myObject.data.savedArray = nameOfArrayObject;
myObject.data.savedXML = nameOfXMLObject;
myObject.data.userName = userName_txt.text;
```

A particular piece of data can be erased from a shared object using null, as in the following example:

```
myObject.data.userName = null;
```

If userName were a piece of data in the shared object, the preceding script would delete it.

You can delete an entire shared object by using the clear() method of the SharedObject class:

```
myObject.clear();
```

Extracting data from a shared object is similar to creating data in one:

```
userName_txt.text = myObject.data.userName;
```

In the userName_txt text field, the preceding script will display the value of userName in the shared object. If this variable doesn't exist in the shared object, the value displayed in the text field will be undefined.

When the SWF file session ends (that is, the movie is closed or exited), all the information under the data property of your shared object is automatically written to the shared object file, ready to be retrieved using the getLocal() method described earlier. You can force a shared object to be written and saved at any time by using the flush() method. For example:

```
myObject.flush();
```

This line of ActionScript forces your shared object and all the data it contains to be saved. Because myObject references the shared object named "stuff_I_saved", this is the object that will actually be saved.

Flash stores all shared objects in a central location on the user's hard drive—the exact location depends on where the movie resides that created the shared objects.

On Windows XP, all shared objects are stored in the following general directory where *<username>* is the name of the user who was logged on when the shared object was created: Documents and Settings*<username>*\Application Data\Macromedia\Flash Player\.

On a Mac, the location is as follows: System Folder\Preferences\Macromedia\Flash Player\.

Note *Depending on the version of your operating system, the location of shared object files might vary somewhat. To locate shared object files on your machine, search for files with a .sol extension.*

These are both general paths—that is, when a movie creates a shared object, a new subdirectory is created at one of the previously mentioned locations. For example, if you were to view a movie at the following URL:

www.electrotank.com/fun/games/MiniGolf.swf

any shared object created by this movie would, by default, be saved at the following path on a Windows machine:

Documents and Settings*<username>*\Application Data\Macromedia\Flash Player\ electrotank.com\fun\games\MiniGolf

Notice that this subdirectory's path structure matches that of the URL.

Because a movie played locally (such as a projector) doesn't exist at a URL, Flash will save shared objects that it creates to a localhost directory:

Documents and Settings*<username>*\Application Data\Macromedia\Flash Player\localhost

All these directory paths are default paths in which shared object data is stored. You actually have a lot of latitude about where a shared object is stored or retrieved from within the general directory. Using the previous example, imagine playing a movie at the following URL:

www.electrotank.com/fun/games/MiniGolf.swf

This movie has the following shared object:

```
myScores = SharedObject.getLocal("scoreData");
```

This shared object is saved to the following path in Windows XP:

Documents and Settings\<*username*>\Application Data\Macromedia\Flash Player\ electrotank.com\fun\games\MiniGolf\scoreData.sol

Flash will look for this same location again when the movie is played from that URL; however, the getLocal() method lets you add an optional directory path where the shared object should be saved. Assuming that the movie at the aforementioned URL has this shared object declaration:

```
var myScores:SharedObject = SharedObject.getLocal("scoreData", "/fun");
```

the shared object would be saved to the following path:

Documents and Settings\<username>\Application Data\Macromedia\Flash Player\ electrotank.com\fun\scoreData.sol

Armed with this knowledge, you can create movies at different locations that use the same shared object—useful if you want all the movies on your site to reference a "master" shared object containing information about the user. Simply save a shared object in the main (/) directory.

Be careful when using a single shared object across movies. Any one of the shared objects has the potential of overwriting the data it contains with new data.

A single movie can create, save, and load multiple shared objects simultaneously.

> **Note** *You can configure the amount of data that a given URL can store by using the Flash player. If you right-click the window of an open SWF file and select Settings, you'll see the Local Storage controls. You can block any site from storing information on your machine.*

In this exercise, you'll create a journal that saves text entries in an array as a shared object.

1. Open *journal1.fla* in the Lesson13/Start folder.

You will notice one frame with four layers, named according to their contents. The Stage contains two text fields that will be used to display information. The large text field in the center, `journalBody_txt`, will be used for journal entries. The smaller text field at the bottom of the screen, `entryNumber_txt`, will be used to display the current journal entry number. The Buttons layer contains the Prev, Next, New, and Save buttons, which have instance names of `previous_btn`, `next_btn`, `new_btn`, and `save_btn`, respectively.

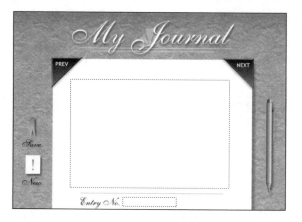

This application will allow you to start a new journal entry, save it, and browse through the entries you've created.

2. With the Actions panel open, select Frame 1 in the Actions layer and then add the following script:

```
var myJournal:SharedObject = SharedObject.getLocal("JournalObject");
```

This line of ActionScript creates a reference to the shared object `JournalObject`. This object can be read and modified using the `myJournal` reference set up here. When using `myJournal` in the following scripts, we're actually working with the shared object named `JournalObject`.

3. Add the following conditional statement just below the line of script you added in Step 2:

```
if (myJournal.data.journal == undefined) {
  myJournal.data.journal = [];
}
```

This statement looks in the shared object for an array named journal. If it doesn't find one (undefined), the action within the statement creates the journal array.

Note *If an array is created, it automatically becomes part of the shared object when the movie is exited or the shared object is saved using the flush () method.*

The journal array will appear undefined the first time the movie is played. Each subsequent time the movie is played, the array will exist and this action will be ignored.

Note *It's a good idea to check for undefined data values in a shared object, which allows you to assign default values the first time a movie is played by the user.*

4. **Add the following function definition at the end of the current script:**

```
function displayEntry(num:Number) {
   var entry:String = myJournal.data.journal[num - 1];
   if (entry != undefined) {
      entryNumber_txt.text = num;
      journalBody_txt.text = entry;
   }
}
```

This function does two things: It sets the value of two text fields on the Stage— entryNumber_txt and journalBody_txt—based on the value of num. Then, a conditional (if) statement is used to specify what should occur if the user has saved an entry in the journal.

As shown in Step 3, when the application is first used (as opposed to reopening it after adding an entry), an array named journal is created on the shared object. By default, a new array object always has a length of 1, indicating that it contains a single value at index 0, which is initially a value of undefined. The first time the application is used, myJournal.data.journal[0] contains a value of undefined. This value doesn't change until the user deliberately saves an entry into that index number.

In Step 5, we will script a call to this function:

```
displayEntry(myJournal.data.journal.length);
```

The first time the application is used, the length of the journal array will be 1; therefore, the function call will look like this:

```
displayEntry(1);
```

The first line in the displayEntry() function that we just defined uses the parameter value passed to it (in this case, 1) to set the value of entry. That line of script gets evaluated this way:

```
entry = myJournal.data.journal[1 - 1]
```

Or broken down further:

```
entry = myJournal.data.journal[0]
```

As already mentioned, if the user has never saved a journal entry at index 0 (such as the first time the application is used), entry is assigned a value of undefined; otherwise, it will contain the text of the first entry.

The conditional (if) statement looks at the value of entry and performs an action only if the value of entry is *not* undefined. If entry has a value of undefined, the function does nothing, and the entryNumber_txt and journalBody_txt text fields will be empty. This occurs only when the user has never saved a journal entry. After the user has saved at least one entry in the journal, the actions in the conditional statement are executed.

Assume that the user has saved 9 entries and then reopens the application. In this circumstance, the displayEntry() function we just defined will be called and passed a parameter value of 9:

```
displayEntry(9)
```

Note *This function call is added and explained a bit more in the next step.*

As a result, the value of entry within the function is assigned a value representing the text of the 9th entry in the journal (which is actually stored in index 8 of the journal array, as explained later in this lesson). This will cause the actions in the conditional statement to execute because entry is no longer undefined. The first action displays the value of the number passed to the function in the entryNumber_txt text field, which in this case is 9. The second action displays the value of entry in the journalBody_txt text field.

The reason for subtracting 1 from the value of num, as shown in the first line of the function definition, is that the index (within the journal array) in which each entry is saved is always one fewer than its actual entry number. The 5th entry is saved in index 4, the 6th entry in index 5, and so on because array indexes begin at 0, but we want our entry numbers to begin with 1. Therefore, this conversion keeps them in sync. Several of the scripts that follow employ similar logic.

This script is probably the trickiest to understand of the entire project. Be sure to review it several times until you feel comfortable with how it works.

5. Add the following function call to the end of the current script:

```
displayEntry(myJournal.data.journal.length);
```

Because this function call exists on Frame 1, it's executed as soon as the movie plays. The displayEntry() function (which was defined in Step 4) is called and passed a value based on the length value of the journal array in the shared object. This will display the final entry that the user made before exiting the movie. For example, if the journal array has three entries, the displayEntry() function is passed a value of 3, and the third journal entry is displayed. If the journal array has just been created (as described in Step 3), it will contain a single empty element; therefore, a length of 1 gets sent to the function.

6. Add the following function definition to handle saving data:

```
function save() {
    var num:Number = Number(entryNumber_txt.text) - 1;
    myJournal.data.journal[num] = journalBody_txt.text;
    myJournal.data.flush();
}
```

As mentioned earlier in this lesson, data is automatically saved to a shared object when a movie is exited. By using the flush() method, as shown here, you can save data at any time while the movie is playing. This function will be called when the Save button is clicked (see Step 11). Let's take a look at how this function works.

The first line in the function creates a variable named num. The value of this variable is set to the current value displayed in the entryNumber_txt text field, minus 1. The Number() function is used to make sure num contains a numerical value. The num value is used in the next line of the function to reference the appropriate array index of the current journal entry as it relates to the current entry number. As mentioned in Step 4, the number displayed in the entryNumber_txt text field is actually 1 more than the associated array index it references, which is why 1 is subtracted from the current entry value in the first line of script. (Keep reading: This information will make more sense in a moment.)

The next line in this function definition uses the value of num to update the journal array with the text displayed in the entryNumber_txt text field. As always, the best way to understand this is by using a sample scenario. Imagine that the current entry number displayed in the entryNumber_txt text field is 9. When this function is called, num would be set to a value of 8 (9 minus 1). The second line in the function would be evaluated as follows:

```
myJournal.data.journal[8] = journalBody_txt.text;
```

This will place the text in the journalBody_txt text field into index 8 of the journal array. Note again that the current *entry number* is 9, but the currently referenced *index number* of the array is 8 (see Step 4 for more on this topic). This line of script can affect the data in the array in two ways: If index 8 was previously empty (undefined), it will now contain text; if it previously included text, that text will be overwritten.

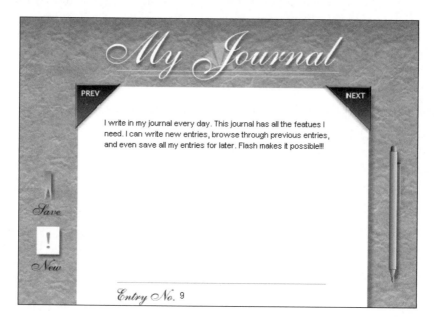

The last action in the function uses the flush() method to force the data and shared object to be saved to the user's hard drive. For our project, that will include all the entries that exist in the journal array.

7. Add the following function definition to create a new journal entry:

```
function newEntry() {
    entryNumber_txt.text = myJournal.data.journal.length + 1;
    journalBody_txt.text = "";
    Selection.setFocus("journalBody_txt");
}
```

The first action in this function sets the current journal entry number (entryNumber_txt text field) to the length of the journal array, plus 1. If the journal array has 2 entries, it has a length of 2. Adding 1 will cause 3 to appear in the entryNumber_txt text field. This action causes all new entries to be inserted at the *end* of the array. The last two actions in this definition are used to empty the journalBody_txt text field and then to give it focus so that the user can immediately begin typing his or her entry. To better understand this, let's take a look at how this function works in harmony with the save() function discussed in the Step 6.

Assume that there are two entries in the journal array, which means that the array has entries at index positions 0 and 1 (important to remember) and that it has a length of 2. When the function in this step is executed, the entryNumber_txt text field displays 3 (the length of the journal array plus 1), and the journalBody_txt text field will be emptied. The user now types text into this text field and clicks the Save button, which calls the save() function defined in Step 6. At that point, the save() function subtracts 1 from whatever is displayed in the entryNumber_txt text field, which in turn saves the current text in the journalBody_txt text field to index position 2 of the journal array. The journal array now contains three entries at index positions 0, 1, and 2, and its length is 3. If the function is called again, the process begins again.

8. Add the following function definition, which will be used to display the next entry in the journal:

```
function nextEntry() {
    var num:Number = Number(entryNumber_txt.text) + 1;
    if (num > myJournal.data.journal.length) {
        num = myJournal.data.journal.length;
    }
    displayEntry(num);
}
```

When executed, this function displays the next journal entry in the array. It does this by assigning a value to num based on the current numerical value displayed in the entryNumber_txt text field, plus 1. This value represents the next journal entry to be displayed. To prevent our application from displaying an entry that doesn't exist, the value of num is compared against the total number of entries in the journal array (the length property of journal). If the value of num is greater (as the if statement determines), you're attempting to display a nonexistent entry. In that case, the action within the if statement resets the value of num to the length property value of the journal array, in effect causing the last entry in the array to be displayed instead. The final action in this function calls the displayEntry() function and passes it the value of num, enabling it to display the appropriate journal entry.

9. Create the following function to display previous journal entries:

```
function previousEntry() {
  var num:Number = Number(entryNumber_txt.text) - 1;
  if (num < 1) {
    num = 1;
  }
  displayEntry(num);
}
```

This function works similarly to the function described in Step 8. num is given a value representing the current entry number minus 1. The if statement prevents the application from displaying anything beyond journal entry 1. Here's how it works.

Suppose that the user is currently viewing entry 6. When this function is called, num is assigned a value of 5 (6 minus 1), and that value is checked to make sure that it's not less than 1. Because it's more than 1, the action within the if statement is ignored, and the displayEntry() function is called and passed a value of 5, displaying journal entry 5.

If the user is viewing entry 1 when this function is called, num would initially be assigned a value of 0. The if statement would determine that this value is indeed less than 1 and change its value to 1. The displayEntry() function would then be passed a value of 1. Because entry 1 is already being displayed, it will appear as if nothing has changed onscreen. As mentioned, this mechanism prevents browsing past entry 1 because no entries exist at entry 0 or less.

10. Add the following *onRelease* event handler for the *new_btn* instance:

```
new_btn.onRelease = function() {
  newEntry();
};
```

When the user clicks the new_btn button instance, the newEntry() function is called, advancing the current entry number by 1 and clearing the journalBody_txt field so that new text can be entered.

11. Add the following *onRelease* event handler for the *save_btn* instance:

```
save_btn.onRelease = function() {
  save();
};
```

When the user clicks the save_btn button instance, the save() function is executed, at which point the current text in the journalBody_txt field either replaces an existing entry or is added as a new entry in the journal array (as described in Step 6).

12. Add the following *onRelease* event handler for the *previous_btn* instance:

```
previous_btn.onRelease = function() {
   previousEntry();
};
```

The call to the previousEntry() function changes the display to show the journal entry created before the current one that's displayed.

13. Finally, add the following *onRelease* event handler for the *next_btn* button instance:

```
next_btn.onRelease = function() {
   nextEntry();
};
```

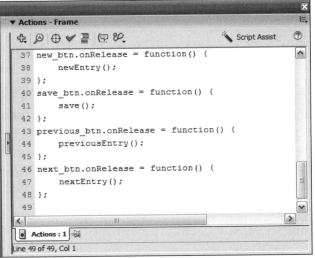

This ActionScript simply calls the nextEntry() function when the button is clicked. The screen is then updated to display the next entry in the list of journal entries.

14. Choose Control > Test Movie to test your work. Enter some text as a journal entry. Click the Save button to save the entry and then click the New button to create a new journal entry. Click the Save button, and restart the movie.

When you restart your movie, the shared object will be loaded as described in Steps 2–3, and any data previously saved can be browsed using the Prev and Next buttons.

15. Close the test movie and save your work as *journal2.fla*.

Thus far in this lesson, you have learned the basics of creating, retrieving, and saving shared objects.

You can also use shared objects to save any of the following (for example):

- User's name
- Last frame visited
- User's music preference
- Date of user's last visit
- User's ordering preferences
- Scores (for games)
- Appointments, addresses, lists
- Property values (x, y, alpha, rotation, and so on) of elements

Using the WebServiceConnector Component

Through the use of the WebServiceConnector component, a Flash movie can connect to a Web service and load information from it. A *Web service* is a server-side application that accepts data, performs a service based on that data, and returns a result. For instance, a Web service might allow you to feed it a zip code and, as a result, return the weather in the specified area. Another Web service could find all the spelling mistakes in a string of text fed to it, correct the spelling errors, and return the modified text.

To send data to a Web service, the data must be formatted in XML. More precisely, the XML must meet the SOAP (Simple Object Access Protocol) standard. Fortunately, you don't need to learn this standard. The WebServiceConnector component handles the process of converting data to XML (the data you send to the Web service) in the appropriate format, sending it to the Web service as well as receiving and parsing the response. This means that you can communicate with Web services without having to worry about formatting the request properly or figuring out how to interpret the returned XML. The WebServiceConnector component handles everything.

The WebServiceConnector component has four parameters:

- WSDLURL. This parameter is the URL for the file that defines the Web service operation. When this parameter is entered, the Flash authoring environment automatically attempts to load the destination file. This allows the authoring environment to display information related to the Web service in the Schema tab of the Component inspector, which will be discussed later in this lesson.

- operation. After the file located at WSDLURL is loaded, the operation parameter allows you to select from a drop-down list the operation that you want to execute. Many Web services provide only one operation, such as getPrice, whereas other Web services may provide several types of operations, such as SendICQmessage, SendMSNmessage, and SendAIMmessage.

- multipleSimultaneousAllowed. This is a drop-down list in which you can choose true or false. The default value is true. If true is selected, the component makes web requests to the Web service whenever it is asked to do so, even if it hasn't received a response from a previous request. If false, it won't make any more requests until a response to the current request has been received.

- suppressInvalidCalls. You can select either true or false from a drop-down list for this parameter. The WSDL file loaded via the WSDLURL parameter specifies what type of data is required to process the request. If suppressInvalidCalls is set to true, and your Web services request doesn't contain the specified type of data, the request is not sent. If suppressInvalidCalls is set to false, the request is sent, no matter what type of data is entered.

As mentioned a moment ago, the Schema tab of the Component inspector is dynamically populated based on the file at the WSDLURL property and the value of the operation property. It defines what information you should send and what information you should expect as a result. For example, there is a Web service that will give you the physical distance between two zip codes. If you enter its WSDLURL into the component and select the getDistance operation, the Schema table updates to show the following image.

There are two main areas in the schema: params and results. The params property contains the variables that you should send with the Web service request, which in this case consist of two zip codes. The results property is usually just a string.

You use the params property on the Schema tab to learn what information you should send to the Web service. You then create an array in the component instance called params and assign it values in the order in which they appeared in the params property on the Schema tab. For example, if we gave the WebServiceConnector component an instance name of zip_ws, we would add the params array like this:

```
zip_ws.params = ["27609", "90210"];
```

The first zip code in the array corresponds to the first property in the Schema, fromZip. The second one corresponds to the second property in the Schema, toZip.

To get the component instance to perform the service request, you must invoke the trigger() method. For example:

```
zip_ws.trigger();
```

The trigger() method tells the component to take the params property, format a request, send the request, and wait for a response. The response fires an event called the results event. You must add a Listener to capture that event. For example:

```
function distanceReceived (ev:Object) {
   var distance:String = ev.target.results;
}
zip_ws.addEventListener("result", distanceReceived);
```

This code adds a Listener to the `zip_ws` WebServiceConnector component and calls the `distanceReceived` function when the `results` event is fired.

Note www.xmethods.com *contains an extensive listing of Web services you can use in your applications.*

In the following exercise, you will get a chance to use everything introduced in this section. You will use a language translation Web service to create an application that enables you to translate English into a number of other languages.

Note *The WebServiceConnector component uses XML.sendAndLoad to communicate with the Web service; therefore, it is subject to the same security restrictions found when loading data onto one domain from another. For you to be able to use a Web service from an application sitting on a domain, the target domain (that is, where the Web service is located) must grant you access via its crossdomain.xml file. As a result, it will work properly when run from your hard drive, but won't from your website (unless you convince them to put up a crossdomain.xml file).*

1. Open *Translator1.fla* **in the Lesson13/Start folder.**

There are three layers on the main Timeline: Actions, Assets, and Background. The Actions layer will contain the ActionScript that you will be adding to this project. On the Assets layer are a ComboBox component with an instance name of `language_cb`, two TextArea components named `input_ta` and `output_ta`, and a Button component named `translate_btn`.

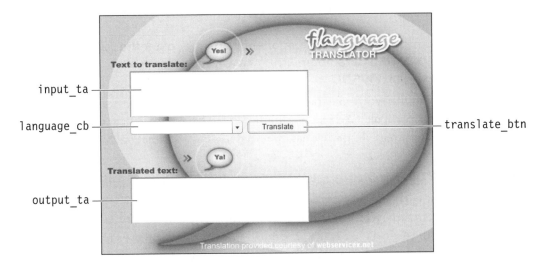

When this project is complete, you will be able to enter text in the input_ta TextArea component, select a translation language using the language_cb ComboBox component instance, and click the translate_btn Translate button. The Web service will then be sent a request containing the text to translate, as well as information about the selected language to translate it into. The Web service will translate the text and send the result back to the application, where it will be displayed in the output_ta TextArea component.

Communication with the Web service is handled by an instance of the WebServiceConnector component, which we'll add to our project next.

2. **Open the Components panel and drag an instance of the WebServiceConnector component onto the Stage. Place it to the left of the visible Stage area so that it doesn't get in the way of the other assets.**

You have now added an instance of the WebServiceConnector component to your project. Over the next few steps, you will configure this component to do what you need.

3. **Select the WebServiceConnector component and give it an instance name of *translator_ws*.**

This name will be used in our scripts to communicate with the component.

4. **With the component still selected, open the Component inspector.**

The Component inspector should open showing three tabs: Parameters, Bindings, and Schema. In the steps that follow, you will work with the Parameters tab and the Schema tab.

5. **On the Parameters tab of the Component inspector, enter the following URL into the *WSDLURL* parameter: *http://www.webservicex.com/ TranslateService.asmx?WSDL*.**

This is the URL for the WSDL file that defines exactly how the WebServiceConnector should talk to this particular Web service. In the WSDL file, the only data that interests us is the information regarding what data we need to send and what data we expect to be returned.

As soon as you enter the *http://www.webservicex.com/TranslateService.asmx?WSDL* URL and deselect that particular parameter, the Flash authoring system loads that file into the authoring environment. When the file is loaded, you will be able to select a Web service operation from the operation parameter drop-down list shown on the Parameters tab. The Schema tab will update depending on the operation selected.

Note *You must be connected to the Internet to complete Step 5. Flash cannot load the WSDL file if you are not connected to the Internet.*

6. On the Parameters tab, click the *operation* drop-down list. Select Translate.

For this particular Web service, there is only one operation from which to choose.

You will not need to change any of the other parameters of this component instance.

7. Select the Schema tab in the Component inspector. Notice that there are now two fields listed below *params* (*LanguageMode* and *Text*).

The params object on the Schema tab defines what data should be sent to the Web service. From what we see here, we determine that we need to send a string, LanguageMode, which represents the language of the text being sent as well as the language to which the text should be translated. In addition, we need to send a string, Text, which represents the text to be translated.

Although the Schema tab gives you some idea of what you're supposed to send, it doesn't tell you everything. For example, the LanguageMode string accepts strings such as "EnglishTOFrench" (which stands for "English to French"). The only way you know this information is by actually reading about the Web service from wherever you found the Web service. For this example, the Web service was found when browsing through *Xmethods.com*. The listing for this Web service described exactly what the Web service does and exactly what the Web service needs to get the job done.

The following list shows just a few of the many acceptable LanguageMode string values:

- EnglishTOFrench—English to French
- EnglishTOGerman—English to German
- EnglishTOChinese—English to Chinese
- EnglishTOSpanish—English to Spanish

The Text string simply holds the text that you want to be translated.

In the next few steps, you will create an array called on the WebServiceConnector instance params and will assign values. The params array holds the information that will be sent to the Web service.

You are now ready to ready to add the ActionScript needed to complete this project.

8. Select Frame 1 in the Actions layer and open the Actions panel. Add the following code:

```
language_cb.dataProvider = [{label:"English to French", data:"EnglishTOFrench"}, ¬
    {label:"English to German", data:"EnglishTOGerman"}, {label:"English to ¬
    Chinese", data:"EnglishTOChinese"}, {label:"English to Spanish", data: ¬
    "EnglishTOSpanish"}];
```

You'll remember that language_cb is the name of the ComboBox component instance in our project. By setting the dataProvider property of the component instance equal to an array, we automatically populate the contents of the component. Each element in the array represents one item in the ComboBox and has two properties: label and data. When the Flash movie is published, the ComboBox shows the text entered in each of the label properties. When an item is selected, the value property of the ComboBox is set to the data property associated with the selected item.

If a user selects English to German, for example, the value of the ComboBox component instance is changed to "EnglishTOGerman". This value will be used when the Translate button is clicked.

9. Add the following function to the frame:

```
function translationReceived(ev:Object) {
    var str = ev.target.results;
    output_ta.text = str;
}
```

In a moment, we will script our project to execute this function when a response from the Web service has been received. The ev parameter is a reference to the Event object created specifically for this event. (See Lesson 10, "UI Components," for more information about Event objects.)

The first line of this function creates a variable named str. This variable is assigned a value based on the results property of the Web services component in our project. This can be a tricky concept, so let's look at an example of how this will work.

As mentioned earlier, when a WebServiceConnector instance receives a response from the Web service with which it's communicating, that information is stored in the results property of the instance. Because receiving a response from the Web service executes this function, ev.target (as used in the function) is a reference to the translator_ws component instance in our project; therefore, ev.target.results is a reference to the information the Web service has sent back to our component instance. In the end, the value of str is the string value sent back from the Web service.

The second line in this function displays the value of str (the resulting translated text) in the output_ta component instance.

10. Add the following function, which asks the WebServiceConnector component instance to do its job:

```
function translate() {
    var direction:String = language_cb.value;
    var textToTranslate:String = input_ta.text;
    translator_ws.params = [direction, textToTranslate];
    translator_ws.addEventListener("result", translationReceived);
    translator_ws.trigger();
}
```

This function is executed when the Translate button is clicked (ActionScript to handle this action is added in the next step). A variable called direction is set. It gets its value from the value property of the language_cb ComboBox component instance. For example, if the user has selected English to French, direction is assigned a value of "EnglishTOFrench".

The next variable created is textToTranslate. This variable value is the text from the input_ta TextArea component.

The next line creates an array in the translator_ws instance called params. This array is used to store the data that will be sent to the Web service. Remember that the Schema tab listed the data to be sent to the Web service in this order: LanguageMode, Text, with LanguageMode (the first parameter) represent a value such as "EnglishTOFrench", and Text (the second parameter) represents the text to translate. The names used for these parameters (as shown on the Schema tab) are really not as important as their order. In other words, the first parameter should hold a value representing how to translate the text, and the second parameter should hold the text to translate. The params array we added to the translator_ws instance holds the data sent to the Web service, stored in the correct order.

The next line of the function registers the translationReceived() function (defined in Step 9) to listen for the results event in relation to the translator_ws instance. When the translator_ws instance receives a response from the Web service, the translationReceived() function is executed.

The last line of the function tells the translator_ws WebServiceConnector component instance to perform the request. This is done by invoking the trigger() method.

11. Add the following ActionScript to capture the *click* button event:

```
var buttonListenerObject:Object = new Object();
buttonListenerObject.click = function() {
  translate();
};
translate_btn.addEventListener("click", buttonListenerObject);
```

You should be familiar with this type of ActionScript by now. We create a Listener object for the button instance and then add a function called click to the Listener object. Finally, we register the Listener object to listen for that event when fired by the translate_btn instance.

In summary, when the translate_btn is clicked, the translate() function is called. translate() puts the data to be sent into the WebServiceConnector instance (by setting its params property), tells the instance to call the translationReceived() function when the results have been received, and finally triggers the connection process.

12. Add this final line of ActionScript to the frame:

```
input_ta.text = "Enter text here...";
```

This line of ActionScript forces the input_ta TextArea instance to show text when the application is launched. The user can remove this displayed text (by deleting or typing over the displayed text), and then enter new text.

```
▼ Actions - Frame                                                    Script Assist
1  language_cb.dataProvider = [{label:"English to French", data:"EnglishTOFrench"},
2  function translationReceived(ev:Object) {
3      var str = ev.target.results;
4      output_ta.text = str;
5  }
6  function translate() {
7      var direction:String = language_cb.value;
8      var textToTranslate:String = input_ta.text;
9      translator_ws.params = [direction, textToTranslate];
10     translator_ws.addEventListener("result", translationReceived);
11     translator_ws.trigger();
12 }
13 var buttonListenerObject:Object = new Object();
14 buttonListenerObject.click = function() {
15     translate();
16 };
17 translate_btn.addEventListener("click", buttonListenerObject);
18 input_ta.text = "Enter text here...";
```

Actions : 1

Line 18 of 18, Col 38

13. Choose Control > Test Movie to test your work. Enter some English text into the *input_ta* instance, choose the destination language from the drop-down list, and click the Translate button.

If you're connected to the Internet, your text should be translated and displayed in the output_ta component.

When you click the Translate button, the WebServiceConnector component formats a request for the Web service, sends the request, and waits for a response. When a response is received, the results event is fired and the text is displayed for the user to see.

14. Close the test movie and save your work as *Translator2.fla*.

You have successfully created an application that uses the WebServiceConnector component. Now that you know how to use this component, you can hook into any number of Web services to enhance the functionality of your projects.

What You Have Learned

In this lesson, you have:

- Learned about the data formats that Flash can accept (pages 319–321)
- Discovered how GET and POST are used to transfer data (pages 321–322)
- Gained experience using the LoadVars object to communicate with a server-side script (pages 323–334)
- Learned about policy files and how they're used (pages 334–336)
- Saved and retrieved data locally using shared objects (pages 336–348)
- Created a language translation application using the WebServiceConnector component (pages 348–357)

14 XML and Flash

Imagine what it would be like if every electrical appliance in your home had a different type of plug. Chances are you'd end up putting most of those gizmos back in the cupboard and doing the task manually. Or what if none of the screwdrivers or wrenches in your tool shed even came close to fitting the screws, nuts, and bolts that hold stuff together? Fortunately, neither scenario is likely because people figured out long ago that by creating products according to guidelines, or *rules of standardization*, they could have far more productive societies.

In essence, standards facilitate linkages between disparate items—battery and flashlight, Macromedia Flash and multiuser game server, and so on. And on the web, where tons of data are transferred every second, having a standardized way of moving data among systems is essential. The powerful and easy-to-use XML has become one standard.

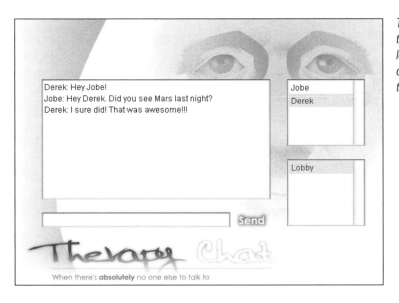

The simple chat application that you will script in this lesson shows you how to connect a Flash application to an XML socket server.

In this lesson, we'll introduce you to the XML format as well as show you how to use the XML class and the XMLSocket class in Flash. By lesson's end, you will have made Flash talk to ASP pages for user login and registration, and you will have created a very simple real-time chat application using a socket server.

What You Will Learn

In this lesson, you will:

- Learn about the XML format
- Create new XML instances
- Learn how to parse an XML document
- Send and load XML from the server
- Use methods, properties, and events of the XML class
- Learn about the XMLSocket class and socket servers
- Build a simple real-time chat application

Approximate Time

This lesson takes approximately one and one half hours to complete.

Lesson Files

Media Files:

Lesson14/Assets/AddUser.asp
Lesson14/Assets/UserLogin.asp
Lesson14/Assets/XMLExample.mdb
Lesson14/Assets/InstallElectroServer.exe
Lesson14/Assets/ElectroServer.as
Lesson14/Assets/Wddx.as
Lesson14/Assets/WddxRecordset.as

Starting Files:

Lesson14/Start/loginRegister1.fla
Lesson14/Start/Chat1.fla

Completed Projects:

Lesson14/Completed/loginRegister2.fla
Lesson14/Completed /Chat2.fla

XML Basics

Although the name Extensible Markup Language (XML) sounds a bit cryptic, don't worry: the format itself is actually quite easy to understand. In a nutshell, XML provides a way of formatting and structuring information so that receiving applications can easily interpret and use that data when it's moved from place to place. Although you may not realize it, you already have plenty of experience structuring and organizing information. Consider the following example.

Suppose you want to write a letter to a friend. You structure your thoughts (information) in a format you know your friend will recognize. You begin by writing words on a piece of paper, starting in the upper-left corner, and breaking your thoughts into paragraphs, sentences, and words. You could use images to convey your thoughts or write your words in a circle, but that probably would confuse your friend. By writing your letter in a format familiar to your friend, you can be confident that your message will be conveyed—that is, you will have transferred your thoughts (data/information) to the letter's recipient.

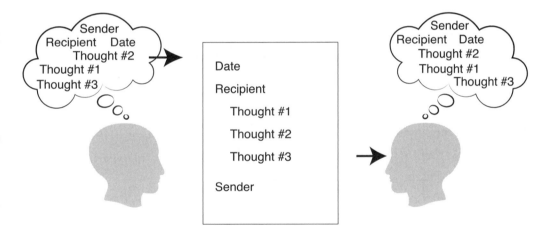

You can use XML in much the same way—as a format for conveying information. For example, if you want to send data out of Flash for processing by a web server, you format that data as XML. The server then interprets the XML-formatted data and uses it in the manner intended. Without XML, you could send chunks of data to a server, but the server probably wouldn't know what to do with the first chunk or the second, or even how the first chunk related to the second. XML gives meaning to these disparate bits of data so the server can work with them in an organized and intelligent manner.

XML's simple syntax resembles HTML in that it employs tags, attributes, and values—but the similarity ends there. Where HTML uses predefined tags (for example, <body>, <head>, and `<html>`), in XML you create your own tags—that is, you don't pull them from an existing library of tag names. Look at the following simple XML document:

```
<MyFriends>
  <Name Gender="female">Kelly Makar</Name>
  <Name Gender="male">Mike Grundvig</Name>
  <Name Gender="male">Free Makar</Name>
</MyFriends>
```

Each complete tag (such as `<Name></Name>`) in XML is called a *node*, and any XML-formatted data is called an *XML document*. Each XML document can contain only one *root node*; the document just shown has a root node called `MyFriends`, which in turn has three *child nodes*. The first child node has a *node name* of `Name` and a *node value* of `Kelly Makar`. The word `Gender` in each child node is an *attribute*. Attributes are optional, and each node can have an unlimited number of attributes. You'll typically use attributes to store small bits of information that are not necessarily displayed onscreen—for example, a user identification number.

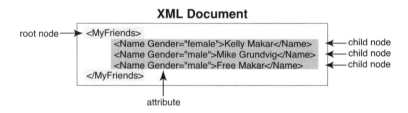

XML Document

The tags in this example (which we made up and defined) give meaning to the bits of information shown (`Kelly Makar`, `Mike Grundvig`, and `Free Makar`).

The next XML document shows a more extended use of XML:

```
<AddressBook>
  <Person>
    <Name>Kelly Makar</Name>
    <Street>121 Baker Street</Street>
    <City>Some City</City>
    <State>North Carolina</State>
  </Person>
  <Person>
    <Name>Tripp Carter</Name>
    <Street>777 Another Street</Street>
    <City>Elizabeth City</City>
    <State>North Carolina</State>
  </Person>
</AddressBook>
```

This example shows how the data in an address book would be formatted as XML. If there were 600 people listed in the address book, the `Person` node would appear 600 times with the same structure.

So how do you create your own nodes and structure? How does the destination (ASP page, socket, and so on) know how the document is formatted? And how does it know what to do with each piece of information? The simple answer is that this intelligence has to be built into your destination. Thus, if you were planning to build an address book in Flash and wanted the information it contained to be saved in a database, you would send an XML-formatted version of that data to an ASP page (or another scripted page of choice), which would then *parse* that information and insert it into the appropriate fields in a database. The important thing to remember is that the ASP page must be designed to deal with data in this way. Because XML is typically used to transfer rather than store information, the address book data would be stored as disparate information in database fields, rather than stored as XML. When needed again, that information could be extracted from the database, formatted as XML by a scripted page, and sent along to Flash or any other application that requested it.

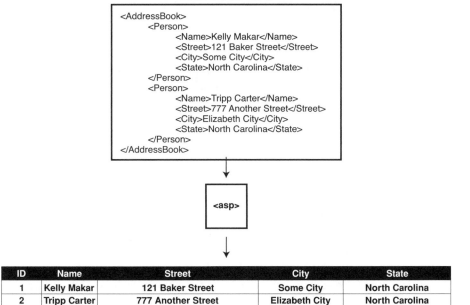

XML Document

```
<AddressBook>
    <Person>
        <Name>Kelly Makar</Name>
        <Street>121 Baker Street</Street>
        <City>Some City</City>
        <State>North Carolina</State>
    </Person>
    <Person>
        <Name>Tripp Carter</Name>
        <Street>777 Another Street</Street>
        <City>Elizabeth City</City>
        <State>North Carolina</State>
    </Person>
</AddressBook>
```

`<asp>`

ID	Name	Street	City	State
1	Kelly Makar	121 Baker Street	Some City	North Carolina
2	Tripp Carter	777 Another Street	Elizabeth City	North Carolina

Web pages often use text files that contain XML-formatted information—for example, a static XML file for storing information about which ASP pages to call, or what port and IP to connect to when attempting to connect with a socket server.

Now that you know the basics of the XML format, here are some rules you need to follow when you begin using it:

- You cannot begin node names with the letters *XML*; many XML parsers break when they see XML at the beginning of a node name.
- You must properly terminate every node—for example, you would terminate <Name> with </Name>. The slash (/) inside the final tag indicates that a node is completed (terminated).
- You must URL-encode all special characters—which you can do by using the escape() function in Flash. Many parsers interpret certain unencoded characters as the start of a new node that is not terminated properly (because it wasn't a node in the first place). An XML document with nonterminated nodes won't pass through an XML parser completely. Attributes are less forgiving than text nodes because they can fail to pass through the parser on characters such as a carriage return or an ampersand. If you URL-encode the text, you won't experience this trouble.
- Most XML parsers are case-sensitive, which means that all tags of the same type must have the same case. If you start a node with <Name> and terminate it with </name>, you're asking for trouble.
- You can have only one root node.

One more thing to note before you begin working with XML is that the clean XML structure shown in these examples is not necessary. The carriage returns and tabs are there to make it easier for *us* to read. These tabs and carriage returns are called *white space*, and you can add or delete white space without affecting the overall structure.

Using the XML Class

It's time to start using some XML! Nearly everything you do with XML in Flash involves the XML class and falls into one of the following categories: formatting XML, parsing XML (extracting the information), loading XML, or sending XML. With the XML class, you can load XML from an external source such as a static file or a server-side script. After an XML document is loaded, you can access its information using the methods and properties of the XML class. You can also use the methods and properties of the XML class to create your own XML document. After this document is created, you can use it in a Flash movie or send it out to a server-side script. This section covers the ActionScript you need to accomplish these goals.

Formatting XML

The XML class in Flash has several methods, most of which you can use to create and format XML documents. The truth is, though, you're unlikely to employ them because they're difficult to use—and there's a better way. We'll show you how to create a string and then convert it into an XML class instance, a much easier (and more common) way of formatting XML.

To create an XML instance in Flash, you must use the XML class constructor. Here's how you would create an empty XML instance:

```
var myXML:XML = new XML();
```

To populate the instance with XML-formatted data when it's created, you can pass (inside the parentheses of the constructor) the name of a variable that holds an XML-formatted string or another XML instance.

Suppose you want to create the following XML document in Flash:

```
<MyFriends>
   <Name Gender="female">Kelly Makar</Name>
   <Name Gender="male">Free Makar</Name>
</MyFriends>
```

You would do two things:

1. Create the document as a string.

2. Convert the string to an XML instance by using the XML class constructor new XML().

Here's an example:

```
var myString:String = "<MyFriends> ¬
   <Name Gender=\"female\">Kelly Makar</Name> ¬
   <Name Gender=\"male\">Free Makar</Name></MyFriends>";
var myXML:XML = new XML(myString);
```

This code creates the XML document as a string and converts it to an XML instance called myXML. This instance can then be sent to the server using the send-related methods described later in this section of the lesson.

Parsing XML

The word *parse* simply means to analyze something or break it down into its parts. When someone speaks of writing a script to parse an XML document, they're talking about writing a script that extracts information from that XML document. The XML class has many properties to help you do this. We'll use the XML instance just discussed, myXML, to illustrate the use of a few of the most common properties.

firstChild: This property points to the first node in the tree structure. For example, myXML.firstChild.firstChild returns:

```
<Name Gender="female">Kelly Makar</Name>
```

The first child node of the XML document is the root node (MyFriends), and the root node's first child is Name, as shown.

childNodes: This property returns an array of the child nodes at any given point in the tree structure. For example:

```
var myArray:Array = myXML.firstChild.childNodes
```

Here, myArray contains two elements whose values are the same as those of the two Name nodes.

nextSibling: This property points to the next node in the same level of the tree structure. Thus,

myXML.firstChild.firstChild.nextSibling returns:

```
<Name Gender="male">Free Makar</Name>
```

attributes: This property returns an associative array of attribute names. For example:

```
myXML.firstChild.firstChild.nextSibling.attributes.Gender returns:
```

```
"male"
```

myXML.firstChild.firstChild.nextSibling.attributes.Gender

```
<MyFriends>
        <Name Gender="female">Kelly Makar</Name>
        <Name Gender="male">Free Makar</Name>
</MyFriends>
```

These examples represent the most commonly used properties of the XML class; others work in the same way, referencing different parts of the tree structure.

Loading XML

Typically, you'll only work with XML in Flash when you're loading or sending out the XML. To load XML from a remote source, do the following:

1. Create an XML instance.

2. Use the `load()` method of the XML class to load XML-formatted data from an external source. For example:

```
var myXML:XML = new XML();
myXML.load("http://somedomain.com/info.xml");
```

Although in this example the document being loaded is a static XML file, it doesn't have to be. You can also point to an ASP page (or another scripted page) whose result is an XML document.

To determine when the XML has finished loading into an instance, you use the `onLoad` event available to the XML instance. You can define this event to call a function when the document is finished loading. Consider the following example:

```
function init () {
   //parse script here
}
var myXML:XML = new XML();
myXML.onLoad = init;
myXML.load("http://somedomain.com/info.xml");
```

As the next-to-last line shows, when the XML document is finished loading, the `init()` function will be called. In the `init()` function, you write special code to interpret the XML. For example, if you're expecting an XML-formatted address book, you write some special code to walk the XML nodes, pulling out the data within them. We'll show some simple parsing examples later in this lesson.

Sending XML

The XML class allows you to send XML to a URL. It also enables you to send XML and load the resulting document simultaneously.

To send XML to a URL, use the `send()` method and specify a destination URL:

```
var myXML:XML = new XML("<Message><Text>Hi!</Text></Message>");
myXML.send("http://somedomain.com/somedestination.asp");
```

To send XML and receive a response, all in one shot, use the `sendAndLoad()` method of the XML class. With this method, you must specify an XML instance whose contents you want to send, a URL in which to send the XML document, and an XML instance in which to receive the response. As with the load() example described earlier, you must define an onLoad event to handle the loaded XML. Here's an example:

```
var URL:String = "http://www.myDomain.com/UserLogin.asp";
function init () {
  trace(objToReceive);
}
var xmlToSend:String = ¬
  "<Login><Username>Jobem</Username><Password>hayes</Password></Login>";
var objToSend:XML = new XML(xmlToSend);
var objToReceive:XML = new XML();
objToReceive.onLoad = init;
objToSend.sendAndLoad(URL, objToReceive);
```

This ActionScript creates an XML instance (objToSend) containing login information and then sends that information to a URL, where it waits for a response from the destination. When the response is fully loaded into the receiving XML instance (objToReceive), the init() function is called.

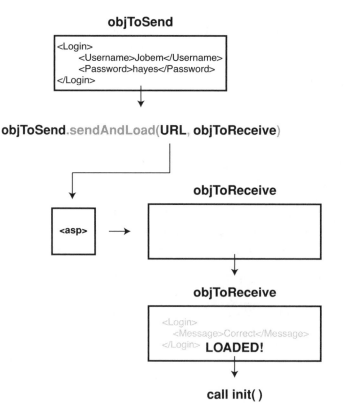

Now that you know a little bit about the XML format and the XML class, it's time to put that knowledge to use. In the following exercise, you'll format a few simple XML documents, perform some easy parsing, and use sendAndLoad() to create a simple Flash application that acts as a registration/login screen.

The Flash file used in this section communicates with ASP pages. To fully build and test this file, you'll need access to a server in which you can run ASP scripts (this usually means a Windows server). To test the files in this exercise, you'll need to upload two ASP files (AddUser.asp and UserLogin.asp) and one Microsoft Access database file (XMLExample.mdb) to the same directory on a Windows server. These files can be found in the Lesson14/Assets folder.

> **Note** *The ASP pages used in this lesson read and write to the database file. On most Windows servers, the permissions settings allow this exchange to take place. If you're having trouble getting the ASP files to perform correctly, ask your administrator or ISP to change the permissions settings to allow your ASP pages to access the database.*
>
> *We understand that not everyone reading this book has access to a Windows server. Because there are so many different server languages, it would be impossible to create supporting files for all of them. We chose ASP because of its ease of use and universality. Lack of a Windows server shouldn't diminish the value of the instructions that follow, however, because everything is explained in detail anyway.*

The AddUser.asp page accepts an XML document structured as follows:

```
<Register>
  <Username>jobem</Username>
  <Email>jobe@electrotank.com</Email>
  <Password>secret</Password>
</Register>
```

If the user was registered properly, this page (AddUser.asp) returns the following result:

```
<Register>
  <Message>User Inserted</Message>
</Register>
```

If a user of the same name already exists, the ASP page returns this result instead:

```
<Register>
  <Message>User Exists</Message>
</Register>
```

The UserLogin.asp page accepts an XML document structured as follows:

```
<Login>
  <Username>jobem</Username>
  <Password>secretword</Password>
</Login>
```

If the information provided was correct, this page returns the following result:

```
<Login>
  <Message>Login Correct</Message>
</Login>
```

If the information provided was incorrect, the page returns this result instead:

```
<Login>
  <Message>Login Incorrect</Message>
</Login>
```

1. Open *loginRegister1.fla* in the **Lesson14/Start directory.**

This file already includes all the frames, text fields, and buttons needed for this example. The file contains four layers: the Labels layer contains the frame labels we need; the Actions layer is where we'll write all the ActionScript; the Assets layer contains text fields (in the form of TextInput component instances) and buttons; and the Background layer contains the interface graphics.

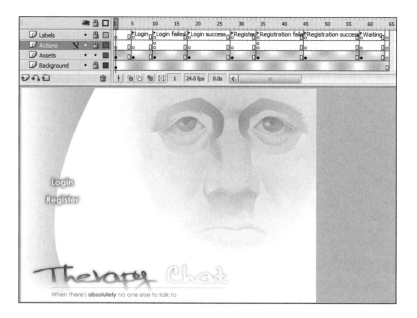

2. With the Actions panel open, select Frame 1 of the Actions layer and add a **stop()** action.

By placing a stop() action here, we prevent the movie from playing automatically.

3. Add the following script to the frame:

```
login_btn.onRelease = function() {
  _root.gotoAndStop("Login");
};
```

There is a button on the Assets layer on Frame 1 that has an instance name of login_btn. The script in this step assigns a function to the onRelease event handler for that button. The user clicks this button to go to the login frame, where he or she can log in.

4. After the **login_btn** event handler, add the following script:

```
register_btn.onRelease = function() {
  _root.gotoAndStop("Register");
};
```

This script adds an onRelease event handler to the register_btn button instance. The user clicks this button to go to the register frame to register a new account.

5. Move the playhead to the frame labeled Login. At this label are two TextInput component instances (*username_ti* and *password_ti*) and a button instance called **submit_btn** on the stage. With the Actions panel open, select the frame on the Actions layer at that label and add the following line of script:

```
var loginURL:String = "http://www.yourdomain.com/UserLogin.asp";
```

The variable loginURL points to the ASP page that accepts the login XML document (located at the domain where you uploaded it). The ASP page parses the document that you send and returns an answer to let you know whether the user provided the correct information. This URL should include the full path to the UserLogin.asp file that you uploaded.

6. With the same frame still selected, add the following script:

```
var objToReceive:XML;
submit_btn.onRelease = function() {
  var xmlToSend:String = "<Login><Username>" + ¬
    username_ti.text + "</Username><Password>" + password_ti.text ¬
    + "</Password></Login>";
  var objToSend:XML = new XML(xmlToSend);
  objToReceive = new XML();
  objToReceive.onLoad = loginResponse;
  objToSend.sendAndLoad(loginURL, objToReceive);
  _root.gotoAndStop("Waiting");
};
```

The first line of this script creates a variable named objToReceive, which will eventually hold an XML instance. Next, a function is defined. This function is called when the user clicks the Submit button, with an instance name of submit_btn. The function begins by using the values entered in the username_ti and password_ti TextInput component instances to format the XML that we're sending to the ASP page and then places that formatted data into a string variable named xmlToSend.

Next, we create a new XML instance named objToSend and pass it the XML-formatted string we just created. The reason for doing this is that the sendAndLoad() method only works with XML instances—we can't apply it to a string.

Next, we create a new instance named objToReceive. This is the XML instance into which the ASP page's response is loaded. Using the onLoad event, we tell the objToReceive instance to call the loginResponse() function after the XML data has been loaded into it. We'll create the loginResponse() function in the next step.

The next action in the function invokes the sendAndLoad() method by specifying the instance to send, the destination URL, and the instance in which to load the response. Finally, the last action sends the Timeline to a frame named Waiting. This frame informs the user that the information was sent, but no response has been returned. The movie stops on this frame until it receives a response from the server.

You may wonder why objToReceive (which is used to receive incoming XML) was created *outside* the function definition, but objToSend (used to hold and then send outgoing XML) is created *within* the function definition because any variables or instances created within the function itself (using the var keyword) are considered local to the function, and thus are deleted from memory as soon as the function has finished executing, which takes only a split second. Although the sending of XML can be accomplished within the timeframe of the function's execution, it might take several seconds for the resulting XML to load into objToReceive, which is why that instance must exist *after* the function has finished executing. If it was deleted when the function was finished executing, there would be no instance into which to load the resulting XML.

7. Add the following function definition after the one you added in Step 6:

```
function loginResponse() {
    var response:String = objToReceive.firstChild.firstChild.firstChild.nodeValue;
    if (response == "Login Correct") {
      _root.gotoAndStop("Login Success");
    } else if (response == "Login Incorrect") {
      _root.gotoAndStop("Login Failed");
    }
}
```

The function in this step is called as soon as the last byte of XML is loaded into the XML instance called objToReceive, as described in Step 6. The function in Step 7 parses the XML response from the server. The loginResponse() function creates a variable named response and sets its value based on the data extracted from the returned XML document. Remember that the response of the UserLogin.asp page is in this format:

```
<Login>
  <Message>Login Correct|Login Incorrect</Message>
</Login>
```

As a result, response will have a value of either Login Correct or Login Incorrect, depending on what's extracted from this XML document. An if statement then uses this value to send the Timeline to the frame labeled either Login Success or Login Failed. This action moves from the Waiting frame, which is used as an interim location while waiting for a response from the server.

8. Move the playhead to the frame labeled **Register**. At this label are three TextInput component instances (**username_ti**, **email_ti**, and **password_ti**) and a button with an instance name of **submit_btn** on the stage. With the Actions panel open, select the frame on the Actions layer at that label and add the following line of script:

```
var registrationURL:String = "http://www.yourDomain.com/AddUser.asp";
```

This is the ASP page that accepts the registration XML-formatted document. It will process the information and return a result. Be sure to enter the correct path to the file that you uploaded.

9. With the same frame still selected, add the following script:

```
var objToReceive:XML;
submit_btn.onRelease = function() {
  var XMLtoSend:String = "<Register><UserName>" + username_ti.text ¬
    + "</UserName><Email>" + email_ti.text + "</Email><Password>" ¬
    + password_ti.text + "</Password></Register>";
  var objToSend:XML = new XML(XMLtoSend);
  objToReceive = new XML();
  objToReceive.onLoad = registrationResponse;
  objToSend.sendAndLoad(registrationURL, objToReceive);
  _root.gotoAndStop("Waiting");
};
```

The ActionScript in this step is similar to that used in the Login frame label defined in Step 6—the only differences are in the format of the XML and some reference names. Notice that the XML document here contains three pieces of user information: `username_ti.text`, `email_ti.text`, and `password_ti.text`. This is the information entered into the TextInput instances by the user. The destination script will parse this document and extract the information.

When the user clicks the Submit button, the contents of the three text fields are used to format an XML document. That XML document is then sent to the `AddUser.asp` page to be parsed, and the relevant content is added to the database. The ASP page returns a response, which is captured by the function added in Step 10.

10. Add the following function definition after the one you added in Step 9:

```
function registrationResponse() {
  var response:String = objToReceive.firstChild.firstChild.firstChild.nodeValue;
  if (response == "User Inserted") {
    _root.gotoAndStop("Registration Success");
  } else if (response == "User Exists") {
    _root.gotoAndStop("Registration Failed");
  }
}
```

The function in this step is called when the last byte of information is loaded into `objToReceive`. This function is similar to the `loginResponse()` function defined in Step 7. Remember that the `AddUser.asp` page returns a document of this format:

```
<Register>
  <Message>User Inserted|User Exists</Message>
</Register>
```

As a result, `response` will have a value of either `User Inserted` or `User Exists`, depending on what is extracted from this XML document. An `if` statement then uses this value to send the Timeline to the frame labeled Registration Success or the frame labeled Registration Failed.

11. Choose Control > Test Movie to test your work. Click the Register button and submit some information. Reopen the movie and then try to log in.

You have just created a simple application that illustrates some uses of the XML class. Test it a few times to make sure that you're comfortable with the ActionScript.

12. Close the test movie and save your work as *loginRegister2.fla*.

Now you're ready to start creating some advanced data-driven applications.

Using Socket Servers

A *socket server* is an application that can accept "socket" connections. Socket connections are persistent, which means that they let you remain connected to a server rather than making a connection just long enough to download information before disconnecting. Unlike a scripted page, a socket server is an application that's always running. It can accept simultaneous connections from multiple computers and exchange information among them. While you're connected to a socket server, you can send or receive information at any time. Using socket connections to continually transfer data to and from the server is how most chats and multiplayer games are created in Flash.

A key principle to understand about using socket connections with Flash is that you don't have to request information to get information—for example, in a chat application, a message can be *pushed* into Flash at any time without Flash having to ask for it.

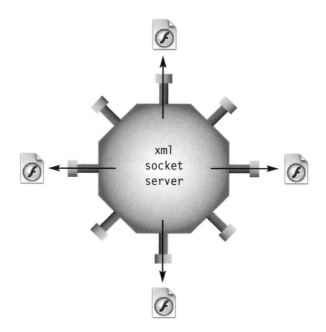

Introduction to the XMLSocket Class

This section provides a basic introduction to Flash's built-in XMLSocket class. This discussion is simply a guide to the use of this built-in class, so you can familiarize yourself with the general concepts needed for plugging your applications into nearly any socket server. The exercise that follows makes use of a special socket server that wraps most of the functionalities you're about to learn into a simple-to-use class. But more on this in a bit. Let's look at the inherent way Flash communicates with a socket server.

Before you can connect a Flash movie to a socket server, you must create a new XMLSocket instance, using the constructor for the XMLSocket class. You can then use the methods of the instance to connect to a server and exchange information. In this section, we'll show you how to create and use an XMLSocket instance while also using the XML class methods and properties introduced earlier in this lesson.

To create a new XMLSocket instance, you must use the constructor for XMLSocket. Here's an example:

```
var server:XMLSocket = new XMLSocket();
```

This line of ActionScript creates a new XMLSocket instance named server. To connect the XMLSocket to a server, you simply employ the connect() method using the following syntax:

```
server.connect(hostName,port)
```

The hostName parameter is the IP address on which the socket server resides—usually a numeric sequence (for example, 65.134.12.2). IP addresses such as 127.0.0.1 or localhost are valid references to your own computer. If you type **http://localhost** into your web browser's address bar, it would try to connect to your computer as if it were a website. The port parameter refers to the port on which the server is listening. Flash can connect only to ports higher than 1024. For example:

```
var server:XMLSocket = new XMLSocket();
server.connect("localhost", 9999)
```

You can close a connection with a socket by using the close() method:

```
server.close();
```

To send information via the socket connection, simply use the send() method and pass in the instance you want to send. For example:

```
server.send("<Text>Hi</Text>");
```

The XMLSocket class can respond to the following types of events:

- onConnect—This event fires when the connection is accepted or fails.
- onXML—This event fires when information arrives via the socket connection. This action lets you know that new information has arrived so that you can use it.
- onClose—This event fires when the connection with the socket is lost. This event will not fire as a result of purposely closing the connection from Flash using the XMLSocket.close() method.

As we did with the onLoad event in the XML class, we have to define these event handlers with the XMLSocket instance that we create. For example:

```
function serverConnected (success:Boolean) {
  trace(success);
}
server.onConnect = serverConnected;
```

Here the serverConnected() function is called when the onConnect event is fired. The success parameter in the function definition has a value of true if the connection was successful and false if the connection was unsuccessful.

The onXML event is used as follows:

```
function xmlReceived (data:XML) {
  trace(data);
}
server.onXML = xmlReceived;
```

The xmlReceived() function is called each time information arrives via the socket. The data parameter contains the XML document pushed into Flash.

The onClose event handler can be defined and used as follows:

```
function socketClosed () {
  //notify the user
}
server.onClose = socketClosed;
```

You would typically use this type of event to let the user know that a connection has been lost.

ElectroServer 3

To utilize the functionality of any socket server, you can't just upload a script into the CGI-bin of your website or place it in a normal web-accessible directory. Usually written in Java, C, C++, or Visual Basic, socket servers generally require root-level access to the web server. This usually means that you must be running your own dedicated server to install and use a socket server. Fortunately, this isn't as scary as it sounds. As a matter of fact, you can set up a socket server on your own personal computer so that you can develop with it, which is a recommended and common practice when developing applications that use a socket server.

For the next exercise, we'll show you how to get a socket server up and running on your local machine so that you can go on to build a simple chat application that connects to the socket server. To test it, you'll need to use Windows 98, Windows 2000, Windows XP, Windows ME, or newer.

The accompanying CD-ROM contains the installer for a Java-based socket server called ElectroServer 3. To get the latest version of ElectroServer or to find more examples, please visit *www.electro-server.com.*

Note *ElectroServer 3 is supported by any operating system that supports the JRE. This includes Macintosh OS-X and higher, Linux, UNIX, Windows, and so on. For non–Windows installation instructions for ElectroServer 3 see www.electro-server.com.*

The next exercise guides you through the steps to get ElectroServer 3 up and running on your Windows computer.

1. To install and start ElectroServer 3 on Windows, open the Lesson14/Assets directory. Double-click the file called *InstallElectroServer.exe* to install ElectroServer 3, and follow the series of prompts to completion. You don't need to change any of the default options during the installation process.

You have just installed ElectroServer 3, the socket server that we'll use in the next exercise to build a Flash chat. If you left the default options selected while installing ElectroServer 3, it also installed several example files onto your hard drive.

2. To start ElectroServer 3, click Start > All Programs (or Program Files) > Electrotank > ElectroServer 3 > Start ElectroServer.

ElectroServer 3 should start without any problem.

By default, ElectroServer 3 will connect to the *127.0.0.1* IP address, which is the IP address by which your computer refers to itself. Also, the default port on which ElectroServer 3 will exchange data is 9875. Both the IP and the port are configurable, but you won't need to change the settings for the chat exercise.

ElectroServer Class

In the next exercise, you'll build a chat program that communicates with ElectroServer 3. When being developed, a socket server must be programmed to look for a certain protocol. XML is a protocol, but even deeper than that, the socket server must look for XML in a certain structure—a protocol within a protocol. For example, if you want to send an XML-formatted login request from Flash to ElectroServer 3, it must use this format:

```
<XmlDoc>
  <Action>Login</Action>
  <Parameters>
    <Name>myName</Name>
    <Password>myPassword</Password>
  </Parameters>
</XmlDoc>
```

ElectroServer 3 reads the Action node, and then knows what else to look for. When it sees that the Action is `Login`, it knows to expect a `Name` node and a `Password` node. You must use a specific XML protocol for every socket server. XML itself is a standard, but the structure of the XML is specific to the socket server being used.

Does this sound daunting? You can send or receive 100 or so different XML packets in ElectroServer 3 to accomplish tasks such as sending a message, creating a room, and so on. There is good news, though: The ElectroServer class is included with this lesson. The ElectroServer class internally handles all the XML formats that need to be sent or received. You can talk to ElectroServer 3 easily through the ElectroServer class, without having to write a single line of XML!

> **Note** *Within the directory of this project's lesson files is a file named ElectroServer.as. This file defines the ElectroServer class and its capabilities. During exporting or compiling of this movie, Flash uses the contents of this file to enable the exported movie to utilize the functionality of the ElectroServer class. It's important that this file (and its supporting files, named* Wddx.as *and* WddxRecordset.as) *exist in the same directory as the completed project file; otherwise, an error will occur when you export the movie.*

To send a chat message to the server, this is all you need to do:

```
ElectroServer.sendMessage("public", "Hello world!");
```

This line of ActionScript executes the sendMessage() method of the ElectroServer class. The first parameter, "public", tells the ElectroServer class to send a public message to the entire room. The second parameter is the message to send.

To send a private message to a user named Derek, you would use this line of ActionScript:

```
ElectroServer.sendMessage("private", "Hello Derek!", "Derek");
```

Note *Documentation for every method, property and event of the ElectroServer class can be found in a file named* Class_Documentation.html *in the directory* Program Files\Electrotank\ElectroServer 3\Examples\Flash MX 2004 *on your hard drive. To find the most up-to-date ElectroServer class and documentation, visit* www.electro-server.com.

It's time to build a simple chat application using ElectroServer 3. A few more basic concepts as well as specific methods and events of the ElectroServer class will be discussed as we go along.

1. Open *Chat1.fla* in the Lesson14/Start folder.

The file contains four layers: the Labels layer, which contains the labels for the movie; the Actions layer, where we'll keep the ActionScript; the Assets layer, containing the text fields and buttons; and the Background layer, which contains the interface graphics.

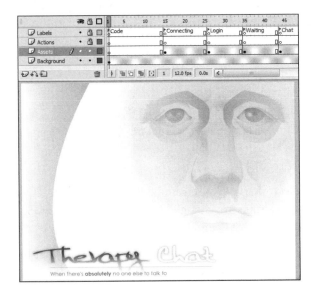

We'll begin by scripting the code to get a user connected to ElectroServer 3, logged in, and joined to a room. A *room* is nothing more than a collection of users. When a user sends a chat message, it's automatically sent to everyone in the room. ElectroServer 3, like most socket servers, supports multiple rooms. Many rooms can exist at once, each with users. A user can switch from one room to another, as you'll see later in this exercise.

After we've scripted our project to the point where a user can log in and join a room, we'll add the ActionScript needed to display the user list and room list and allow the user to chat. All of this can be done in about 80 lines of code!

2. **With the Actions panel open, select Frame 1 of the Actions layer and add the following script:**

```
var es:ElectroServer = ElectroServer.getInstance();
```

The ElectroServer class is a *static class* (also known as a *singleton*), which means that only one instance of it can exist within your movie. To create this instance of the ElectroServer class, simply call the getInstance() method directly on the class, and it will return a reference to itself. The line of code in this step creates a variable named es, which is our reference to the instance of the ElectroServer class.

For the rest of this exercise, the ElectroServer class will be accessed by using the es reference created in this step.

> **Note** *We can create an instance of the ElectroServer class only because of the ElectroServer.as file that exists in the same directory as this project file. This .as file is loaded during the process of exporting the project file SWF, enabling all the functionality of the ElectroServer class that we'll script in the following steps.*

3. **Using the following code, set the IP and port to which the chat should connect, and load the policy file:**

```
var ip:String = "127.0.0.1";
var port:Number = 9875;
System.security.loadPolicyFile("xmlsocket://"+ip+":"+port);
es.setIP(ip);
es.setPort(port);
```

When you installed ElectroServer 3, it created default settings that it would use for its operation. Unless these settings are changed, when you start ElectroServer 3 it will bind to your local IP address (*127.0.0.1*) and listen on port 9875.

The first two lines of ActionScript create variables to store the IP and port. The third line of ActionScript loads the policy file from ElectroServer. This is a very important line of code if you are planning on having your SWF file and ElectroServer on different domains or IPs. By including that line of ActionScript, the chat file will be given permission to exchange information with ElectroServer.

The final two lines of ActionScript tell the ElectroServer instance which IP and port to use. The ElectroServer class instance will not attempt to connect to ElectroServer 3 until you invoke the connect() method. We'll do that later in the exercise.

4. With the same frame selected, add the following code to capture the connection response from ElectroServer 3:

```
es.onConnection = function(success:Boolean, error:String) {
   if (success) {
      gotoAndStop("Login");
   } else {
      msg_txt.text = error;
   }
};
```

In a moment, we'll create the script that connects our application to ElectroServer 3. When the connection happens, an onConnection event occurs, which is what this script handles. Two parameters are passed to the function when the onConnection event is fired: success and error.

The first parameter, success, is a Boolean value. If true, the connection was a success, and the user is taken to the Login frame label to log in. If false, the connection failed. If the connection failed, the second parameter, error, is passed to the function. This parameter contains a string that explains what went wrong. When a failed connection occurs, the else part of the statement is executed. This part of the statement displays the error message in the text field named msg_txt. This text field exists at the Connecting frame label on the Timeline. To understand how this works, it's important to realize that one of the last scripts we will place on this frame (in Step 9) will move the Timeline of our application to the Connecting frame label, where it will wait for a response from the server. If an error occurs, the part of our script that reads as follows will display the error message in the msg_txt text field on the Connecting frame label because our application is paused at that label:

```
msg_txt.text = error
```

What can cause the connection to fail and what kind of error messages are generated? If the connection failed because the ElectroServer class could not find ElectroServer 3 (possibly due to a wrongly specified IP or port, firewall issues, or the fact that the server was not running), error will contain a string that reads, "Could not establish a server connection." Otherwise, an error will be generated dynamically from the server. The server could deny a connection because it has reached its connection limit, which is 20 simultaneous users in the free license version.

Before proceeding further, take a look at the essential steps necessary for chatting using ElectroServer 3. The user must do the following successfully:

1. Connect to ElectroServer 3.

2. Log in to ElectroServer 3, which assigns you a username.

3. Join a room.

In Step 4, we scripted what happens when the connection occurs. In the steps that follow, we'll script our application to take care of the login process as well as the process of joining a chat room.

5. Add the following script to capture the login response:

```
es.loggedIn = function(success:Boolean, error:String) {
   if (success) {
      joinRoom();
   } else {
      msg_txt.text = error;
   }
};
```

On the frame labeled Login, which will be covered later in this exercise, the user is allowed to enter a username and a room name, and click a button to send a login request to the server. The server will then send back a response either allowing or denying the login request. The loggedIn event is triggered when the server responds to a login request.

Similar to the onConnection event, the loggedIn event has two parameters: success and error. If success is true, the login attempt was successful and the joinRoom() function is called. If success is false, the login attempt was not successful and an error string is placed in the msg_txt field. A user might receive an error if attempting to log into the server with a username that's already being used.

6. Add the following function to handle joining a user to a room:

```
function joinRoom() {
   var roomOb:Object = new Object();
   roomOb.roomName = roomToJoin;
   es.createRoom(roomOb);
}
```

Before discussing this function, it's important to realize that on the frame labeled Login there are two TextInput component instances: username_ti and room_ti. The user will use these text input boxes to enter a username and the name of the chat room that he or she wants to join. A script we will be adding to that frame will take the room name that the user enters and convert it to a variable named roomToJoin, which is used by the function in this step (third line down). Now let's look at how this function works.

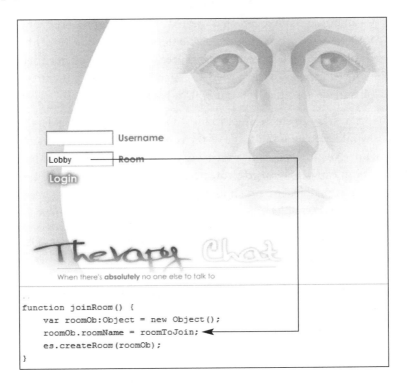

As shown in Step 5, when the login response from the server is a success, the joinRoom() function is called, and the room that was specified by the user in the login screen is created. Here's how.

There are two methods of the ElectroServer class that are appropriate to mention here: createRoom() and joinRoom(). The joinRoom() method tells ElectroServer 3 that you want to join a specified room. Here's an example:

```
es.joinRoom("Sports");
```

If a room called Sports exists, you will join it. If it doesn't exist, an error will be returned by the server. This error is captured in the roomJoined event, which we'll script in the next step.

With the createRoom() method, you can create a room that doesn't yet exist. If you attempt to create a room that already exists, internally the ElectroServer class will capture the error and attempt to join you to that room instead.

Because the createRoom() function more easily facilitates joining a room, we use that in our function.

In the joinRoom() function—not to be confused with the joinRoom() method of ElectroServer 3—an object named roomOb is created and given a property named roomName. The value of roomName is the string that the user enters into the room_ti field on the Login frame. This object is then passed into the createRoom() method, which either creates the room (based on the properties of the passed-in object), if the user is the first person in that room, or joins the user to that room if it already exists.

It might seem like overkill to create an object just to store a single variable: the name of the room. This would be true if the name of the room were the only configurable property of a new room; however, many default properties of a room can be overridden if requested. For example, a room can be password-protected, hidden from the room list, set to allow a maximum number of people, and much more. For simplicity, our room needs only to be given a name, so the roomOb object has a single property (roomName) attached to it.

Note *To learn about advanced properties, see the ElectroServer class documentation on the CD-ROM.*

7. **To capture the ElectroServer 3 response to attempting to create/join a room, add the following code:**

```
es.roomJoined = function(Results:Object) {
    if (Results.success) {
        gotoAndStop("Chat");
    } else {
        msg_txt.text = Results.error;
    }
};
```

In Step 6, you added the joinRoom() function, which requests that a room of a certain name be created. If that room doesn't exist, it's created, you're automatically joined to it, and the roomJoined event is fired. If the room already exists, internally the ElectroServer 3 class captures that error and attempts to join you to it, and the roomJoined event is fired. Here we've scripted what should occur when this event is fired.

An object is passed into the roomJoined event handler when it's triggered. This object contains two properties: success and error. If success is true, the user has successfully been joined to the room and is taken to the Chat label, which contains the elements that facilitate chatting. If there was an error joining the room, the error is shown in the msg_txt field (which exists on the Connecting label).

8. Add the following line of script at the end of the current script:

```
_global.style.setStyle("themeColor", 0xE5EEF4);
```

This line of script colors all our component instances a light shade of blue to match the overall color of our design.

9. For the final action on this frame, add this line of script:

```
gotoAndStop("Connecting");
```

```
1  var es:ElectroServer = ElectroServer.getInstance();
2  var ip:String = "127.0.0.1";
3  var port:Number = 9875;
4  System.security.loadPolicyFile("xmlsocket://"+ip+":"+port);
5  es.setIP(ip);
6  es.setPort(port);
7  es.onConnection = function(success:Boolean, error:String) {
8      if (success) {
9          gotoAndStop("Login");
10     } else {
11         msg_txt.text = error;
12     }
13 };
14 es.loggedIn = function(success:Boolean, error:String) {
15     if (success) {
16         joinRoom();
17     } else {
18         msg_txt.text = error;
19     }
20 };
21 function joinRoom() {
22     var roomOb:Object = new Object();
23     roomOb.roomName = roomToJoin;
24     es.createRoom(roomOb);
25 }
26 es.roomJoined = function(Results:Object) {
27     if (Results.success) {
28         gotoAndStop("Chat");
29     } else {
30         msg_txt.text = Results.error;
31     }
32 };
33 _global.style.setStyle("themeColor", 0xE5EEF4);
34 gotoAndStop("Connecting")
```

This step moves the Timeline of our chat application to the Connecting frame label. In the next step, we'll add the code that asks the ElectroServer class to connect to ElectroServer 3.

10. On the frame labeled Connecting in the Actions layer, add the following two lines of script:

```
msg_txt.text = "Connecting..."
es.connect();
```

The first line of ActionScript populates the msg_txt text field with some text informing the user that the application is attempting to establish a connection. The next line calls the connect() method of the ElectroServer class. The connect() method takes the IP address and port (set in Step 3) and uses them to try to find ElectroServer 3 to establish a connection. The result is captured in the onConnection event (created in Step 4).

11. Move to the frame labeled Login. In the Actions layer, add the following variable declaration and button event handler:

```
var roomToJoin:String;
login_btn.onRelease = function() {
  var username:String = username_ti.text;
  roomToJoin = room_ti.text;
  if (username.length > 2 && username.length < 15) {
    es.login(username);
    gotoAndStop("Waiting");
  }
};
```

This frame includes two TextInput instances named username_ti and room_ti, and a button with an instance name of login_btn. When login_btn is clicked, the onRelease event handler shown here is called. It populates the variable roomToJoin with the contents the user entered into the room_ti instance (remember that the value of roomToJoin is used in the script added in Step 6). It also checks to make sure that the username entered is a reasonable size—more than 2 characters, but fewer than 15 characters. If the username has an acceptable length, the login() method of the ElectroServer class is called, passing in the username, and the application moves to the Waiting frame label.

Internally, the ElectroServer class takes the username, formats an appropriate XML document, sends it to ElectroServer 3, and waits to hear a response. When a response is received, the loggedIn event (scripted in Step 5) is fired.

12. Add the following line of script to the Waiting frame in the Actions layer:

```
msg_txt.text = "Waiting…";
```

When the user clicks the login button on the Login frame, he or she is taken to the Waiting frame to wait for a response from the server, which will trigger the loggedIn event we scripted in Step 5. As shown in that script, if the loggedIn event captures an error, the msg_txt field will display that error; otherwise, the joinRoom() function is called to join the user to a room and, as a result, to take the user to the Chat frame label (as described in Steps 6 and 7). The elements enabling the user to chat are at this frame.

13. Move to the Chat frame.

This is the frame from which all users who have successfully connected to ElectroServer 3, logged in, and joined a room will chat. Notice that the TextArea component on the screen has an instance name of chatBox_ta, which will be used to display the chat messages. To the right of this instance are two List components with instance names of roomListBox_lb and userListBox_lb. As you can probably guess, the roomListBox_lb instance will be used to show the list of rooms that exist on the server, and userListBox_lb will display the list of users in your current room.

Below the chatBox_ta instance is a TextInput instance in which the user can type a chat message. It has an instance name of msgBox_ti. The button with the instance name send_btn is used to send a chat message.

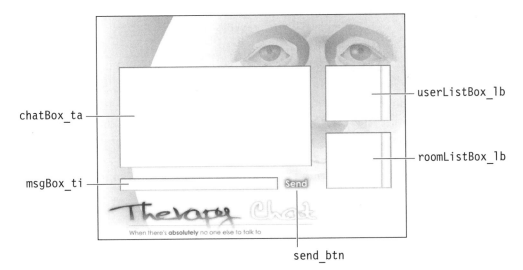

14. Select the frame on the Chat label in the Actions layer and open the Actions panel. Enter this button's **onRelease** event handler:

```
send_btn.onRelease = function() {
  var msg:String = msgBox_ti.text;
  if (msg.length > 0) {
    es.sendMessage("public", msg);
    msgBox_ti.text = "";
  }
};
```

This script is executed when the Send button is clicked. A variable called msg is created to store the contents of the msgBox_ti instance. If the length of the message to send is greater than 0, the sendMessage() method of the ElectroServer class is executed. The first parameter of this method, "public", informs the ElectroServer class that the message is intended for everyone in the room. The second parameter contains the message to send. In addition to sending a message, the content of the msgBox_ti instance is erased so the user can type another message.

You have just created the script needed to send a chat message to everyone in the room.

15. Add the following event handler to capture the chat messages coming in from ElectroServer 3:

```
es.messageReceived = function(type:String, message:String, from:String) {
  chatBox_ta.text += from + ": " + message + newline;
  chatBox_ta.vPosition = chatBox_ta.maxVPosition;
};
```

This script assigns an event handler to the messageReceived event, which is triggered whenever an incoming message is received from the server. When this event is fired, it is passed three parameter values. The first parameter, type, can be a value of either "public" or "private". In this exercise, all messages are public messages, so we don't need to worry about using that first parameter. However, in a full-featured chat front-end, you would want to know whether an arriving message was public or private. If it's a private message, you might want Flash to play a sound or color-code the text to give an indication to the person chatting that he or she just received a private message.

The second parameter, message, contains the chat message that has arrived. The final parameter, from, contains the username of the person who sent the message.

The first line of script inside the function adds a line of text to the chatBox_ta TextArea component. It starts with the name of the user who sent the message, adds a colon and the contents of the message, and finally adds a newline so the next message received will be on its own line.

Next, the script sets the scroll position of the text in the chatBox_ta component. In a chat application, incoming messages are typically appended to the bottom of the text field, and the field is automatically scrolled to the bottom. This line of script sets the scroll position of the chatBox_ta instance to be the maximum scroll position possible.

16. To display the list of users in the room, the userListUpdated event must be captured and used. Add the following script at the end of the current script:

```
function showUsers() {
    var userlist:Array = es.getUserList();
    userListBox_lb.setDataProvider(userlist);
}
es.userListUpdated = showUsers;
showUsers();
```

First we create a function called showUsers(). This function grabs the most recent user list from the ElectroServer class using the getUserList() method and stores it as an array called userlist. As a result, the userlist array will contain one object for each user in the room. Each of these objects has a property named label that contains the username of the user that the object represents. If there are seven users in the room, the getUserList() method will return an array containing seven items; the array is stored in the array named userlist.

The second line in the function takes the userlist array instance and passes it into the setDataProvider() method of the userListBox_lb List component instance. The result is that the userListBox_lb is populated with a list of all of the usernames in the room.

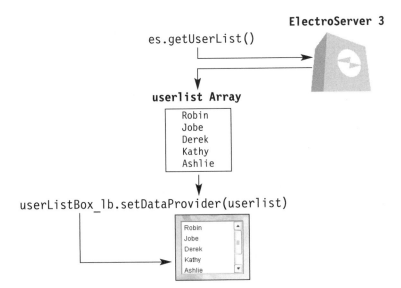

On the first line of script below the function definition, we assign the showUsers() function to the userListUpdated event. This event is triggered by the server automatically whenever the list of users in the room changes. Thus, whenever someone enters or leaves the chat room, the showUsers() function is called, and the user list shown in the userListBox_lb instance is updated.

The last line of script calls the showUsers() function manually because when we first arrive at the Chat frame we want to display the current list of users. If we didn't call the showUsers() function manually, the current user list wouldn't display in the userListBox_lb instance until the next person came into the room or left the room, causing a userListUpdated event to fire.

17. To show the list of rooms, add the following code:

```
function showRooms() {
    var roomlist:Array = es.getRoomList();
    roomListBox_lb.setDataProvider(roomlist);
}
es.roomListUpdated = showRooms;
showRooms();
```

This script is almost identical to the script that captures and displays the user list. The showRooms() function grabs the room list (an array of objects, each representing one room) from the ElectroServer class and passes it into the setDataProvider() method of the roomListBox_lb List component instance.

The showRooms() function is then assigned as the event handler for the roomListUpdated event. Every time something about a room list changes, such as the number of people in a room or the addition/removal of a room, this event is fired.

Finally, the showRooms() function is manually called so that the current list of rooms can be displayed. After that, it will be called only when the roomListUpdated event fires.

18. To allow a person to click the name of a room to join that room, add the following script:

```
var roomClickListenerObject:Object = new Object();
roomClickListenerObject.change = function(eventObject:Object) {
    var room:String = eventObject.target.value;
    es.joinRoom(room);
};
roomListBox_lb.addEventListener("change", roomClickListenerObject);
```

When users arrive at the Chat frame, they will see the list of rooms in the roomListBox_lb instance. As the list of rooms changes, the box will update. The script that you just added gives the user the ability to click any room in the list and be joined to that room automatically.

We first create an object and then create a function called change on the object. Finally, we assign this object as an event listener to the roomListBox_lb component instance. The change event is fired whenever a user changes the selected room in the roomListBox_lb instance. Usually, this is accomplished by the user's clicking a room in the list, although it can also be accomplished using the keyboard.

When the change event is fired, an Event object is passed into the event handler. We extract the name of the item that was selected and give it a variable name of room. The value of that variable is then passed into the joinRoom() method to join the user to that room.

When users join a new room, they receive an updated user list, which is handled by code we have added to this frame. So, by simply clicking the name of a room, the user will be joined to that room, and the list of users will change to display the list of users who are in that room.

19. Start ElectroServer 3.

The default IP and port for ElectroServer 3 are 127.0.0.1 and 9875. When you start ElectroServer 3, it will attempt to bind itself to your local IP and listen on the default port.

It's now time to test your chat application.

20. Choose File > Export > Movie to export this project to a *SWF* file in this lesson's directory on your hard drive. Navigate to that directory and double-click the exported *SWF file*. Log in and send some chat messages.

You should see your chat messages appear in the chatBox_ta TextArea component. Try opening more than one copy of this SWF file and log in with different usernames. You should be able to see all the users in the userListBox_lb List component.

Try to log in two users with the same username to see whether you receive an error. Log users into separate rooms and try to join a room by clicking the room name.

21. Close the test movie and save your work as *Chat2.fla.*

You accomplished a lot in this exercise. You created a basic chat application using the ElectroServer class, a little bit of ActionScript, and some components.

If you're interested in creating a more advanced chat room, look through the ElectroServer class documentation on the CD-ROM or download some source files from *www.electrotank.com/ElectroServer/*.

You can modify this chat to do any of the following:

- Enable password-protected rooms
- Allow private messaging
- Let a user create a new room from the Chat frame label
- Build in support for emoticons

What You Have Learned

In this lesson, you have:

- Learned the basics of XML format (pages 361–364)
- Used several of the XML class methods and properties (pages 364–368)
- Created a simple Flash registration and login application (pages 369–375)
- Explored XML socket servers (pages 376–380)
- Built a real-time Flash chat application using the ElectroServer class (pages 381–394)

15 External Interface

Macromedia Flash 8 introduces a new way for Flash applications to communicate with the environment hosting Flash Player. When deploying applications to the web, that most frequently means communicating with the browser. The ExternalInterface class provides a way to make synchronous calls to JavaScript functions (something not previously available) as well as a simple way in which to call ActionScript functions from JavaScript. Using ExternalInterface you can build integrated applications utilizing functionality native not only to Flash Player, but also functionality of the environment within which Flash Player is embedded.

Using ExternalInteface, you can build integrated Flash/HTML applications such as the quiz application from this lesson.

What You Will Learn

In this lesson you will:

- Learn how to call JavaScript functions from Flash Player
- Call ActionScript functions from JavaScript

Approximate Time

This lesson takes approximately an hour to complete.

Lesson Files

Media Files:

None

Starting Files:

Lesson15/Start/emailTester1.fla
Lesson15/Start/counter1.fla

Completed Projects:

Lesson15/Completed/emailTester2.fla
Lesson15/Completed/counter2.fla

Getting Started with ExternalInterface

The ExternalInterface class is the preferred way in which you make JavaScript to Flash and Flash to JavaScript function calls when you are publishing Flash 8 content. The class is only available starting in Flash Player 8. If you plan to publish content to a previous version of Flash Player, you'll need to use something such as the Flash/JavaScript Integration Kit. You can read more about the Flash/JavaScript Integration Kit at *http://weblogs.macromedia.com/flashjavascript*.

ExternalInterface is designed to work with ActiveX as well as the NPRuntime API. What that means is that it works with InternetExplorer 5.0 and higher on Windows as well as with Netscape 8.0 and higher, Mozilla 1.7.5 and higher, and Firefox 1.0 and higher on Windows and Macintosh, and Safari 1.3 and higher on Macintosh. At the time of this writing, NPRuntime does not yet work with Opera. If you are building an application that must work in a browser that does not support ActiveX or NPRuntime, you can consider the Flash/JavaScript Integration Kit.

The ExternalInterface class is in the flash.external package. That means that if you want to reference the class you'll either have to use the fully qualified class name (flash.external.ExternalInterface) or you'll have to import the class before referencing it. Importing the class is generally recommended because it makes your code more succinct and readable. The following import statement imports the class so that you can simply reference the class as ExternalInterface at any point following the import statement. The following import statement is implied in every short example in the remainder of this lesson:

```
import flash.external.ExternalInterface;
```

Configuring HTML for Basic ExternalInterface Calls

If you want to use ExternalInterface to enable Flash-to-JavaScript and JavaScript-to-Flash communication, you'll have to configure the HTML so that the allowScriptAccess parameter (<object> tag) and attribute (<embed> tag) is set to always. The default HTML published by Flash assigns a value of sameDomain to allowScriptAccess, so if you've published the HTML from Flash, you'll need to edit it. The following illustrates where you can locate the `allowScriptAccess` parameter and attribute:

```
<object classid="clsid:d27cdb6e-ae6d-11cf-96b8-444553540000" ¬
    codebase="http://fpdownload.macromedia.com/pub/shockwave/cabs/ ¬
    flash/swflash.cab#version=8,0,0,0" width="550" height="400" ¬
    id="Example" align="middle">
    <param name="allowScriptAccess" value="always" />
    <param name="movie" value="Example.swf" />
    <param name="quality" value="high" />
    <param name="bgcolor" value="#ffffff" />
    <embed src="Example.swf" quality="high" bgcolor="#ffffff" ¬
        width="550" height="400" name="Example" align="middle" ¬
        allowScriptAccess="always" type="application/x-shockwave-flash" ¬
        pluginspage="http://www.macromedia.com/go/getflashplayer" />
</object>
```

Calling JavaScript Functions from ActionScript

There are potentially many reasons to call JavaScript functions from a Flash movie embedded within an HTML page. JavaScript has access to data that is not immediately accessible to Flash Player. For example, JavaScript can determine which browser is being used. It's possible that you might want to capture that data and send it to the server for logging purposes. By calling a JavaScript function from Flash, it's possible to retrieve that data and then you can use standard ActionScript APIs (LoadVars, XML, and so on) to send that data to the server. Another possibility that you'll see in the first task of this chapter is that you can call JavaScript functions from Flash to use JavaScript functionality that's not available natively within ActionScript.

Regardless of what you want to accomplish by calling JavaScript functions from Flash, the way in which you make the call is the same. The `ExternalInterface.call()` method is a static method that requires at least one parameter specifying the name of the function to call. The function name must be specified as a string, and the value must be the name of the function in the container (that is, the JavaScript function) that you want to call. The following code calls a function named `testFunction()`:

```
ExternalInterface.call("testFunction");
```

You can pass parameters to the JavaScript function by adding them to the parameter list of the `ExternalInterface.call()` method. For example, if you want to pass four string parameters to `testFunction()`, the code might look something like the following:

```
ExternalInterface.call("testFunction", "a", "b", "c", "d");
```

As a simple example, the following code opens a JavaScript alert window with a message that says "This alert was opened by ExternalInterface.":

```
ExternalInterface.call("alert", ¬
    "This alert was opened by ExternalInterface.");
```

Note that alert() is a standard, built-in JavaScript function that opens a new alert window.

One feature that ExternalInterface has that previous Flash-to-JavaScript communication options didn't have is that the call() method is synchronous, so if the JavaScript function returns a value, it is returned by the call() method. For example, if testFunction() is defined so that it returns a string, the following code would assign the return value to a variable called browserStr:

```
var browserStr:String = ExternalInterface.call("testFunction");
```

Using JavaScript Functionality from Flash

In the first task in this lesson, you'll build an application that allows Flash to leverage JavaScript functionality that's not available in ActionScript. You'll use JavaScript regular expressions to test whether the email address that the user has entered looks like a valid email address (it follows the rules of a properly formatted email address).

Regular expressions are patterns that can describe strings in a generalized fashion. Regular expressions are useful for searching for substrings and testing whether a string is in a valid format. Regular expressions are built into JavaScript, but not Flash. However, by using ExternalInterface you can run a regular expression test in JavaScript, and return the result to Flash. Because the focus of this book is on ActionScript, not regular expressions, it's beyond the scope of this book to discuss regular expressions in detail. For the purposes of this task, we'll provide the JavaScript regular expression code. (If you want to learn more about regular expressions there are many good resources online. One helpful resource is *www.regular-expressions.info*.)

1. Open *emailTester1.fla* from the Lesson15/Start directory.

The Flash document contains all the assets you'll need to complete the task. Note that there are two layers on the main Timeline: Actions and Components. There are four component instances on the Components layer. At the top is a Label instance with an instance name of emailTestLbl. Below that is an unnamed Label instance and a TextInput instance with an instance name of email. Below that is a Button instance named send.

2. Select the keyframe on the Actions layer and open the Actions panel by pressing F9. Add the following import statement to the Script pane:

```
import flash.external.ExternalInterface;
```

Import the class to make the remainder of the code more readable.

3. Add the following line of code to assign a listener function to the click event for the button:

```
send.addEventListener("click", checkEmail);
```

The preceding code tells Flash Player to call the checkEmail() function when the user clicks the button.

4. Define the `checkEmail()` function so it calls a JavaScript function called testEmail and passes it the value from the email TextInput component. Assign the return value to the `emailTextLbl` Label component.

```
function checkEmail():Void {
   emailTestLbl.text = ExternalInterface.call("testEmail", email.text);
}
```

The `checkEmail()` function is called each time the user clicks on the send button. The function calls a JavaScript function (`testEmail()`) in the container HTML page. It passes that function the text from the TextInput component, and it assigns the return value to the `emailTestLbl` Label instance.

5. Publish the SWF file as well as the HTML page.

To test the ExternalInterface functionality, you have to publish the SWF file to a container such as an HTML page.

6. Edit the HTML page and set the `allowScriptAccess` parameter and attribute to `always`.

As noted previously, the `allowScriptAccess` parameter and attribute must be set to `always`.

7. Define the `testEmail()` JavaScript function by placing the following code within the `<head>` tag of the HTML page:

```
<script language="JavaScript">

function testEmail(stringValue) {
   var re = /\b[A-Z0-9._%-]+@[A-Z0-9._%-]+\.[A-Z]{2,4}\b/i;
   return re.test(stringValue);
}

</script>
```

The `testEmail()` function uses native JavaScript regular expression functionality to test whether the string that was passed to the function is in a valid format to be an email address. It returns a Boolean value. The topics of regular expressions and JavaScript are beyond the scope of this book. However, you can read more about regular expressions at *www.regular-expressions.info* and you can read more about JavaScript at *www.w3schools.com/js*. The regular expressions site has a page specific to regular expressions and JavaScript. You can read that page at *www.regular-expressions.info/javascript.html*.

8. Test the application in a web browser.

Type valid and invalid email address values into the TextInput instance, and click the send button. The Label instance above will display either true or false.

Calling ActionScript Functions from JavaScript

Calling ActionScript functions from JavaScript is necessary to make integrated hybrid applications using Flash and HTML. Often, an existing application will exist in HTML/ JavaScript, and you'll want to integrate some Flash-enabled functionality such as video or animation. In such cases it's frequently necessary that the HTML page be able to communicate to Flash.

There are two things you must configure properly before you can call an ActionScript function from JavaScript. Let's look at each of them in the following two sections.

Registering an ActionScript Function

To call an ActionScript function from JavaScript, you must first register the function using the ExternalInterface.addCallback() method. The method requires three parameters:

- **methodName:** A string specifying the name of the function as it is to be callable from JavaScript
- **instance:** The ActionScript object to which the function is scoped when called via JavaScript
- **method:** The reference to the function/method that you want to register

The following example defines a function called `increment()` that increments a variable called `count`. It then registers the function so that it can be called from JavaScript with the name `incrementCount`.

```
function increment():Void {
   count++;
}
ExternalInterface.addCallback("incrementCount", this, increment);
```

Getting a Flash Object Reference

In the HTML page that embeds the SWF file, you must have a reference to the Flash object to be able to call the registered function(s). To retrieve a reference to the Flash object, you must make sure that you specify a name parameter for the <object> tag and a name attribute for the <embed> tag. If you published the HTML from Flash, the name parameter and attribute values are the same as the SWF filename by default. For example, if the filename is example.swf, then the name parameter and attribute will have the value `example`.

After you determine that the name parameter and attribute have valid values, the next step is to retrieve a reference to the Flash object using that value. However, you can retrieve the reference only after the Flash object exists. One way to ensure that the object exists before trying to reference it is to use the onLoad handler for the <body> tag. The onLoad handler will get called only after the HTML content, including the Flash object, has loaded. You can tell the browser to call a custom JavaScript function when the onLoad handler is called. For example, the following code calls a function called `initialize()` when the HTML content has loaded:

```
<body onLoad="initialize();">
```

You can then define the function (`initialize()`) so it retrieves a reference to the Flash object. How you can reference the Flash object differs between browsers. Every supported browser references the Flash object in the same way, with the exception of Internet Explorer on Windows. Most browsers reference the Flash object in the following way:

```
window.document.FlashObjectName
```

Internet Explorer references the object as follows:

```
document.FlashObjectName
```

It's relatively simple to write a function that detects the browser so that it can retrieve the correct Flash object reference. The following code declares a variable called flashObject. The `initialize()` function (which you can assume is called by the onLoad handler) checks which browser is being used and it then assigns the correct reference to the variable. In the following code, assume that the name parameter and attribute for the `<object>` and `<embed>` tags is `example`.

```
<script language="JavaScript">
var flashObject;

function initialize() {
   if(navigator.appName.indexOf("Microsoft") != -1) {
     flashObject = document.example;
   }
   else {
     flashObject = window.document.example;
   }
}
</script>
```

After you retrieve a reference to the Flash object, you can call any registered functions directly from that object. For example, if the Flash object has a function registered as `incrementCount`, you can call the function in the following way.

```
flashObject.incrementCount();
```

Note that you can pass parameters to the function as you would any function. The following passes two parameters—a number and a Boolean value—to a function registered as `testFunction()`.

```
flashObject.testFunction(5, true);
```

Building a Quiz Application

In this task you'll build a quiz application utilizing the JavaScript-to-Flash and Flash-to-JavaScript communication you learned in this lesson. The quiz uses a timer that is built in Flash. The quiz is built using JavaScript. Each time a new question is displayed, JavaScript has to notify the timer to start. When the timer stops, it has to notify JavaScript to disallow responses to the current question.

1. Open *counter1.fla* from the Lesson15/Start directory.

The document contains the assets you need to complete this task. On the main Timeline there are three layers: Actions, Hand, and Face. The Hand and Face layers have instances of movie clip symbols on them. The instance on the Hand layer is named `handClip`. The artwork within the symbol is aligned so that the bottom of the line is at 0,0; when it is rotated, the point around which it rotates is the bottom of the line.

2. Select the keyframe on the Actions layer and open the Actions panel by pressing F9. Then add the following two import statements to the Script pane:

```
import flash.external.ExternalInterface;
import mx.transitions.Tween;
```

You'll use ExternalInterface to enable Flash-to-JavaScript and JavaScript-to-Flash communication. The Tween class is used to rotate the hand on the timer.

3. Declare a variable to use for the programmatic tweens.

```
var watchTween:Tween;
```

You'll want to have a reference to the current Tween object so that you can stop it if necessary.

4. Register a function called `startCountdown()` so that it can be called from JavaScript. The function referenced is called `startCountdown()`, and the name of the function as it is callable from JavaScript is also `startCountdown()`.

```
ExternalInterface.addCallback("startCountdown", this, startCountdown);
```

The `startCountdown()` function that you'll define in the next step causes the hand to rotate.

5. Define the `startCountdown()` function so it starts a new Tween object that rotates `handClip` 360 degrees. Define the function so it accepts a parameter that specifies the duration of the tween in seconds. Add a listener object to the Tween object so it gets notified when the tween completes.

```
function startCountdown(seconds:Number):Void {
  watchTween.stop();
  watchTween = new Tween(handClip, "_rotation", null, 0, 360, seconds, true);
  watchTween.addListener(true);
}
```

You want to initially stop any existing tween, so if the timer is reset while a previous tween was in progress, the `onMotionFinished()` function won't get called for the aborted tween. Use a Tween object to rotate the hand 360 degrees in the specified number of seconds.

6. Define an `onMotionFinished()` function that gets called when the tween completes. Define the function to call a JavaScript function called `stopCountdown()`.

```
function onMotionFinished():Void {
  ExternalInterface.call("stopCountdown");
}
```

When the hand has rotated 360 degrees, Flash Player will call onMotionFinished(). In turn, have the function call the JavaScript function called stopCountdown().

7. Publish the SWF file and HTML page.

You'll need to test the application in a web browser, so publish the necessary files.

8. Edit the HTML page. Make sure that allowScriptAccess is set to always and note the name parameter and attribute values.

If you saved the Flash document as counter1.fla, the name parameter and attribute will likely have the value of counter1. If you've made any changes to filenames, and the name parameter and attribute have different values, you can either rename them or you can simply make necessary changes in the code that follows in the next few steps.

9. Define an onLoad handler for the <body> tag so that it calls a function named initialize().

```
<body bgcolor="#ffffff" onLoad="initialize();">
```

The initialize() function will then get called after the HTML content has loaded. You can use the function to retrieve the Flash object reference.

10. Define a <script languge="JavaScript"> section within the document <head> tag. Define a variable called countdownTimer to store a reference to the Flash object and define an initialize() function that assigns the correct reference.

```
<script language="JavaScript">

  var countdownTimer;

  function initialize() {
    if(navigator.appName.indexOf("Microsoft") != -1) {
      countdownTimer= window.document.countdownTimerObject;
    }
    else {
      countdownTimer= document.countdownTimerEmbed;
    }
  }
</script>
```

The preceding code simply retrieves the correct Flash object reference and assigns it to the countdownTimer variable.

11. Add an HTML form below the **<object>** and **<embed>** tags. Use the following HTML code:

```
<form name="quiz">
  <textarea name="message" cols="50" rows="5"></textarea>
  <br />
  <input type="radio" value="true" name="response"
onClick="userRespond(true);" />true
  <br />
  <input type="radio" value="false" name="response"
onClick="userRespond(false);" />false
  <br />
  <input type="button" name="next" value="Next"
onClick="displayNextQuizItem();" />
</form>
```

Notice that the form has a name of quiz. That's important because it's how you can reference the form from JavaScript. You'll use the message textarea to display quiz questions as well as the number of correct responses. The two radio buttons both have the same responses: one is for true responses and the second is for false responses. Each has an onClick handler that calls a custom JavaScript function called userRepond(). In the case of the true radio button, it passes the function a value of true, and in the case of the false radio button, it passes the function a value of false. The button calls a custom JavaScript function called displayNextQuizItem() when clicked.

12. Within the **<script>** tag, define an array of the quiz questions, an array of correct responses, an array for storing the user responses, and an index variable to iterate through the quiz questions.

```
var quizItems = ["The ExternalInterface class is used primarily ¬
    for displaying bitmaps within Flash.", "ExternalInterface ¬
    was introduced in Flash Player 5.", "ExternalInterface.call() ¬
    works synchronously so that any value returned by the ¬
    function is available to Flash Player immediately after ¬
    invoking call().", "ExternalInterface works only if every ¬
    movie clip within the SWF is unrotated."];

var correctResponses = [false, false, true, false];
var responses = new Array(correctResponses.length);
var quizIndex = -1;
```

The quizItems array contains four elements, as does the correctResponses array. The elements of the arrays correspond to one another. For example, the correct response to the first quiz question is false, whereas the correct response to the third quiz question is true. The responses array, though initially empty, will also have elements that correspond to the elements of the `quizItems` and `correctResponses` arrays. For example, the user's response to the first quiz question is stored in the first element of the `responses` array. The `quizIndex` is the index of the current element from the `quizItems` array. Initialize the variable to -1 so that when it is first incremented it will correspond to the first element of the `quizItems` array.

13. Update the `initialize()` function so that it disables the textarea and radiobuttons when the quiz starts.

```
function initialize() {
  if(navigator.appName.indexOf("Microsoft") != -1) {
    countdownTimer= window.document.countdownTimerObject;
  }
  else {
    countdownTimer= document.countdownTimerEmbed;
  }
  document.forms.quiz.elements.message.disabled = true;
  document.forms.quiz.elements.response[0].disabled = true;
  document.forms.quiz.elements.response[1].disabled = true;
}
```

When the quiz starts, make the textarea and radiobuttons disabled so that the user cannot click on them. To start the quiz, the user has to click the next button—the only form element that's not disabled.

14. Define a function to display the next quiz item.

```
function displayNextQuizItem() {
  quizIndex++;
  if(quizIndex >= quizItems.length) {
    displayResponses();
    return;
  }
  document.forms.quiz.elements.message.disabled = false;
  document.forms.quiz.elements.message.value = quizItems[quizIndex];
  document.forms.quiz.elements.response[0].checked = false;
  document.forms.quiz.elements.response[1].checked = false;
  document.forms.quiz.elements.response[0].disabled = false;
  document.forms.quiz.elements.response[1].disabled = false;
  countdownTimer.startCountdown(5);
}
```

The preceding function might seem daunting at first. However, as you look more closely, you'll see that it's not too difficult. It starts by incrementing `quizIndex` so that it effectively moves to the next quiz question. It then checks whether the quizIndex value corresponds to a valid element in quizItems. If it doesn't, you know that the user has completed the quiz. Therefore, it calls the function that displays the number of correct responses.

Assuming that the user hasn't yet completed the quiz, the function continues by enabling the message textarea and radiobuttons. It resets the states of the radiobuttons so they are deselected, and it displays the text of the current quiz question in the textarea. It also calls the startCountdown() function for the timer Flash object, passing it a value of 5 seconds. If you want to allow the user more time to respond to each quiz question, you can simply use a number greater than 5.

15. Define the **userRespond()** function for handling user responses.

```
function userRespond(response) {
    responses[quizIndex] = response;
}
```

When the user responds, log the response in the responses array.

16. Define the **stopCountdown()** function that is called from Flash when the timer stops.

```
function stopCountdown() {
    document.forms.quiz.elements.message.disabled = true;
    document.forms.quiz.elements.response[0].disabled = true;
    document.forms.quiz.elements.response[1].disabled = true;
}
```

When the timer stops, you'll recall, it calls a JavaScript function named stopCountdown(). The function needs only to disable the message textarea and the radiobutton instances so the user can no longer respond.

17. Define the **displayResponses()** function to display how many correct responses the user got during the quiz.

```
function displayResponses() {
    document.forms.quiz.elements.message.disabled = false;
    var correct = 0;
    for(var i = 0; i < correctResponses.length; i++) {
        if(responses[i] == correctResponses[i]) {
            correct++;
        }
    }
    document.forms.quiz.elements.message.value = correct + " correct responses";
}
```

The displayResponses() function loops through each element in the correctResponses array and compares the user's responses to the correct responses. It then displays the number of correct responses in the message textarea.

18. Test the application.

Open the HTML page in a browser. Click the Next button to start the quiz. Reply to each item before the timer stops. Click Next to continue to the next item. Once you've responded to each item the quiz will score, and it will tell you how many correct responses you got.

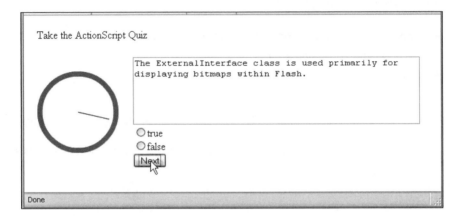

What You Have Learned

In this lesson you have:

- Learned that ExternalInterface is the recommended way in which to build hybrid, integrated applications with Flash and container technologies (pages 397–399)
- Used the ExternalInterface.call() method to call JavaScript functions from Flash (pages 399–402)
- Used the ExternalInterface.addCallback() method to register an ActionScript function so that it is callable from JavaScript (pages 402–410)

16 Sound and Video

Few things enhance the way we experience something more than sound does. Not only does sound provoke an almost instantaneous emotional response, it also provides dimension. When standing in the middle of a crowded room, you can close your eyes and easily determine the relative position of people and clattering items just by listening. In a Macromedia Flash presentation you can employ sound to provide your user with context as well as to create an engaging experience.

In addition to sound we'll work with video in this lesson. The Flash Player can load external files at runtime. This ability allows you to create some fun and interesting applications.

Flash's sound controls will make this basketball sound like the real thing.

In the coming exercises, we'll demonstrate Flash's versatile sound controls by emulating a bouncing basketball inside an arena. We'll also use a media component and cue points to build an application that loads and plays an external video.

What You Will Learn

In this lesson, you will:

- Explore the uses of sound with ActionScript
- Learn how to create a Sound instance
- Drag an object within a visual boundary
- Control the volume of a Sound instance
- Control the panning of a Sound instance
- Add sounds to your movie by using the `attachSound()` method
- Learn how to use the MediaPlayback component
- Set up cue points in a video to make the application change over time

Approximate Time

This lesson takes approximately one and one half hours to complete.

Lesson Files

Media Files:

Lesson16/Assets/bluezone.flv
Lesson16/Assets/cue0.jpg
Lesson16/Assets/cue1.jpg
Lesson16/Assets/cue2.jpg
Lesson16/Assets/cue3.jpg
Lesson16/Assets/cue4.jpg
Lesson16/Assets/cue5.jpg
Lesson16/Assets/cue6.jpg

Starting File:

Lesson16/Start/basketball1.fla
Lesson16/Start/video1.fla

Completed Project:

Lesson16/Completed/basketball6.fla
Lesson16/Completed/video2.fla

Controlling Sound with ActionScript

Although most of us can enjoy listening to music without thinking too much about what we're hearing, the vibrations that make up even the most elementary sounds are actually far from simple—a fact made evident by the processing-power requirements of most audio-editing programs. Despite the complexity of even the simplest audio clip, however, sounds can be broken down into three basic characteristics:

- **Length.** A sound's *length* can provide sensory cues about size (the short chirp of a small-car horn compared with the roar of a semi-truck's horn) and urgency (the tinkle of a viciously shaken dinner bell compared with the long bong of a lazy Sunday church bell).

- **Volume.** A sound's *volume* provides clues about distance. Louder sounds give the feeling of closeness, whereas quiet sounds imply distance. A sound that gradually goes from quiet to loud, or vice versa, creates a sense of movement.

- **Panning.** *Panning* represents the position of the sound from left to right or right to left. Like volume, panning allows you to determine the relative position of the element making the sound. If you were to close your eyes at a tennis match, you could accurately determine the position of the ball (left or right of the net) simply by the "pop" of the ball being smacked by the racket.

With Flash, you can control sound characteristics simply by editing sound instances on the Timeline—a solution that works well for presentations that don't require audience or user participation. However, if you want to give your user control—allowing the user to move and slide things around—you need a more dynamic solution. Fortunately, you can easily emulate and control all these sound characteristics via ActionScript.

Creating a Sound Instance

To control sounds dynamically, you must use *Sound instances*. One of the most important points to realize about Sound instances is that you associate each one with a particular Timeline in your movie at the time you create the sound. To dynamically control sound on the root Timeline, you need to create a Sound instance and associate it with the root Timeline. To dynamically control sound in a movie clip instance, you have to create a Sound instance associated with that Timeline.

> **Note** Although a particular Timeline can contain several layers of sounds, it should be understood that when a Sound instance is created and associated with a particular Timeline, all sounds in that Timeline will be controlled equally using that single Sound instance. Setting the volume of that Timeline's Sound instance to 50 will relatively decrease all sounds on all layers of that Timeline by 50 percent.

The syntax used to create Sound instances is quite simple:

```
var soundInstanceName:Sound = new Sound (Target);
```

Let's break it down:

- `soundInstanceName` denotes the name of your new Sound instance. You can assign any name you want; just make sure that the name describes the sounds that it controls and that you follow the same rules for naming your Sound instance as you would for naming variables: no spaces, punctuation marks, or numbers as the first character of the name.
- The syntax `new Sound` is ActionScript's way of creating a new Sound instance.
- `(Target)` is where you indicate to the Timeline which target path will be associated with this Sound instance.

After you create a Timeline-associated Sound instance, you control that Timeline's sound (for example, volume and panning) by referencing in your scripts the name of the Sound instance, *not* the target path or instance name of the Timeline.

Let's look at a real example. To create a Sound instance to control the sound in a movie clip instance named `myMovieClip_mc`, you use the following syntax:

```
var mySound:Sound = new Sound (myMovieClip_mc);
```

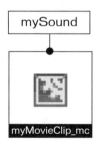

After you create a Sound instance associated with the movie clip instance `myMovieClip_mc`, you would use the `setVolume()` method of the Sound class to dynamically adjust the volume to 50 percent, as the following syntax shows:

```
mySound.setVolume(50);
```

As mentioned earlier, the goal of this lesson's project is to simulate the sound of a basketball bouncing around the court. In the exercise that follows, we'll create a Sound instance—the first step in producing that bouncing ball.

1. Open *basketball1.fla* in the Lesson16/Start folder.

This file contains six layers: Background, Ball, Ball Score, Score Fields, Watermark, and Actions:

- The Background layer contains the background graphics.

- The Ball layer contains the basketball graphic, which is a movie clip instance appropriately named `basketball_mc`. We'll be looking at this instance's Timeline in a moment because it plays a part in the functionality of our project.

- The Ball Score layer contains a movie clip named `score_mc` (placed in front of the goal) that will be used to simulate the ball swishing into the goal. We'll be working with this instance later in the lesson.

- The Score Fields layer contains a couple of text field instances named `indiana_txt` and `northCarolina_txt` that will eventually be used to display scores. We'll discuss these in a later exercise as well.

- The Watermark layer contains a see-through graphic that appears on the lower-right portion of the stage, simply to give our project a realistic "television station" feel.

- The Actions layer will contain most of the scripts for this project.

indiana_txt   northCarolina_txt   score_mc

basketball_mc

2. Double-click the `basketball_mc` movie clip instance to open its Timeline.

This movie clip contains three layers: Sound, Graphic, and Shadow. The Sound layer simply contains a "bounce" sound on Frame 5. This sound plays at the same time the bouncing ball appears to hit the floor. The Shadow and Graphic layers contain a couple of tweens to emulate the look and movement of a bouncing basketball.

Because the movie clip's Timeline doesn't include a `stop()` action, playback will continue to loop, giving the effect of a continuously bouncing ball.

3. Choose Edit › Edit Document to return to the main Timeline.

Now it's time to create a Sound instance associated with the `basketball_mc` movie clip instance. This object will allow us to control the volume and panning of the bounce sound as the user drags the ball around the court.

4. With the Actions panel open, select Frame 1 of the Actions layer and add the following script:

```
var bounce:Sound = new Sound(basketball_mc);
```

The only function of this line of script is to create a new Sound instance named `bounce` that's associated with the `basketball_mc` Timeline. Because the bouncing sound is part of this Timeline, we can dynamically control the volume and panning of that sound by controlling the `bounce` Sound instance.

5. Choose Control › Test Movie to see the movie play.

In its current state, our project doesn't appear very dynamic. You can't drag the ball around, and the bouncing sound maintains a consistent volume and pan throughout. We'll remedy this situation as we progress through this lesson. The important point to realize is that as soon as the movie begins to play, a Sound instance is created. The bounce inside the `basketball_mc` instance won't sound different until we modify our new Sound instance.

6. Close the testing environment to return to the authoring environment. Save the current file as *basketball2.fla*.

We'll build on this file as we progress through this lesson.

Dragging a Movie Clip Instance Within a Boundary

Being able to drag the ball movie clip instance around the screen is critical to our project's interactivity. The ball's position onscreen will determine the volume and panning of the bouncing sound. If we were to allow users to freely drag the basketball_mc movie clip instance onscreen, however, our scene would not be realistic because the user could drag and bounce the ball over the crowd, the backboard, and so forth. Obviously, we need to restrict dragging to the area denoted by the court.

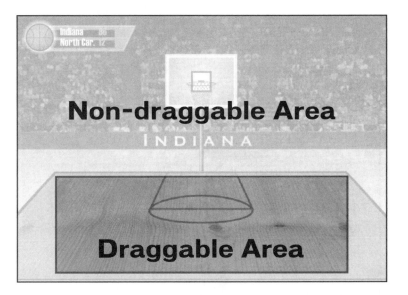

There are several ways of scripting so that an object can be dragged only within a certain area. In this exercise, you'll learn how to control the draggable area by tracking the mouse's movement and allowing dragging to occur only when the mouse pointer is within a certain area onscreen.

1. Open *basketball2.fla*.

Continue using the file you were working with at the end of the preceding exercise.

Before you continue, it's important to think through the problem at hand; that is, how to drag the ball movie clip instance in sync with the mouse movement and how to constrain that dragging to a specific area onscreen.

The first objective is to establish the draggable area, or *boundary*, of our screen. In Flash, you define a boundary by determining four coordinates: top, bottom, left, and right. Our script will use these coordinates to restrict movement within that area. For this exercise, the coordinates that represent the four sides of our boundary will be as follows:

Top boundary = 220

Bottom boundary = 360

Left boundary = 60

Right boundary = 490

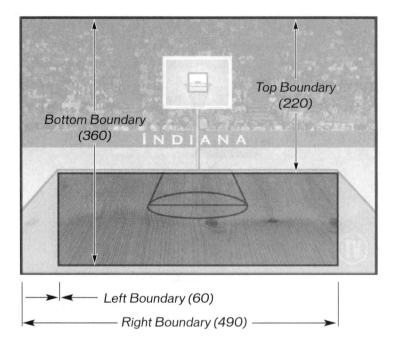

As shown by the arrows, all coordinates are based on the distance of that side from the top and left sides of the stage.

Note *An easy and visual method of determining boundary coordinates is to draw a simple box on the stage. Resize it and position it in the area that will serve as the boundary in the scene. Select the box and then open the Info panel. Using the information in the X, Y, W, and H boxes, you can determine the four coordinates of your boundary: Y is the top boundary, X is the left boundary, Y + H is the bottom boundary, and X + W is the right boundary. After you determine the four coordinates of your boundary, delete the box. There are other, more dynamic ways of setting a border, but this technique is the most straightforward.*

Because we want the basketball to move only when the mouse pointer is within the boundary, in scripting terms we need to check for a condition before the ball can be dragged. Logically, this might be translated as follows: *If the mouse pointer's position is within the coordinates of the boundary, drag the* basketball_mc *movie clip instance; otherwise, stop dragging.*

We'll need to instruct the script to check for this condition on a regular basis because the mouse is in frequent motion. Using the onMouseMove event handler, we can check for this condition each time the mouse is moved. This will allow our script to act instantly to enable or prevent the basketball_mc movie clip instance from being dragged.

We now have all the information necessary to proceed.

2. With the Actions panel open, select Frame 1 of the Actions layer. After the line of script from the preceding exercise creating the bounce Sound instance, add the following lines of script:

```
var leftBoundary:Number = 60;
var rightBoundary:Number = 490;
var topBoundary:Number = 220;
var bottomBoundary:Number = 360;
```

These variables contain the *x* and *y* coordinates of our boundary.

Next, we'll add an if statement that constantly checks the position of the mouse and allows the ball to be dragged only if the mouse pointer is within the boundary we just defined.

3. Add the following lines at the end of the current script:

```
this.onMouseMove = function() {
  if (_xmouse > leftBoundary && _ymouse > topBoundary && ¬
    _xmouse < rightBoundary && _ymouse < bottomBoundary) {
    basketball_mc.startDrag(true);
  } else {
    stopDrag();
  }
}
```

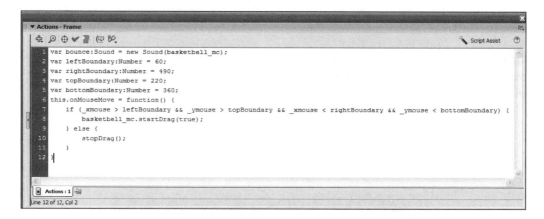

Using an onMouseMove event handler, the if statement is analyzed each time the mouse is moved.

With this if statement, we're checking to determine that four conditions are true. If they are, dragging will commence; if not, dragging will cease. We're checking the current horizontal and vertical positions of the mouse pointer (_xmouse and _ymouse, respectively) to see how they compare with the boundaries we defined earlier.

Let's look at a couple of possible scenarios to understand the logic behind this if statement. Suppose that during playback of the movie, the mouse pointer is moved to where its horizontal position (_xmouse) is 347 and its vertical position (_ymouse) is 285. By plugging in these values as well as the values that define our boundaries, the if statement would look similar to the following:

```
if (347 > 60 and 347 < 490 and 285 > 220 and 285 < 390)
```

In this circumstance, the if statement would evaluate to true because all the conditions are true—347 is greater than 60 and less than 490, and 285 is greater than 220 and less than 390. In this scenario, dragging is allowed.

Let's look at one more scenario. Suppose that during playback of the movie, the mouse pointer is moved to a horizontal position of 42 and a vertical position of 370. If we plug in these values, the if statement looks like this:

```
if (42 > 60 and 42 < 490 and 370 > 220 and 370 < 390)
```

In this circumstance, the if statement evaluates to false because not all the conditions are true—42 is *not* greater than 60 (the first condition in the statement).

When the if statement evaluates to true, the startDrag() action is triggered and the basketball_mc instance becomes draggable. The true parameter value used in this action causes the center of the basketball_mc movie clip instance to be locked to the vertical and horizontal positions of the mouse pointer.

> **Note** The *startDrag()* action is not the only way to drag a movie clip instance. In our script, we could replace this action with the following:
>
> ```
> basketball_mc._x = ._xmouse;
> basketball_mc._y = ._ymouse;
> ```
>
> These two lines would cause the x and y coordinates of the basketball_mc movie clip instance to mimic the x and y coordinates of the mouse pointer, so it appears to be dragged. The advantage of this technique is that it allows you to drag multiple movie clip instances simultaneously. In contrast, the *startDrag()* action allows only one movie clip instance at a time to be dragged. In our script, this is sufficient because the basketball is the only item that needs to be draggable.

When the if statement evaluates to false, the stopDrag() action is triggered, causing the ball to stop being dragged. Because this if statement is evaluated with each movement of the mouse, the dragging process can be stopped and started frequently, depending on the current position of the mouse pointer.

4. **Choose Control › Test Movie to see how the movie operates.**

In the testing environment, move your mouse around the court. When the mouse pointer is moved within the boundary we defined, dragging will occur, causing the ball to appear as if it's bouncing around the court. Move the mouse pointer outside this boundary, and dragging stops.

5. **Close the testing environment to return to the authoring environment. Save the current file as** *basketball3.fla.*

Controlling Volume

Everything we've done to this point has been in preparation for the next several exercises. Although controlling the volume of a movie clip instance with an attached Sound instance is a straightforward task, we plan to take an extremely dynamic approach to the process.

Remember in the first exercise of this lesson that we created a Sound instance named bounce and associated it with the basketball_mc movie clip instance. This movie clip instance contains a bouncing sound that plays when the ball appears to hit the floor. To adjust the volume of this Sound instance, you would use the following syntax:

```
bounce.setVolume(70);
```

This line of script uses the setVolume() method to set the volume of the bounce Sound instance to 70 percent. Because this particular Sound instance is associated with the basketball_mc movie clip instance, the volume of all sounds on that Timeline will be adjusted accordingly. Volume can be set anywhere from 0 (muted) to 100 (100 percent).

Because ActionScript is such a dynamic scripting language, we can also use a variable name to set the volume rather than hard-coding it as demonstrated previously. If the value of the variable changes, so does the amount of the volume adjustment. Take a look at the following example:

```
bounce.setVolume(myVariable);
```

This line of script adjusts the volume of the bounce Sound instance to the current value of myVariable. As the value of myVariable changes, so does the volume of the bounce Sound instance. We'll use this dynamic approach for this exercise.

The project's background was designed to provide a sense of depth, with the bottom of the basketball court seeming close to the user and the top of the court seeming distant. The court itself is a close visual representation of the boundary we scripted in the preceding exercise. With this fact in mind, our goal is simple: we want to set the volume of the bounce Sound instance based on the vertical position of the ball within the boundary. When the ball is at the top of the boundary, the bouncing sound will be at 50 percent volume, giving a sense of distance. As the ball moves toward the bottom of the boundary, the bouncing sound should get louder (to a maximum of 100 percent), so the ball sounds as if it's getting progressively closer.

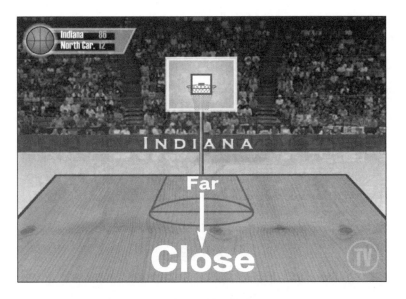

To achieve this objective, we need to do a couple of tasks. We want to create a variable and constantly update its value to a number between 50 and 100. We'll determine this value by figuring the vertical distance (as a percentage value) between the mouse pointer and the top side of our boundary in relation to the overall vertical size of the boundary. Sound confusing? Let's review the formula for figuring percentages and take a look at a sample scenario. Here's the formula we'll be using:

1. Determine the overall height of the area.

2. Determine the height of the portion for which the percentage must be figured.

3. Divide the size of the portion by the overall size and then multiply by 100.

Remember that the top boundary in our script is 220, and the bottom boundary is 360. With the first part of the preceding formula, we determine the overall height of the area—that is, the vertical size of the boundary—by subtracting 220 (the top boundary) from 360 (the bottom boundary). This gives us a value of 140 (360 − 220). Next, we need to determine the height of the portion for which the percentage must be figured. Suppose the mouse pointer has a vertical position of 310. We subtract 220 (the top boundary) from 310 (the current position of the mouse pointer). This gives us a value of 90 (310 − 220), which means that the mouse pointer is currently 90 pixels from the top boundary. Finally, we divide the size of the portion (90) by the overall vertical size of the boundary (140) and then multiply that result by 100. Mathematically, our equation would look like this:

$(90 / 140) * 100 = x$

$(.6428) * 100 = x$

$x = 64.28$ or 64.28%

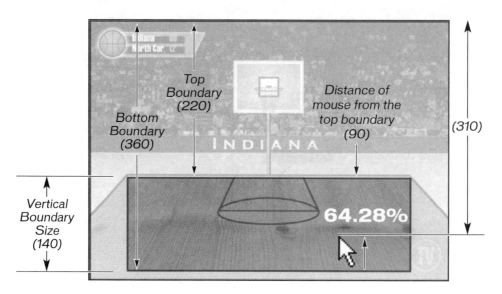

If x were a variable in our movie, we could set the volume of our bounce Sound instance to the value of this variable by using the following syntax:

```
bounce.setVolume (x)
```

Because the value of *x* is currently 64.28, the volume of the bounce Sound instance is set to that value; however, because the mouse is constantly moving, the value of *x* is always changing—as is the volume of the bounce.

We have one more mathematical issue to deal with. Using our current percentage-generating equation, we have a percentage range between 0 and 100, with 0 indicating that the mouse is at the top of the boundary and 100 indicating that it's at the bottom. We want a percentage range between 50 and100, where 50 is generated when the mouse is at the top of the boundary, and 100 is generated when it's at the bottom. We can easily accomplish this goal by dividing the percentage value generated (0 to 100) by 2 and then adding 50. For example, suppose the percentage value is 50:

$50 / 2 = 25$

$25 + 50 = 75$

Using the conversion formula, you can see how a value of 50 (normally midway between 0 and 100) is converted to 75 (midway between 50 and 100). Let's look at one more example:

20 / 2 = 10

10 + 50 = 60

A value of 20 is one-fifth the value between 0 and 100, and the converted value of 60 is one-fifth the value between 50 and 100.

At this point, the overall logic we'll use to accomplish volume control looks like this:

1. Each time the mouse is moved, if the mouse pointer is within the boundary, determine the vertical distance of the mouse pointer (as a percentage between 0 and 100) from the top boundary.

2. Divide this value by 2 and then add 50.

3. Plug this value into a variable.

4. Use this variable's value to set the volume of the bounce Sound instance.

Now let's add this functionality to our movie.

1. Open *basketball3.fla.*

Continue using the file you were working with at the end of the preceding exercise. This should be basketball3.fla.

2. With the Actions panel open, select Frame 1 of the Actions layer. After the four lines of script defining the sides of the boundary (following the line var bottomBoundary:Number = 360;), insert the following line of script:

```
var boundaryHeight:Number = bottomBoundary - topBoundary;
```

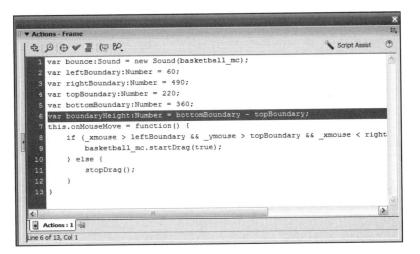

This step creates a variable named boundaryHeight and assigns it the value of bottomBoundary - topBoundary. The two lines of script directly above this line indicate that bottomBoundary = 360 and topBoundary = 220. Written out, this line of script would look like this:

$$boundaryHeight = 360 - 220$$

or

$$boundaryHeight = 140$$

This value represents the vertical size of our boundary and will be used to determine percentage values as described previously.

> **Note** Although we could have directly assigned a value of 140 to the boundaryHeight variable, using an expression is much more dynamic. This way, if you ever change the value of topBoundary or bottomBoundary, the value of boundaryHeight would automatically be updated. A well-thought-out script contains few hard-coded variables; be conscious of where you can use expressions.

3. Insert the following line of script after the `basketball_mc.startDrag (true)` action:

```
var topToBottomPercent = (((( _ymouse - topBoundary) / boundaryHeight) *¬
    100) / 2) + 50;
```

```
▼ Actions - Frame
1  var bounce:Sound = new Sound(basketball_mc);
2  var leftBoundary:Number = 60;
3  var rightBoundary:Number = 490;
4  var topBoundary:Number = 220;
5  var bottomBoundary:Number = 360;
6  var boundaryHeight:Number = bottomBoundary - topBoundary;
7  this.onMouseMove = function() {
8      if (_xmouse > leftBoundary && _ymouse > topBoundary && _xmouse < rightBoundary && _ymouse < bottomBoundary) {
9          basketball_mc.startDrag(true);
10         var topToBottomPercent = (((( _ymouse - topBoundary) / boundaryHeight) * 100) / 2) + 50;
11         bounce.setVolume(topToBottomPercent);
12         basketball_mc._xscale = topToBottomPercent;
13         basketball_mc._yscale = topToBottomPercent;
14     } else {
15         stopDrag();
16     }
17 }

Actions : 1
Line 10 of 17, Col 1
```

This line creates the variable `topToBottomPercent` and assigns it a value based on an expression that is the mathematical representation of the percentage formula we discussed earlier. Three dynamic values are needed for this expression to be evaluated: `_ymouse` (the vertical position of the mouse pointer), `topBoundary` (which currently equals 220), and `boundaryHeight` (which currently equals 140). The multiple parentheses denote the order in which each part of the expression is evaluated. The following steps demonstrate how this expression is evaluated:

1. Evaluate `_ymouse` - `topBoundary`.
2. Divide the result by `boundaryHeight`.
3. Multiply by 100.
4. Divide by 2.
5. Add 50.

There are two unique aspects of the location of this line of script, which is nested within the onMouseMove event handler. The expression that determines the value of `topToBottomPercent` is evaluated almost every time the mouse is moved; therefore, the value of the variable is constantly changing based on the current position of the mouse pointer. We say *almost* because this line of script is also nested within the `if` statement that checks whether the mouse is within the boundary. This variable's value is set/updated only when the mouse is within the boundary. Because this variable's value will soon be used to set the volume of the bounce Sound instance, you should understand that nesting it within the `if` statement prevents changes to the volume of the sound whenever the mouse pointer is outside the boundary.

4. Add the following line of script after the line added in Step 3:

```
bounce.setVolume(topToBottomPercent);
```

This line simply sets the volume of the bounce Sound instance based on the current value of the `topToBottomPercent` variable. Because the value of this variable is being updated constantly, the volume of the bounce Sound instance will be updated as well.

This line is nested within the onMouseMove event handler as well as in the `if` statement that looks for movement within the boundary, so the volume of the bounce Sound instance is updated each time the mouse pointer is moved within the boundary.

5. Add the following lines of script after the line added in Step 4:

```
basketball_mc._xscale = topToBottomPercent;
basketball_mc._yscale = topToBottomPercent;
```

These two lines of script add a bonus effect to our project. Using the current value of the topToBottomPercent variable, these lines adjust the _xscale and _yscale properties of the basketball_mc movie clip instance. The ball is scaled in size at the same time that the volume of the bounce Sound instance is set. In other words, although the volume is being adjusted to provide an auditory sense of the ball's movement, the ball's size is being comparably adjusted visually to give the project a greater sense of reality. Because these lines are nested within the onMouseMove event handler as well as in the if statement that looks for movement within the boundary, the size of the ball movie clip instance is updated each time the mouse pointer is moved within the boundary.

6. Choose Control > Test Movie.

In the testing environment, move your mouse pointer around the court. As the ball is dragged upward, its size and bounce volume decrease, making the ball seem to move away. As the ball is dragged downward, its size and bounce volume increase, making the ball seem to move closer.

7. Close the testing environment to return to the authoring environment. Save the current file as *basketball4.fla*.

Controlling Panning

Although the volume of a sound gives a sense of distance, panning helps determine its left/right position. Similar to setting the volume of a Sound instance, setting a Sound instance's panning is straightforward, as the following example demonstrates:

```
bounce.setPan (100);
```

This code causes the bounce sound to play out of the right speaker only. You can set a Sound instance's panning anywhere between -100 (left speaker only) and 100 (right speaker only), with a setting of 0 causing the sound to play equally out of both speakers.

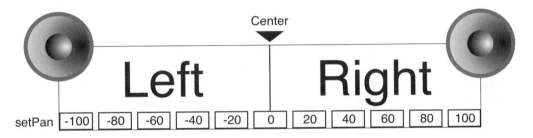

As with the setVolume() method, the setPan() method can use the value of a variable to set a Sound instance's panning more dynamically, as the following example demonstrates:

```
bounce.setPan (myVariable);
```

We'll use a variable to set the pan of the bounce Sound instance. As in the preceding exercise, this variable will contain a percentage value between -100 and 100 (encompassing the entire spectrum of panning values). We'll base the pan setting of the bounce Sound instance on the horizontal distance of the mouse pointer from the center point in either the left or right section.

To make this technique work, we must do the following:

1. Determine the horizontal size of the draggable boundary and then split it in two, essentially breaking the boundary into two "sections," left and right.
2. Establish the position of the horizontal center.
3. Determine the mouse pointer's current horizontal position (at the exact center or in the left or right section) each time it's moved.

If the mouse pointer is at the exact center point, the pan is set to 0. If the mouse is left of the center point (in the left section), the pan is set to a value between -100 and 0. This value represents the horizontal distance (percentage-based) of the mouse pointer from the center point in relation to the overall size of the section. Likewise, if the mouse pointer is right of the center point (in the right section), the pan is set to a value between 0 and 100, which represents the horizontal distance (percentage-based) of the mouse pointer from the center point in relation to the overall size of the section.

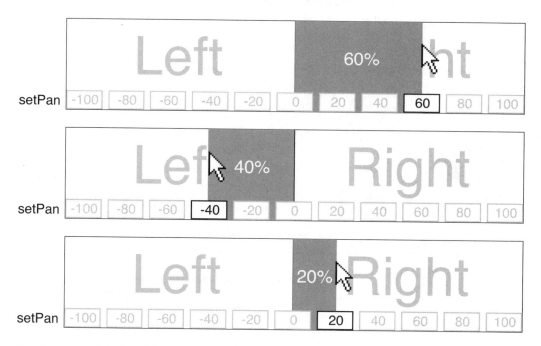

Don't worry if you're confused. We've already discussed most of the principles for translating this logic into ActionScript; we just need to adapt them a bit.

1. Open *basketball4.fla*.

Continue using the file you were working with at the end of the preceding exercise.

2. With the Actions panel open, select Frame 1 of the Actions layer. After the line of script var **boundaryHeight:Number = bottomBoundary - topBoundary**, insert the following line of script:

```
var boundaryWidth:Number = rightBoundary - leftBoundary;
```

This line creates a variable named boundaryWidth and assigns it the value of rightBoundary - leftBoundary. The lines of script directly above this one indicate that rightBoundary = 490 and leftBoundary = 60. This is how the line of script looks when written out:

boundaryWidth = 490 – 60 or boundaryWidth = 430

This value represents the horizontal size of the boundary and will be used to determine the size of the left and right sections of the boundary.

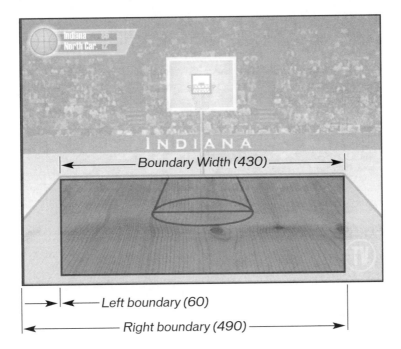

3. Add the following line of script after the line added in Step 2:

```
var sectionSize:Number = boundaryWidth / 2;
```

This step creates a variable named sectionSize and assigns it a value based on the value of boundaryWidth / 2. At this point, boundaryWidth has a value of 430. This line of script written out would look like this:

sectionSize = 430 / 2 or sectionSize = 215

You need to know the size of these sections to determine what percentage values to use for setting the pan of the bounce Sound instance.

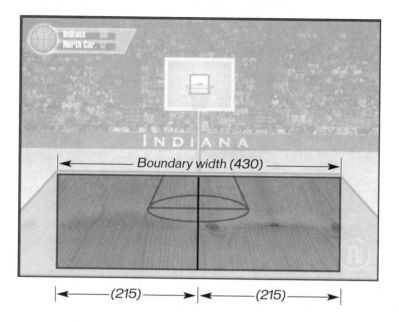

4. Add the following line of script after the line added in Step 3:

```
var centerPoint:Number = rightBoundary - sectionSize;
```

This step creates a variable named `centerPoint` and assigns it the value of `rightBoundary` - `sectionSize`. At this point, `rightBoundary` has a value of 490 and `sectionSize` has a value of 215. Here's how this line of script would look when written out:

centerPoint = 490 − 215

or

centerPoint = 275

This value denotes the horizontal location of the center point of the boundary—the place where the left and right sections meet. This variable plays a critical role in the panning process because it allows us to determine which section the mouse pointer is in—and thus whether the bounce Sound instance should be panned left or right. If the mouse pointer's horizontal position (_xmouse) is greater than centerPoint (275), we know that the mouse pointer is in the right section; if it's less than 275, we know the mouse pointer is in the left section.

5. After the line `basketball_mc._yscale = topToBottomPercent;` in the script (within the `onMouseEvent` handler), insert the following lines of script:

```
var panAmount = ((_xmouse - centerPoint) / sectionSize) * 100;
bounce.setPan(panAmount);
```

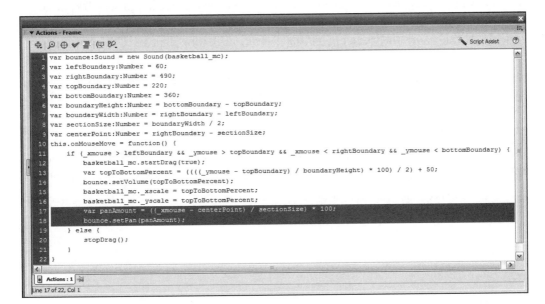

The variable panAmount is created in the first line. The expression that sets the value of panAmount is based on the percentage-generating equation we used to set the volume. After the value of panAmount has been established, this variable is used to set the pan for the bounce Sound instance. The expression is set up to generate a value between 100 and -100 for panAmount.

To help you understand how this section of script works, we'll look at a couple of scenarios. Let's assume that the mouse pointer's horizontal position (_xmouse) is 374 when the expression that sets the value of panAmount is evaluated. By plugging in the values for centerPoint (275) and sectionSize (215), we can break down this expression in the following way:

panAmount = ((374 − 275) / 215) * 100

or

panAmount = (99 / 215) * 100

or

panAmount = .4604 * 100

or

panAmount = 46.04

After the value of panAmount has been determined, the next line of script sets the pan of the bounce Sound instance based on the value that the expression assigned to the panAmount variable. At this point, the value of panAmount is 46.04. Setting the pan to this amount will cause it to sound 46.04 percent louder in the right speaker than in the left, indicating that the ball is on the right side of the basketball court. Visually, the ball will appear on the right side of the court as well because the mouse pointer's horizontal position (374) is greater than that of centerPoint (275), indicating that the mouse pointer (and thus the basketball_mc movie clip instance) is 99 pixels (374 − 275) to the right of the center point.

Now let's look at another scenario. Assume that the mouse pointer's horizontal position is 158. Plugging all the necessary values into our expression, we can break it down as follows:

panAmount = ((158 − 275) / 215) * 100

or

panAmount = (−117 / 215) * 100

or

panAmount = −.5442 * 100

or

panAmount = −54.42

In this scenario, panAmount is set to a negative number (−54.42). This is the result of subtracting 275 from 158 at the beginning of the expression. Because 158 − 275 = −117 (a negative number), the expression evaluates to a negative value—ideal because we need a negative value to pan our sound to the left. After the value of panAmount has been determined, the next line of script sets the pan of the bounce Sound instance based on the value that the expression assigned to the panAmount variable (−54.42). This causes the bounce to sound 54.42 percent louder in the left speaker than in the right, indicating that the ball is on the left side of the basketball court. Visually, the ball will appear on the left side of the court as well because the mouse pointer's horizontal position (158) is less than that of centerPoint (275), indicating that the mouse pointer (and thus the basketball_mc movie clip instance) is −117 pixels (158 − 275) to the left of the center point.

If the mouse pointer's horizontal position is equal to that of centerPoint (275), the expression sets the value of panAmount to 0, causing sound to come out equally from the left and right speakers. This in turn indicates that the ball is in the center of the court.

Because the two lines of script in this step are nested within the onMouseMove event handler as well as in the if statement that looks for movement within the boundary, the sound is panned each time the mouse pointer is moved within the boundary.

6. Choose Control › Test Movie to see how the movie operates.

In the testing environment, move your mouse pointer around the court. As you drag the ball, not only does the bounce's volume change but so does the location of the sound—moving from left to right and vice versa.

7. Close the testing environment to return to the authoring environment. Save the current file as *basketball5.fla*.

Attaching Sounds and Controlling Sound Playback

In nondynamic projects, sounds are placed directly on and controlled from the Timeline. If you want a sound to play in your movie, you must drag it from the library onto the Timeline and then indicate when and how long it should play, as well as how many times it should loop on playback. Although this may be a fine way of developing projects for some, we're ActionScripters—we want control! That's why in this exercise we show you how to leave those sounds in the library and call on them only when you need them. Using other methods available to Sound instances, you'll learn how to add sounds and control their playback on the fly.

When you create a Sound instance in Flash, one of the most powerful things you can do with it is attach a sound—in essence, pulling a sound from the library that can be played or halted any time you want. To do this, you must assign identifier names to all the sounds in the library. After these sounds have identifier names, you can attach them to Sound instances and control their playback and even their volume and panning, as we discussed earlier in this lesson.

For example, let's assume that there's a music soundtrack in the project library with an identifier name of rockMusic. Using the following code, you could dynamically employ this sound in your project and control its playback:

```
var music:Sound = new Sound();
music.attachSound("rockMusic");
music.start(0, 5);
```

When executed, the first line of this script creates a new Sound instance named music. The next line attaches the rockMusic sound (in the library) to this Sound instance. The third line starts the playback of this Sound instance, which in effect starts the playback of the rockMusic soundtrack because it's attached to this Sound instance. The 0 in this action denotes how many seconds into the sound to start playback. For example, if the rockMusic soundtrack includes a guitar solo that begins playing 20 seconds into the soundtrack, setting this value to 20 would cause the sound to begin playback at the guitar solo rather than at the sound's beginning. The second value in this action, which we've set to 5, denotes how many times to loop the sound's playback. In this case, our soundtrack will play five times before stopping.

Note *You can set all of these values using variables or expressions—opening a world of possibilities.*

In the following exercise, we show you how to attach a random sound from the library to a Sound instance and trigger its playback whenever the mouse button is pressed. We'll also set up our script so that pressing any key halts the sound's playback.

1. Open *basketball5.fla.*

Continue using the file you were working with at the end of the preceding exercise.

The Ball Score and Score Fields layers of our project contain assets we'll use in this exercise. The Ball Score layer contains a movie clip instance named score_mc above the basketball goal. This instance contains two frames labeled Empty and Score. At the Empty frame label, the instance is, well, empty. This is its state when it first appears in the project. At the Score label is a short animation used to simulate the basketball going through the net as if a score were made. A script we'll be adding shortly will play this animation in various circumstances.

The Score Fields layer contains two text fields: indiana_txt and northCarolina_txt. These fields will be used to display updated scores under various circumstances. (This will become clear shortly.)

Before we begin scripting, we need to look at some of the assets in the library.

2. Choose Window > Library to open the Library panel.

The library contains a folder called Dynamic Sounds, in which you'll find four sounds that have been imported into this project. These sounds exist only within the library; they have not been placed on our project's Timeline yet.

3. Click on Sound 0 to select it. From the Option menu in the library, choose Linkage.

The Linkage Properties dialog box appears. This is where you assign an identifier name to the sound.

4. Choose Export for ActionScript from the Linkage options, and give this Sound an identifier name of Sound0.

The reason we used an identifier name ending in a number is that our script generates a random number between 0 and 2: when 0 is generated, Sound0 plays; when 1 is generated, Sound1 plays; when 2 is generated, Sound2 plays. The number at the end of the identifier name is therefore crucial.

After you assign an identifier name to the sound, click OK.

5. Repeat Steps 3 and 4 for Sound 1 and Sound 2 in the library. Give Sound 1 an identifier name of Sound1 and Sound 2 an identifier name of Sound2.

> **Note** Library item names can contain space; identifier names cannot. When assigning identifier names, follow the naming rules that apply to variables.

At this point, you have given three of the sounds in the Dynamic Sounds folder identifier names of Sound0, Sound1, and Sound2. The other sound, named Nothing but Net, has already been given an identifier of Net. This sound will be used in a moment to simulate the sound that a basketball net makes when a ball swishes through it.

6. With the Actions panel open, select Frame 1 of the Actions layer. After the line of script that creates the **bounce** Sound instance, insert the following line of script:

```
var dynaSounds:Sound = new Sound();
```

This step creates a new Sound instance called dynaSounds. This Sound instance will eventually be used to randomly play one of the sounds in the library (Sound 0, Sound 1, or Sound 2).

Notice that when we created this Sound instance, we didn't associate it with a Timeline. This means that our new Sound instance will be associated with the entire project—a "universal" Sound instance, so to speak.

7. Add the following line after the script added in Step 6:

```
var netSound:Sound = new Sound ();
```

```
1  var bounce:Sound = new Sound(basketball_mc);
2  var dynaSounds:Sound = new Sound();
3  var netSound:Sound = new Sound ();
4  var leftBoundary:Number = 60;
5  var rightBoundary:Number = 490;
6  var topBoundary:Number = 220;
7  var bottomBoundary:Number = 360;
8  var boundaryHeight:Number = bottomBoundary - topBoundary;
9  var boundaryWidth:Number = rightBoundary - leftBoundary;
10 var sectionSize:Number = boundaryWidth / 2;
```

This line creates another Sound instance named netSound that will be used to play the sound in the library with an identifier of Net.

8. Add the following lines at the end of the current script:

```
this.onMouseDown = function() {
    var randomSound = random(3);
    dynaSounds.attachSound("Sound" + randomSound);
    dynaSounds.start(0, 1);
}
```

This onMouseDown event handler causes these lines of script to be triggered whenever the mouse is clicked anywhere on the stage. The expression random(3); generates one of three values between 0 and 2 and assigns this value to the randomSound variable. The next line attaches a sound from the library to the dynaSounds Sound instance, based on the current value of randomSound. If the current value of randomSound is 2, this would be the same as writing the following line of script:

```
dynaSounds.attachSound("Sound2");
```

With each click of the mouse, a new number is generated, and the sound attached to this Sound instance can change. The last line of the script plays the current sound attached to this Sound instance. For the two parameters of this action, 0 causes the sound to play back from the beginning; the second parameter value of 1 causes the sound to play back once.

9. Insert the following conditional statement within the **onMouseDown** event handler, just after **dynaSounds.start(0, 1);**:

```
if(randomSound == 0){
    northCarolina_txt.text = Number(northCarolina_txt.text) + 2;
    netSound.attachSound("Net");
    netSound.start(0, 1);
    score_mc.gotoAndPlay("Score");
}else if(randomSound == 1){
    indiana_txt.text = Number(indiana_txt.text) + 2;
    netSound.attachSound("Net");
    netSound.start(0, 1);
    score_mc.gotoAndPlay("Score");
}
```

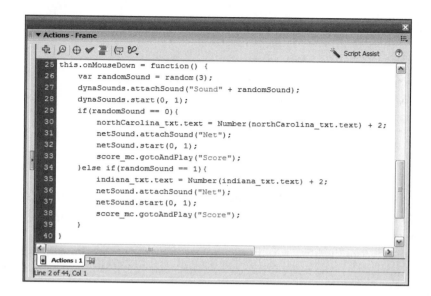

```
25  this.onMouseDown = function() {
26      var randomSound = random(3);
27      dynaSounds.attachSound("Sound" + randomSound);
28      dynaSounds.start(0, 1);
29      if(randomSound == 0){
30          northCarolina_txt.text = Number(northCarolina_txt.text) + 2;
31          netSound.attachSound("Net");
32          netSound.start(0, 1);
33          score_mc.gotoAndPlay("Score");
34      }else if(randomSound == 1){
35          indiana_txt.text = Number(indiana_txt.text) + 2;
36          netSound.attachSound("Net");
37          netSound.start(0, 1);
38          score_mc.gotoAndPlay("Score");
39      }
40  }
```

Because this conditional statement was placed within the onMouseDown event handler, it's evaluated every time the mouse button is pressed, and one of the sounds in the library is randomly played (as discussed in Step 8).

Before we explain what this conditional statement does, it's important that you realize how the three sounds in the library sound. The sound with an identifier of Sound0 is a clip of a booing crowd. Sound1 is a crowd cheering! Sound2 is a referee's whistle. Because this project was built with the Indiana basketball fan in mind, whenever Sound0 (booing) is attached to the dynaSounds Sound instance, we want team North Carolina to score two points, the cumulative total of which will be displayed in the northCarolina_txt text field instance in the upper-left corner of the stage. Whenever Sound1 is attached (cheering), team Indiana is given two points, displayed in the indiana_txt text field. When Sound2 is attached, neither team gets a point.

So how do we know which sound is being attached with each mouse click? Simple—by evaluating the value of randomSound, which is what the conditional statement does. If it has a value of 0, Sound0 has been attached, and team North Carolina has scored. If it has a value of 1, Sound1 has been attached and team Indiana has scored.

With that in mind, the conditional statement says that if randomSound has a value of 0, update the value shown in the northCarolina_txt text field to its current value plus 2, attach the sound in the library with the identifier of Net to the netSound Sound instance, play that sound, and send the score_mc instance to the frame labeled Score. All this transpires to give the realistic feel of team North Carolina scoring a point (which will happen very rarely!).

If randomSound has a value of 1, the second part of the conditional statement is executed, which essentially performs the same actions as the first part, except that team Indiana's score is updated.

10. **Add the following lines at the end of the current script (below the onMouseDown event handler):**

```
this.onKeyDown = function() {
    dynaSounds.stop();
}
Key.addListener(this);
```

The onKeyDown event handler causes this line of script to be triggered whenever a key is pressed. When this action is executed, playback of the dynaSounds Sound instance is stopped, regardless of where it is in its playback. The last line causes the Key object to listen for this event.

11. **Choose Control > Test Movie to see how the movie operates.**

In the testing environment, clicking the mouse causes a random sound from the library to play. The sound stops if you press a key while the sound is playing.

12. **Close the testing environment to return to the authoring environment. Save the current file as *basketball6.fla*.**

This step completes the project! You should now be able to see how dynamic sound control enables you to add realism to your projects—and in the process makes them more memorable and enjoyable. You can do all kinds of things with sounds, including loading them from an external source, which we described in Lesson 13, "External Data Connections."

Loading and Controlling External Video

With the growing popularity of broadband, the use of video in applications continues to escalate. Fortunately for us, so do Flash's capabilities for loading and playing video. The Flash Player 8 and later support video files with an alpha channel. This allows for some interesting and creative uses of video in Flash applications.

Video can be imported as a library item in Flash, or can be loaded externally at runtime. External video clips have some great advantages over embedded clips:

- The clip can be edited separately from the SWF files that use it.

- The clip can be progressively downloaded as it plays, making it unnecessary for the entire clip to load before it can be viewed.

- The clip can play at a different frame rate than the SWF file in which it's loaded, ensuring that the video clip always plays at the intended frame rate.

To use an external video clip in a Flash project, it must first be converted to the FLV (Flash Video) file format. Flash has the built-in capability to import most video formats (including AVI and QuickTime), which can then be exported to the FLV file format for use as an externally loaded clip. Although this is a sufficient means for creating FLV files, you might want to create, edit, and eventually export a video from your favorite video-editing application, such as Adobe Premiere.

After you have a usable FLV file, you need to know how to load it into Flash as well as how to control it and communicate with it. The direct way is by creating an instance of the Video class and then loading video into that instance via instances of the NetConnection and NetStream classes. If that sounds like too much work, you're absolutely right. A more elegant solution is to use the incredibly versatile and powerful Media components that ship with Flash 8 Professional. These components allow you to work with these built-in classes to handle the most demanding video-related tasks, including the use of cue points.

The Media components come in three forms:

- **MediaDisplay.** This component is used as a container for loading and playing either external FLV or MP3 files. Graphical playback controls are not provided with this component, but the loaded file can be controlled by using methods of the component, including play() and stop(), or by setting property values such as volume. This component is useful for inserting media into your project without the added intrusion of playback controls.

- **MediaController.** This component complements the MediaDisplay component by providing playback controls for controlling media loaded into a MediaDisplay instance. Media is never loaded into or played by the MediaController; the MediaController is used only for controlling playback in a MediaPlayback or MediaDisplay instance. This component allows you to place media in one location on the screen, via the MediaDisplay component, and control it from another location on the screen. Associating an instance of the MediaController component (named controller) with an instance of MediaDisplay component (named display) is as simple as this:

```
controller.associateDisplay(display);
```

- **MediaPlayback.** This component contains the combined functionality of both the MediaDisplay and MediaController components.

MediaDisplay Component   *MediaController Component*   *MediaPlayback Component*

Although the Component inspector provides a visual way of configuring Media component instances, there are a number of properties, methods, and events that can be used to configure and control Media component instances via ActionScript. All these components inherit functionality from the Media class, which means that instances of the components can be controlled and configured using common commands. Let's look at what you can do with Media component instances.

One of the most important tasks a Media component instance can perform is to load media. This can be done using the setMedia() method:

```
myMediaComponent.setMedia("myVideo.flv", "FLV");
```

This line loads myVideo.flv into the Media component instance named myMediaComponent. Because Media components can also load MP3 files, the second parameter of the setMedia() method is used to define the media type. Loading an MP3 file into the same instance would look like this:

```
myMediaComponent.setMedia("mySong.mp3", "MP3");
```

Note *Media cannot be loaded into instances of the MediaController component.*

After media has been loaded into an instance, its playback can be controlled via ActionScript using the play(), pause(), and stop() methods. Here's an example of the play() method:

```
myMediaComponent.play();
```

Note *Of course, the playback of media is also controlled automatically via playback controls when using the MediaController and MediaPlayback instances.*

Media component instances generate various events, allowing your application to react to such actions as a click of the Play button, the end of playback, or a volume adjustment by the user. Reacting to these events requires Listener objects. For example:

```
var myListener:Object = new Object()
myListener.volume = function(){
  //actions
}
myMediaComponent.addEventListener("volume", myListener);
```

Here, myListener is set up to react to volume changes in the myMediaComponent instance.

Media component instances can generate unique events in response to *cue points*. Cue points are used to mark points of time during a media file's playback. When playback reaches a point in time marked as a cue point, the component instance playing the media fires a cuePoint event. This event can be captured by a Listener, which can be scripted to react to that particular cue point. For example:

```
myMediaComponent.addCuePoint("liftoff", 54);
myListener.cuePoint = function(eventObj:Object){
  //actions
}
myMediaComponent.addEventListener("cuePoint", myListener);
```

This script adds a cue point named liftoff to the myMediaComponent instance. This cue point is fired 54 seconds into the playback of the loaded media. The Event object sent to the cuePoint event handler when the event is fired contains the name of the cue point ("liftoff") so that the event handler can be scripted to take action based on that specific cue point's being reached.

In this exercise, you'll use an instance of the MediaPlayback component to load and play an external video file. You'll add cue points so that the application can react to specific points during the video's playback.

1. Open *video1.fla* in the **Lesson16/Start folder.**

This project contains four layers: Background, Boxes, Media Component, and Actions. Our project's static graphics are on the Background layer. There are two elements of interest on the Boxes layer: a movie clip named cueBox_mc and a text field named cue_txt. Our application will eventually load a JPG file into the cueBox_mc instance in response to a specific cue point's being reached. The cue_txt text field will display text associated with that loaded JPG file .

The Media Component layer holds an instance of the MediaPlayback component named display. We'll load and play back our video clip within this instance.

The Actions layer will contain all the script for this project.

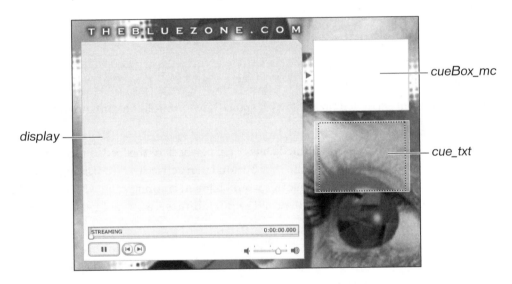

As with the other projects in this lesson, we'll start by reviewing the external files that this project will use.

2. Using your operating system's directory-exploring application, navigate to the **Lesson16/Assets directory and locate *bluezone.flv*, *cue0.jpg*, *cue1.jpg*, *cue2.jpg*, *cue3.jpg*, *cue4.jpg*, *cue5.jpg*, and *cue6.jpg*.**

The bluezone.flv file is the external Flash video file that our application will load. The other files represent snapshots of various points in the video file's playback. Our application will eventually load each of these snapshots, using cue point functionality.

cue0.jpg cue1.jpg cue2.jpg cue3.jpg cue4.jpg cue5.jpg cue6.jpg

> **Note** The video file for this project was graciously provided by Brooks Patton, who helped co-author two of Derek Franklin's first Flash books. He brilliantly wrote, produced, and directed this commercial, which Derek feels is one of the best he's ever seen. Thanks, Brooks!

3. Return to Flash. With the Actions panel open, select Frame 1 of the Actions layer and add the following script:

```
display.autoPlay = true;
display.activePlayControl = true;
display.controllerPolicy = "on";
display.totalTime = 60;
```

These four lines of script tell the display instance how it should be configured before we load any media into it.

The first line tells the instance to immediately begin playback of the loaded media file. The next line tells the instance to show the Play button in an active state, indicating that the media file is playing. You would think this would happen automatically with the autoPlay property set to true, but it doesn't. If autoPlay is set to false, activePlayControl must also be false.

The next line indicates that the component's playback controls should always be visible. By default, this property is set to "auto", which causes the playback controls to slide into visibility whenever the user mouses over the playback control area.

The last line indicates to the component instance that the media to be loaded is 60 seconds long. We specify this setting so the playback slider/indicator can accurately reflect the playback progress of the loaded file. Again, you would think that this would be known automatically by the instance, but it's not.

> STREAMING   0:00:18.874

> **Note** The totalTime property doesn't need to be set in order for the rest of the functionalities of the component instance to work properly.

Before we script the display instance to load the video file, let's set it up to open a URL when playback of the loaded file is complete.

4. Add the following script:

```
var displayListener:Object = new Object();
displayListener.complete = function(){
  getURL("http://www.thebluezone.com");
}
display.addEventListener("complete", displayListener);
```

Here we've created the displayListener object and scripted it to open a URL in response to the firing of a complete event. We've also registered this object to listen for this event from the display instance. When the loaded video file has completely played, *www.thebluezone.com* opens in a browser window.

5. Add the following script to load the external video:

```
display.setMedia("bluezone.flv", "FLV");
```

This loads bluezone.flv into the display instance.

Let's do a test.

6. Choose Control > Test Movie.

As soon as the movie appears, the external video file is loaded and begins to play. You can interact with any of the playback controls to see the effect they have on the video's playback. As you've seen, using a Media component instance makes adding external video to your project a breeze.

Let's return to the authoring environment to add several cue points.

7. Close the test movie to return to Flash. With the Actions panel open, select Frame 1 of the Actions layer and insert the following script, just below the line `display.addEventListener("complete", displayListener);`:

```
display.addCuePoint("0", 1);
display.addCuePoint("1", 8);
display.addCuePoint("2", 14);
display.addCuePoint("3", 31);
display.addCuePoint("4", 35);
display.addCuePoint("5", 53);
display.addCuePoint("6", 56);
```

This script creates seven cue points in the display instance. The first cue point is named "0" and is set to trigger one second into the media's playback. The next cue point is named "1" and is set to trigger eight seconds into the media's playback. The remaining cue points are self-explanatory. The name of the cue points can be any string value you choose. We've named them for specific reasons, which we'll explain in a moment.

> **Note** If you load a different media file into the display instance, these cue points still exist. Because these cue points may not be appropriate for the newly loaded file, you can use the removeAllCuePoints() method to delete them all quickly:
>
> ```
> display.removeAllCuePoints()
> ```

8. Insert the following script just below `display.addCuePoint("6", 56);`:

```
var cueTextArray:Array = new Array();
cueTextArray[0] = "Potential Fluffy victim";
cueTextArray[1] = "Sweet, innocent Fluffy appears";
cueTextArray[2] = "Fluffy is crammed into dial-up pipe";
cueTextArray[3] = "Fluffy enters The Blue Zone";
cueTextArray[4] = "Fluffy's revenge!";
cueTextArray[5] = "Faceful of Fluffy";
cueTextArray[6] = "Blue Zone information";
```

This script creates an array named cueTextArray, which is then filled with short snippets of text. Each of these snippets is displayed in the cue_txt text field when its corresponding cue point has been reached. It should be noted that the index position of each snippet relates to the name of a cue point added in the preceding step (the cue point named "0" relates to the snippet in index position 0 of this array).

It's time to bring together our cue points, the text snippets in cueTextArray, and our external JPG files to complete the functionality of this project.

9. Insert the following script just below the closing brace of the `displayListener.complete` event handler:

```
displayListener.cuePoint = function(eventObj:Object){
  var index = Number(eventObj.cuePointName);
  loadMovie("cue" + index + ".jpg", "cueBox_mc");
  cue_txt.text = cueTextArray[index];
}
display.addEventListener("cuePoint", displayListener);
```

```
    1 display.autoPlay = true;
    2 display.activePlayControl = true;
    3 display.controllerPolicy = "on";
    4 display.totalTime = 60;
    5 var displayListener:Object = new Object();
    6 displayListener.complete = function(){
    7     getURL("http://www.thebluezone.com");
    8 }
    9 displayListener.cuePoint = function(eventObj:Object){
   10     var index:Number = Number(eventObj.cuePointName);
   11     loadMovie("cue" + index + ".jpg", "cueBox_mc");
   12     cue_txt.text = cueTextArray[index];
   13 }
   14 display.addEventListener("cuePoint", displayListener);
   15 display.addEventListener("complete", displayListener);
   16 display.addCuePoint("0", 1);
   17 display.addCuePoint("1", 8);
   18 display.addCuePoint("2", 14);
   19 display.addCuePoint("3", 31);
   20 display.addCuePoint("4", 35);
   21 display.addCuePoint("5", 53);
   22 display.addCuePoint("6", 56);
   23 var cueTextArray:Array = new Array();
   24 cueTextArray[0] = "Potential Fluffy victim";
   25 cueTextArray[1] = "Sweet, innocent Fluffy appears";
   26 cueTextArray[2] = "Fluffy is crammed into dial-up pipe";
   27 cueTextArray[3] = "Fluffy enters The Blue Zone";
   28 cueTextArray[4] = "Fluffy's revenge!";
   29 cueTextArray[5] = "Faceful of Fluffy";
   30 cueTextArray[6] = "Blue Zone information";
   31 display.setMedia("bluezone.flv", "FLV");
```

The first part of this script creates a cuePoint event handler on the displayListener object, and the last line of the script registers that object to listen for that event from the display instance. Because we added seven cue points to the display instance in Step 7, this event handler will be triggered seven times by the time the video has played through. Let's look at how the event handler works.

The event handler is passed an Event object when the event is fired. This Event object contains the name and time of the cue point that fired the event. The name of the cue point is accessible using this syntax:

```
eventObj.cuePointName
```

and the time of the cue point with the following syntax:

```
eventObj.target.time
```

When our third cue point is fired, the event objects will have the following values:

```
eventObj.cuePointName// has a value of "2"
eventObj.target.time// has a value of 14
```

All we're really interested in is the name property of the cue point that triggered the event. The first line within the event handler converts this value to a number and assigns it to the index variable. The remaining two lines in the event handler use this value. A loadMovie() action loads one of the external JPG images into the cueBox_mc instance. Which JPG is loaded depends on the value of index. When the first cue point is reached, cue0.jpg is loaded; when the next cue point is reached, cue1.jpg is loaded; and so on.

The last line in the event handler displays one of the text snippets in the cueTextArray in the cue_txt instance. Again, the snippet displayed depends on the current value of index.

When the cue point named "0" is fired, cue0.jpg is loaded and the text snippet at index position 0 of the cueTextArray is displayed; when the cue point named "1" is fired, cue1.jpg is loaded and the text snippet at index position 1 of the cueTextArray is displayed, and so on.

Our scripting is complete, and now it's time to do one final test.

10. Choose Control > Test Movie.

When the movie appears and the video begins to play, simply sit and watch as cue points are reached and the cuePoint event handler does its job. Utilizing this event is a great way to synchronize other elements in your movie to the playback of a video, or even an MP3 file.

11. Close the test movie to return to Flash, and save this file as *video2.fla*.

This step completes the exercise and this lesson. As you've learned, Flash provides many tools and a lot of flexibility when your project calls for the use of external media assets.

What You Have Learned

In this lesson, you have:

- Learned why and how you create Sound instances (pages 413–416)
- Controlled an object's movement within a visual boundary (pages 417–421)
- Controlled the volume of a Sound instance based on the vertical position of the mouse pointer (pages 422–428)
- Controlled the panning of a Sound instance based on the horizontal position of the mouse (pages 429–435)
- Added random sounds to your project and controlled the playback, looping, and stopping of sounds dynamically (pages 435–441)
- Loaded an external video into a Media component and created cue points to trigger actions (pages 441–450)

17 Printing and Context Menus

Flash gives you a great amount of control over the process of printing content within the Flash movie window. You can print content that is not displayed onscreen as well as print the content within specific movie clips, frames, or levels. Unlike printing web pages from your browser, in which all graphical content is printed as bitmaps, Flash gives you the option to print certain graphical content as a bitmap or vector image (which produces results that are crisp and colorful). In addition, Flash allows you to gather information about a user's printer such as the dimensions of the paper and the default paper orientation so that printing can be customized even further. All this printing control is made possible by Flash's built-in PrintJob class.

Flash's printing capabilities give you a high level of control over many aspects of printing Flash content, including the area to print.

In this lesson, you will learn how to use the PrintJob class to print content in various ways. You will also be introduced to the ContextMenu class so that you can add your own custom print options to the context menu (the menu that appears when you right-click or Ctrl-click on a Macintosh).

What You Will Learn

In this lesson, you will:

- Distinguish between printing from Flash and printing from the browser
- Learn how to use the PrintJob class
- Print content as a bitmap or vector
- Create a custom context menu
- Add custom items to a context menu

Approximate Time

This lesson takes approximately forty-five minutes to complete.

Lesson Files

Media Files:

None

Starting Files:

Lesson17/Start/PrintArea1.fla
Lesson17/Start/ContextMenu1.fla

Completed Projects:

Lesson17/Completed/PrintArea2.fla
Lesson17/Completed/ContextMenu2.fla

Flash Printing versus Browser Printing

Despite all the interactive and exciting ways in which you can use Flash to create powerful multimedia presentations, sometimes it's appropriate to add print functionality to an application. Printing functionality is both useful and appropriate for the following applications:

- Employee directory
- Word processor
- Drawing program
- Quiz with a results screen at the end

There are three ways to print Flash content:

- Using the standard web page print option found in all web browsers if the movie is being viewed in a browser window
- Right-clicking (Ctrl-clicking on a Macintosh) the SWF file being played in the web browser and then selecting the Print option from the context menu that appears. Support for this feature was first officially introduced with the Flash Player 5, although there was limited support in certain versions of the Flash Player 4
- Having content printed as the result of ActionScript

Let's look at some of the advantages and disadvantages of each option.

Printing from the browser. Most people know how to print with the browser's Print command, but it doesn't give them much control over what's printed. When using this option, *everything* on the page is typically printed in addition to the desired Flash content, including text, graphics, buttons, banner ads, and any form elements that might be visible. The user ends up printing a bunch of extra distracting stuff that probably has no importance to him or her.

Printing from the context menu. Right-clicking (Ctrl-clicking on a Macintosh) a SWF file and choosing the Print option from the context menu that appears is a better option because it allows the user to focus printing efforts on the content within the SWF file; however, there are a few problems with this option. Users may not know that the context menu option even exists. Also, when printing with this command, only frames on the main Timeline are printed; considering the fact that a Flash movie can contain many Timelines, this restriction is somewhat limiting. And if you can deal with the first two obstacles, be aware that when you print using the context menu Print option, color and transparency effects used in the movie are lost. This could result in a printed page that looks nothing like you expected.

Note *For brevity, we'll assume right-click functionality for the opening of a Flash context menu in the remainder of this lesson. It should be understood that Ctrl-clicking on a Macintosh is the equivalent to right-clicking on a Windows computer.*

Printing using ActionScript. Using ActionScript to print from Flash provides much more control over the printing process and the results, making printing Flash content easier and more efficient for the end user.

Using ActionScript, you have the following print capabilities:

- Print a level or specific movie clip, even if it's not visible
- Print a specific frame within a level or movie clip
- Specify the dimensions surrounding the movie clip or level that you want to print
- Print content as vectors
- Print content as a bitmap
- Perform various printing tasks, using various printing options, by opening a single Print dialog box

Using the PrintJob Class

The PrintJob class is a built-in Flash class that gives the programmer control over what can be printed in a SWF file as well as how it's printed. To use the PrintJob class, a new instance of the class must be created.

```
var myPrintJob:PrintJob = new PrintJob();
```

With this script, a new instance of the PrintJob class is created and referred to as `myPrintJob`.

To tell the PrintJob object what content to print, you must use the `addPage()` method of the PrintJob class. We'll get to this soon. Before you can use the `addPage()` method to add all printable content to the print job, however, you must first call the `start()` method of the PrintJob class:

```
var myPrintJob:PrintJob = new PrintJob();
var result:Boolean = myPrintJob.start();
```

The first line of this script creates the instance of the PrintJob class. The second line invokes the `start()` method. The moment that the `start()` method is called, a pop-up window (specific to the operating system) asks whether the user wants to proceed with printing. If the user selects Print, the Boolean value `true` is returned and stored as the value of the variable `result`. If the user doesn't have a printer installed or cancels the print pop-up window, the Boolean value `false` is returned. This feature allows you to program an application to react one way if the user successfully initializes the print option, and another if the user cancels the print request or doesn't have a printer. For example:

```
var myPrintJob:PrintJob = new PrintJob();
var result:Boolean = myPrintJob.start();
if (result) {
   //Successfully initialized print action
   //Add pages to print here
} else {
   //User does not have printer or user canceled print action
}
```

result = true   result = false

Note *After the `start()` method is called but before the user responds to the pop-up window, Flash is paused and no frames are executed. All animations and code halt until the user responds.*

If the value of `result` is `true`, the user has a printer and has chosen the Print option. It's then time to use the `addPage()` method of the PrintJob class to add the printable content. The syntax for invoking the `addPage()` method looks like this:

```
myPrintJob.addPage(target, printArea, options, frameNumber);
```

The `addPage()` method has four parameters:

* `target`. This option defines the Timeline where the page lives that you want to print. If this parameter is entered as a number, it's interpreted as pointing to a level of the movie. If the value entered is a string, it points to a movie clip.

- printArea. This parameter expects an object with four properties: xMin, xMax, yMin, and yMax. These properties together form a rectangle determining the printable area of the target. All of these measurements are relative to the registration point of the target. For example, if xMin has a value of -300, the left border of the printable area is 300 pixels to the left of the registration point of the target. By default, leaving the printArea parameter blank prints the entire dimensions of the movie clip (or what can fit on the printed page).

- options. This setting specifies whether the page should be printed as a bitmap image or as vector graphics. The parameter value needs to be an object with a single property, printAsBitmap. This property has a Boolean value. If true, the page is printed as a bitmap. If false, it's printed as vector graphics. By default, leaving the options parameter blank prints the page as vector graphics. By printing as a bitmap you can print movies that maintain their transparencies and color effects, as shown onscreen.

- frameNumber. This parameter is a number specifying the frame within the target to be printed. It works only with frame numbers, not frame labels. By default, if this parameter is blank, the currently displayed frame of the target is printed.

All the parameters of the addPage() method are optional except target.

Let's look at some examples of this method in use. The following script creates a new PrintJob class instance, starts the print request, and adds a page to be printed. The currently displayed frame of the myClip_mc movie clip instance will be printed as vector graphics.

```
var myPrintJob:PrintJob = new PrintJob();
var result:Boolean = myPrintJob.start();
if (result) {
  myPrint.addPage("myClip_mc");
} else {
  //User does not have printer or user canceled print action
}
```

To use the default value of a parameter, enter null. The following line adds Frame 5 of the myClip_mc movie clip instance to the PrintJob class instance, and specifies that it should be printed as a bitmap:

```
myPrint.addPage("myClip_mc", null, {printAsBitmap:true}, 5);
```

To specify the dimensions of a movie clip to be printed, you must define the printArea (second parameter) using an object, as shown here:

```
myPrintJob.addPage(0, {xMin:30, xMax:250, yMin:27, yMax:300});
```

The target is level 0. This addPage() method instructs Flash to print all content in level 0 on the current frame that's shown between the *x* positions of 30 and 250, and the *y* positions of 27 and 300. Only content found within these dimensions will be printed.

You can add pages from various Timelines to a single PrintJob instance, allowing the user to print content from those various Timelines from a single Print dialog box:

```
myPrintJob.addPage("invitation_mc", null, {printAsBitmap:true}, 2);
myPrintJob.addPage("map_mc", null, {printAsBitmap:false}, 1);
myPrintJob.addPage(1, null, {printAsBitmap:true}, null);
myPrintJob.addPage("guestList_mc", null, {printAsBitmap:true}, 4);
```

To add all frames of a Timeline to a print job, use a looping statement:

```
for(i = 1; i <= myMovieClip_mc._totalframes; ++1){
   myPrintJob.addPage("myMovieClip_mc", null, null, i);
}
```

With each loop, a page is added to the print job. The current value of i specifies by which frame in the myMovieClip_mc instance to print for that page. This loop continues until i is greater than the number of frames in the instance.

Note *Remember that a Timeline needn't be visible to add frames from that Timeline to a print job. This feature allows you to create hidden content in your movie that might only be appropriate for printing purposes, such as coupons, instructions, or maps that don't fit into your project's overall design.*

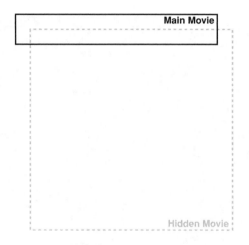

After all pages have been added to a PrintJob instance, you invoke the `send()` method of the PrintJob class to start the printing.

```
myPrintJob.send();
```

After you're done with the instance of the PrintJob class, you should delete it.

```
delete myPrintJob;
```

Tip *Don't leave instances around that no longer have any use; that's a waste of memory.*

A complete script for creating a print job will look something like this:

```
var myPrintJob:PrintJob = new PrintJob();
var result:Boolean = myPrintJob.start();
if (result) {
  myPrintJob.addPage("invitation_mc", null, {printAsBitmap:true}, 2);
  myPrintJob.addPage("map_mc", null, {printAsBitmap:false}, 1);
  myPrintJob.addPage(1, null, {printAsBitmap:true}, null);
  myPrintJob.addPage("guestList_mc", null, {printAsBitmap:true}, 4);
  for(i = 1; i <= myMovieClip_mc._totalframes; ++1){
    myPrintJob.addPage ("myMovieClip_mc", null, null, i);
  }
```

```
    myPrintJob.send();
    delete myPrintJob;
} else {
    //User does not have printer or user canceled print action
}
```

In the following exercise, you'll dynamically select part of an image and print it.

1. Open *PrintArea1.fla* in the Lesson17/Start folder.

There are four layers on the main Timeline: Actions, PrintArea Box, Interface, and
Animals. The Actions layer is where you'll add the ActionScript for this exercise. The
PrintArea Box layer contains a movie clip instance named box_mc. The Interface layer
contains the main interface graphics for this application, and the Animals layer contains
six frames of animal pictures.

When this exercise is complete, you can navigate images using the Left arrow and Right
arrow keys on the keyboard. Clicking an image and dragging down and to the right draws
a box on top of the image. As soon as the user releases the mouse button, a print command
is sent to print the area of the image that was just selected. The box_mc movie clip is resized
as the mouse moves, to give the impression that the user is selecting part of the image.

2. With the Actions panel open, select Frame 1 of the Actions layer and add the following script:

```
stop();
box_mc._visible = false;
```

The first action prevents the Timeline from moving forward until we tell it to do so. The second line makes the box_mc movie clip instance invisible initially. We only want it to be shown if the user has pressed the left mouse button and dragged to create a selection.

3. Add the following variable to track the state of the mouse:

```
var down:Boolean = false;
```

The movie initializes with the mouse button up. When the left mouse button is pressed, the down variable changes to true.

4. Add the following four variables to track the print area dimensions:

```
var xMin:Number;
var xMax:Number;
var yMin:Number;
var yMax:Number;
```

To specify the area of a target to print, you specify four values: xMin, xMax, yMin, and yMax. These values are declared here with no value. When the mouse button is pressed, the xMin and yMin values are set. As the mouse moves, the xMax and yMax values are set.

5. Add the following **onMouseDown** event to handle initializing the selection:

```
this.onMouseDown = function() {
    down = true;
    xMin = _xmouse;
    yMin = _ymouse;
    box_mc._x = xMin;
    box_mc._y = yMin;
};
```

When the left mouse button is pressed, the down variable's value is set to true. The minimum selection values, xMin and yMin, are set based on the mouse position when the event occurs. These two values are immediately used to position the box_mc movie clip.

6. To handle scaling the selection as the mouse moves, add the following script:

```
this.onMouseMove = function() {
  updateAfterEvent();
  if (down) {
    box_mc._visible = true;
    xMax = _xmouse;
    yMax = _ymouse;
    box_mc._width = xMax - xMin;
    box_mc._height = yMax - yMin;
  }
};
```

The updateAfterEvent() function is a built-in function in Flash. It tells Flash to redraw graphics onscreen after the mouse moves, rather than waiting until the end of the current frame. This technique gives smoother results to objects that change as the mouse moves.

Every time the mouse moves, a conditional statement is evaluated. It states that if down is true (as it is when the mouse button is pressed), the box_mc instance is made visible. Next, the values of xMax and yMax are set based on the current position of the mouse. Finally, the box_mc movie clip instance's dimensions are set based on the distances between the minimum values (captured when the mouse button was pressed) and the maximum values (which change as the user moves the mouse around). The end result is that the box_mc movie clip instance scales as the mouse moves to emulate selecting.

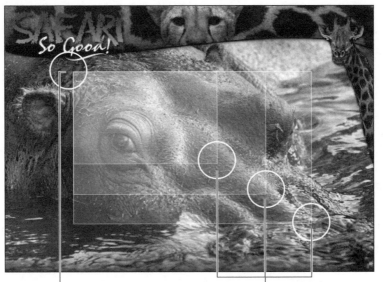

onMouseDown   onMouseMove

7. Add the following script to capture the **onMouseUp** event:

```
this.onMouseUp = function() {
   down = false;
   box_mc._visible = false;
   printImage();
};
```

When the mouse button is released, the down variable is set back to false, and the box_mc movie clip becomes invisible again. Then the printImage() function is called; this function uses the dimension variables from the selection process to print an area of the image. Let's create that function next.

8. At the end of the current script, add the following function definition:

```
function printImage() {
   var myPrintJob:PrintJob = new PrintJob();
   var result:Boolean = myPrintJob.start();
   if (result) {
      myPrintJob.addPage(0, {xMin:xMin, xMax:xMax, yMin:yMin, ¬
         yMax:yMax}, {printAsBitmap:true}, _currentframe);
      myPrintJob.send();
   }
   delete myPrintJob;
}
```

This function is called after the user has clicked, dragged, and released the mouse button. A new instance of the PrintJob class is created and stored as myPrintJob; then the start() method is called, the result of which is stored as the value of the result variable.

If the value of result is true, the user has a printer and has opted to continue the printing process. The addPage() method is then called, and the target Timeline to print is set as level 0. The second parameter passes in an object whose properties are the dimensions that were gathered during the selection process. The third parameter specifies that the image should be printed as a bitmap. The fourth parameter specifies that the frame to print is the current frame where the main Timeline resides. Thus, if the user has navigated to Frame 6, a portion of the hippo graphic, as defined by the selection dimensions, will print.

After the addPage() action, the function sends the added page to the printer by using the send() method. When the send() method is called, the Flash Player sends all the added pages (a single page in this case) to the printer to be printed.

The last line in this function deletes the instance of the PrintJob class because we're done with it.

The last thing we need to do is add the script to enable the user to navigate the animal images.

9. At the end of the current script, add the following function definition:

```
this.onKeyDown = function(){
  if(Key.isDown(Key.RIGHT)){
    nextFrame();
  }else if(Key.isDown(Key.LEFT)){
    prevFrame();
  }
}
Key.addListener(this);
```

You should be familiar with how this script works. When the onKeyDown event occurs, a conditional statement checks whether the key pressed down is the Left arrow or Right arrow key. If the Left arrow key is pressed, the main Timeline moves to the next frame. If the Right arrow key is pressed, the main Timeline moves to the previous frame. If any other key is pressed, nothing happens.

Let's test our work.

10. Select Control › Test Movie. Select a portion of the image and then release the mouse button to print it.

After you select a portion of the image, a print window should pop up, opened by your operating system. If you proceed with the print job, the selected area of the image will be printed.

Note   *The ActionScript that we added in this exercise supports selecting a portion of the image by clicking and dragging down and to the right. Using more advanced ActionScript, we could have supported selecting in any direction.*

11. Close the test movie and save your work as *PrintArea2.fla*.

You have successfully created a simple application that uses the PrintJob class. You can print a specific area of an image with this application.

Creating Custom Context Menus

The context menu appears when you right-click a Flash movie (Ctrl-click on a Macintosh). There are three different types of Flash context menus:

- **Standard menu.** Appears when you right-click anything in a Flash movie except a text field.
- **Edit menu.** Appears when you right-click a text field that's editable or selectable.
- **Error menu.** Appears when a Flash movie fails to load within a web page and you right-click in the empty area.

The error menu cannot be changed, but the standard and edit context menus can be customized to display new items or remove the built-in default items. All the built-in context menu items can be removed except for the Settings item and the Debugger item.

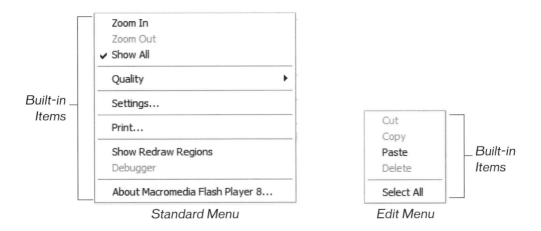

Built-in Items — Standard Menu

Built-in Items — Edit Menu

The Flash Player includes two built-in classes to assist you in creating a customized context menu:

- **ContextMenu.** This class allows you to create a new context menu, hide built-in menu items (Zoom In, Zoom Out, 100%, Play, Stop, and so on), and keep track of customized items.

- **ContextMenuItem.** Each item in a context menu is an instance of this class. The ContextMenu class has a property (array) called customItems. Each element in that array is an instance of the ContextMenuItem class.

The ContextMenu class and the ContextMenuItem class are used together to build custom context menus.

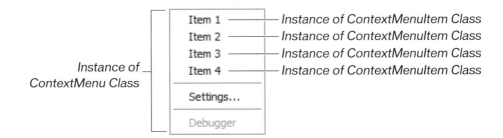

Instance of ContextMenu Class — Item 1, Item 2, Item 3, Item 4, Settings..., Debugger. Item 1—4 labeled: Instance of ContextMenuItem Class.

When creating a new instance of the ContextMenu class, you can specify a function to be called when that ContextMenu is displayed:

```
var myContextMenu:ContextMenu = new ContextMenu(menuHandler);
```

The menuHandler() function is executed just before the context menu appears. Script within the function can be used to evaluate certain conditions within the application, and items on a context menu can be dynamically added, removed, enabled, or disabled. For example, a Save item can be disabled if nothing has changed since the last time the user saved.

You can dynamically change the function a context menu calls before it appears, by redefining its onSelect event handler. For example:

```
myContextMenu.onSelect = anotherFunction;
```

As a result of this script, the onSelect event handler is reassigned from its initial value to that of anotherFunction. The myContextMenu instance will call anotherFunction() instead of menuHandler()—or whatever function you passed into the ContextMenu constructor when creating it—when the context menu is selected (but before it appears).

When creating custom context menus, you might want to remove the default items that appear. To hide the built-in items in a context menu, you call the hideBuiltInItems() method:

```
myContextMenu.hideBuiltInItems();
```

With this method, all built-in items are hidden from the context menu except the Settings and Debugger items.

Note *In editable text fields, standard items such as Cut, Copy, Paste, Delete, and Select All are not removable.*

Instances of the ContextMenu class have only one property: customItems. This is an array that stores the custom ContextMenuItem objects that form the custom items that appear on the menu. To add a custom item to a ContextMenu object, you add it to the customItems array for that object:

```
myContextMenu.customItems.push(new ContextMenuItem("Next Page", ¬
    nextPageHandler));
```

This statement adds a new ContextMenuItem object to the customItems array of the myContextMenu object. The first parameter is the text to be displayed in the menu. The second parameter is the callback function for that item. When the item is selected from the context menu, the callback function is called.

```
myContextMenu.customItems.push(new ContextMenuItem("Next Page", nextPageHandler))
```

```
Next Page
Settings...
Debugger
```

```
myContextMenu.customItems.push(new ContextMenuItem("Previous Page", previousPageHandler))
```

```
Next Page
Previous Page
Settings...
Debugger
```

```
myContextMenu.customItems.push(new ContextMenuItem("First Page", firstPageHandler))
```

```
Next Page
Previous Page
First Page
Settings...
Debugger
```

Custom menu items in a context menu can be referenced in the following manner:

```
myContextMenu.customItems[0] // first custom menu item
myContextMenu.customItems[1] // second custom menu item
myContextMenu.customItems[2] // third custom menu item
```

Knowing this, you can enable and disable menu items dynamically:

```
myContextMenu.customItems[1].enabled = false;
myContextMenu.customItems[3].enabled = false;
```

Disabled menu items still appear on the custom context menu, but they're dimmed and won't function when clicked. Menu items are enabled by default.

You can dynamically change the function that a context menu item calls when selected by redefining its onSelect event handler. For example:

```
myContextMenu.customItems[0].onSelect = differentCallbackFunction;
```

Note *Just to clarify, the context menu itself has a callback function that is executed just before the menu appears, and each context menu item has a callback function that's executed when that item is selected from the menu.*

To use a custom context menu, it has to be assigned to a particular movie clip, button, or text field instance. The assignment causes that custom menu to appear when the instance is right-clicked. Here's the syntax:

```
myClip_mc.menu = myContextMenu;
```

When the mouse is right-clicked over the myClip_mc movie clip instance, the myContextMenu context menu is displayed.

Note *A single custom context menu can be associated with as many movie clip, button, and text field instances as you want.*

When using custom context menus, the Timeline with the highest depth always captures the right-click mouse event, which causes its custom menu to be displayed. For example, if two movie clips are overlapping, and each has an associated custom context menu, the clip that's at a higher depth is the one whose menu is shown when the mouse is right-clicked over that clip. This principle also applies to the main Timeline. If the mouse is not over a movie clip that has a custom menu, but the main Timeline (_root) has a custom menu, the custom menu for _root will be displayed.

In the following exercise, you'll create a custom context menu. The end result will be an interactive refrigerator note. You'll be able to add text to the note, clear the note, mark it as "urgent", and print it.

1. Open *ContextMenu1.fla* in the Lesson17/Start folder.

This file has three layers: Background, Text Field, and Actions. The Background layer contains the graphics for the project. The Text Field layer contains an input text field instance with the name entry_txt. Frame 1 of the Actions layer is where you'll add the ActionScript for this project.

When the project is complete, you'll be able to add text to the editable text field; when you right-click, you'll be able to select Print Fridge Note from the custom context menu.

2. Select Frame 1 in the Actions layer, open the Actions panel, and add the following line to create a new instance of the ContextMenu class:

```
var myContextMenu:ContextMenu = new ContextMenu(menuHandler);
```

This code creates a new instance of the ContextMenu class, named myContextMenu. This custom context menu will eventually be associated with the entry_txt text field. When the mouse is right-clicked over that field, this menu (and the menu items we'll eventually add to it) will appear. We'll add three custom items to this menu that give the user the following options:

- Print any text in the entry_txt text field
- Delete any text in the entry_txt text field
- Reformat any text in the entry_txt text field so that it's red and consists of uppercase characters

In the constructor, a reference to a function called menuHandler() is passed in. This function is called whenever this menu is opened (the user right-clicks the entry_txt text field). Let's create that function next.

3. Add the following **menuHandler()** function definition below the current script:

```
function menuHandler() {
  var numberOfItems = myContextMenu.customItems.length;
  if (entry_txt.text.length > 0) {
    for(var i = 0; i < numberOfItems; ++i){
      myContextMenu.customItems[i].enabled = true;
    }
  } else {
    for(var i = 0; i < numberOfItems; ++i){
      myContextMenu.customItems[i].enabled = false;
    }
  }
}
```

This function is called just before the myContextMenu menu appears. The purpose of this function is to enable and disable custom items on that menu on the fly, depending on whether the entry_txt text field contains any text. If there *is* text in that field, custom items on the context menu are enabled; otherwise, the custom items are disabled.

The function begins by creating a variable named numberOfItems. The value of this variable is based on the number of custom menu items that have been added to the myContextMenu instance. In this project, that instance will eventually have three items added to it; thus, the value of numberOfItems is 3. The value of this variable will be used in a moment.

Next, a conditional statement evaluates whether the user has entered any text into the entry_txt text field. If the field contains text, the first part of the statement uses a loop to quickly enable all the custom items on the `myContextMenu` instance. If no text is found, all the items are disabled.

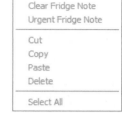

entry_txt *Contains Text*   entry_txt *Is Empty*

After this function has executed, the menu appears. Now let's add some custom items to the `myContextMenu` instance.

4. Add the following line of script just below the **menuHandler()** function:

```
myContextMenu.customItems.push(new ContextMenuItem("Print Fridge Note", ¬
   printHandler));
```

This line of script adds a new ContextMenuItem instance to the `customItems` array of the `myContextMenu` instance. This step defines the first item that will appear when the menu is opened.

The first parameter of the ContextMenuItem constructor method contains the text that we want to appear in the menu representing this item. The second parameter is the callback function that should be executed when the item is selected. We'll create the callback function next.

5. Add the following script to define the **printHandler()** callback function:

```
function printHandler() {
  var myPrintJob:PrintJob = new PrintJob();
  var result:Boolean = myPrintJob.start();
  if (result) {
    myPrintJob.addPage("entry_txt");
    myPrintJob.send();
  }
  delete myPrintJob;
}
```

This function is called when Print Fridge Note is selected from the context menu. The first line creates a new instance of the PrintJob class. The second line attempts to initialize the printer, capturing the result of printer initialization. If no printer exists or the user cancels the print request, the result variable has a value of false. If the user proceeds with the print request, the result variable is set to true.

If result is true, we use the addPage() method of the PrintJob class to add contents of the entry_txt text field to be printed. The remaining default parameters for the addPage() method are acceptable, so we don't need to set them.

Next, the page is sent to the printer, and the myPrintJob instance is deleted.

Let's add the remaining two items to our custom context menu.

6. Add the following script at the end of the current script:

```
myContextMenu.customItems.push(new ContextMenuItem("Clear Fridge Note", ¬
    clearHandler));
function clearHandler() {
    entry_txt.text = "";
}
```

This script adds another custom item to the customItems array of the myContextMenu instance. "Clear Fridge Note" is the text for this item, and the clearHandler() function is called when this item is selected. The clearHandler() function is created with the three remaining lines of script. Its only task is to remove any text from the entry_txt text field.

7. Add the following script below the current script:

```
myContextMenu.customItems.push(new ContextMenuItem("Urgent Fridge Note", ¬
    urgentHandler));
function urgentHandler() {
    entry_txt.textColor = 0x990000;
    entry_txt.text = entry_txt.text.toUpperCase();
}
```

This step adds one more custom item to the myContextMenu instance. The text for this item is "Urgent Fridge Note", and the function called when this item is selected is urgentHandler(). This function takes the text entered into the entry_txt field, makes it red, and converts it to uppercase characters.

8. Add the final line of script:

```
entry_txt.menu = myContextMenu;
```

This step associates the myContextMenu instance with the entry_txt text field. If the user right-clicks this text field, the custom context menu appears; otherwise, the custom menu won't be shown.

9. Select Control › Test Movie to test your work. Type some text in the text field, open the custom context menu, and select a custom menu item.

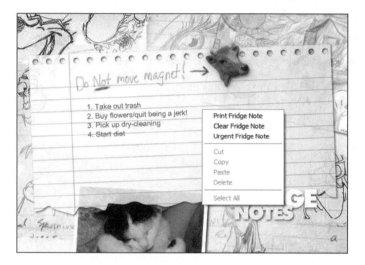

Notice that if the text field is blank, the custom menu items are disabled in the context menu. They're visible, but not selectable. If the text contains at least one text character, the menu items become available. This is the result of the menuHandler() function created in Step 3.

10. Close the test movie and save your work as *ContextMenu2.fla*.

This step completes the exercise and this lesson.

Custom context menus provide a great way for users to interact with an application— without having to manually search for a particular button or control. If you use this new Flash feature, be sure to make users aware of it.

What You Have Learned

In this lesson, you have:

- Learned the differences between Flash printing and browser printing (pages 453–454)
- Used the PrintJob class to print both vectors and bitmaps (pages 454–464)
- Created a custom context menu (pages 464–472)

18 Maximum-Strength SWF Files

Over the last several years, Macromedia Flash has gained the respect of programmers as a tool to develop applications. The majority of these applications are used in web browsers and loaded over the Internet. There are a few amazing software packages designed to assist you in creating Flash applications designed to run outside the browser as a stand-alone executable file. These programs let you add functionality to your Flash applications that you couldn't get from authoring the file from within Flash. In this lesson, you'll learn about some of these programs, and experience working with one of them.

In this lesson, you'll use a third-party tool to create a Flash game with a uniquely shaped playback window.

What You Will Learn

In this lesson, you will:

- Learn about the fscommand() function
- Enhance a Flash executable file by using a third-party tool
- Configure movie functionality using HTML and FlashVars

Approximate Time

This lesson takes approximately one and one half hours to complete.

Lesson Files

Media Files:

Lesson18/Assets/background.gif
Lesson18/Assets/bullet.gif
Lesson18/Assets/contactus.gif
Lesson18/Assets/leftsidebar.gif
Lesson18/Assets/placeholder.gif
Lesson18/Assets/resources.gif
Lesson18/Assets/resourcesdivider.gif
Lesson18/Assets/welcomeheader.gif
Lesson18/Assets/whatsnew.gif
Lesson18/Assets/mask.bmp
Lesson18/Assets/highest_score.txt

Starting Files:

Lesson18/Start/Game1.fla
Lesson18/Start/NavBar1.fla
Lesson18/Start/home1.htm
Lesson18/Start/news1.htm
Lesson18/Start/contact1.htm

Completed Projects:

Lesson18/Completed/Game1.exe
Lesson18/Completed/Game1.swf
Lesson18/Completed/Game2.fla
Lesson18/Completed/NavBar1.swf
Lesson18/Completed/NavBar2.fla
Lesson18/Completed/home2.htm
Lesson18/Completed/news2.htm
Lesson18/Completed/contact2.htm

Understanding fscommand()

The `fscommand()` function enables a Flash movie to communicate with the application that's currently holding the movie. The following are examples of applications that hold (*host*) Flash movies:

- Stand-alone Flash Player
- Web browser
- Executable that displays the Flash movie, such as those created by third-party tools discussed later in this lesson; or executables created using C++, Visual Basic, and so on

> **Note** *The ExternalInterface class that was introduced with Flash 8 is generally more powerful than using `fscommand()` because with ExternalInterface your application can call specific functions (and receive responses) in the application that is holding the SWF file, such as a web browser. However, the `fscommand()` function is still useful if exporting to Flash 7 or older, or exporting for use in a projector.*

It's simple to use `fscommand()` from within Flash. The `fscommand()` function accepts two parameters: a command name, and optional extra information. The extra information is used as a parameter of the command:

```
fscommand("command_name", "optional extra stuff");
```

When Flash executes an `fscommand()`, the host application receives notification that a command has been sent to it. The name of the command is sent, as well as any optional parameter data. The host application must be programmed to deal with these incoming commands; it looks at the name of the incoming command and reacts accordingly, using any optional parameter data to complete the task.

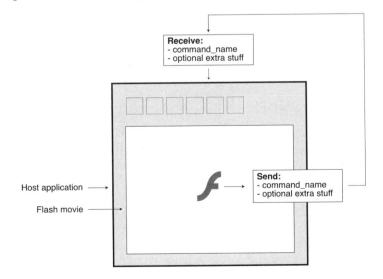

Let's explore in detail some of the previously mentioned uses of the `fscommand()` function.

Controlling the Stand-Alone Flash Player (Projectors)

Using the Publish settings in Flash, you can publish a Flash movie as a *projector*. A projector file typically contains your movie as well as the Flash Player. Opening the file causes your movie to play in its own application window (the Flash Player/Projector window). The `fscommand()` function can be used in your movie so that it can communicate with the projector in various ways. There are six built-in `fscommand()` functions that the stand-alone player can execute:

```
fscommand("quit")
```

This command closes the stand-alone player window.

```
fscommand("fullscreen", true)
```

or

```
fscommand("fullscreen", false)
```

This command forces the stand-alone player to play at full screen (if `true`) or at the defined movie size (if `false`).

```
fscommand("allowscale", true)
```

or

```
fscommand("allowscale", false)
```

This command determines what happens if the user resizes the projector window while your movie is playing. If `true`, the movie is scaled to fit 100% in the resized stand-alone player window. If `false`, the player window is still resizable, but the movie playing inside it remains at its original size.

```
fscommand("showmenu", true)
```

or

```
fscommand("showmenu", false)
```

Right-clicking (Ctrl-clicking on a Macintosh) a movie playing in the stand-alone player opens a context menu. The minimal version of this menu is shown if this `fscommand()` parameter is set to `false`. The full menu is shown if `true`.

```
fscommand("exec", fileName)
```

This command executes (opens) another application (such as an .EXE file on Windows). The parameter is the filename of the application to open. Applications opened using this command must reside in a folder named *fscommand*. This folder must reside in the same directory as the projector.

```
fscommand("trapallkeys", true)
```

or

```
fscommand("trapallkeys", false)
```

If true, all key events are sent to the Flash Player. If false, certain key events such as accelerator keypresses are not sent.

Any of these commands can be executed from within your movie using syntax similar to the following:

```
myButton_btn.onRelease = function(){
    fscommand("quit");
}
```

Stand-alone fscommand() functions have no effect on Flash movies played outside the stand-alone player.

Executing AppleScripts with fscommand() Functions

AppleScript is a built-in scripting language for the Macintosh operating system. AppleScripts (files containing AppleScript code) are used to tell the operating system to perform tasks such as these:

- Batch processing
- File conversion and manipulation
- Performing tasks at specified times

One of the more powerful aspects of using the exec fscommand() in a Macintosh-based projector is its capability to execute an AppleScript. Let's look at a simple example.

> **Note** *This is not intended to be extensive instruction on how to create AppleScripts, but rather a simple demonstration of how AppleScripts can be executed via Flash. For more information on AppleScript, visit www.apple.com/applescript/.*

The following AppleScript opens the file named catalog.pdf on the My CD disk:

```
tell application "Finder"
activate
select file "catalog.pdf" of disk "My CD"
open selection
end tell
```

To execute this AppleScript from Flash, you name it (for example, launchCatalog), save it in the fscommand folder and create a script within your Flash movie similar to the following:

```
myButton_btn.onRelease = function(){
   fscommand("exec", "launchCatalog");
}
```

When myButton_btn is clicked, the launchCatalog AppleScript is executed, and catalog.pdf opens.

Communicating with a Web Browser

When a Flash movie is embedded in an HTML page and the page is viewed in a web browser, the fscommand() function enables the Flash movie to communicate with the browser via JavaScript. This feature allows you to do tasks such as open alert boxes, resize the browser, and other JavaScript activities.

Note *Because the success of this communication depends on the specific browser and version, some Flash developers limit their use of the fscommand() function. For more information about using the fscommand to communicate with a browser, visit www.macromedia.com.*

Tip *If exporting for use in the Flash 8 player or later, ExternalInterface is the better choice for communication with JavaScript in the web browser. See Lesson 15 for more information on ExternalInterface.*

Creating an Enhanced Executable (Projector)

Several companies make software to extend the functionality of a Flash movie. Most of these products take a SWF file and wrap it within a powerful executable shell. This shell can be considered a high-tech "box" that contains your SWF file. The box has been programmed with the capability to perform all sorts of tasks that a typical SWF file can't do. The SWF file controls this powerful box by sending specialized commands to it. Depending on the box, Flash uses fscommand() functions or a custom API provided by this box. Think of the

SWF file as the interface and brains of the resulting application, and the box (executable) as the facilitator. These are two of the most popular products that extend Flash:

- Zinc—Multidmedia (MDM) Limited (*www.multidmedia.com*)
- SWF Studio—Northcode (*www.northcode.com*)

The following figure illustrates how a SWF file interacts with a Flash wrapper such as Zinc. The white box is the SWF file and the gray box that houses it is the wrapper. The SWF communicates with the wrapper, in this case telling it to save a new text file called myText.txt with the word "Hello" in it. The wrapper accepts the command from the SWF and saves the file to the hard drive.

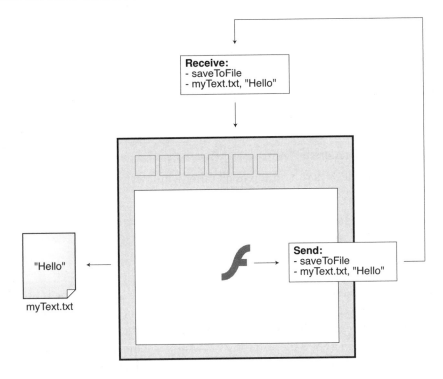

Note At this time, only Zinc provides a way to create Applications for both Windows and Mac OS-X.

These applications extend Flash's capabilities with hundreds of commands. Typically, you open the application (such as Zinc), locate the SWF file that makes use of special commands, adjust a few settings, and click the Build button, which creates an .EXE file.

When opened, this file contains and plays your SWF movie, and is sent commands by your movie. The end result is a powerful Flash movie.

The following are a few of the tasks that can be accomplished through the use of one of the identified third-party tools:

- Create or remove text files or directories
- Upload and download files from the Internet
- FTP files from the Internet
- Force the computer to display the Flash content in DirectX mode
- Open a file browse pop-up window to allow a user to locate a file or location
- Save a screenshot of the Flash content or a specific area within the Flash content
- Set the desktop wallpaper on the user's computer

Although most of the extended functionality that you gain from these software products comes from executing commands in ActionScript, several configurable options can be set directly from the software's interface (to be applied to the executable file that's created):

- Disable right-click
- Remove window borders
- Make the window always run on top of all other windows
- Assign a custom icon to the executable
- Include additional files in the executable

Using Zinc

Zinc is an excellent program created by Multidmedia Limited (MDM). Zinc is used to take a SWF file and to create a PC application, Mac application, or even a Pocket PC application from it. The latest version of Zinc no longer uses fscommand() functions for communication between a SWF file and the Zinc wrapper. Zinc now provides an easy-to-use API that allows Flash to communicate synchronously with it. So Flash can execute a method on the API provided by Zinc and get a response in that same line of code. In earlier versions of Zinc and in other tools like it, fscommand() functions have been used, which typically had a response delay of at least one frame.

You'll see how easy Zinc is to use in the next lesson, in which you'll create an enhanced stand-alone Flash application. But first you need to install it!

Install the Zinc trial version (Windows only) of Zinc on your computer by following these steps:

1. Locate the file zinc_trial_setup.exe in the Software folder on the CD-ROM for this book and double-click the file to open it.

2. Follow the installer's instructions to install Zinc.

3. After installation, launch the application.

When launching Zinc for the first time, you get a pop-up window asking what type of application you want to create. The choices range from PC applications to Mac or Pocket PC applications. In this book, we'll cover only the PC desktop applications. Click Desktop Application.

You can control a variety of Zinc settings (see figure). The following is a brief overview of some of the most important available options and settings:

Tab	Description
Input File	Zinc creates an executable file for various platforms that hold at least one SWF file. On this tab, you specify the location on your hard drive for that SWF file. In addition to the input file you can specify the name and location of the file to be created.
Style	On this tab, you can change visual properties of the file and the window in which it launches, including properties such as various window styles and their settings.
Size/Position	On this tab, you can specify the size of the window and where on the screen it should position itself when launched.
Input Devices	On this tab, you can define how you want the window to respond to certain keypresses, mouse interactions, joysticks, or even touch screens!
Flash Settings	This tab allows you to specify a few playback options for the Flash file, such as quality and background color.

Now that you're acquainted with Zinc's interface, let's use it to create an enhanced Flash game. This game creates a text file (used for holding a high score), shakes the projector window, and even talks to you!

1. Open *Game1.fla* in the Lesson18/Start directory.

Notice that there are five layers—Background, Assets, Top Bubbles, Actions, and Labels—as well as three frame labels (which we'll discuss in a moment). The Labels layer contains no content. It's just used to place empty frames that are given a frame label. The Background layer contains the project's background graphics. The Assets layer contains most of the remaining visual elements for the game, except for a bitmap of some bubbles on the Top Bubbles layer (this graphic was added to give the game some depth). As usual, the Actions layer will contain the ActionScript used in this project.

The game that you'll build is very simple. You move a ship left and right using the Left arrow and Right arrow keys. You can fire a projectile upward from the ship by using the spacebar. Bubbles appear from the left side of the screen and move to the right. The goal is to destroy as many bubbles as you can within a certain time limit. When finished, your score is saved to a text file if you have attained a new high score.

The Initial frame label will contain script to load the current high score data from a text file. Also on this label is a button that we'll use to begin gameplay. When the user clicks the button, the Timeline moves to the Game label, which contains the script and assets for playing the game. After the game's time limit has been exceeded, the Timeline moves to the Game Over label, where the current score is saved to a text file if the score is higher than the previously saved high score.

Other than a few specific commands used in this exercise, all the ActionScript used in this project should be familiar from earlier lessons. There are functions, arrays, duplicated movie clips, and the hitTest() method. Instead of dissecting each script line by line, we'll focus more on what a group of code accomplishes, and in some cases how it relates to the use of Zinc.

Before we begin scripting, you should be aware of two important assets you'll use in the exercise, both of which are contained in the Lesson18/Assets directory. Both of these assets must be in the same directory as the final project file. The first asset is a text file named highest_score.txt. This file contains the variable declaration score=0. We'll explain this in a moment. The second asset is a file named mask.bmp, which is a black-and-white bitmap image that acts as a mask for the game application's window.

2. Move the playhead to the Initial frame label.

This frame contains two important assets: a text field named score_txt that displays the current high score, and a button instance named play_btn that moves the Timeline to the Game frame label. We'll script both of these elements in a moment.

3. With the Actions panel open, select the frame in the Actions layer (at the Initial frame label) and add the following line of ActionScript:

```
mdm.Forms.MainForm.showMask("mask.bmp");
```

When the resulting SWF file is wrapped in a Zinc executable file, this line of ActionScript talks to that Zinc shell. In this case, the command tells the executable file to apply the specified bitmap file as a mask to the playback window. The end result is an executable file in the shape defined by the black-and-white image of the bitmap.

When Zinc is used to create an executable from a SWF file, it injects some ActionScript into your SWF file. This ActionScript is an API that you can use to interact with Zinc. All commands start with mdm. The Zinc help system is very helpful in showing you what lines of ActionScript are needed to call certain commands.

A Zinc application can be just one window, which is typical, or it can handle many. These windows are called Forms. Each form has a name and can be individually masked. In our case, we have only one form and it is the main form for the entire application. Therefore, to mask the main form we use the line of ActionScript just added:

```
mdm.Forms.MainForm.showMask("mask.bmp");
```

4. Add the following script to load and display the previously saved high score:

```
var highscore:Number;
function scoreLoaded() {
    score_txt.text = "Most bubbles destroyed: "+ lv.score;
    highscore = Number(lv.score);
}
var lv:LoadVars = new LoadVars();
lv.onLoad = scoreLoaded;
lv.load("highest_score.txt");
```

This script creates an instance of the LoadVars class and loads the contents of the highest_score.txt text file into it. When the text file is loaded, the string "Most bubbles destroyed: 37" is displayed in the score_txt text field. The number of bubbles destroyed varies depending on the current value of score in the loaded text file.

The first line of the script in this step declares highscore as a variable on the main Timeline. In the scoreLoaded() function, when the text file is loaded the value of score in the file sets highscore's initial value. The highscore variable is declared on the main Timeline because we need to keep it around for the duration of gameplay. At the end of the game, the current score is compared to this value to determine whether a new text file containing the updated high score should be created.

5. Add the following script for the Play button:

```
play_btn.onRelease = function() {
    gotoAndStop("Game");
};
stop();
```

When the play_btn button instance is clicked, the Timeline moves to the Game frame label.

The final action list keeps the movie from playing automatically when the application is opened.

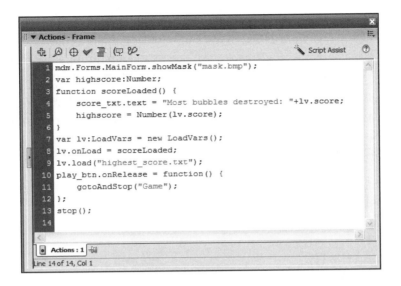

```
1  mdm.Forms.MainForm.showMask("mask.bmp");
2  var highscore:Number;
3  function scoreLoaded() {
4      score_txt.text = "Most bubbles destroyed: "+lv.score;
5      highscore = Number(lv.score);
6  }
7  var lv:LoadVars = new LoadVars();
8  lv.onLoad = scoreLoaded;
9  lv.load("highest_score.txt");
10 play_btn.onRelease = function() {
11     gotoAndStop("Game");
12 };
13 stop();
14
```

6. Move the playhead to the Game frame label.

This frame contains three movie clip instances: `bubble_mc`, `ship_mc`, and `projectile_mc`. The ship is controlled with the arrow keys, allowing it to move left or right depending on which arrow key is pressed. The `bubble_mc` clip is duplicated at certain times, with the duplicates acting as potential targets. The `projectile_mc` clip is duplicated when the spacebar is pressed. These duplicates are used to shoot down (pop) bubbles as they move across the screen.

7. With the Actions panel open, select the Actions layer at the Game frame label and add the following actions:

```
var ship_speed:Number = 2;
var projectiles:Array = new Array();
var projectile_speed:Number = 4;
var bubble_speed:Number = 3;
var shooting:Boolean = false;
var bubbles:Array = new Array();
var game_length:Number = 60 * 1000;
var hits:Number = 0;
var depth:Number = 0;
```

The ship, projectiles, and bubbles all move at their own speeds. A speed value is the amount that the object can move (in pixels) during one frame. The variables ship_speed, bubble_speed, and projectile_speed define these speeds.

Arrays of projectiles and bubbles are also created, named projectiles and bubbles, respectively. These arrays store and keep track of bubbles and projectiles that are created and used during gameplay. Using arrays makes it easy to loop through the existing projectiles and bubbles to check for collisions or to remove them all from the screen.

The hits variable stores the number of bubbles destroyed. The depth variable stores the current highest unused depth. The game_length variable stores the amount of time that the game lasts, in milliseconds (we set it to last 60 seconds). The shooting variable stores a value of false. These variables will be discussed later.

8. Add the following onEnterFrame event at the end of the current script:

```
this.onEnterFrame = function() {
    generateBubbles();
    captureKeyPresses();
    moveProjectiles();
    moveBubbles();
    detectCollisions();
};
```

This onEnterFrame event executes these five functions (none of which have been created yet) for every frame:

- generateBubbles() creates a new bubble at a random time.
- captureKeyPresses() checks whether the arrow keys or spacebar have been pressed. Depending on which key is pressed, this function moves the ship left or right, or fires a projectile.
- moveProjectiles() moves fired projectiles upward.
- moveBubbles() moves bubbles to the right.
- detectCollisions() loops through the projectiles and bubbles looking for collisions.

Let's add these functions next and briefly discuss how they work.

9. Add the generateBubbles() function at the end of the current script:

```
function generateBubbles() {
    if (random(50) == 0) {
        ++depth;
        var name:String = "bubble" + depth;
        var clip:MovieClip = bubble_mc.duplicateMovieClip(name,depth);
        bubbles.push(clip);
        clip._xscale = clip._yscale = 50 + random(50);
    }
}
```

If random(50) evaluates to 0, a new bubble is created. Statistically, this process should occur once every 50 frames. When a new bubble movie clip instance is created, a reference to it is stored in the bubbles array. The generated bubble instance is given a random size by setting its _xscale and_yscale properties to values between 50 and 100.

10. Create the **captureKeyPresses()** function:

```
function captureKeyPresses() {
    if (Key.isDown(Key.LEFT) && ship_mc._x> 185) {
        ship_mc._x -= ship_speed;
    } else if (Key.isDown(Key.RIGHT) && ship_mc._x < 370) {
        ship_mc._x += ship_speed;
    }
    if (Key.isDown(Key.SPACE) && !shooting) {
        shooting = true;
        shoot();
    } else if (!Key.isDown(Key.SPACE)) {
        shooting = false;
    }
}
```

If the Left arrow or Right arrow key is pressed, and ship_mc is within a horizontal boundary of 185 on the left and 370 on the right, the ship_mc instance is moved the amount of ship_speed in the appropriate direction. The boundary exists to prevent the instance from moving beyond the area of water in the tub.

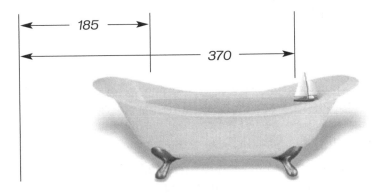

If the Spacebar is pressed and the value of the shooting variable is false, the shoot() function is called, and shooting is set to true. If the spacebar is not pressed, shooting is set to false again, which ensures that the game player has to press the spacebar once for every shot. Without this condition, the game player could hold down the spacebar to have a continuous barrage of shots fired. That's not fair to the bubbles!

11. Add the shoot() function at the end of the current script:

```
function shoot() {
    ++depth;
    var name:String = "projectile" + depth;
    var clip:MovieClip = projectile_mc.duplicateMovieClip(name, depth);
    clip._x = ship_mc._x;
    clip._y = ship_mc._y;
    projectiles.push(clip);
}
```

This function is called when the spacebar is pressed. It creates a new projectile, positions it on top of the ship_mc movie clip instance (so it appears that the projectile is being fired from the ship), and adds a reference to the new projectile in the projectiles array.

12. Now create the moveProjectiles() function:

```
function moveProjectiles() {
    for (var i:Number = projectiles.length - 1; i >= 0; --i) {
        var clip:MovieClip = projectiles[i];
        clip._y -= projectile_speed;
        if (clip._y < 40) {
            clip.removeMovieClip();
            projectiles.splice(i, 1[al]);
        }
    }
}
```

At this point in the book, you're used to seeing for loops; however, this is the first time that we've used a for loop to count backward. This function serves two purposes: moving any projectiles that have been created as a result of the user pressing the spacebar and removing the projectiles if they get too high on the screen.

This loop processes every projectile instance referenced in the projectiles array. With every iteration, each instance referenced in the array is moved up on the screen by the amount of projectile_speed. If the *y* position of the currently referenced movie clip instance goes past 40, the instance is removed. The instance is removed in two steps: It's physically removed from the screen by using the removeMovieClip() method; then the reference to the instance in the `projectiles` array is deleted, using the `splice()` method of the Array class.

You may wonder why this particular loop call requires i to be counted backward (`--i`). Think of the references to projectile instances in the `projectiles` array as a stack of nine books, with the book at the bottom of the stack having an index value of 0, and the topmost book having an index value of 8. Now suppose you're given the task of removing the books at positions 1 and 4. If you remove the book at index 1, the remaining books on top of that book drop down one position; the book that was formerly at position 2 is now at position 1, the book that was at position 3 is now at position 2, and so on. This creates a problem when you remove the book at position 4 because it has been dropped to position 3. Removing the book at position 4 actually results in removing the book that was formerly at position 5. The book that was originally at index 4 is skipped altogether.

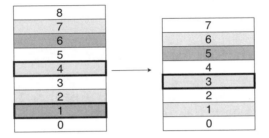

The same kind of logic problem would exist in our loop if we removed items by starting at index 0 and working our way up. By working backward, we eliminate this problem. Here's how.

Returning to the book illustration, if book 4 is removed first, books 5 through 8 are all dropped one position. But that's okay because you're working backward; the book at position 1 is still at position 1. When the time comes to remove it, it's right where it needs to be. Our backward loop solves this problem in the same way when removing projectiles.

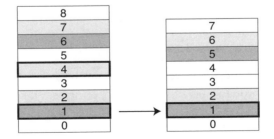

13. Create the `moveBubbles()` function:

```
function moveBubbles() {
  for (var i:Number = bubbles.length - 1; i >= 0; --i) {
    var clip:MovieClip = bubbles[i];
    clip._x += bubble_speed;
    if (clip._x > 550) {
      clip.removeMovieClip();
      bubbles.splice(i, 1);
    }
  }
}
```

This function works like `moveProjectiles()`, except that it handles the movement and deletion of bubble instances. They are moved to the right at the rate of `bubble_speed` and removed when they breach the rightmost boundary of the project.

14. Next, create the `detectCollisions()` function:

```
function detectCollisions() {
  for (var i:Number = projectiles.length - 1; i >= 0; --i) {
    var projectile_clip:MovieClip = projectiles[i];
    for (var j:Number = bubbles.length - 1; j >= 0; --j) {
      var bubble_clip:MovieClip = bubbles[j];
      if (projectile_clip.hitTest(bubble_clip)) {
        ++hits;
        projectile_clip.removeMovieClip();
        projectiles.splice(i, 1);
        bubbles.splice(j, 1);
        bubble_clip.play();
        mdm.Application.shake(5);
      }
    }
  }
}
```

This function has a nested loop. For every projectile in the `projectile` array, the entire `bubble` array is looped through, and a `hitTest()` is performed. If `hitTest()` returns a value of `true`, a collision has occurred between the projectile being tested and a bubble instance.

If a collision is detected, the `hits` variable is incremented, the projectile is removed, and the bubble is removed from the `bubbles` array. The bubble is told to play a "bursting" animation. The final frame in the `bubbles_mc` movie clip has an action assigned, `this.removeMovieClip()`, which removes the bubble clip as soon as the bubble has burst.

The final action that occurs if a collision is detected is the execution of the Zinc command: `shake`. The `shake` command tells the application to shake the playback window the number of times listed as the second parameter. When a collision is detected, the playback window shakes five times.

15. Create the `gameOver()` function to handle ending the game:

```
function gameOver() {
  clearInterval(gameID);
  for (var i:Number = projectiles.length - 1; i >= 0; --i) {
    var clip:MovieClip = projectiles[i];
    clip.removeMovieClip();
    projectiles.splice(i, 1);
  }
  for (var i:Number = bubbles.length - 1; i [a2]>= 0; --i) {
    var clip:MovieClip = bubbles[i];
    clip.removeMovieClip();
    bubbles.splice(i, 1);
  }
  gotoAndPlay("Game Over");
}
var gameID:Number = setInterval(gameOver, game_length);
```

The last line of script shown here uses `setInterval()` to tell the `gameOver()` function to execute after the game has been played for one minute, which is the length of time specified in the `game_length` variable created in Step 7.

When executed, the `gameOver()` function takes four actions: It first clears the interval so that the `gameOver()` function is not called again in another 60 seconds. Then it uses a couple of looping statements to loop through and remove any outstanding projectile and bubble instances. Finally, it sends the movie to the Game Over frame label.

16. Move the playhead to the Game Over frame label.

This frame contains the text showing that the game has ended. There is also a button named `playagain_btn` that moves the Timeline back to the Initial frame so that the game can be played again.

No ActionScript will actually be assigned to this frame; instead it will be assigned to the next frame because of the command used. Typically, when these commands are placed on a frame, they're executed *before* the visual content of the frame is rendered. Therefore, execution of commands on the Game Over frame label technically occurs while the user still sees the content of the Game label (albeit just for a split second). By putting these commands on the next frame, we let the visual content of the Game Over frame label render on the screen first, before the execution of the commands.

17. Select the frame in the Actions layer directly after the Game Over frame label and add the following script:

```
if (hits != 1) {
  var message:String = "Game Over! You destroyed "+ hits + "bubbles!";
} else {
  var message:String = "Game Over! You destroyed " + hits + "bubble!";
}
mdm.Application.say(message);
```

Both Windows 2000 and Windows XP come with a speech pack built in, allowing them to render strings of text to voice. This script formats a dynamic message and has Windows play the message using the mdm.Application.say method. The parameter specifies a variable whose value is the text to speak.

> **Note** If you're testing the game on a *Windows 98 or Windows 95 machine* (which doesn't have a built-in speech engine), don't include this portion of script, or you'll get an error at the end of the game.

18. Add the following script to handle saving a high score:

```
if (hits > highscore) {
  var saveTo:String = "highest_score.txt";
  var saveContent:String = "score=" + hits;
  mdm.FileSystem.saveFile(saveTo, saveContent);
}
```

At the end of the game, this conditional statement compares the value of hits (the number of bubbles hit) with the value of highscore (which is the current high score, as discussed in Step 4). If hits has a greater value, a new high score has been achieved and needs to be saved. The mdm.FileSystem saveFile method saves the new score to a text file, which is loaded at the beginning of the next game.

This method accepts two parameter values, separated by commas. The first line within the conditional creates a variable named saveTo, which represents the name of the target text file. The second line creates a variable named saveContent, which contains the text that will be saved. The value of this variable is created by adding the string "score=" to the value of hits. If hits has a value of 53, for example, the text score=53 is written to the highest_score.txt file, overwriting any existing text in the file.

19. Add the following button event handler and stop() action at the end of the current script:

```
playagain_btn.onRelease = function() {
  gotoAndStop("Initial");
};
stop();
```

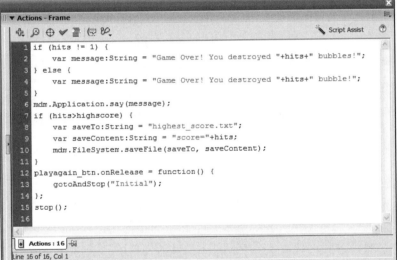

When the playagain_btn button instance is clicked, the user returns to the Initial frame label, in which the high score is reloaded and the game can be replayed. A stop() action is added here to keep the movie from playing.

The scripting of our file is complete. The last tasks are creating a SWF file and then wrapping that file in an executable generated by Zinc.

20. Choose File > Publish to create a SWF file.

In the previous step you completed all scripting needed to make this application function. For Zinc to create an executable file it takes a SWF file and spits out an executable file. In this step you create the SWF file that Zinc needs.

Next you will be using Zinc to create an executable file.

Note *This step assumes that the default publish settings are used.*

21. With Zinc open, select the Input File tab. At the bottom of the tab is the option Please Select An Input File. Use this option to browse to and select the *Game1.swf* file on your hard drive.

Obviously, this is where you select the file that you want to convert into a Zinc executable.

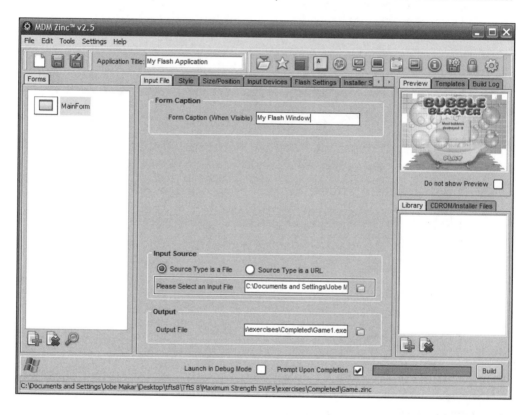

22. At the bottom of the same tab is the option Output File. Use this option to select the name and directory for the output file. This should be the default directory that contains the mask image and *highest_score.txt* file.

In this step, you told Zinc what to name the output executable file, and where to put it. There is a Build button on the bottom right. When clicked, it will take the input file, process it, and create the output file.

23. Click the Style tab. In the lower-left corner of the tab, click the **No Border** radio button.

This option setting is necessary for the bitmap mask to fit the movie properly.

24. Click on the Input File tab again. Click the Build button to generate the executable file.

A progress bar appears as Zinc creates an executable file. When complete, a dialog box asks whether you want to launch the file. Select Cancel.

25. Check your working directory for a file named *Game1.exe*. Double-click this file to launch your game!

Immediately upon launching, the game's playback window is masked based on the all-white portions of the mask.bmp image. The Initial frame label is shown first, and the current high score (which is 0) is loaded. Play the game and watch the special Zinc commands we added in action. When you hit a bubble, the playback window shakes. At the end of the game, the application talks to you (on Windows 2000/XP) to let you know how many hits you made. If you've achieved a new high score, it's saved to the highest_score.txt file.

26. Close the executable file by pressing the Escape key and then close Zinc. Return to the Flash authoring environment and save your work as *Game2.fla*.

You have created an enhanced executable file using Zinc. Zinc and other third-party tools offer hundreds of custom commands to enhance your content. You might find it interesting to read through the help files for Zinc to learn about the other available commands. You might also want to play around with different Zinc options when creating your executable files, such as assigning an icon to the file or having it fade in when the file is opened.

If you're bored with plain ol' ActionScript (yeah, right), learning to use third-party tools such as Zinc can open up a new and powerful means of creating incredibly dynamic applications.

Using FlashVars

Have you ever had a situation in which a single Flash movie could be used in a number of different ways, aside from simple tweaks? For example, imagine having a Flash movie that loads and plays external MP3 files. To use this movie to play 10 different MP3 files would require you to open the original FLA file, manually edit a small section of the code that specifies the MP3 to load, and export 10 different SWF files. Or you might have to script the movie to load the information from a database. The first option is too much work and has the potential of turning into a bandwidth nightmare. Even if each SWF file contained only a single line that was different, you would still have 10 different SWF files. If each file was 30 KB in size, placing them all on a single page would result in a 300 KB download. The second option, setting up your movie to load data from a database, is generally fine, but might be too complex a solution in some situations. Fortunately, there's a third option that fits nicely in the middle: the FlashVars parameter.

FlashVars, introduced in Flash MX, is an HTML <object> and <embed> parameter/attribute that provides a quick and easy way to pass data into a movie embedded in an HTML page. Immediately upon loading the movie, the data passed in can tell the movie to do something. This essentially provides a means to configure a SWF file via HTML without having to physically open the original FLA file and edit its code. In other words, a single SWF file can be used for multiple purposes. For example, suppose that a particular SWF file plays MP3s. If you embed that SWF file in an HTML page, with a few adjustments to the FlashVars parameter in the <object> and <embed> tags you can easily define which MP3 file that particular instance of the SWF file should play. The greatest benefit about this functionality is that a single SWF file can be repurposed multiple times throughout your entire site, and your visitor needs to download it only once. Your site's overall performance is enhanced.

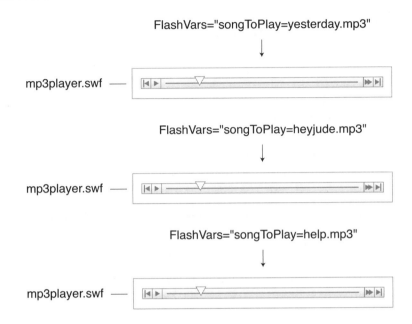

As mentioned earlier, FlashVars is an `<object>` and `<embed>` parameter. Implementation varies depending on which tag is used. For example, within the `<object>` tag, FlashVars is used within a nested `<param>` tag:

```
<PARAM NAME=FlashVars VALUE="songToPlay=heyjude.mp3">
```

The attribute `NAME=FlashVars` tells the Flash player to push the contents of the `VALUE` attribute into the Flash movie when the movie is loaded. The content pushed is variable data loaded into the main Timeline of the SWF file. In this example, a single variable named `songToPlay` with a value of `"heyjude.mp3"` is pushed in.

Note *All variable values pushed into an SWF file using FlashVars are initially considered strings by Flash. Using some of the conversion tools provided by ActionScript, you can convert values to other data types within Flash.*

Within the `<embed>` tag, FlashVars is an attribute that can be added with the following syntax:

```
FlashVars="songToPlay=heyjude.mp3"
```

In both sample scripts, we've shown only how the FlashVars parameter can be used to pass in a single variable and its value; however, more variables can be added by placing an ampersand (&) between name/value pairs, as shown in the following example:

```
<PARAM NAME=FlashVars ¬
  VALUE="songToPlay=heyjude.mp3&volume=80&imageToShow=forest">
```

This example pushes three variables—songToPlay, volume, and imageToShow—into the SWF file when it's loaded. You can add up to 64 KB of variables by using FlashVars.

What if you need to use characters other than letters or numbers? When setting the value portion of the FlashVars parameter, special characters must be escaped by converting them to URL-encoded strings. This conversion is necessary because HTML uses special characters such as <, >, ?, @, and so on for interpreting how to render and process a page. Converting the special characters to URL-encoded strings makes them invisible to HTML.

Fortunately, you don't have to learn how to escape a string of characters. Flash provides the escape() function, which handles most of the dirty work. Let's look at an example.

Suppose that you want to pass the email address *santa@clause.com* into a Flash movie by using FlashVars. This string contains both an at (@) symbol and a period (.) that must be escaped before the string can be used. You can create an escaped version of the string with the following script:

```
var str:String = "santa@clause.com"
trace(escape(str));
```

When this script is executed, the Output panel shows the following:

```
santa%40clause%2Ecom
```

Next, you copy this escaped version of the email address and paste it as the value for the FlashVars parameter, as shown here:

```
<PARAM NAME=FlashVars VALUE="email=santa%40clause%2Ecom">
```

Variable values are automatically unescaped by Flash after they're pushed in; therefore, Flash sees santa%40clause%2Ecom as its actual value of santa@clause.com.

All variables are passed into Flash before Frame 1 of a Flash movie is executed, which allows you to script your movie to react to this passed-in data immediately upon loading and playing.

In the following exercise, you'll create a simple Flash navigation bar for a website. You'll use the FlashVars parameter so that this same navigation bar (SWF file) can be used on multiple HTML pages but appear unique on each page.

1. Open *NavBar1.fla* in the Lesson18/Start directory.

This movie has three layers—Background, Buttons, and Actions. The Actions layer will contain all the script for this project. The Buttons layer contains three movie clip instances: home_mc, news_mc, and contact_mc. These instances will act as both movie clips and buttons. In a moment, we'll look at the Timeline of one of these instances.

The SWF file created by this authoring file is used as a navigation bar on a three-page website. Each of the three movie clip instances on the Buttons layer represents a section of the site: Home, News, and Contact. When one of these instances is clicked, the user is taken to the appropriate HTML page. Using FlashVars, data is passed to our single SWF file on each of these pages, enabling it to react in a certain way based on the current HTML page that has been loaded. For example, when the News page is visited, the News button on the navigation bar is highlighted and disabled, and a unique audio clip plays.

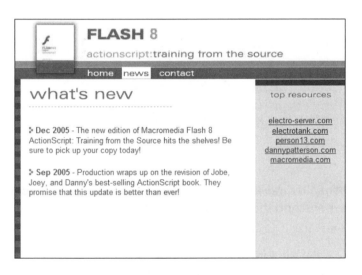

Our SWF file will be scripted to use these passed-in variables:

- currentPage is a value representing the content of the current HTML page, such as "Home", "News", or "Contact"

- homeFileName represents the name of the HTML file to load when the Home button is clicked. For example, we want home2.htm to open when the Home button is clicked, so homeFileName is assigned a value of home2

- newsFileName represents the name of the HTML file to load when the News button is clicked

- contactFileName represents the name of the HTML file to load when the Contact button is clicked

Before we begin scripting, it would be a good idea to get acquainted with some of the elements in the movie that play a role in its end functionality.

2. Choose Window › Library to open the Library panel.

Notice that the library contains three sounds named Sound1, Sound2, and Sound3. Each sound has been given an identifier so that it can be dynamically attached using the attachSound() method. This will be explained in greater detail in a moment.

3. Double-click one of the movie clips instances on the Buttons layer to view its Timeline.

The Timeline consists of three layers and two frames. The main point to note is that when the playhead is moved to Frame 2, the clip appears highlighted. All three instances on the Buttons layer are constructed this way. This structure plays an integral role in how the navigation bar works.

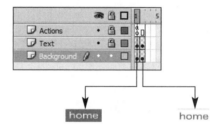

4. Return to the main Timeline. With the Actions panel open, select Frame 1 of the Actions layer and add the following line of script:

```
var soundEffect:Sound = new Sound();
```

This line simply creates a Sound object that will be used in a moment to play a unique sound, depending on the page to which the user has navigated.

5. Add onRelease event handlers to each of the clip instances:

```
home_mc.onRelease = function() {
  getURL(homeFileName + ".htm");
};
news_mc.onRelease = function() {
  getURL(newsFileName + ".htm");
};
contact_mc.onRelease = function() {
  getURL(contactFileName + ".htm");
};
```

This script assigns onRelease event handlers to the home_mc, news_mc, and contact_mc movie clip instances. When any of these instances is clicked, it opens a URL based on the value passed into the movie using FlashVars (homeFileName, newsFileName, or contactFileName), plus the extension ".htm". For example, if we use FlashVars to set the value of newsFileName to news1, and then click the news_mc instance, news1.htm opens. Using FlashVars in this manner gives us the flexibility to change the URLs that are opened by the movie, without having to open the movie in the authoring environment and manually editing it there.

6. Next, add the following conditional statement:

```
if (currentPage == "Home") {
  home_mc.gotoAndStop(2);
  soundEffect.attachSound("Sound1");
  soundEffect.start(0, 1);
  delete home_mc.onRelease;
} else if (currentPage == "News") {
  news_mc.gotoAndStop(2);
  soundEffect.attachSound("Sound2");
  soundEffect.start(0, 1);
  delete news_mc.onRelease;
} else if (currentPage == "Contact") {
  contact_mc.gotoAndStop(2);
  soundEffect.attachSound("Sound3");
  soundEffect.start(0, 1);
  delete contact_mc.onRelease;
}
```

Each of the three web pages (which you'll set up later in this exercise) uses FlashVars to pass in a variable named currentPage. The value of currentPage is "Home", "News", or "Contact", depending on the page that's loaded. For example, when the Home page is loaded, currentPage has a value of "Home". This conditional statement looks at that value when the movie is loaded and takes one of three sets of actions based on that value. Let's consider a scenario.

When the user visits the Contact page, currentPage has a value of "Contact". As a result, the last portion of this conditional statement is executed. The contact_mc movie clip is moved to Frame 2, in which the instance appears highlighted (indicating to the user that he or she is currently on the Contact page). Next, Sound3 in the library is attached to the soundEffect Sound object and played. The last action deletes the onRelease event handler from the contact_mc instance. This is done because if the Contact page is currently loaded, there's no need for that event handler, which is just used to navigate to the Contact page.

This step completes the scripting of our movie. Next, we'll export it to a SWF file and place an instance of it on three HTML pages, using FlashVars to set it up to react differently on each page.

7. Choose File › Export › Export Movie to export this movie as *NavBar1.swf* in the Lesson18/Start directory.

Next, we'll embed this SWF file in several HTML pages.

8. Using your favorite HTML editor, open *home1.htm* in the Lesson18/Start directory.

The main thing to be aware of in this file is the placeholder.gif image at the top of the page. Each of our starting HTML files has this image. In the steps that follow, we'll swap this image for the NavBar1.swf file generated in Step 7.

9. Swap the placeholder image for the *NavBar1.swf* movie (embed the SWF movie in place of the placeholder image). View the HTML source for the page, locate the **<param>** tags (nested in the **<object>** tags), and add the following tag:

```
<param name="FlashVars" ¬
    value="currentPage=Home&homeFileName=home2&newsFileName=news2 ¬
    &contactFileName=contact2">
```

This step adds the FlashVars parameter to the `<object>` tag. The `value` portion of the tag contains four variables and their values, separated by ampersands (&):

```
currentPage=Home
homeFileName=home2
newsFileName=news2
contactFileName=contact2
```

When the SWF file is loaded on this page, it receives these variable values and reacts to them, as discussed in Steps 5 and 6. As a result, when this page is loaded, the Home button appears highlighted and disabled, a sound plays, and clicking the remaining navigation buttons in the movie opens news2.htm or contact2.htm, as appropriate.

10. **With the HTML code still visible, add the following attribute to the `<embed>` tag:**

```
FlashVars="currentPage=Home&homeFileName=home2&newsFileName=news2 ¬
    &contactFileName=contact2">
```

This step adds the FlashVars attribute to the `<embed>` tag, giving browsers that use that tag (such as Netscape) access to the FlashVars functionality.

Note   *Dreamweaver 8 supports the capability to add FlashVars tags to Flash content in an HTML page.*

11. **Save this file as *home2.htm*.**

The only thing left to do is edit our two remaining HTML pages.

12. **Open *news1.htm* in the Lesson18/Start directory. Edit this page in a fashion similar to that described in Steps 9 and 10, but change the value of `currentPage` to `News` (`currentPage=News`) in both the `<object>` and `<embed>` tags.**

When the SWF file is loaded on this page, it's passed the same four variables as discussed in Step 9, but the revised value of `currentPage` on this page causes the News button to appear highlighted and disabled, and a different sound plays, as defined by the conditional statement in Step 6.

13. **Save this file as *news2.htm*.**

Finally, let's edit one more page.

14. Open *contact1.htm* in the Lesson18/Start directory. Edit this page as described in Steps 9 and 10, but change the value of `currentPage` to `Contact` (`currentPage=Contact`) in both the `<object>` and `<embed>` tags.

The revised value of `currentPage` on this page causes the Contact button to appear highlighted and disabled, and a different sound plays, as defined by the conditional statement in Step 6.

15. Save this file as *contact2.htm*.

The last step is to test your work.

16. Double-click *home2.htm* to open it in your default browser. When the page loads, click the navigation buttons in the Flash movie.

As you click the buttons, one of the three HTML pages is loaded. Each time a page loads, the FlashVars code on that page passes variable data into the SWF file that tell it how to react on that page. This allows you to use a single 20 KB SWF file on three different pages to take different actions, as opposed to creating three different SWF files to accomplish the same goal. As mentioned earlier, this can be a plus to someone visiting your website because they'll be required to load only a single SWF file, not three.

Remember, FlashVars not only allows you to use a single SWF file in unique ways on different HTML pages (as demonstrated in this exercise), but you can also use a single SWF file multiple times on a *single* HTML page, with each instance configured to show a different frame, load a different MP3, show different text, or whatever your imagination suggests. This is an often overlooked yet powerful tool.

17. Close your browser. Return to Flash and save the file as *NavBar2.fla*.

This completes the exercise, lesson, and the book! We hope that you've learned a lot and had fun along the way. If you are interested in learning even more about ActionScript and Flash then check out *www.peachpit.com* for more ActionScript titles.

What You Have Learned

In this lesson, you have:

- Learned about `fscommand()` functions (pages 475–480)
- Enhanced a Flash movie with Zinc and special Zinc commands (pages 480–496)
- Configured movie functionality using HTML and FlashVars (pages 496–504)

Index

events

  common component events, 241

  component-specific events, 241–242

  definition, 4

  dispatching, 281–287

  types, 163

extends keyword, 147

external data. *See also* data transfer

  formats supported

    data sources, 321

    loading into Flash, 319–320

    policy files, 334–336

ExternalInterface class

  application with two-way
    JavaScript/Flash communication,
    404–410

  calling functions

    ActionScript from JavaScript,
    402–404

    JavaScript from ActionScript, 398–399

  configuring HTML for calls, 397–398

  JavaScript regular expressions, 399–402

  registering ActionScript functions,
    402–403

F

FileReference class, listeners, 171, 172

FileReferenceList class, listeners, 172

filters

  appending, 208–209

  assigning to objects, 205

  constructing, 204–205

  deleting, 209

  retrieving, 208

  types, 204

  updating, 209

  using, 206–211

Find button, 14–15

FlashVars parameter, 496–498

  navigation bar for website, 498–504

floodFill() method, 222–225

flush() method, 341, 343, 344

focusIn events, 245, 255

FocusManager component, 258–262

focusOut events, 242

for loops, 80–81, 84–85

for...in loops, 81–82

forward slashes (//), comments, 7, 10

frames, code placement, 31

fscommand() function

  communicating with web browsers, 478

  executable projectors

    SWF Studio, 479, 480

    Zinc, 479–496

  executing AppleScripts, 477–478

  stand-alone projectors, 476–477

  versus ExternalInterface class, 475

functions

  arguments array, 45

  creating, 40–43

  objects, 34–35

  parameters, 43–53

  returning results, 54–60

  syntax, 39–40

G

gameOver() function, 491

generateBubbles() function, 486

get() method, 141–142

getBytesLoaded() method, 323

shared objects
  data transfer, 319, 320, 321
  saving data, 336–348
SharedObject class
  callback methods, 166
  dynamic classes, 131
  saving data, 336–348
shoot() function, 488
Show Code Hint button, 14–15
showRooms() function, 392
showUsers() function, 391, 392
Singleton design patterns, 128
socket servers. *See* XMLSocket class
Sound class, 109, 131
  callback methods, 166
  characteristics, 413
  instances, 413–414
  sound simulation of basketball
      bouncing on court, 414–416
    attaching sounds, 435–439
    controlling panning, 429–435
    controlling sound playback, 435,
        439–441
    controlling volume, 422–428
    moving ball within boundaries,
        417–421
spacing/indentions, 8–9
Stage class, 109
  listeners, 171, 172
start() method, 462
startCountdown() and stopCountdown()
    functions, 405, 409
startDrag() and stopDrag() methods,
    280, 421
startHintInterval() method, 191
static classes, 382
static methods, 145–146

static properties, 144–145
  versus static methods, 146
stop() method, 416
strict data typing, 26–30
String class, 109, 116–118
String data type, 26
strings and quotation marks, 7
StyleSheet class, 110
  callback methods, 166
subclasses, 146
submitChoice() function, 330, 331
subtraction operator (–), 10
superclasses, 146
  overriding properties or methods, 148
SWF files
  exact domain matching, 334
  saving data with shared objects, 336–348
switch/case statements, 68–69, 71, 72
syntax. *See also* dot syntax
  Check Syntax button, 14–15
  classes, 128–132
  definition, 3
  functions, 39–40
  variables, 25–26
System class, 110
  callback methods, 166
  listeners, 172

T

ternary (conditional) operator (?:), 69
testEmail() JavaScript function, 401
testFunction() function, 398
text files, data transfer, 320
  LoadVars class, 323

4808

TR
897.7
.M344

2006